I0188715

The Growth and Destruction of the Community of Uscilug (Ustilug, Ukraine)

Translation of
Kehilat Ustila be-vinyana u-ve-hurbana

Original Book Edited by:
Aryeh Avinadav

Originally published in Israel, 1961

A Publication of JewishGen, INC
Edmond J. Safra Plaza, 36 Battery Place, New York, NY 10280
646.494.5972 | info@JewishGen.org | www.jewishgen.org

An affiliate of New York's Museum of Jewish Heritage – A Living Memorial to the Holocaust

The Growth and Destruction of the Community of Uscilug (Ustilug, Ukraine)
Translation of ***Kehilat Ustila be-vinyana u-ve-hurbana***

First Printing: October 2021, Cheshvan 5782

Editor of Original Yizkor Book: Aryeh Avinadav
Project Coordinators: Mitch Fahrer
Layout and Name Indexing: Jonathan Wind
Reproduction of Photographs: Sondra Ettlinger
Cover Design: Rachel Kolokoff Hopper

Printed in the United States of America by Lightning Source, Inc.

Library of Congress Control Number (LCCN): 2021947486

ISBN: 978-1-954176-21-8 (hard cover: 312 pages, alk. paper)

About JewishGen.org

JewishGen, INC. is a non-profit organization founded in 1987 as a resource for Jewish genealogy. Its website serves as an international clearinghouse and resource center to assist individuals who are researching the history of their Jewish families and the places where they lived. JewishGen provides databases, facilitates discussion groups, and coordinates projects relating to Jewish genealogy and the history of the Jewish people. In 2003, JewishGen became an affiliate of the **Museum of Jewish Heritage—A Living Memorial to the Holocaust** in New York.
Please visit https://www.jewishgen.org/ to learn more.

Executive Director: Avraham Groll

About the JewishGen Yizkor Book Project

The **JewishGen Yizkor Book Project** was organized to make more widely known the existence of Yizkor (Memorial) Books written by survivors and former residents of various Jewish communities throughout the world. Later, volunteers connected to the different destroyed communities began cooperating to have these books translated from the original language—usually Hebrew or Yiddish—into English, thus enabling a wider audience to have access to the valuable information contained within them. As each chapter of these books was translated, it was posted on the JewishGen website and made available to the public.
Please visit https://www.jewishgen.org/Yizkor/ to learn more.

Director of JewishGen Yizkor Book Project: Lance Ackerfeld

About the JewishGen Press

JewishGen Press (formerly the Yizkor Books-in-Print Project), the publishing division of JewishGen.org, provides a venue for the publication of non-fiction books pertaining to Jewish genealogy, history, culture, and heritage. In addition to the Yizkor Book category, publications in the Other Non-Fiction category include Shoah memoirs and research, genealogical research, collections of genealogical and historical materials, biographies, diaries and letters, studies of Jewish experience and cultural life in the past, academic theses, and other books of interest to the Jewish community. We are not considering works of fiction at this time.
Please visit https://www.jewishgen.org/press/ to learn more.

Director of JewishGen Press: Joel Alpert
Managing Editor - Jessica Feinstein
Publications Manager - Susan Rosin

Notes to the Reader

The images in the original book were reproduced from photographs from the time of the first edition. These reproductions were already of poor quality, being pre-war and at least 30 or more years old. As a result the images in the book are not very good and the best achievable.

A reader can view the original scans of the book on the websites listed below.

The original book can be seen online at the New York Public Library site:

https://digitalcollections.nypl.org/items/494df2b0-58a4-0133-0dbc-00505686d14e

or at the Yiddish Book Center web site:

https://www.yiddishbookcenter.org/collections/yizkor-books/yzk-nybc314072/kehilat-ustilah-be-vinyanah-uve-hurbanah

To obtain a list of all Shoah victims from Uscilug (Ustilug), the reader should access the Yad Vashem web site listed below; one can also search for specific family names using family name option. These lists are continually updated by Yad Vashem, so it is worthwhile to periodically search these lists.

There is more valuable information (including the Pages of Testimony, etc.) available on this website: http://yvng.yadvashem.org

A list of all books available from JewishGen Press along with prices is available at: https://www.jewishgen.org/press/

Credits for Book Cover

Front Cover Photo:
Courtesy of Mitch Fahrer. A photo of his grandmother, Ruth Bernstein Mamet, (back row, left) and several friends and classmates in 1920, just months before she departed for the United States with her family.

Back of Front Cover Photo:
Courtesy of Mitch Fahrer. Names of those represented in the photograph (not in order):

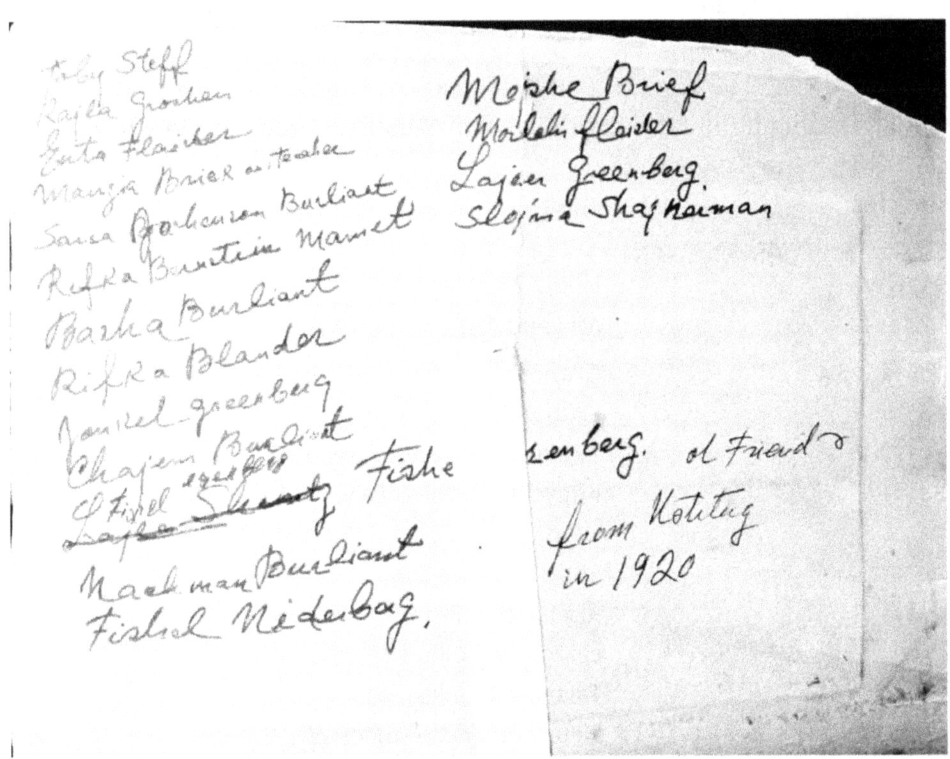

Toby Steff, Razla Grosbien, Manza Brier (Teacher), Sarra Jachcuson Burliant, Rifka Bernstein Mamet, Rifka Blander (Mitch Fahrer's relative who likely perished at Sobibor, there is no existing photo of her and she cannot be identified in this photo), Jankel Greenberg, Chaim Burliant, Fishel Isenberg, Nachman Burliant, Fishel Niederberg, Moshe Brief, Morlelin Fleisher, Lajeer Greenberg, Sloima Shaynerman

Front and Back Cover Background:
A mother writing to her son in the Polish army, page 46

Front and Back Cover Background Photograph:
Winter Grass by Rachel Kolokoff Hopper

Back Cover Photo:
Market Square, page 17

Back Cover Bible Verse: *Jeremiah 8;23*, page 207

GeoPolitical Information

Ustyluh, Ukraine is located at: 50°52' N, 24°09' E and 280 miles W of Kyyiv

	Town	District	Province	Country
Before WWI (c. 1900):	Ustilug	Vladimir	Volhynia	Russian Empire
Between the wars (c. 1930):	Uściług	Włodzimierz	Wołyń	Poland
After WWII (c. 1950):	Ustilug			Soviet Union
Today (c. 2000):	Ustyluh			Ukraine

Alternate Names for the Town:
Ustyluh [Ukr], Ustilug [Rus], Uściług [Pol], Ustila [Yid], Ustiluh, Austile, Ostila, Ustilla, Oustiloug

Nearby Jewish Communities:

Horodło, Poland 5 miles WNW
Volodymyr Volynskyy 8 miles E
Hrubieszów, Poland 11 miles WSW
Kryłów, Poland 13 miles SSW
Skryhiczyn, Poland 14 miles NW
Dubienka, Poland 17 miles NW
Dolsk 20 miles NNE
Pavlivka 22 miles SE
Uchanie, Poland 23 miles W
Turiysk 23 miles NE
Lokachi 24 miles ESE
Varyazh 24 miles S
Ozyutichi 25 miles E
Lukov 25 miles NNE
Milyanovichi 25 miles NNE
Grabowiec, Poland 26 miles W
Lyuboml 26 miles NNW
Tyszowce, Poland 26 miles SW
Kupychiv 26 miles ENE
Wojsławice, Poland 26 miles W
Sokal 27 miles SSE
Kiselin 29 miles E
Łaszczów, Poland 29 miles SW
Tartakiv 30 miles SSE
Sielec, Poland 30 miles WNW
Ozeryany 30 miles ENE
Świerże, Poland 30 miles NW

Jewish Population in 1897: 3,212

Map of Ukraine with **Ustyluh** indicated

TABLE OF CONTENTS

Table of Contents translated by Yocheved Klausner

In Memory of Our Town (Foreword)	A. A.	3
Generations and Eras		
Ustyluh (Ustylug)	Rabbi Dov Takatch	8
On the Banks of Rivers	Aryeh Avinadav	12
In Light of Memories	Elyhau Schlachter	47
Personalities and Activities		
Kindness of Youth (a bundle of memories)	Tzila Fleischer	58
Torah Va'avodah Movement in Ustiluh	A. Ben–Dov	63
Hechalutz Branch in Ustiluh	Yitzhak Farber	66
Hashomer Hatzair and Other Youth Movements in Ustiluh	Zvi Hadari (Pomerantz)	69
The Cultural Center in Ustiluh	Sima Rutenberg (Goldberg)	74
Figures	E. Schlechter	77
In Memory of Moshe Shpirer	Yakov Biterman	82
Leibale Helfman	Yehudit Sapir–Chen (Helfman)	83
Two Figures– Two Destinies	A. Ben–Dov	84
Three Who Dared to Protest	Moshe Zemel	88
Concealed Lights	Mina Sheinman	90
Grandfather's Home	Menashe Secharbrot	91
Fillins – Institutions and Organizations	M.K.A.	93
Figures from the Pre–Holocaust Generation		95

In Fire and in Blood 99

On the Ruins of Our Town Yeshayahu Meltzman 99

The Tale of Two Sisters Arie Avinadav 109

Confession (An Elegy) A. Achi–Frida 113

The Fate of One Family Bezalel Halperin 114

The Last Greetings Yitzhak Farber 116

From the Claws of Death Esther Goldman 118

Yiddish Section

Flowers and Tears

At the Mass Grave of Ustiluh 130

Ustiluh – Its Rich Past Rabbi Dr. Aharon Wertheim 130

My Town – Ustiluh Dr. Aharon Rosmarin 132

The School System and Children's Education in Ustiluh Baruch Goldberg 136

The Teacher and His Circle Yaakov Zipper 138

The Phenomenal Matmid [dilligent Yeshiva student] Baruch Goldberg 147

Nachman Burlyant, Z"L Tzila Fleisher 150

For God and For People Malka Chometzki (Reiz) 151

Avraham (Avrom'ke) Reiz Tzila 153

A Vanished Dream Eliezer Reiz 159

The Ustiluh Youth – From 1917 to 1922 Chaim Weinshel 161

Links in a Chain Bernard Ginsburg 164

The Tear That Was Not Shed Bella Eichenboim-Terner 173

The Destruction of Ustiluh Nachman Burlyant 178

The Massacre in Piatidan (poem) Kehat Kliger 180

A Stroll Yossel Burlyant, z"l, 182

Ustiluh in the Old Days (a poem) Tzirl 183

The "Revenge" Battalion Shmuel Diamant 184

Victims of the Shoah 196

Yizkor

May God Remember 208

A Scroll of Remembrance (Necrology) 211

Fallen for the Homeland – may God avenge their blood

Yakov Cohen 265

Yehuda Fleisher 267

Aaron Blander 268

Avraham Korenfracht 270

Passed Away

R'Moshe and Breindel Rosmarin 271

Feiga from across the river (Eichenboim) 273

Yosef Eidelshteyn 274

Aaron Dror (Shovalev) 276

Reuven Rotenberg 277

Yenta Gurevitz 278

Zehava (Golda) Eidelshteyn 279

Memories of Rivka Reiter, z"l 280

Ben Zion Goldhaber 281

Pinhas Sapir–Chen 282

Rivka Ingber 284

Rivka Wasserman 285

Yossel and Nachman Burlyant 285

Vision of the Dry Bones 286

The Surviving Remnant 289

List of Former Ustiluh Residents in Israel 290

Name Index 293

Foreward

The region where Ustilug is located has changed hands many times throughout history. Sometimes part of Poland, sometimes Russia, and presently as part of Ukraine, the name of the town has equally changed about as many times.

To help future generations searching for information about their ancestors, we provide the following list of names that has been given to the town of Ustilug. In the Ustilug Yizkor Book translation from Yiddish, the spelling by the original authors has not been modified.

Austile; Austiller; Ostila, Ostilla; Uscilug; Ustile; Ustilug: Ustiluh; Ustyluh

Mitch Fahrer

קהילת אוסטילה
בבנינה ובחורבנה

עורך

אריה אבינדב

בהוצאת ארגון יוצאי אוסטילה בישראל ובתפוצות

[Page 2]

Publication committee:

Tzila FLEISHER. Aryeh AVINADAV, Eliyahu SHLACHTER, Sima ROTENBERG, Yitzhak FARBER, Betzalel HALPERIN

Printed by A. Strod and Sons, Tel Aviv

[Page 3]

In Memory of the Thousands of Martyrs from Ustiluh

[Page 4] blank [Page 5]

In Memory of Our Town (Foreword)

By A.A.

Translated by Ala Gamulka

We present this book, for future generations, in memory of our town. It is now sixteen years since the final destruction by the Nazis and their collaborators of our town Ustile.

For a long time, we were shaken by the news of the terrible truth about the fate of our town and our relatives. We could not grasp the fact that the contact we had with our dearly beloved was completely broken. We had left them there in the hope that we would still be able to see them some day, perhaps even in our country. It was not meant to be. The shock was so great and the pain was penetrating. We could not find a way to express our deep sadness and mourning. We could not even think of publishing a Yizkor book as it entailed a great deal of concentration, emotional peace and time to reflect.

In the meantime, life went on. Eventually, we were able to calm down and the first steps were taken to commemorate our destroyed community and its martyrs.

At a meeting of the former residents of our town, held on 19 Elul, 1959 in Jerusalem, we placed a memorial tablet in the Holocaust cellar on Mount Zion. Attached to it was the list of those who perished. One deed carries another– Eliyahu SHLACHTER proposed the publication of a Yizkor Book. At the same time, the author of this article agreed to be the editor.

Truthfully, we must note that the proposal did not meet with any enthusiasm among those in the audience. Perhaps they did not believe that it was feasible. Member P., one of those active in the organization, expressed his doubts by whispering to me: "You will have to write the entire book" …i.e.: there will not be a book!

To our surprise, and to his, the member was wrong. He actually contributed an article. Here is our book.

B.

We take special responsibility to point out what had been done for our town prior to the publication:

[Page 6]

a. In the newspaper "Hatsofeh" of 21 Sivan1943, an article entitled "The Jewish village in Poland" was published. It was written by yours truly and talks about Ustiluh, its past and its bitter end.

b. In the collection "Volyn Anthology", booklet 1, published in Nissan, 1945, there was a concise article about Ustiluh. It was written by Rabbi Dov TKATCH of Ludomir, now in Tel Aviv.

c. In the above–mentioned anthology, booklets 16–17 from Heshvan 1953, written by yours truly, there is an article about Ustiluh. There is also a correction to the article by Rabbi Tkatch.

d. As we began to prepare the book, we received a booklet in memory of the destruction of Ustiluh. It had been published in New York in January 1948. The emotional articles were written by Rabbi Aaron WERTHEIM and the brothers Nachman and Yossel BORLIANT, z"l,. They are included here.

C.

It was not an easy undertaking.

Half a year after the decision was made, we still had not received any material from our members. When we contacted Yad Vashem in Jerusalem, we were directed to the two articles published in the "Volyn Anthology" …

It was only after our first mailing in Shevat, 1960 that we began to receive the "first crop" – articles of remembrance and pictures. Some of them were inappropriate for publication due to the content and were returned to the senders. However, the fact there was some forward movement spurred us to continue to send mailings. We exchanged correspondence with members in our country, in the United States and Canada, Cuba and Argentina. The purpose was to explain and to encourage the writing. It was not enough. In order to obtain material on the Holocaust period we were obliged to go to the homes of some of our members and to write down their shocking stories.

We continued to collect material and to prepare until the holiday of Passover. We then sent the book to the printer.

As to the financial situation– it was less encouraging. As I write these lines, we are still asking ourselves:

" How will we receive help?"

We must emphasize this fact in order to reply to a certain complaint, as follows:

As we announced in our first mailing, it was our intention to publish the book in Hebrew only. However, after some deliberation, we agreed that it was necessary to follow the wishes of the authors, whether in Hebrew or in Yiddish. Member G. from Argentina said that not everyone can read Hebrew and the book should be done entirely in Yiddish. If we did not agree, then we should use both languages.

Our reply was as written above.

[Page 7]

D.

Now we go to the contents of the book.

We do not pretend that that the book is complete. There will be those who will find flaws and literary lapses. However, in spite of this, it is obvious that the book presents a magnificent memorial to the Jews of Ustiluh in general, and to its martyrs, in particular.

At the beginning we said that the book will serve future generations. We must elaborate:

The first section deals with the history of the village, its atmosphere and stories of certain personalities. It is not merely intended as a history, but we, the present generation of former residents of Ustiluh, have a personal need to do it. We are thus reminded of our childhood and our youth. We have hidden longings for those times. These memories are the spice of human life. It had faded during the evil times…

People retain pictures of their youth as special assets. However, these pieces of paper are silent. They only hint at what was… The book reminds one of various events and happenings that one witnessed and perhaps even participated in.

In contrast, the second section depicts the Holocaust period. It is equally meant for our generation and those to come. We see in these stories a window to what took place and a warning to all those in the Diaspora. One must not have confidence in foreign nations. If not for the naïve trust of the victims of the Nazi beast and in the enlightenment of the German people, who knows how many of them would have been saved. Thousands, if not millions, could have evaded torture and death.

This double assessment directed us in the preparation of the book with its different topics.

E.

An excerpt from one of our mailings to the members:

"It is our opinion that a Yizkor Book should not only contain eulogies. We are interested in describing the village in all its nuances, light and dark and the special conditions which influenced its development. We tend to emphasize more its qualities and look at its defects with humor, with understanding".

In addition, we also say:

In our literature we have the expression: "Town and mother in Israel". The town can be compared to one's mother. Mother is loved, even if she is physically impaired. One does not falsify her picture in order to correct the impairment. In the same, way, one's hometown, with all its faults, is beloved.

[Page 8]

(See the article by Dr. – "My shtetl Ustiluh"). We described our village as it was etched in our childhood memories.

In order to be true to the special character of our village, we dedicated an important part to the description of the Hassidic atmosphere in it. We were assisted by two learned men whose articles are published in the Yiddish section.

In addition, it was our opinion that private recollections are only to be published if they pertain to general events. We did not really insist on this. There were some personal memories that reflected a beautiful Jewish life in many of our homes.

F.

We must emphasize a few more facts that may cause a reaction in our readers. It is best to explain them here:

The readers will find some descriptions of scenery or events that are repeated in various places. In order to continue the flow and for other reasons, it was decided, most of the time, not to leave out some of them.

a. Since the book was divided into two sections, Hebrew and Yiddish, we were unable to do an accurate separation according to topics. The present version made better sense than to intermingle articles in both languages.

b. As to old, new and mixed spelling in Yiddish, we decided to publish the articles as they were written. We, ourselves, use the new.

G.

In conclusion, we must thank all the members who helped to accomplish the job: those on the publication committee who worked tirelessly and the authors of the articles and stories, especially the Survivors who shed tears and suffered pain and those who sent pictures. We thank everyone who helped financially and in other ways to produce this memorial to our village and our beloved martyrs.

You should all be blessed. 23 Nissan 1961

[Page 9]

Generations and Eras

Inquire of the former generation, and apply yourself to what their fathers have searched out

(Job 8:8)

[Page 10] Blank [Page 11]

Ustyluh (Ustylug)

by Rabbi Dov Takatch

Translated by Zvi Kaniel

The following translations were commissioned by Avigail Frij, whose maternal grandparents were from Ustilug (Kopp and Kultin Families)

Ustiluh is a small town, roughly 10 versts west of Vladimir –Volynsk, on the banks of the Bug River. As the surrounding area is heavily forested, about seventy years ago, Ustiluh residents used to send off wooden rafts down the river toward Danzig. For this reason, people used to call Ustiluh "little Danzig." Forestry and lumber manufacturing were prominent industries in the area. Merchants, agents, supervisors, clerks, lumber workers, wagon drivers, and all sorts of suppliers came to Ustiluh. People moved to and from the town in large numbers. Many of the local townspeople, as well as those who lived in the surrounding area, earned their living from the lumber trade; quite a few of them did rather well, and some became wealthy. Besides this, many Jews were shopkeepers and tradesmen of various kinds, as in so many other East European towns. This is how they lived for many generations.

In 1847, the Jewish community of Ustiluh numbered 1487. The census of 1897 showed that there were 3,212 Jews, of a total of 3,590 residents. In 1935, there were still more than 3,000 Jews in the town.

Most of the Jews were simple, upright folk, followers of the Chassidic *Rebbes* of Trisk, Rozhin, Karlin, Neskhiz and Radzin. The Chassidic *Rebbes*, Reb Mordeche'le, Reb Pinchasl, and Reb Moshele, all descendants of the Ba'al Shem Tov, also resided in Ustiluh. In later years, the renowned *tzaddik* Reb Leiezerel zt"l, resided there. Tragically, Reb Leiezerel suffered a fatal accident not long after moving to town. He died unexpectedly on his way to immerse in the *mikveh*. This caused much anguish and a deep sense of mourning among the townspeople for a long time. Over the generations, many other great Torah scholars likewise made their homes in Ustiluh.

The town had a number of shuls. The Danche shul, which was built by the widow of the wealthy Reb Dan. This G–d fearing woman had a reputation for generosity. Besides having built the shul in memory of her late husband, during her lifetime she paid for the upkeep of the shul and the salaries of its rabbi and other officials. She also arranged and paid for the construction of the local ritual bath.

The local Study Hall, known as the "laymen's Study Hall, was located on Vinehauser Street at the foot of the mountain. In this Study Hall the cantor was Reb Wolf from Terestzanska, a pious learned man, who possessed a beautiful voice. Although there was a Study Hall in his hometown where a regular minyan davened, he would come to Ustiluh for Rosh Hashana and Yom Kippur.

There was another large Study Hall in the center of town which most of the town's Jews attended. There were also several Shtiblach belonging to the various Chassidic groups that had settled in town.

[Page 12]

Among the many outstanding citizen of Ustiluh were Reb Michel Schwartz and Reb Abba Schwartz, wealthy and generous Jews whose names and fame spread throughout the area. Their homes were havens for all the needy and hungry people in town. Other noted philanthropists in town were Reb Yosef Shamayas, Reb Wolf Jacobs, and Reb Lipa (known as "the great"). These G–d fearing men donated lavish sums to charity and performed countless acts of kindness. There were two ritual slaughters in those days in Ustiluh: Reb Leibush and Reb David.

The Ustiluh community dwelled in peace for many generations, as people raised their children to continue in their forefathers' traditions. However, the First World War had a devastating effect on the Jews of Ustiluh, whose situation was already quite difficult by then.

After the war, when the Allies redrew the border that bisected the Volhynian region between Russia/Ukraine (U.S.S.R) and Poland, the border came near Ustiluh. This change as well had an adverse effect on life in Ustiluh and on the incomes of its Jewish population. The town's fortunes plummeted and many of its Jews moved away. Those who remained suffered from loss of income and unemployment.

It should be noted that the Polish government built a rail line from Ludomir (Vladimir–Volynsk) to Warsaw through Ustiluh, and the connections on the Bug were disrupted.

In time, the financial situation in town improved. The local Jewish school expanded. Its founders named it "The Yaakov Cohen School" after Yaakov Cohen, who was killed in Ramat Hakovesh in Eretz Yisrael during "the disturbances" (1929 Arab riots). The two libraries in town (one for Hebrew/Jewish books, and the second for Yiddishists and others) were managed by the local Zionists throughout that period. The local orphanage, which housed 22 children, was controlled by the Zionists, along with nearly all the town's public institutions.

Most of these public institutions were Zionist–oriented. Ustiluh's "Hechalutz" organization was influential, and the Zionist movement flourished.

During those years, the townspeople invited the Rebbe Reb Piniele, son–in–law of the Belzer Rebbe, to settle in Ustiluh. His arrival was accompanied by great pomp and a regal welcoming. The Belzer Rebbe also came, along with his considerable entourage, in honor of the occasion. The Jews of Ustiluh put on a huge celebration that lasted several weeks. Nevertheless, Reb Piniele resided in Ustiluh for only a short time, because the town's dwindling resources could not provide for his upkeep. He eventually left Ustiluh and moved to Pzemishil in Galicia. Subsequently, two rabbis remained in town: Rav Benzion Reider, a great Torah sage, and Rav Yehoshua Shintop.

The bloody campaign of the accursed Nazis obliterated the Jewish community in Ustiluh. May Hashem avenge their blood.

Editor's Notes:

We have cited the honored rabbi's account in its entirety, as it was printed in the first booklet "Volyn Anthologies" (Yalkut Volyn, Nissan 1945), which was the first account published in Israel about Ustiluh. We wish, however, to call attention to what we feel are a number of inaccuracies, and to clarify a number of relevant points.

A. To the best of our knowledge, already in 1935, the Jewish population in Ustiluh numbered about 4,000 people.

B. There were two ritual baths in town: that of "Danche" and a second in the bathhouse near the Bug River.

[Page 13]

C. The Study Hall known as "the "laymen's Study Hall "or "the Rav's" was not identical with the Vinehauser *Study Hall*. The former was higher up, while the latter not far from it, in the vicinity of the Vinehauser.

D. The philanthropists mentioned by the rabbi, except for Reb Wolf Jacobs (Yokhenzon) were deceased several decades before the Holocaust.

E. To the best of our knowledge, the last ritual slaughterers in Ustiluh were Reb Avraham Schlachter, Reb David Blinder, and Reb Nachum Stoliar. Reb Leibush had passed away many years earlier.

F. The border between Ukraine–Russia and Poland after the First World War did not come near Ustiluh; it lay about 100 km. east, near Austra–Ostrog. It is true, however, that during the First World War, when German and Austrian forces occupied the region, the Bug River served as a sort of border. Although forces of the same armies occupied both sides of the river, even so, to cross the bridge spanning the river, one had to procure a permit that cost 15 gold rubles.

Students at the First Hebrew School

[Page 14]

The Northern Bridge on the Bug, the "Golden Bridge" During the Austrian Conquest

[Page 15]

Tashlich on the Bug
In the background the house of R. Liptche Eisenberg

[Page 16]

On the Banks of Rivers
(A Few Sketches on the Town's Way of Life)

by Aryeh Avinadav

Translated by Zvi Kaniel

Note: For privacy reasons, the names of the central characters in this essay are fictitious.)

A. The Town of Rozhe–Yampol, also known as Ustiluh

Only a few select people know the town's ancient name. That is, in any case, what Shmulik thought. How then did he know? He spent much time with the *Dayan* (rabbinical judge) Rav Hirsch David, during which he became familiar with the laws of marriage and divorce. The divorce document written in town specified: "The City of Rozhe–Yampol, that is called Ustiluh, located on the River Bug and the River Liova, and on flowing springs."

Shmulik's father Yossel told him how the town's name changed.

"A local Polish noblewoman named Rozhe decided to name the village after herself–Rozhe–Yampol. The fields surrounding the town were fertile, and the local people mostly cultivated wheat there. Over time, many Jews moved to Rozhe–Yampol to take advantage of the economic opportunities that were developing there.

"In those early days, there was no railroad system in the country. So, people built granaries along the lower slope that faces the Bug River basin. Wooden troughs carried the grain down from the granaries to the river's edge, where it was loaded onto rafts and barges.

"Ships anchored underneath the lower mouth of the gutters, and were filled with wheat, rye, and other types of grains, for transshipment to Germany, whose crop yield did not suffice to support its populace.

"After the number of Jewish families of merchants, bureaucrats, and workers increased, they realized that they needed a shul and a ritual bath. Builders and carpenters began arriving, along with tailors, shoemakers, and other assorted craftsmen. Stores opened to furnish the townspeople with their needs, and eventually, the village became a town.

"When, after a long life, the noblewoman died, her children sold off the lands they inherited from her and moved from the area. The town fathers afterward decided to change the town's name to Ustiluh, i.e., "*usti luh*" – the confluence where the Luga (river) spills into the Bug. The Poles called it "*usti Luga.*"

The town's new name helped maintain the Luga River's original name as well. People used to refer to the town as "Stav" (lake in Polish), since at that spot, because the flow of its waters in the wide river delta was slow and unrecognizable. At that spot stood the mill that belonged to the town benefactor's son.

[Page 17]

Years later, the Bug River's importance declined when it stopped serving as a commercial waterway. From that point, people mostly used the river for bathing and washing laundry. While at the same time, the "Stav" (swamp; river Luga) acquired renewed importance. As the river was readily accessible, it became the major source of drinking water for most of the townspeople. Fishing succeeded there more than at the Bug. It provided swamp grass for the festival of Shavuot. And, of course, the mill.

Although the bill of divorce written in Ustiluh only mentioned the two rivers, the fact is that another rather small river ran near the town's southern edge, where some wineries were situated. It flowed by the Constantine Mountains, that faced each other like Mount Gerizim and Mount Eval, and emptied into the Bug. Knowledgeable folk claimed that this smaller river also had an official name: Studianka. However, who would bother with such a troublesome name. Second, how could this pint–sized river be more notable than "the Swamp?"

Regarding the Constantine Mountains, some claimed they were artificial mountains, constructed during the Napoleonic Wars, and served for much the same purpose during the Pòlish Uprising of 1863. Children burrowing on those hills often unearthed coins dating from different periods.

While it is difficult to ascertain the historical truth regarding the origin of these hills, it was evident that Shmulik was not claiming they were named for the Roman Emperor Constantine the Great. Or, the mad Russian Tsar Constantine Pavlovich. The mountains were named after a gentile shoemaker, whose work hut and pigsty were located between the two hills.

Indeed, Constantine was a known personality in town, since he spent most of his time hanging out with some of the town loafers, exchanging jokes in acerbic Yiddish. He bought the Jews' chametz before Pesach from one of the *dayanim*. Every year for eight days, Constantine owned most of the town.

In fact, rivers encircled Ustiluh on three sides. What about its eastern flank? Turns out that the Creator dug there the "Balboa," a lake that swarmed with gold–colored fish. It was a favorite of many local housewives, because these fish could survive for a while on dry land.

Adjacent to the "Balboa" on two sides of the road leading to the provincial town of Ludomir lay the Jewish and Catholic cemeteries. Close to the latter was a church, for the most part concealed by the surrounding trees. Only its red roof sporting two crosses was visible between the leaves. From here until the first houses on Ludomir Street in Ustiluh stood rows of old Sumac trees that shaded the entire road.

Approaching the workshop section of town, the noise of the pounding blacksmith's hammer and the racket of the rope maker's spinning wheel could be heard. Here, one passed the Ukrainian Church, whose green, cross topped roofs thrust with impudence toward the clear blue sky, here in the midst of this Jewish town....

[Page 18]

Ludomir Street terminated at a commercial center. From here, to the right, the street veered downhill to the confluence of Luga ("the Stav") and Bug rivers. To the left were the wineries and the gentiles' houses. Directly opposite stood the town square bound by shops and stands on three sides. On the fourth side stood the large, two story brick building known as "Vogenfeld's Wall."

Within this area and surrounding it resided the 4,000 residents of Ustiluh, most of whom were Jewish. A small minority of Ukrainian farmers and Polish city people also lived there. The Ukrainians lived on the gentiles' street. Among other things, they served as the town's "*Shabbat goy.*" They were coarse and deceitful, but forthright people. In contrast, were the Poles, who were scattered all over town. Most of them operated pork shops, while a few of them were skilled workers. They treated the Jews with courtesy, but harbored much malice in their hearts.

At the end of "the Bug" street lived a family who belonged to the Neskhiz Shtiebel. Every evening, when the setting sun turned the sky purple, the children became terror stricken because that signified that "the wicked were being burned in hell. At the same time Jews stood in silent prayer in three of the shuls on that street. All the while, plumes of white smoke and flames arose from the edge of the street. The jarring squeal of slaughtered pigs sliced the air, followed afterward by the pungent aroma of scorched pig hairs.

The Neskhiz Shtiebel had the annual task of housing the army conscripts, who were always exhausted from chronic lack of sleep. This was not surprising since they would sit up night after night playing cards and munching sunflower seeds.

The aforementioned family had a son, Victor, who used to fraternize with the other Jewish youth, reading, writing and speaking in proper Yiddish. To no one's surprise, he was a shrewd card player as well. Victor used to spend time with the other boys in town. But, when the latter finally left to get some sleep or to explore the town's southern streets, Victor enjoyed thumbing through books. The next morning, any book that you might pick up had a bold inscription on its front page: Victor Sokolovsky.

B. Holy and Profane

There were twelve shuls in Ustiluh, corresponding to the Twelve Tribes of Israel. There were shuls for the homeowners the craftsmen, the cattle dealers, and the various Chassidic groups.

There were a similar number of Heders (elementary schools) for children. After a time, the local intelligentsia opened a new school –The Renovated Cheder. The *Hassidim* who frowned on this new school's curriculum called it "*HaCheder HaMesukan* " ("The Dangerous Cheder").

The intelligentsia even formed their own prayer group that they called "*Beit Yaakov*." Local wits used to call it "The *Goshen Shtiebel*," based on the phrase "And throughout the Land of Goshen where the Children of Israel dwelled there was no barad (hail,) (barad=beard) as all its members were clean shaven.

[Page 19]

In those days, threatening a wind was gusting through the local Study Halls. It closed the Gmara books, and drove the boys out into the "big world." There were, however, small groups or individuals who maintained their Talmud studies, even continuing to use the traditional soul–stirring tune that the Jewish people passed down from earlier generations.

In the traditional schools, the curriculum remained unchanged. The children sat in their classrooms chanting the Hebrew verses of the Torah they learned, translating them into Yiddish. The sing–song of their studies spilled out into the street. In the winter evenings, throngs of children on their way home from *cheder*, lanterns in hand, crunched the snow to the tempo of their continued singing.

This sweet melody sung when studying Torah in Heder soothed and restored the soul. However, reciting the weekly portion on Friday according to the cantillation marks, captivated listeners even more. This chanting was as delicious as the special rolls dipped in meat sauce that they received for lunch in honor of the upcoming Shabbat.

The "*ma'hapach pashta*" asks a simple ("*pashta*") question[1]. The "*zakef katan*" upholds ("*zakef*") it. The "*meircha tipcha*" and "*munach etnachta*" come to explain the matter until everything is clarified ("*tipcha*" and "*etnachta*"). But, the "*pazer*" and the "*zakef gadol*" are not satisfied, raising various objections, while the "*kadma ve'azla*" was perplexed. The "*telisha ketana*" also complained. In the end, the "*telisha gedola*" explains the matter to the satisfaction of all.

The vigorous debate continued until suddenly a new sound was heard. "They're grinding spice for the fish and the baked foods." The sound of the grinder and the aroma of the spices and fish proclaimed the approaching Shabbat Queen. The sounds and smells comingled with the children's vigorous singing ignited a fire of enthusiasm for the forthcoming Shabbat.

The anticipation reached its peak when the tiny flames of the Shabbat candles were kindled with humble yearnings toward the skies of Shabbat, with Hashem's loyal, Chosen People turning to the west, welcoming the Shabbat Bride into their homes.

Along with the Shabbat splendor and charm came a sense of humility. All the Jewish homes became lodgings for the holy Shabbat and her ministering angels. The humble abode of Mott'l the porter along with the wealthy Yokeanzons' grand mansion. The unlearned soldier's shack and the house of the local Rav that overflowed with Torah and exalted Jewish knowledge.

Shabbat stroked the little children's heads as they waited eagerly for their father's *Kiddush*. The holy day's quiet sanctity refreshed their mothers. Thus, young and old sang the praises of Shabbat with heartfelt joy and reverence.

Ustiluh's populace, in particular the Hassidic groups, knew well how to take advantage of the blessed Shabbat repose. Pleasures that provided reward both in this world and in the World to Come.

[Page 20]

This is not the stuffed geese, fine delicacies and delightful wines that adorned the Yokhenzon family table, and perhaps those of a dozen other well to do Jews in town. It was rather at the morning *Kiddush* in the Shtiebel over a glass of whiskey and some sesame cakes. The participants usually followed up with stories of *tzaddikim* and *Hassidim*, and capped the occasion with some spirited dancing.

This is how the Ustiluh community spend their Shabbat – in the fine manner of Hassidism throughout Eastern Europe. *Davening* (praying), the Shabbat meals, an afternoon rest, partaking of some cherry wine and delicious Shabbat treats. Later in the day, a lesson from a *maggid* (town preacher[2]). A communal third Shabbat meal, followed by the evening prayers that concluded the holy day. After all the celebrating, they conducted a Melaveh Malka meal with friends, where stories of the holy Ba'al Shem Tov and his disciples were told. *Hassidim* considered relating these stories on Saturday night a providential omen for success in earning a living and for increased fear of Heaven.

This is how the Jews of Ustiluh began their new week – brimming with belief and trust.

However, the difficulties of earning a living sometimes seem to intrude on one's belief and trust. “A person's sustenance is as difficult as the parting of the Red Sea” (Masechta Pesachim 118a). This was evident back in the days of the Ustiluh community's daily struggle to earn a living. Most Jewish villages throughout the Pale of Settlement fared the same.

At the crack of dawn, the peddler or craftsman awoke, prayed the Shacharit service, often punctuated by coughs and yawns. Often with his usual bundle of merchandise at his side ready to begin his trek through the area's villages. Occasionally, he arrived at some hamlet, only to discover that others had already visited there. He meandered from one place to another throughout the week. His food consisted of dark bread, some vegetables, herring, and some baked potatoes. At night, he slept on the ground on a bundle of straw. After a week of toil and suffering, he returned home shattered and exhausted with a few coins in his pocket.

When a farmer arrived in the marketplace, half a dozen storekeepers, standing at their stores' entrance:

“Hey friend, come here. At my store you'll get everything for the lowest prices….” The farmer paid a quick visit to each of the six shops one after the other. However, usually he did not buy anything, because perhaps in the seventh or eighth shop he might find even lower prices.

However, not all the shops were identical. In one, David Moishe's condemns a gentile woman for digging through the entire barrel of herring until she found one that she liked. While in the shop across the street, Daniel Feige's sat in his fabric shop quietly learning from a holy book. Apparently, his most recent bankruptcy did not disturb his composure, and in fact, as a result of it, his youngest daughter got married soon afterward.

True, some shopkeepers were relatively well off. But, even the worst off were in a much better position not only than that of the peddlers, but even of those who had “regular jobs” such as teachers, scribes and clerks. These, however, were not the lowest income jobs. It would seem that the matchmakers were part of the lowest income bracket. It is difficult in our times to grasp the degree of poverty so many Jews endured at that time (early 20th century) in Poland.

[Page 21]

Market square

The resident craftsmen – the tailors, cobblers, carpenters, blacksmiths, and others –faced an unusual situation. If they were experts in their fields, they earned a better living. But they were pitiable *because* they were "craftsmen."

Ustiluh's Jewish population governed itself according to pedigree. All the town idlers and anyone who conducted business outdoors were all part of this dull pastime called pedigree. So, the craftsmen who were then preoccupied with their work forfeited their share of the pedigree show.

Why was Ustiluh so preoccupied with matters of pedigree? Many years earlier, the town hosted a "big wedding," in which 70 "white Hassidic rabbis" participated. From that moment on, the town became, at least in the eyes of its Jewish residents, elevated to a special status. Ever since that wedding, they guarded their blue–blooded lineage with intensity. When a local family would engage a matchmaker to seek a match for a daughter, the girl's mother made sure to spell out in detail the family history and its living and deceased members' activities. The matchmaker had to know that there was not a single craftsman in the family!

If this was the situation with a simple groom, when it came to a match involving a contender for the rabbinate, pedigree played an even greater part in any proposed matrimonial arrangement. The boy had to have an impeccable pedigree, descended from eminent Hassidic rabbis. Moreover, the boy's outward appearance had to reflect his noble station.

[Page 22]

Indeed, the Jews of Ustiluh cherished and respected their marvelous young Rabbi Yosef ("Yossel") Wertheim. It is not clear if they revered the Rabbi because of his Hassidic leanings. The town's Hassidic residents – who drove the clean–shaven educated people out of their midst – were surprised to find the Rabbi not too sympathetic to their cause. In fact, the Rabbi did his best to draw the educated people back toward Torah observance by involving them in communal affairs.

Neither did the Rabbi's considerable scholarship play a decisive role in the community's admiration for him. Because the town's Jewish populace, save a few scholars, were more involved in Hassidism than in Torah learning.

The Rabbi recognized this from the very beginning of his tenure in Ustiluh. At his acceptance sermon in the Great House of Study, he noted the unique situation in which he found himself. Citing the phrase in Psalms (45:2) "My heart overflows with a good matter; I say: 'my work concerns a king.", Rabbi Wertheim explained if my words are directed at Kings, an appellation for Torah Sages, then (continues the quote: – my tongue is the pen of a ready writer. I can speak straight without allegories. However, if the situation is– "You are finer than the children of men." If you must first find favor in people's eyes (i.e., they cannot appreciate the speaker's erudition), then ("grace is poured upon your lips." Meaning, the speaker has to employ different language, a "graceful" manner of speech that unlearned listeners will appreciate....

The Ustiluh community accepted him. He was a brilliant orator who also spoke fluent Russian. He represented the townspeople to the local authorities when a local business venture needed some permits, or to demand that the government withdraw some cruel, foolish decree.

This position vis a vis the government allows us to understand the behavior of Pinchas the intermediary. when he appeared in the local shuls on Shabbat announcing, "I hereby proclaim by order of the Rabbi and with the agreement of the town dignities, that.... The intermediary would cast a knowing glance toward those sitting along the eastern wall of the shul. His eyes said it all. "Okay, no one had asked their opinion; he just meant it as a form of speech. But I am sure none of you would dare undermine my mission."

Ustiluh was fortunate. Not only were they proud of their Rabbi but also of their town's patron. Imagine having a well to do, good–hearted son, and a son–in–law a Torah scholar. Such a home had the best of both worlds: that of the good–hearted son's generosity together with the son–in–law's radiant Torah study and wisdom.

A certain school teacher named Wolf Jacobs was a contemporary of Yossel David Chaim's. Years later, he became known as the wealthy Yokhenzon. In his younger years, Yossel's father–in–law, although not considered one of the wealthier citizens of Ustiluh, supported him. Yossel, as he sat and learned Torah in the Trisker Shtiebel, seemed to be a typical Torah student, one of many in town. He stood out, however, by forever reiterating his desire and intention to become wealthy.

The years of support from his father–in–law ended and Wolf Jacobs Yokhenzon began supporting himself by selling lumber. He achieved breathtaking success as his dealings expanded far beyond Ustiluh's town limits. He owned entire forests throughout the region, a flour mill and a sawmill in the city of Ludomir, along with other holdings. Nevertheless, Wolf did not forget his roots, and continued living in Ustiluh.

[Page 23]

He employed dozens of family members in permanent jobs, and hundreds of others in temporary positions. He generously contributed to local charity institutions, and sustained several needy families in town.

Yokhenzon, unlike most other nouveau riche, had a large family. His sons furthered their education in other countries, and his daughters married professional men. But, Yokhenzon himself, like his earlier persona, Wolf Jacobs, wore a small felt cap on his head. Some claimed he still studied Torah on a regular basis.

His wife Sheindel comported herself in a similar, unassuming manner like her husband. She also assisted several communal charity organizations, and distributed cash and food parcels to the needy.

Even the couple's more "progressive" sons and daughters were raised in the spirit of simplicity and restraint

Over all, the Jews of Ustiluh were satisfied with the quality of life in their town. Of course, not everyone was content with their lot, as the case of Wolf Jacobs demonstrated. Some people always seemed to aim for more....

C. Protected by Faith

In memory of my father, an exemplary *chassid,*
Reb Dov ben Moshe Herschels
And in memory of my mother,
the righteous Bat Sheva
May their souls reside in the Garden of Eden

Yossel took leave of his rabbi the day after Yom Kippur to journey home. Early Friday morning, together with a group of Hassidim, he crossed the Russian border, reaching the town of Krilov. He found the nearest synagogue put on his tallit and Tefillin and prayed the morning prayers. One of the local Jewish residents invited him for breakfast. After the meal, as he rose to leave, his host begged him to stay for Shabbat. Yossel refused, as he had to get home that day, since Sunday was the eve of Sukkot. True, he owned a readymade Sukkah. But, such an important mitzvah, in which one's entire body is submerged (in the Sukkah), requires preparation and not just to rush into it straight from one's journey home.

After plentiful thanks and exchanged good wishes Yossel took leave of his hosts. His host accompanied him to the marketplace hoping to find a wagon destined to travel toward Ustiluh. When they did not find any, Yossel began his trek on foot, hoping that somewhere along the road he might meet up with a wagon traveling in the desired direction.

When he arrived at the first village on his route home, he asked about any available wagons that could bring him to his hometown, but there were none. Potato harvesting season and wheat planting occupied all the workers, so not one wagon ventured out of town.

[Page 24]

Attempting to shorten his route, Yossel veered off the main thoroughfare and cut through some side roads. At day's end he still was far from home.

Yossel came into a dense oak forest. Some local farmers assured him that the forest was only three kilometers long, but it seemed to him like he had been trudging without end.

In the afternoon it seemed as if all the forest creatures were napping. Peace and quiet reign throughout the area, save for an occasional lone bird twittering a soft melody, similar to the enraptured singing of some Hassid.

Silence enveloped Yossel as he trekked through the forest. In the background, as if contemplating their fate were the falling autumn leaves. Crunching the carpet of yellow–red leaves underfoot produced a soft undertone of pain of those who have been cut off from the living world. The changing color of those leaves still attached to the branches signified their realization that with every gust of wind, many more of them will fall to the earth.... Thus, each leaf waits in submission for its turn. No one is able to cancel this judgment. Such is the destiny of man as well, and of Yossel.

True, these leaves had seen better days, when they held tight to the tree's branches and drew their nourishment from them. Then, they were a fresh green color, bringing joy to all who beheld them. Whereas he, Yossel, most of his days were filled with heartache and suffering.

Already from childhood, Yossel's life was marred with trauma. His father earned a living from government–regulated products such as tobacco and whiskey. Occasionally, Yossel encountered bushy–mustached policemen entering their home, whose very appearance provoked a sense of dread. The police were checking real or imagined "violations" of the agreement with the government. Most of the time, his father managed to sway the officer's conclusions by means of some carefully placed "inducements" throughout the house. These successful outcomes, however, did not alleviate the constant fear and tension every time these uniformed officials visited their home. One day, an investigating officer caught his parents flagrantly breaking the law. This time, no financial stimuli would help, and Yossel's parents were sentenced to six months in jail.

Yossel did not really have much of a childhood. At his father's behest, he became engaged to Dina when he was fourteen years old. From then on, he had to conduct himself as an upcoming young man. At age seventeen, he married his wife. His father–in–law, who ran a tavern in town, promised to support him for ten years, allowing him to study Torah undistracted. He succeeded in his studies, but, later, tragedy struck when several of his children died young.

In the meantime, the Polish Army drafted Yossel. He tried to maim himself – a common practice in those days – to save himself from the clutches of the gentile army, but, did not succeed.

[Page 25]

As his enlistment day drew closer, and being in good health, he had to flee to far–off Lublin, where he spent a year as a teacher teaching one of the affluent inhabitants' children. When he sensed the authorities were closing in on him, Yossel escaped to Galicia, where he dwelled in the court of the Hosiatin Rabbi for a year or two.

Yossel's recollection of the aged rabbi evoked other, pleasant memories of the early years after his marriage, when he had first discovered his rabbi.

The Shtiebel in which Yossel prayed and studied served all the *Hassidim* who belonged to the various Rozhin descendants' courts. Yossel's father David Chaim belonged there. He prayed in the Shtiebel and contributed to the annual effort to raise funds for the rabbi's salary. But he did not visit any *tzadikim*. Hence, Yossel had to choose for himself a spiritual guide whom he would follow. He traveled from one town to another, visiting whichever *tzadikim* he could find. When he settled on a younger, lesser known *rebbe*, his friends asked him why he chose someone about whom nothing of note had ever been observed. Yossel smiled, telling them he had noticed and heard quite a bit about this *rebbe*. He saw the *rebbe's* holy hand cupped to his ear trembling when they recited Kaddish. He heard his voice shuddering with pure fear of Heaven. He then understood the rationale behind the *rebbe's* reputation for silence and tranquility fulfilling the phrase "For You (Hashem) silence is Your praise." (Psalms 65:2)

The pleasant memories had passed and Yossel recalled his latest life experiences.

Upon ascending the throne, Czar Nicholas II of Russia declared a blanket amnesty for everyone who had avoided previous military conscription. This meant no one would be punished for evading the draft, on condition they would now appear at the draft board for enlistment. Yossel returned home and after enduring three grueling years in the army, was finally discharged from military service.

Now, Yossel began working to develop his family's economic resources. He built a windmill in town, and began selling wheat. He did not, however, achieve much success in these ventures. His windmill suffered some large–scale damages, and his other business dealings did not generate much income. Finally, Yossel had to liquidate the remains of his business affairs. He moved into his father's house, and began a "temporary" teaching career until he found some other form of income that suited his nature. For the past fifteen years, he visited the "older *rebbe*" and now the younger one, requesting a blessing for "ample income." Each time, however, the response came: "find favor (in men's eyes) and success." This was the *rebbe's* way of recommending at least another year as a teacher....

This time, after receiving the *rebbe's* usual blessing, Yossel mustered up enough courage to request a different source of income, something better....

"I understand what you're asking," said the *tzaddik*. However, consider this. "You don't want to be a teacher. Another fellow wants to teach but is unqualified. What will happen to all these Jewish children?"

Yossel could think of nothing to say in response. Accepting the *rebbe's* ruling and his fate, "finding favor and success" would have to suffice. At least he would not have to ingratiate himself with the townspeople, as did other teachers. He would enjoy a degree of respect from his students, as was the situation had been until now.

[Page 26]

If Yossel had been someone of higher spiritual stature, he would have rejoiced in his good fortune: that of teaching Torah to Jewish children, as the *tzaddik* insisted. However, Yossel's material needs for income hounded him without end. In particular, he needed to provide for his three surviving children. Three out of ten were left. Their pale appearance and scruffy clothing broke his heart. His wife Dina, was a right–minded woman who never complained why God was doing this to her. Although she accepted God's decree with equanimity, she agonized in her heart over her family's physical condition. Yossel's contemplations ended with a start as he suddenly realized that the path upon which he was walking had disappeared, leaving him lost in the forest. Standing for a moment, he deliberated what to do. He listened for a sound of man or beast, but, heard nothing. Retracing his steps, Yossel turned to the side, and the path indeed had disappeared. He decided to continue walking straight in the hope of eventually get out of the forest. In the meantime, the hour grew later, and he worried that he would not reach any village before dark. The thought of being trapped in the forest at night terrified him. A cold sweat covered Yossel from head to toe, as he was convinced he heard wolves howling and wild boar grunting. Suddenly, a thought flashed through his mind. God has tested him with many challenging situations in his life, and he successfully passed them all; he would pass this one too. He resolved that once darkness settled in; he would not walk beyond the limits of Shabbat.

After he made this resolution, all fear and weakness disappeared. With newly emboldened steps, he continued walking through the forest. A short time later, the blue sky began poking through the trees before him. He was leaving the forest and entering a wide–open area. In the distance, he saw white houses belonging to local farmers.

Trembling with excitement, he hurried forward until he came upon a little stream winding through the bushes and river grass. Several women crouched at the creek's edge scrubbing clothes to the accompaniment of singing and animated chatter.

"Excuse me ladies, what is this village's name?

All at once, they stopped their washing and stared at Yossel with inquiring eyes. "This village is called Veischetin

"How far is it to Ustiluh?

"Six versts.

“Are there any Jews here?

“What do you think? Libka is here.

Yossel headed straight to the water, rinsed his hands, and uttered words of thanks to Hashem. He arrived at Libka's yard, where her husband was cutting hay with another farmer. Yossel asked for some water, over which he recited a blessing and drank. As he put the cup down, he announced: “I'll be spending Shabbat here!”

The master of the house was confused. “Why? There's enough time for you to get home.

“No,” Yossel proclaimed. “I'm not budging from here. All I wish from you is somewhere to sleep. I have my own food.

“That's not what I mean,” Libka apologized. It's just that a Jew such as yourself will be bored on Shabbat at my place where you won't find even one book from which to learn.” (Yossel would later learn that Libka had difficulty reciting Kiddush, which was why he did not want outsiders present at his Shabbat table.)

[Page 27]

“If I provide you with a wagon and horses, will you continue on home?

“Agreed.”

At once Libka turned to his farmer colleague asking, “Ivan, will you take this man to his hometown?”

“Yes, for five gold coins.”

Yossel did not quibble over the price, and even agreed to pay in advance. Ivan released his horses from the wheat cutting shaft and hitched them to the wagon.

As the setting sun approached the tree tops and its golden rays reflecting on the straw roofed villages houses, they set off for Ustiluh. Soon after leaving Veischetin, Yossel grabbed the whip from Ivan's hands and began lashing the horses to drive them ever faster.

“Are you trying to kill my horses?” stammered the farmer. “Do you think that your five gold coins will buy me new horses?”

As they approached the outskirts of Ustiluh, Shabbat candles were beginning to flicker one after the other in the windows.

D. The Fire

Friday night, Shabbat Bereishit, Yossel and his family were awakened from their sleep by insistent banging on the windows. “Fire, help!”

They rushed out in their pajamas to see the baker's house engulfed in flames. Men ran back and forth with buckets both empty and full. Shrieking women wrung their hands in despair. Children stood by weeping in helplessness. Yossel's widowed sister Rachel joined the firefighting effort. Only Dina stood by composed, awaiting her husband's instructions. The children stood near them shuddering with fear. Five–year–old Shmulik sobbed as he clung to his mother. Yossel quickly assessed the situation.

"Dina, take the children to Vogenfeld's house. The flames won't reach there. Rachel and I will try to save whatever we can from the house."

At that moment, Yossel's friend Pinchas Lichtman arrived. His house was far from the blaze, so he hurried over to see if there was anything he could do to help.

The two of them, Yossel and Pinchas, salvaged whatever they could from the house, placing it all in a pit behind the house. In the meantime, Bieliankin, a Polish aristocrat who lived nearby, arrived with a company of volunteer firefighters. The nobleman barked orders into a megaphone, and the firemen swung into action. All the local water carriers lined up with their wagons delivering water to the rubber fire hose that dosed the flaming inferno. The fire seemed to peter out.

[Page 28]

But, all of a sudden there arose a gust of wind from the direction of the burning house. Along the entire length of the street there were wooden houses, many covered with straw roofs. The structures were built close to one another, and flames leaped from roof to roof and from wall to wall. They engulfed the windows and doorways, soon becoming one huge horrifying conflagration that enveloped entire rows of houses.

The firefighters were unable to control the fire, and soon lost patience with the entire operation. Bieliankin screamed into the bullhorn until he was too hoarse to speak. The firemen dropped the fire hose and instead took up logs to break down the burning houses.

The rest of the town's residents did their best to assist them.

All this time, the houses on the opposite side of the street, including Yossel's, remained unaffected by the fire, the blazing fire reflecting on their walls.

Suddenly, the wind changed direction and came howling down the street. Sheaves of straw and sparks shot onto two of the houses, one of which was Yossel's.

Pinchas Lichtman, who, at that moment, was dragging a large parcel out of the house noticed this and hollered to Yossel

"Quick, bring water. The roof is on fire."

Yossel shook his head in resignation.

"I'm not doing any more. It's bad enough that I carried all sorts of things not permitted on Shabbat.

"What are you talking about? Will you allow your house to burn to the ground?"

Rachel wrung her hands lamenting:

"Oy vey, just a few buckets of water can save the house."

"I will not desecrate Shabbat, nor will I allow anyone else to on my behalf," Yossel pronounced without hesitation. "Two weeks ago, God tested me and I almost gave in. Now, I'm facing a more difficult test, and I will stand strong and not yield!

In the morning, instead of the houses that had formerly stood on the street, they found scorched heaps of bricks surrounded by piles of smoldering embers and ash. Smoke arose from some of the mounds. The downcast townspeople shuffled around the charred remnants searching for anything valuable that might have survived the inferno.

The only structure that survived intact was Yaakov the Wagon driver's shack. It was a small structure covered in dried straw from which some weeds sprouted. It was located a short distance from the spot upon which Yossel's house had stood. It seemed almost as if the simple hut was ashamed at having experienced a miracle and remained standing....

Among the remnants of Yossel's house, his oven stood out whole and undamaged. As if it was honored to have protected the Shabbat foods in it.

Yossel spread a cloth over a table he had salvaged from the fire, removed the Shabbat cholent from the oven and placed it on the table. The fragrant aroma of the cholent mingled with the stench of fire that lingered in the air.

Everyone ate in silence, as if they were in mourning. Every so often, some women muttered with sarcasm,

[Page 29]

"*Nu,* it's forbidden on Shabbat!" Yossel objected to this attitude. He called out, "Asher'l, let's sing some Shabbat songs. "Thank God who saves us..."

E. The More Things Change...

"The world runs as it always did." This statement requires some explanation. Is there only one world? Our Sages teach that in the future, God will bestow 310 "worlds" on every *tzaddik.* Even on our planet Earth there are many worlds. Furthermore, in little Ustiluh itself there were many "worlds." The world of the *Hassidim.* The world of the town leaders. The world of the enlightened. The latter were known as "the group of twenty–five" or "the intelligentsia." Other "worlds" large and small also existed in town aside from these three main factions.

For Shmulik, however, there was no question. His clearly defined world consisted of three main elements: his father's house, where he lived, ate, drank, and learned Torah with the older students. The house of prayer – the Shtiebel, and the home of Rav Hirsch David, the *Dayan.* All three provided fulfilling spiritual experiences and pleasure.

The great fire that consumed his father's house and the Shtiebel cast a pall of gloom over Shmulik's world. The family wandered from one small apartment to another, most of which were crowded and uncomfortable. The Heder moved into the large House of Learning while the Shtiebel members rented a private room for prayers.

Neither of these two temporary venues provided a satisfactory solution. These too–small sites cramped the Hassidic atmosphere in town. Within a few years, however, the Shtiebel was rebuilt, this time even bigger and more spacious than its predecessor. The old days had returned.

Twilight on Shabbat afternoon, and in the Shtiebel the participants just finished eating the small piece of challah, and an even smaller portion of herring. As the room fills with lengthening shadows of the waning Shabbat, Yossel leads the singing. Both Shmulik and Yisraelik, the Dayan's grandson, help him, with the rest of the group joining them in song. Even the hoarse voice of Sender the egg seller sounded pleasing within this mellow merger of voices.

The celestial angels accompanying the Shabbat as she prepares to take leave of her celebrants shroud themselves in the darkening Shtiebel. But, the reverberation of their beating wings merges with the elevated but still human singing.

Even the frogs outside that thronged the Bug River banks know the songs and contribute their part to the concert.

The fields beyond the Bug that were owned by Jews also offered up the scent of dried hay in honor of the departing Shabbat Queen.

[Page 30]

From behind Eliezer Tebel's house the rising moon in its splendor began to appear in the Shtiebel's windows. The enthralled choir's melodies affected even the phlegmatic "ruler of the night" as its light shimmered on the faces of all the participants, in accordance with the tempo of their movements.

Shmulik's soul felt as if it were going to burst out of his body. Yet, he was enjoying every moment of this experience.

Every holiday had its own special customs and its own kind of beverage. On the last day of Pesach, everyone gathered in the house of the Dayan for some wine. Whereas during Sukkot they celebrated with beer. They placed a keg of beer in the Shtiebel's huge sukkah that would help get the celebrants into the right frame of mind. But, the Dayan's son Reuvale was nowhere to be found, which would delay the start of the festivities. Yossel volunteered to find his friend Reuvale. Sender the Egg Seller joined him. After Sender joined the search party, Shmulik and Yisraelik also joined up. Sender brought a bucket of water with him, and they began their search for Reuvale.

Reuvaleh's sukkah was attached to his house, and opened on one side to a wood shed. A large wooden chest blocked the doorway. Sender and his companions made their way with tentative steps toward the wood shed. At the same time, Yossel appeared at the *sukkah's* entrance, announcing Happy Holiday, causing the assembled guests to face him. A fancy embroidered cloth that Reuvale had brought from Odessa covered the table, and two tall candles in silver candlesticks stood on it. A bottle of red wine, a few silver goblets, and fine cutlery graced the table. The guests had not yet finished their meal, when suddenly, Boom! The candles went out; all the participants were soaked with the water in Sender's bucket. From the woodshed, they heard the fleeing "intruders" footsteps and muffled laughter.

"Ah, it's hoarse Sender with his two little mischief makers!" exclaimed Moshe Yudel, Reuvaleh's son.

"Shmulik and Yisraelik," added Zelig Varsha.

Reuvale and his wife said nothing. "Pouring of the Water" was a long–standing Jewish custom….

The assembled recited Grace after Meals in the dark, and Reuvale and his sons went with Yossel to the Shtiebel.

The leftover water from may not be carelessly discarded without a thought. Thus, pronounced raspy–voiced Sender. Since some water remained in his bucket, he decided to perform another "mitzvah" with Dudi the carpenter, who was sitting in his sukkah. Sender poured the water on his head. The sopping wet Dudi left his sukkah shouting assorted abuses at them as he pursued them.

In the Shtiebel's sukkah, the first round of drinks was poured and downed. The group burst out in song in honor of the Sukkot holiday. Afterwards, the *Dayan* spoke some words of Torah, as was customary. Yonah, one of the younger men present, cleared his throat several times, indicating that he too, wished to say a few words.

"Nu Yonah, tell us some good words." Yonah complied and began speaking.

"The common practice during the weekdays is to eat simple foods and drink water.

[Page 31]

On Shabbat and holidays however, we eat tasty delicacies and drink wine. In the Sanctuary in Jerusalem, however, wine was poured on the weekdays, and water on the festival (of Sukkot). Why is this? To teach us that water is more precious than wine, as it is said, "he washes his garments in wine." (Bereishit 49:11)

"If that's the case," interjected the elderly Shikel, "why only on Sukkot and not on any of the other festivals?"

"Right, right," the crowd began to call out. They were not thrilled with this opposing interpretation.

"The reason is obvious," continued Shikel. "If they would have poured wine (as a libation) for all the bullocks, rams and sheep that were sacrificed on Sukkot in the Beit HaMikdash , there would be no wine left to drink on Simchat Torah."

This novel explanation was received with enthusiasm by all those sitting in the *sukkah*. Shikel was honored with another glass of beer. Yonah, the younger man, also received an additional cup of beer. But, not in the conventional manner, but rather it was poured on his head through the cracks in the roof of the sukkah, in the spirit of the aforementioned phrase, "he washes his garments in wine." The other guests had their clothes soaked with water, again through the cracks in the roof in accordance with the time–honored custom. All this was courtesy of Shmulik and Yisraelik, who performed their jobs with enthusiasm.

All Ustiluh's residents agreed that the spirited service of God that took place in the Rizhiner Shtiebel was way beyond anything experienced in any of the other Shtiblach. This was because in this Shtiebel Hassidim who followed several different *tzaddikim* prayed together. This led to a mutual influencing of one upon the other. How so? Reuvale the Dayan's son, would relate some of the Torah thoughts from Chortkov . (Reuven was a scholar of note; he published two books on the teachings of the Rizhiner *Rebbes*). He also brought the tunes and cantorial melodies of Manish the Chazzan in Chortkov to Ustiluh. Yossel, upon returning from Hosiatin would repeat the Torah thoughts and musical compositions of his *rebbe*. Even hoarse Sender would "tell over," as Yossel put it (as opposed to actually singing), the songs he heard in Sadigura.

On the anniversary of the death of any of the Rizhiner *rebbe's* six sons, and surely on that of the Rizhiner *rebbe* himself, all the Hassidim joined in the commemorative meal.

The celebration of the anniversary and all the preparations for it was an uplifting experience. A few days in advance, Shmulik would prepare huge lanterns that they placed in the eastern windows of the Shtiebel. On the day of the anniversary, Shmulik and Yisraelik would rise early and travel to Eliah Proviznik, who lived on the far side of the river, to buy fish for the meal.

This man, Eliyahu, leased the rights to operate the pontoon bridge crossing the Bug River from the government. He was also a successful fisherman. He was a tough, muscular man whose red face, adorned with a coarse red beard and a long nose advertised his physical strength. On one occasion, Eliyahu punched out a dozen drunken farmers for insulting him. They claimed that he took too long to move the bridge toward them. Eliyahu prayed in the Shtiebel on Shabbat and holidays. On Simchat Torah he was the one who was always called to perform the Reverse Lifting, since there was no one else in the Shtiebel strong enough to do it. But, Eliyahu did not feel this was his right, but rather paid a hefty price for the privilege of displaying the Torah Scroll in shul. He undertook to provide over the course of the year ample quantities of fish for all the anniversary meals.

[Page 32]

Shmulik's mother Dina, whose house was close to the Shtiebel, was in charge of preparing the meal. He helped her get the food ready. He cleaned the fish, checked the rice and the dried fruits, and chopped wood. Toward evening, all the lamps in the Shtiebel were lit along with hundreds of candles in copper chandeliers and on the windowsills. Two large signs in the eastern windows proclaimed "The Remembrance Day of the holy *tzaddik* ..."

Above the table for Torah reading, a lantern suspended atop a wooden pole, rotated by the man appointed over the chandeliers.

After learning Mishna for the elevation of the deceased *tzaddik's* soul, the assembled sat down to the meal. They broke bread and drank "l'chaim" – "may he (the deceased *tzaddik* being honored) be a good interceder for all the Jews. After eating the fish, a second cup of wine was poured, and Sruli Shifras began chanting an appropriate melody asking the *tzaddik* to remind Hashem about our difficulties and the constant ordeals we faced.

Alas, Sruli stuttered, and so was unable to pronounce some sounds and words without repeating them several times. When, however, he sang, the words flowed from his lips without effort. For this reason, whenever he had a yahrzeit, he would sing the Kaddish. He also had responsibility for singing certain chants for Shabbat and holidays– all of which he sang using his Kaddish melody. Sruli had a small notebook to remind him of the words. The only way to understand those words was if you heard Sruli sing them. He would begin in a soft voice, "Remind Him, speak before Him the Torah and good deeds learned and performed by those now residing in the earth." As there was no suitable response, he raised his voice, as if to complain, Remind Him, speak before Him oy, the Torah, the Torah and good deeds learned and performed by those now residing in the earth." Then, the rest of those present joined in with even more passion, "Remind Him." Why are we so quiet? We should be storming the heavens. Remember their love (for You) and sustain their offspring so that the remnant of Yaakov will not be lost." A Jewish community is gathered to eat and drink, yet they do not forget their main reason for coming together: The Memorial Day for the *tzaddik*, it is in a time of Divine mercy, to beg for compassion for the Jewish people.

Ustiluh's streets were tranquil at this time of night. No light appeared in any of its windows, as if the low houses wrapped in darkness wished to close their eyes during this rest time. Not so the Rizhiner Shtiebel. The light radiating from its windows revealed that it was wide awake even at this late hour. Inside, they danced hands on shoulders, heads lowered, eyes shut, singing a melody without words. Their song poured out into the sleeping town's streets and throughout the world....

[Page 33]

A dog wakes up from all the noise. What nerve, he barked, waking up hard working creatures, disturbing their well–deserved rest. Some annoyed roosters– squawked what was all this celebrating about? Right about now, some Jews are rising for Midnight prayers, and over here they are celebrating?

"It doesn't matter," calls out Gershon Leib the beadle, as if speaking directly to the Master of the Universe. "We'll make up with You. We are dancing in your honor. You've been angry with us for long enough. Save us and take us out of this exile and You will also benefit ...!

The town elders continued striding on their life's journey with confidence, planning to continue this way until their last days on earth. While the children still followed in their footsteps, much of the teen–aged youth were abandoning the Shtiebel and the time–tested traditions in search of an improved life.

One path lead from the Shtiebel to the new life's choices. A fifteen–sixteen–year–old youth traveled to one of the neighboring villages to teach the children of the Jewish millers and bartenders, returning to Ustiluh for the holidays shorn of his beard and side curls, sporting a dapper hat and stiff collar. From this point, it was a short path to forsaking the Torah lifestyle ....

During Shmulik's childhood years, the community distanced such enlightened people from the Shtiebel. They were not fazed by this treatment, and often taunted Yossel and Reuven, "You will yet see Moshe Yudel and Asher with shaven faces."

Such contemptuous words horrified Yossel.

"May your mouths be filled with dust!" He angrily raged at them. "It'll never happen!" Yossel turned out to be right; Moshe Yudel and Asher were the only ones in their group who remained in the House of Learning until their weddings, with a soft fluff of a beard on their faces.

The fathers of these two managed to save their sons from the "dangerous winds" that blew through town in those days. But, in general the parents lost in the struggle for their children, who mostly just slipped out of their grasp.

The would–be enlightened people reached a cross–road. Most of them left town for the bigger cities where they found movements and ideologies that interested them. Most joined the various revolutionary socialist movements. Some, however, returned to Ustiluh to "spread the light of knowledge" by offering private lessons in Hebrew and Russian. These lessons laid the foundation for the "Renovated Heder" and planted the seeds of Zionism in the town.

[Page 34]

F. Hazardous Times

The Jewish residents of the "Pale of Settlement" viewed the heavy clouds gathering in the political skies over Europe in the summer of 1914. On the one hand was the dread of a nightmarish war. Not like the far–off Manchurian War, this war would be fought in their home areas. On the other hand, they dared entertain the hope that the Tsar would lose the war against the enlightened nations, just as he lost the previous war with Japan. Maybe all or most of the "Pale of Settlement" would pass into the hands of the victorious nations. Ustiluh's location made it likely to be included in Austrian territory, which was ruled by a reasonably benevolent monarch. Even if Germany ultimately took over the area, it would still be a great improvement over Tsarist Russia. From an economic standpoint, it could even be better than Austria.

All these possibilities were explained and emphasized in hushed tones in the Shtiebel, after verifying that no one was eavesdropping on them.

Apparently, the local political "analysts" were not aware of the Polish National Renewal Movement, and the future roles France and England would play. However, when the government announced a general military call–up on the eve of Tisha B'Av, all the great hopes evaporated from everyone's heart, to be replaced with utter fear for the future.

That intuition of imminent destruction was demonstrated on Tisha B'Av night. The night that for generations was "predisposed to calamities" Even the young pranksters in town, who had planned the traditional Tisha B'Av shenanigans, immediately sensed that the situation was serious. The shoes that everyone removed (before reading the Scroll of Lamentations) were not mischievously filled with water, and the watering cans remained idle.

"And the entire assembly raised up their voices…" (Numbers 14:1)

The next day, the first reports from the new war reached Ustiluh.

"The Germans have entered Kalish!"

"They've also taken Czestochowa!"

No one knew what to make of these reports. Only a small number of people in the Shtiebel sat on the floor reading the Lamentations. The rest gathered in the yard awaiting the latest news dispatches that some youths brought from the market place. News items that were irrelevant, even if true.

"Notices were posted not to sell whiskey to the recruits."

"So–and–so decided to enlist, and his mother is sobbing in the street."

"A gang of gentiles, apparently draftees, broke the door of X's store, stole a few bottles and disappeared."

"There's a lot of commotion at the police station; cops on horseback are coming and going."

[Page 35]

In the midst of this turmoil arose a rumor that the civilian population was ordered to relocate to the district administrative center. Without bothering to verify the reliability of this strange report, people burst into the Shtiebel shouting to hurry up and finish praying now; and to start reciting "Ali Zion." We have to get out of here!"

Yossel was standing before the Ark, with tears streaming down his face. His choked voice trying to pierce the hearts of the others praying in the Shtiebel. "As the wind shakes the trees in the forest…" (Part of the Lamentations poems).

In the end they learned it was a false alarm. But, the events of the following days were astounding, even amusing.

Some townspeople met a company of Austrian army soldiers in a nearby field. They appeared to be taking a pleasure hike, not carrying out any kind of military maneuvers. The commanding officers spoke to the Ustiluh residents in Yiddish or some language similar to it. When the local Jews were ready to go back to town, the officers handed them bundles of Yiddish leaflets requesting "Our Fellow Jews", residents of Volhynia to assist the army of the pious Emperor Franz–Josef to banish the "Russian pig" from the region.

One of the Jews present was convinced that he recognized one of the officers as "Pechania Kopika."

About a year before the war broke out, a strange ruddy faced man appeared in Ustiluh. He spent the days walking through the town's streets selling perfumed paper strips and various children's' toys. With an enchanting melody, he proclaimed throughout the day, "Pechania Kopika," ("fragrance for a kopek"), "Kopika Pechania." He occasionally publicized the prices for the other merchandise. When children gathered around him, he would demonstrate how to use the toys, like the inflatable peacock, or the talking rooster. But he never entered into a conversation with anyone. Even when people stopped him to buy something, he would not interrupt his sales message. He handed the merchandise to the buyer, accepted the money, all the while announcing "Pechania Kopika." Some said that at the inn where he stayed, he would say in German that he is a Jew. But, beyond that, he never uttered a word about himself.

This fellow spent about a week in town. Although no one purchased any more of his merchandise, he continued to smile at everyone whom he met in the street. Questions about this man's true identity persisted until one day he vanished from town. Now, it became obvious this man was a government spy! The Jews of Ustiluh chuckled how they allowed "Old Efraim Yossel" (Emperor Franz Josef) to dupe them. But there was more to come.

Several years back, a certain Hungarian settled in one of the small nearby towns. As was fashionable with Hungarians, he wore an elegant top hat. He began dealing in animal husbandry, specifically raising horses. A few weeks ago, the Hungarian disappeared. Well, just as no one knew from where he came, no one knew where he went. But, lo and behold, yesterday a company of Austrian infantrymen appeared in town, led by their commanding officer, who walked straight into one of the Jewish owned pubs in town.

[Page 36]

"Good morning, Sara! How are you? Can we have something to eat and drink?"

This Jewess was stunned and speechless. The face and the voice were familiar, but from where? An Austrian Army officer?

The officer laughed heartily.

“Sara, don't you recognize Yonders the Hungarian? It all became clear now, but, where was “Punya,” another shadowy figure who hung around town at the same time as Yonders. In fact, not one Russian soldier was to be seen in the area. As if they were embarrassed to show their faces here.

Why did “they” not come?

Not only did “they” not enter Ustiluh, they completely disappeared from the area. In their place appeared “our” (Austrian) army in a full show of strength. It was like a huge beast leaving its lair in search of prey, walking confidently, unaware of the danger waiting nearby.

For several hours, a seemingly endless stream of infantry, cavalry, and heavy artillery with all their equipment paraded down the main street. Where they came from and where they were going no one knew. They faded away in the horizon, along with their confident victory songs that gradually died down as the soldiers vanished into the distance.

At noon, the column halted in its tracks. From the field kitchens arose fragrant aromas that stimulated everyone's appetite. The soldiers were in an elevated mood as they prepared for their meal. As they began eating the steaming hot, tasty porridge, they suddenly heard the thunder of artillery fire. Although the shell landed in an empty field, it was enough to sow confusion among the troops.

“About face!” Came the hastily issued order that was transmitted from one soldier to the other along the entire length of the column. The soldiers turned around beating a hurried and disorderly retreat back to whence they came.

This time, the civilian population did not wait for orders. Large numbers, particularly of women and children grabbed whatever provisions they could and crossed the new bridge over the Bug River. A bridge that was hastily constructed before the war's outbreak.

Dina, Sima, and Shmulik left with the other refugees, while Yossel, like so many others, remained behind to guard, to whatever extent possible, their property

Jews who lived in the villages west of the River Bug, among them many landowners (not like the Jews of Volyn who were not permitted to own land) and assorted people of means received the refugees with great compassion and concern that “perhaps this will befall us too.” They housed the new arrivals in barns and provided them generously with the vegetables that grew in their gardens.

The local Polish and Ukrainian populace's treatment of the new refugees was at best restrained. As if they had not yet decided how they would handle them....\

[Page 37]

Dina, however, who was born in just such a village, met a peasant woman at the well. An interesting conversation ensued.

“My friend,” sighed Dina, “look how people are uprooted from their little corner of the world. Who knows what will be left from all their hard work?”

“Yes, it's surely a bitter fate. But, if we (non–Jews) had to leave our places, it would be even worse.”

“Why? On the contrary. At least you have your property, your fields that cannot be destroyed or stolen. But, us Jews, if our houses are burned and the merchandise in our stores looted, what do we have left?”

"What do you mean? You people all have gold and silver sewn into your clothes. You'll be able to manage wherever you go. But, us? Should we take our livestock or the produce of the fields with us?"

Dina smiled as she nodded, thinking to herself, what a waste of time to try to talk sensibly with fools. They really believed that all the Jews without exception had hidden caches of money.

Forced inactivity on a summer's day is more difficult than insomnia on a winter's night. All the more so considering the conditions and the mood of the refugees at that time. Under these circumstances, people try to ease their boredom in any way possible. Strangers become friends and discover common interests. Issues that normally would not concern people in the least suddenly become matters of great important.

Only God knows how the refugees found out that a solar eclipse was forecast for that very day. There was no radio, and newspapers did not circulate in the area. Nevertheless, at the appointed time, everyone stood outside equipped with pieces of smoked–covered glass. The visible disk of the sun suddenly began to darken. Everyone placed the glass pieces up to their eyes, which allowed them to view this celestial phenomenon from start to finish.

As to the significance of the eclipse, many different approaches arose among the Ustiluh refugees. The Torah scholars among them quoted the words of our Sages: A diminishment of the sun (i.e., an eclipse) is a bad sign for the enemies of Israel (some read it: for the idolaters). They interpreted this as a sign that the war will continue. This contradicted the rumors simmering among some of the refugees that the war would end shortly. Others explained it as a purely scientific naturalistic phenomenon, which is how they were altogether able to predict the eclipse in advance. Shmulik tried to make peace between the two points of view.

Some reinforced their pessimistic outlook by employing gematria and allusions they claim are written in the Zohar and other Kabbalistic books regarding the War of Gog and Magog. According to all indications this was indeed what was happening.

[Page 38]

Even Reb Yoel the Elder, one of the village notables who was a Torah scholar and a mohel, proved from some book whose author was unknown, "clear indications" that this was in fact, the war of the End of Days that was part of the Messianic tribulations. A subdued feeling of terror took hold of the listeners over what the future bode.

In the interim, more news from the town reached the refugees. News that in the end turned out to be baseless rumors. But this is what was reported:

On the day they all fled Ustiluh, after the shooting subsided, the Austrian army took up positions around the town. Civilian traffic was severely curtailed, but, in the town itself life slowly returned to normal. Meaning: the shop owners were forced to reopen their stores so that the soldiers could buy whatever they needed. The latter, however, were not satisfied with their daylight shopping. Many stores, particularly those that sold food, clothing, and shoes were broken into at night and looted. On the other hand, it appeared possible to earn some money supplying the army with freshly baked bread.

On the third day of the refugees' flight, a Friday, many returned to town. The remainder, however, were not so quick to go back home, preferring instead to remain where they were for Shabbat. It turned out that their homes did not require that much protection, and so, remaining where they were would not cause them any losses. Yet, when it was time to light candles, when both men and women were wearing their weekday clothing to receive the Shabbat, it seemed as if the Holy Queen herself was peering through the door in a silence bathed in pain and degradation.

Someone found two rolls over which he recited kiddush for everyone present and distributed slivers of bread to all. The meal itself, consisted of dried bread with some fresh vegetables without table and chairs, placed over some paper or a soiled cloth in place of a tablecloth.

That night, fourteen–year–old Shmulik was unable to sleep. A small kerosene lamp hung on one of the columns in the middle of the barn. It lit up only a small part of the room. All around the rest of the barn shadows spread out over the straw lining the floor. It seemed to Shmulik that the darkness was stretching further and further, and would soon penetrate his body. He buried his face in the fragrant straw to escape the struggle between light and darkness around him and tried to fall asleep. A tapestry of bright green dots on a black background flooded his mind as if passing endlessly before his closed eyes. In the midst of this decoration darted murky shadows like small clouds. Whenever he closed his eyes in the dark, he would see this speckled tapestry flowing by silently, as if it were being pushed along by some powerful and invisible force. This empty display always aroused in Shmulik a mysterious sadness. It seemed to him like another existence above the known worlds. Perhaps this was the "World of Chaos" in which, according to the Aggadah, the souls of sinners wandered.

This time, Shmulik had a different idea. Was this not the entire display of all the past generations that God reveals to us at night when we sleep? Perhaps billions of souls come forth from the darkness, pass by in a flash, and return to the darkness.

[Page 39]

Shmulik did not have the strength to watch the frightening presentation. He opened his eyes, trying to focus them on the real objects in the barn. Particularly the other people asleep there, snoring blissfully in their slumber. But now they seemed to him so pathetic. Green dots? He felt sorry for them and for himself. A world war? Many tragedies would occur. Hundreds of thousands, maybe millions would die. But, what sort of impression would this make on the â€˜spotted tapestry?' On the destiny of the generations? It would be unable to hold back the deluge for even a moment, as if nothing had happened….

Shmulik awoke to the sound of his mother's gentle voice. It was morning, and the others had already left the barn. Outside the pleasant chirping of birds could be heard, along with the giggling of little girls. "The men are planning to go to the neighboring village where there is a minyan," said Dina. "There's a Torah scroll there too. Hurry up and you can go with them."

Shmulik got dressed and went outside. A sunny, end of summer day greeted him as befitting a Shabbat morning. The dew drops glistening on the stubbles of grain as if winking to him, Shmulik, all your speculating is nonsense. The world is beautiful despite all the problems.

When the refugees returned to their town on Sunday, there was no trace of the army, and town life had mostly returned to normal. Later, they found out that on that very first confusing day, the Austrians left the area retreating back to their country's border. The sole cannon shot was, according to Ustiluh residents, was intended as a double gesture of greeting and farewell. However, the "strategists" in town explained that the Austrians' cannon fire wanted to hold off the Russians until they could safely retreat in an orderly fashion. Of course, the question remained, what were the Austrians strategy? Why did they invade, and why did they retreat at the first hint of an actual war?

The town's strategists had no satisfactory answers to these questions. For lack of a better explanation, they decided that "Efraim Yossel" (Emperor Franz Josef) wanted to lay a trap for "Punya" (Czar Nicholas). The same scheme was attributed to "Velvel" (Kaiser Wilhelm II of Germany), who pulled his troops back from Northwest Poland, allowing "Punya" to enter East Prussia. In the end, the Russian defeat at the Battle of Tannenberg confirmed this.

In any case, it was good for Ustiluh that the war moved away from its environs, and was left to speculating and jokes at "Punya's" expense.

However, when the Russian army advanced toward eastern Galicia laying siege to the fortress town of Pzemishil. Ustiluh' s residents were baffled. These latest developments did not fit with the "entrapment" theory they had promoted earlier. As far as Ustiluh's security was concerned, it was clear that even without the entrapment schemes promoted by some, the situation was more complex than they had imagined.

Pzemishil's stubborn resistance under siege encouraged the local Jews that the situation could change for the better.

However, the more this concealed feeling increased among the Jews, so did the fury of the local Ukrainian farmers increase.

[Page 40]

The latter were convinced that the Jews, using various means, were assisting the enemy; the proof was that they uncovered the secret of Pzemishil's survival.

They never understood why the Jewish peddlers bought large amounts of discarded flax, and … eggs. Now, the matter was obvious to all! For many years, the Jews had planned this war. They sent the aforementioned materials to Austria, who then used them to create an elastic net surrounding Pzemishil. The attacking Russian's bullets and shells simply bounced off the net!

True, nothing lasts forever, and the "wall of eggs" finally collapsed, and Pzemishil was conquered by the Czar's forces. There was, however, the more formidable wall – the Carpathian Mountains that now stood before the advancing Russian army. Those mountains were like a giant altar, upon which a seemingly limitless number of soldiers were sacrificed upon it for many months.

Anyone who had a friend or relative in the army worried about their well–being. It did not matter if the newspapers reported stunning victories for "our" army (Austria), or small tactical retreats "straighten out the front lines…." Ustiluh residents knew how to read between the lines. In any case, everyone understood that the enemy (Russia) was not attacking with peashooters. They were all enveloped in a critical situation.

Regarding military conscription, Ustiluh was not heavily affected, because most draft–age men were able to wriggle their way out of enlistment. From an economic standpoint, the war had no negative effects on the town during those early days of the conflict. On the contrary, most of the town's merchants registered improvement in their finances, some more and some less. As is usual in these cases, the rest of the townsfolks feasted on whatever crumbs were left over.

G. Sword, Pestilence and New Masters

From the killing fields of Galicia, as the retreating Russian army approached Ustiluh, a cholera epidemic now erupted throughout the regional towns and villages. The first victim in Ustiluh was Tzertyl, the wife of Simcha Schwalb. A pious and upright woman whose death, just like her life, was beset with heartache. A terrible fear swept through the town when the small funeral procession made its way to the cemetery, along with the report about the nature of the illness for which there was practically no cure.

True, the townspeople managed to provide Tzertyl with at least a respectable funeral. But, when the number of deaths multiplied, the authorities forbade holding funerals altogether. The dead were taken out and buried privately with few people attending, like a funeral for a miscarried fetus.

At that time, the Talmud Torahs were closed. Worker's apprentices failed to show up in the workshops. There were no minyans in the shuls. Movement throughout the town was drastically reduced, and public activity was almost completely suspended. Whoever did not have to go outside enclosed themselves in their homes with the windows shuttered. They drank much whiskey and consumed quantities of garlic, as recommended by medical experts. The community conducted a wedding in the cemetery between Crazy Isaac and Dumb Frieda Patika – a well–known providential omen to ward off plagues.

[Page 41]

But death continued to laugh at these useless measures. It penetrated the sealed windows and hunted down its victims despite all the medical efforts and the proverbial omens. It snatched its victims without remorse or distinction between families' pedigrees. The horror drowned out the mourners' grieving shrieks, freezing the tears on their cheeks.

Like a fox in a chicken coop, the disease might have continued reaping its harvest of unfortunate victims cowering in their houses. But, as commonly happens in times of crisis, some brave souls, people with a sense of communal responsibility rose to the occasion to help their townspeople. The first to lend a helping hand were those volunteers who were skilled in the only known remedy (at that time): massaging the ill person's body. They managed to save the lives of many stricken people, and after a while, the number of those recovering from the disease became greater than those who perished. Next came the dedicated members of the burial society who did their job without respite. Whenever anyone died, they arrived to remove the deceased as quickly as possible, to prevent the germs from spreading and to spare the other family members additional grief by having their loved one's body in their house. Lastly, were the collectors for charity who continued their holy work of providing the needy with food and drink, as needed.

The plague raged through the town for several weeks, its grim harvest laid to rest in the local cemetery. But, just as the cholera epidemic receded, new misfortunes loomed.

One Sunday morning in the month of Av (August), Ustiluh's residents were surprised to see Russian Army units in town. They arrived the previous night and took up positions along the banks of the Bug River. People who lived in the area were ordered to move to the east side of town. The Russians warned the townspeople not to wander in the streets. The relocation began right away: men, women and children, some in vehicles, some on foot, loaded down with bedding, clothes, and food, began trudging eastward.

In the larger courtyards of the older houses, dozens of families gathered, along with their suitcases and bundles, grouped by which street or Shtiebel they belonged. The scenes were reminiscent of waiting rooms at a train station. People who prayed in the Rizhiner Shtiebel found shelter in the warehouse and yard of Reb Koneh Pomerantz. Reb Koneh was a well to do wheat dealer who inherited the business and the large house from his father, Reb Yehoshua. The man of the house, tall, with a pointy white beard and thick eyebrows, mingled among his agitated guests, encouraging the women with comforting words and the men with a whiff of snuff tobacco from his silver case.

Among the refugees were Yossel and his family, and the Lemberger family, whose mother, a survivor of the cholera outbreak, was still recovering from her illness. She was lying on a pile of pillows, a gaunt figure with a yellow tinged face.

Toward evening, Shmulik's mother realized that she forgot a pillow at home. Without telling anyone, Shmulik ran home to get the pillow.

The streets were empty; the cloudy skies fostered a sense of dread.

[Page 42]

Shmulik panicked and thought to flee back to his mother. He stopped when he realized that Maya Lemberger, who worked for his sister Sima the seamstress, would consider him a coward. He made his way to his house that was near the defensive trenches. Even in this part of town not a soul was to be found.

Shmulik noticed plumes of smoke rising above the Bug River Bridge. He grabbed the pillow and prepared to rush back. Out of nowhere the elderly Yisrael Dovrishes appeared before him.

"Ah, Shmulik," exclaimed the old man. "Come to the Shtiebel; we need a minyan for Mincha." Shmulik stood there dumbfounded. Is this man sane, he wondered?

"Why are you standing there? Come along!"

At that moment, an explosion resonated in the sky. Although it was a short blast, it seemed as if the world's ceiling collapsed and fell to the earth. "Is this the end of the world?" The thought flashed momentarily in Shmulik's mind.

Heaven and earth, however, did not disappear. Both he and the old man were healthy and unscathed. Even the pillow Shmulik held in his hand was undamaged. He did notice that the Bug River Bridge was destroyed, some of its remnants floating on the water.

Maya was the first to notice his return to the courtyard, and announced, "Here's Shmulik!"

He passed the test....

The townspeople huddled in their houses and courtyards for three days and nights, filled with trepidation for what the future would bring. From time to time, the Russians fired shells toward the river probing for some response from the Austrians, but received none.

In the meantime, the guests settled in to their new lodgings. The custom of Ustiluh's women to bake enough challahs on Friday to last for the coming week served them well. No one lacked bread that week. Some of the more pragmatic women remembered to bring along containers of jelly with them to spread on their bread, something that helped those recovering from cholera.

The barrage of bullets in the background no longer seemed to make an impression on anyone. At any rate, the gunfire did not disrupt the women chatting in the courtyard. Yossel found a quiet corner where he could look into "Chovat HaLevavot (Duties of the heart)". Menashe, the head of the Lemberger family preferred a more public venue where he studied Midrash in the traditional singsong melody, murmuring to himself while stroking his beard. All the while, Shmulik, along with the rest of the curious group, peered through the cracks in the gate. They were monitoring the activities and movements of the various military units, infantry and cavalry, as they passed quietly through the town's main street.

In those humid evenings lighting any fires was prohibited. People who were worn out from the daytime idle chatter, found it difficult to fall asleep. Many twisted and shifted from side to side, writhing in the darkness. In contrast, the band of the curious were now following the fires that began appearing everywhere, trying to identify which villages were burning.

[Page 43]

The red skies prompted the men to speculate what was causing the sky's change of color. For the young women and girls, it conferred a mysterious, almost magical sensation. They sat clustered together on wool blankets in a circle, whispering in hushed fearful tones about past happenings and even humorous incidents all at once. On life's frustrations and even a few suicides, which promoted the fables of dead people wandering in the night.

Redemption arrived unexpectedly.

Tuesday afternoon, the probing of the Russian artillery stopped, leaving everyone with an uneasy feeling that the quiet was just temporary. The sound of a horse galloping in the distance was occasionally heard. But, when it grew dark, they heard the sound of marching boots and rattling vehicles that continued for some time.

Later on, the evening became quiet, as silence spread its wings over the countryside. Yet, not all living things were at ease. “The Splendor of Creation” huddled behind locked doors, fearful and nervous about what the future will bring, listening to the dark silence.

Suddenly, someone noticed the northern skies became red. A fire was raging out of control as the glow of the blaze grew stronger spreading throughout the sky. Its reflection lit up the faces of the frightened and helpless people strewn throughout the area.

A few brave individuals opened the gate and went out to verify the fire's location. Slowly and quietly, they advanced toward the flames that were rising above the rooftops, indicating that it was close by. In a moment, the fire reached the main town square, through which the main road passed in its descent to the lake (“Stav”). Baruch Hashem, the fire is beyond the town!

From a hill overlooking the Luga River valley, they could see the long bridge and the flour mill engulfed in enormous flames that were reflected in the lake's waters on the right and the Bug River to the left. Not a soul could be seen in the area, yet with that silent backdrop there was an unusual combination of sounds. The sound of the water spilling into the Bug from the Luga along with the popping noise of wood consumed by the flames, together with the swishing sound made by the huge smoldering trees falling into the river.

The people stood transfixed by the awe–inspiring scene. They returned to their courtyard and announced, “The Stav Bridge is burning; the Russians apparently have fled.”

The people were not quite sure that they were truly safe, so a larger group set out toward the defensive trenches located at town's edge. Proceeding slowly and cautiously, they reached the trenches, only to find them empty. By the light of a few small lanterns, they could see evidence of a hasty withdrawal.

Now from the south came the verification for which they had hoped. From their appearance, they were two German Army soldiers, wearing their steel helmets and rifles in hand. Pale and exhausted they made their way to the group, questioning them on the whereabouts of “the Russ.” Are they still in town? When did they flee, last night? Great, thank you.

[Page 44]

They turned around and disappeared into the night.

The following afternoon, a sizeable German infantry unit arrived, staging an ostentatious entrance. The soldiers' cheery eyes matched the smiling sun that joyfully shone that day sparkling on their steel helmets, illuminating the eyes of Ustiluh's citizens.

They truly arrived as liberators, not as conquerors. The soldiers were relaxing and enjoying a light meal. All at once, Jews of all ages approached them in a first–time encounter with German soldiers, and were amazed at what they found. Tall, blond young men in crisp uniforms. And their rations! White bread, sausages, vegetables, chocolate and beer. No wonder they were clobbering “Punya.”

The Jews struggled to express their feelings in Germanized Yiddish. The soldiers, puffing on their pipes answered them, “Ja, ja…” (“Yes. Yes”). Translation: we don't understand what you are saying, but we know that you are well–intentioned and are our friends.

This peaceful scene quickly evaporated the next day when the “friendly boys” began rounding up some of their “friends” for forced labor reinforcing defensive positions and rebuilding the destroyed river bridges. Ustiluh residents, like all the liberated Jews, considered themselves partners with the conquering German forces. They were not particularly interested in performing forced labor. Especially since a more profitable task was at hand.

The local farmers, including the residents of the Gentile Street, abandoned their homes and followed the retreating Russian army eastward. Their forsaken fields were laden with ripe grain, Now, whoever could, went to check the empty villages, large sacks in hand.

The German army remained in Ustiluh for only two weeks. An essential strategic task awaited them: to strike at the Czar's retreating army. The job of maintaining order in Ustiluh was left to various Austro–Hungarian Army riff raff who entered the town afterwards. Slovakian farmers, old stubborn men served as sanitation workers. Young, arrogant Polish boys were deputized as policemen. Appointed over all the above were German and Hungarian speaking officers. All of these were no less anti–Semitic than the Russians.

The military governor resided in the regional capital city Ludomir. He was a villainous type who stood out in his cruelty. All of his underlings throughout the area did their utmost to find favor in his eyes by imitating his brutal conduct.

The provisional government began rationing food. Bread allocation was shrinking from month to month, to near starvation levels, and travel restrictions were throttling the populace. The wooden bridge that the new rulers built over the Bug River was nicknamed "the golden bridge." The reason was that a permit to cross it required payment of 15 Rubles in gold coins. (In Austrian banknotes, this was a huge sum.)

[Page 45]

On the sprawling lands beyond the Bug, people were telling astounding tales. There was a free economy there, where they sold delicious pastries like in normal times. For sure, no one bought the expensive crossing permit merely for leisure. These people did not complain about the state of emergency, but they were the exception. The general populace suffered great hardship due to the grim conditions. Hunger, however, is a strong motivator. When the supplies and grain from the nearby abandoned villages were finished, the residents, including children, began trying to reach some of the further towns, lugging containers of kerosene, salt, matches, and other goods to barter for grain and beans. Of course, those appointed to uphold law and order did not engage in such activities and tried to catch the criminals. Here was an opportunity for the brave Austrian heroes to level fines, confiscate contraband merchandise, and even send people to jail. This, in addition to various extortion schemes and false accusations that they leveled against the Jewish population while performing their sanitation and administrative duties.

H. Famine

If, during normal times, people are challenged by the long, boring, freezing winter months, all the more so was this the case during troubled times. The cost of staple items rose daily, while peoples' source of income declined. So, we may assume that Ustiluh's citizens looked forward to spring 5676 (1916) with greater than usual excitement. At the very least, in the warming weather they would not need to wrap themselves with extra layers of clothing. As to food, whoever had a small plot of land near his house could raise his own vegetables. Someone who did not have a yard could visit the abandoned fields filled with all sorts of after–growth, from which one could prepare all sorts of dishes that fooled one's digestive tract. Despite this, people were constantly seeking more nourishing stuff to eat.

And so, the local authorities found creative ways to utilize these forsaken fields. The military officer who served as mayor arranged to sow vast areas with grain seeds and potatoes. He employed hundreds of Ustiluh's residents for this work, paying them enough to purchase half a kilogram of bread. Those who felt this wage was too low were free to seek more rewarding employment elsewhere.

Only a few brave souls succeeded in this. Shmulik was not one of them. Following the advice of some friends from the Shtiebel, they traveled around the nearby villages to barter goods for different goods. But this required a degree of flattery, deceit, and other outstanding character traits that Shmulik found intolerable. He decided to go back to planting potatoes for the mayor.

Still, even this work involved some trickery to partially compensate for the unjust wages being paid the workers. But, in this case, the methods used were available to all, and almost everyone succeeded at it.

[Page 46]

When the planting was finished, all the workers kept a few potatoes in their buckets, covering them with their jackets. They carried the buckets on their shoulders, with its opening against their backs as if they were empty. In this way, they marched past the soldier guarding the area singing to themselves:

We pass like free people
Ignoring the Memorial Day
Of his father and mother
Without fear and trepidation
We walk slowly and easily
Please, quietly…

When the next shift of workers arrived and began emptying the buckets, the latter hurriedly hid their pickings under mounds of earth, intending to retrieve them later. Although these efforts repeated themselves daily, only a few people were ever able to salvage their booty. This was because the fields were guarded by soldiers. When the smuggled spuds began sprouting the field was covered with circular growths of potato plants. All the field workers recognized the secret of their unusual appearance.

Even before the end of the potato planting season, the "mounding" procedure began. Now, the workers were permitted to take home whatever was found under the circular thickets. These potatoes were transparent like glass, and so they appeared after cooking them. Those who were unwilling to forego them would fry them. Instead of oil, which was unavailable, they rubbed the frying pan with slices of onion.... The taste was beyond description ....

This particular dish usually appeared on Yossel's Friday night table. but with a twist: the potato "omelets" were put into boiling water so they would have soup in honor of Shabbat. The problem was that the potatoes did not survive the hot environment and disintegrated back to their original state. This was the sole cooked food they ate that night, along with a few slices of corn bread, which people considered the main course. Everyone present at the table tasted one spoonful of the soup and without comment did not eat any more. Yossel himself could not restrain himself and remarked, "This is a bit too much!"

No one sang any traditional Shabbat chants that night. The blessing for the Creator was recited quietly over the corn bread.

Alas, Shabbat that week was a dismal one.

Despite the return of winter, the overall situation somewhat improved. Including that of Yossel. This was because Sima's sewing shop that had been closed due to lack of customers now came back to life. People's clothing became worn out, and they needed at least some warm attire for the winter.

[Page 47]

If they could not afford cloth from a store, which were then few and far between– the military warehouses in town were filled with gray–green rucksacks. Although these were made for military needs, when nothing else was available they could be used to sew clothes. Even His Majesty the Kaiser's loyal soldiers agreed. Dozens of men and women earned some income smuggling these sacks by wearing them underneath their regular clothing.

On occasion, however, Gerstel the commandant of the Ustiluh gendarmerie caught a group of unusually fat individuals walking on the road. He ordered them to remove their clothes (the women were permitted to conceal themselves behind the trees) and to hand over all the "excess" clothing. Those caught returned home much thinner, and received fines and were sometimes jailed. Nevertheless, these activities continued since people needed to make some money. In this way, thousands of gunny sacks made their way to the tailors and seamstresses in town.

Even Shmulik finally found some work. The squads that delivered water to Ustiluh residents employed many workers who built defensive barriers made from the wild forest reeds. When this project finished, he learned how to weave wicker baskets for the water squad personnel, which kept him busy until spring. After that, the army–supplied reeds became dried out and were unusable for weaving baskets. But, at that point, the field jobs began until summer's end.

Translator's Footnotes:

1. This is an imaginary exchange between the cantillation notes (*ta'amim* or *trop*) for reading the Torah. The meaning of each note is taken out of its context to serve as a metaphor for "simple," "broadly explain," "uphold," "attack" or "confront," etc.
2. This was not the local rabbi; it was someone who lectured on ethical topics and self–improvement.

[Page 47]

H1. Criminals in the Priest's House

Translated by Ala Gamulka

Yossel's Heder does not produce much income and Shmulik, too, sits idle at home. Therefore, Yossel decided to try his luck in the villages. Perhaps God will pave his way and he would be able to buy something for reselling or, at least, he could obtain food for the household. There was not much available in town. The two went to one of the distant villages. However, everywhere they went, either the inhabitants were poor (so they said) and never had anything to sell or they had already done so.

They were ready to return home when they noticed that policemen had entered the village. Yossel and Shmulik turned into a lane, went around some yards and went into a Jewish home. A few minutes later, the police officer from Ustiluh stood in the doorway. He was a Pole, around fifty years old, short and fat. He had a moustache like a Cossack and was accompanied by two young helpers.

"Who are and what are you doing here?"- he said to Yossel, intimating that the two Jews were suspected of treason or murder.

"We are from Ustiluh and we came to visit our relatives in this house"

"Ah, you are all related! Do you have an identity paper?"

"Yes. Here it is".

The officer looked at the identity paper: "Yossel Winemaker?" - he murmured and immediately ordered his helpers:
"Look for liquor!"

[Page 48]

Yossel tried in vain to correct the officer's error and to tell him that he does not produce liquor and never dealt in this trade. It was just his surname that he had inherited from his ancestors.

The helpers upended the beds and searched the cupboards and storage. They even went into the attic and any place a bottle could be hidden. Nothing was found. The officer then turned to Yossel:

"Do you have a travel permit?"
The inspectors did not work for nothing. The two criminals were written down in the book and were sent home to await their punishment.

On Friday night, just before candle lighting, the officer appeared and invited Yossel and Shmulik to be imprisoned for three days.

The prison was the former residence of the priest who had fled from his wife with her herd. The house was situated in the church courtyard which was surrounded by a tall stone wall and a beautiful fruit garden. The regular prison did not fulfill the needs in special times. The authorities found this large home suited them perfectly. The rooms were filled with various criminals: smugglers, money traders, profiteers, people who did not follow cleanliness rules, those without travel permits, etc.

Father Kutchkov definitely had not foreseen that his home would be used by young Jews to sing socialist songs and to make fun of the saints and the Tsar. He certainly did not dream that the Jews would be holding a prayer session there.

It was a symbolic gesture- to welcome the Sabbath in that house, across from the cross atop the dome. The cross that looked like a scarecrow in the lush garden.

In the meantime, Yossel and Shmulik. Like the others, were forced to sleep on bare boards. Berel, the lame one, said the boards were much harder than those in his home. In his bed the bones did not ache as much.

This was not the only problem.

Usually, every evening, the guard would bring a pail for body wastes. That night, the guard did not bring it in. He was probably too drunk and the prisoners did not notice. They figured that in case of need, they could knock on the door and the guard would open it. However, the needs were numerous and the guard did not react to the knocks. In the end, the two young men broke the barred window and it became easier…

The situation in the women's room was worse. They knocked and suffered all night. There was no relief.

Shmulik had never before felt how long winter nights as he did during these three days.

[Page 49]

At least they were not alone there. The young men sang, argued and played games. It seems that Yossel's physical condition suffered as a result, but not Shmulik's. Shmulik's spiritual world was enriched by these events.

In the meantime, a new source of work opened up. The railroad passed through Ustiluh and Shmulik found temporary work. All went well, except for the slap he received from an officer from Diari. He had been found to be pushing a wheelbarrow only half filled with earth. This gentile who saw the pale and skinny face of the young man and hit him cannot be considered a human being. So, there is no insult as a result.

I. Poles, Bolsheviks and New Times

There was a rebellion in the Austro-German army and anarchy prevailed. Units and single soldiers wandered about on their way home. Jewish young men who had not ever stood out as courageous, became so and disarmed those who came through town. Even Yisraelik, the friend of Shmulik, used to stand at the gates of town and when a lone armed soldier passed by, Yisraelik would order him: "Take off your gun!" The soldier obeyed. Yisraelik brought all the guns to the attic of the Shtiebel. There were neither stairs nor a ladder leading up to it.

A civilian militia was organized in town. Its first task was to get rid of the remnants of the officers in the local command. These "geniuses" had pressured the residents for the past three years, but they were scared and ran away to the area capital. This, after they gave their guns to the new militia. One of them, Lieutenant Schwartz, was happy when he was permitted to take his beloved horse. The militia commanders looked grand. They were sons of the wealthy families and were dressed elegantly. The officer's belt with its revolver fitted well.

The commanders went around town proudly, preening like peacocks. Mishka Odissist (he spent many years in Odessa), a former revolutionary, would shoot his gun in the air. He repeated: "Oh what a pleasure! A Jewish realm". However, the masses were embarrassed and were full of doubts about the uncertain future.

When it came to the abandoned cattle, goats, wheat, etc., originally owned by the occupiers and left on Beliankin's farm, it was different. It was useful to utilise them. The strong early bird tied a rope to the bull's horns and led him home. Another dragged a sheep or a goat while others filled their bags with anything they found. What would Jews do with bulls? They would slaughter them, of course, and would sell the meat cheaply.

[Page 50]

The truth is that in Ustiluh in those days more beef was eaten than during all the years of the Austrian conquest. So much meat is like the quail in the desert!

The barns and silos were emptied and the people attacked the piles of potatoes in the fields. Suddenly, a small unit of Polish speaking soldiers appeared. They began to disperse the crowds. Anyone who did not throw away his loot was beaten badly.

In the evening, a large meeting was held in the Great House of Study. A discussion about the soldiers ensued. They presented themselves as Polish legionnaires- the first time this was heard in Ustiluh. One young man from Hrobishov jumped on the stage and swore that he recognized the head of the troop as a well-known thief in his town.

Finally, it was decided to get rid of the suspicious soldiers from the town.

The next morning, a group of former soldiers went to the inn where the Poles were staying. They held their guns cocked in front of them. The forced the Poles to leave town immediately, but allowed them to keep their guns.

As the Poles crossed the bridge over the Bug, they turned back and began to fire at the town. some Polish residents in town also fired their guns. The Jewish troop returned fire, but did not notice the enemy within. The battle lasted for an hour. Four people were killed and there were injuries.

The next day, a larger group of legionnaires came to town and began to conduct an inquiry about the incident. The town representatives proved that the militia was defending the town from robbers. Although it was a mistake, the commander of the second group only imposed a monetary fine.

For some reason, the fact that Poland was liberated brought an ugly wave of Anti-Semitism left by the legionnaires from some sections of the army. The plucking of beards with the flesh of the cheeks and the casting of Jews from trains were daily occurrences. Even in Ustiluh one would meet Jews with bandaged faces. Slowly, the authorities became stronger and civil life became more stable. Then the Jewish community in general and in Ustiluh in particular was awakened.

The Balfour Declaration led to the establishment of various Zionist organizations. There were parades, parties, lectures, etc.

The Lag Baomer parade of that year was like the prophecy of dry bones. The voice of the redeemer could be heard.

It is a Sunday and all stores are closed. There are hordes of people in the streets: Jews, Ukrainians, Poles. A spring sun is warming everyone.

The sounds of music are approaching- it is a music of reawakening and victory.

[Page 51]

Here comes the orchestra followed by a parade never before seen in Ustiluh. Blue and white flags are waving in the wind. The members of "Young Generation", girls in white dresses and boys in blue shirts, are marching in rows surrounded by blue and white streamers. They are followed by various Zionist organizations with their own flags and slogans. Finally, the crowd comes streaming from all streets and alleys and joins the parade.

The orchestra stops and powerful singing bursts from among the young people. It envelops the crowd:

Get up you the exiled, remove your burden
Spring sun is shining on you
Wake up from your slumber of exile
Open your eyes, lift up your heads
Understand that you will not find rest here
Let us go eastward!

Not many fully understand the Hebrew words, but the Jewish soul, thirsty for redemption and freedom feels the meaning. Oh, Eretz Israel! Oh, Jewish realm!

Even the gentiles feel, at this great moment, how their neighbors have been degraded up to now. The Poles murmur with envy: "Look, the bloody dogs have finally earned it". The Ukrainians sigh with jealousy: "Soon they will go there to their Palestine".

Yes, the parade made a great impression, but not everyone understood they will not find peace here. Most of the Jews of Ustiluh quickly forgot the parade and its meaning and went back to their lives as before. Only the youth did not forget. They truly intended to fulfill their dreams of two thousand years. In the meantime, there was a great interruption which derailed the hopes they had in their hearts.

The Bolsheviks in Ustiluh. It was a short chapter, amusing at the beginning, but very saddening in the end. It was amusing from the point of view of the change in regimes.

The Poles left the town at night without any shots being fired. In the morning, the forces of the Red Army arrived. They were not received with happiness as the people of Ustiluh were not impressed by the Soviet "liberation". However, they were not really afraid. It was known that it was not common for them to take revenge on Jews. Also, they did not pull beards nor did they throw Jews off the train. These deeds were not known among the Soviets.

Actually, their entrance was peaceful, modest and even amusing. The first soldier to come was barefoot, without a hat, with his rifle hanging across his back. People reacted with laughter.

[Page 52]

"If this is how the Red Army looks" – they whispered with a wink- "We will be fortunate to see them leave". The Red Army "in all its glory" appeared: wearing peasant clothes and rags, Cossacks with Hassidic hats and women's jackets. There was no difference between the soldiers and the officers.

Moshe Burlyant, the town secretary, was not a very courageous man. He was invited by the Soviet commander to his office. When he saw that he was wearing a faded coat and torn boots, he felt he could speak to him like a friend. This is how Moshe Burlyant reported to the large circle in the market place that was waiting for results of the meeting.

What did the commander want? To continue all civic matters without interruption. Of course, there would be a government appointed commissar in town. I said: "as you command, Comrade commander. Ha, ha, ha, Comrade Commander!" They were good customers. Money meant nothing to them. They had bank notes in the form of pages of postage stamps and they would tear rows of them and pay without a receipt. They bought everything available in the stores. It reached the point where the store owners gave up on these paper payments and the stores slowly closed, one by one. The next day, many stores were found to have been broken into and emptied. This was especially true of stores that sold cloth and shoes. The owners came to complain and they were told: "Open your stores in the daytime and no one will steal at night". In other words, give the merchandise in exchange for these papers that were good for toys".

Due to this situation, there was nothing for sale in the stores. Then houses were searched for valuable items. In the morning, people were kidnapped for work on barbed wire fences and unpacking war supplies from the train. The Bolsheviks paid for this work with speeches, music in the market place and nightly performances- but no money.

One of the speeches, in Yiddish, was dedicated to the youth. In order not to arouse suspicion of counterrevolution, members of all youth groups came to the lecture. It was worth listening to it. It was a masterful misinformation and ignorance of Zionist matters. The speaker directed his sarcasm towards Zionism. Any one of those who attended would have been happy to stomp on the bald head of the speaker when he repeated, several times, that Aliyah to Eretz Israel is only meant for rebuilding the Temple and to bring sacrifices. The lecture, of course, was accepted without any arguments. Those sitting in the first few rows even applauded. The speaker descended from the stage with a glowing face, like a general who had won a battle.

The Bolsheviks were trounced on the Vistula in Warsaw and had to retreat. The Commissar stood, in Ustiluh, on the balcony of Meir Weinfeld and orated enthusiastically: "You will no longer be slaves to the Poles! Your children will no longer go hungry! Your earnings for hard work will not be stolen! Your wives and daughters will not be raped!"

[Page 53]

However, it was not the Poles who robbed and raped the women in Ustiluh. Within two days it was the Red soldiers of Bodiano! They even found something to steal in Yossel's house: the boots he wore were taken off his feet. They took Reuven's sheep coat (Sima's husband) and twenty-year-old Shmulik's Sabbath clothes. Shmulik was short and skinny and would not accept the fact they he was robbed. He ran after them to denounce them. However, a gun thrust in front of him stopped his progress.

At night, a time of remembering the covenant, the screams of tortured women pierced the air in town.

The next day, the residents were in their homes and listened to the booms of the artillery aimed at the town. They announced the approaching Poles. It was a miracle that no homes were destroyed.

In the afternoon, one could see through the cracks in the shutters, Soviet armies leaving town. The Poles arrived and filled the homes for the night. They were careful and before going to sleep they checked everywhere to make sure there were no Bolsheviks hiding anywhere. When none were found, they took small mementos that could be put into a pocket or in a bag. Unfortunately, the soldiers in Yossel's house could not find anything. However, to show their victory, they took Dina's Sabbath silk scarf.

The curfew of the last six weeks was lifted and life went back to normal as far as was possible at that time. The children returned to their Hebrew school which had been closed during "liberation". In the evenings one could again hear songs of Zion everywhere.

New times came to town. At least this is what everyone in Ustiluh-young and old- hoped for - better times. True for the Diaspora or the land of their fathers which is calling them from afar.

* * *

There was once a small and pretty town called Ustiluh. It is no longer exists…

In the nineteen years since our story ends, life continued on an even path. Young people were married and established a home and a family. They tried to build a proper base as much as possible. Others did not see their future in town and left. Some made Aliyah to Eretz Israel and others went to the American continent or other cities in the country. People died, either too early or in time, and were mourned properly. Even Yossel, the saintly, honest man, died young after a lengthy illness. He was full of sadness after his son, gentle Asher, died young. Prior to that, Sima was married.

[Page 54]

Her lot was to become a widow before her seventh son was born. He was named after his father. Shmuel also married a woman from a village nearby and moved there. Even Dina did not live to a ripe old age. Her weak heart could not stand the sorrow of her widowed daughter. She died seven days after her son-in-law. In the meantime, Shmuel did not sit still. He had a fairly good economic situation, but he always dreamed of making Aliyah. He managed to do so with his wife and two daughters just before the terrible fire that engulfed his hometown as well as the town of his birth.

Aaron Goldberg and his children going to synagogue

This is what the survivors will speak about.

[Page 55]

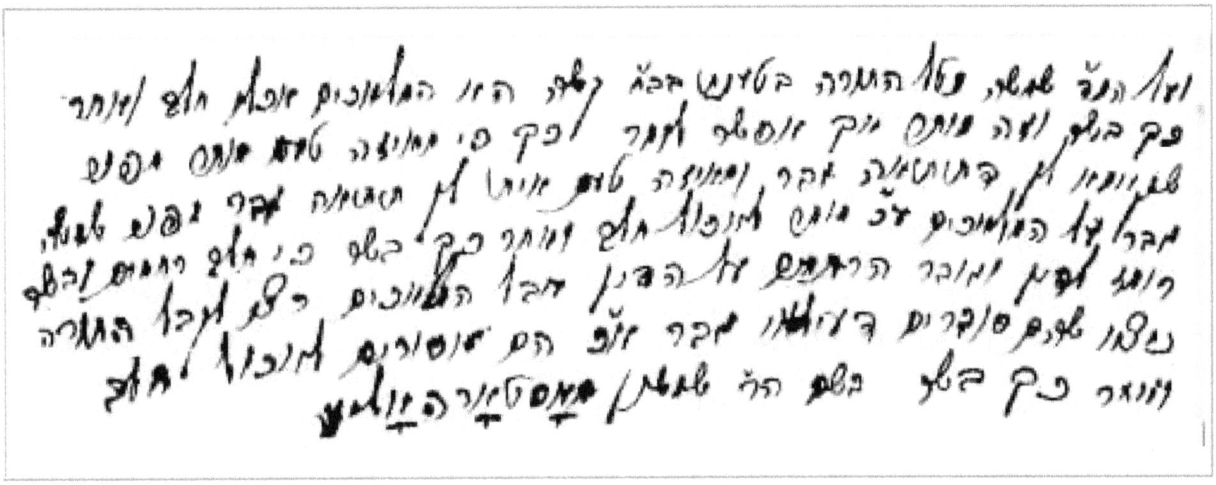

Handwritten letter by R. Dov Tabakhandler (for page 23)

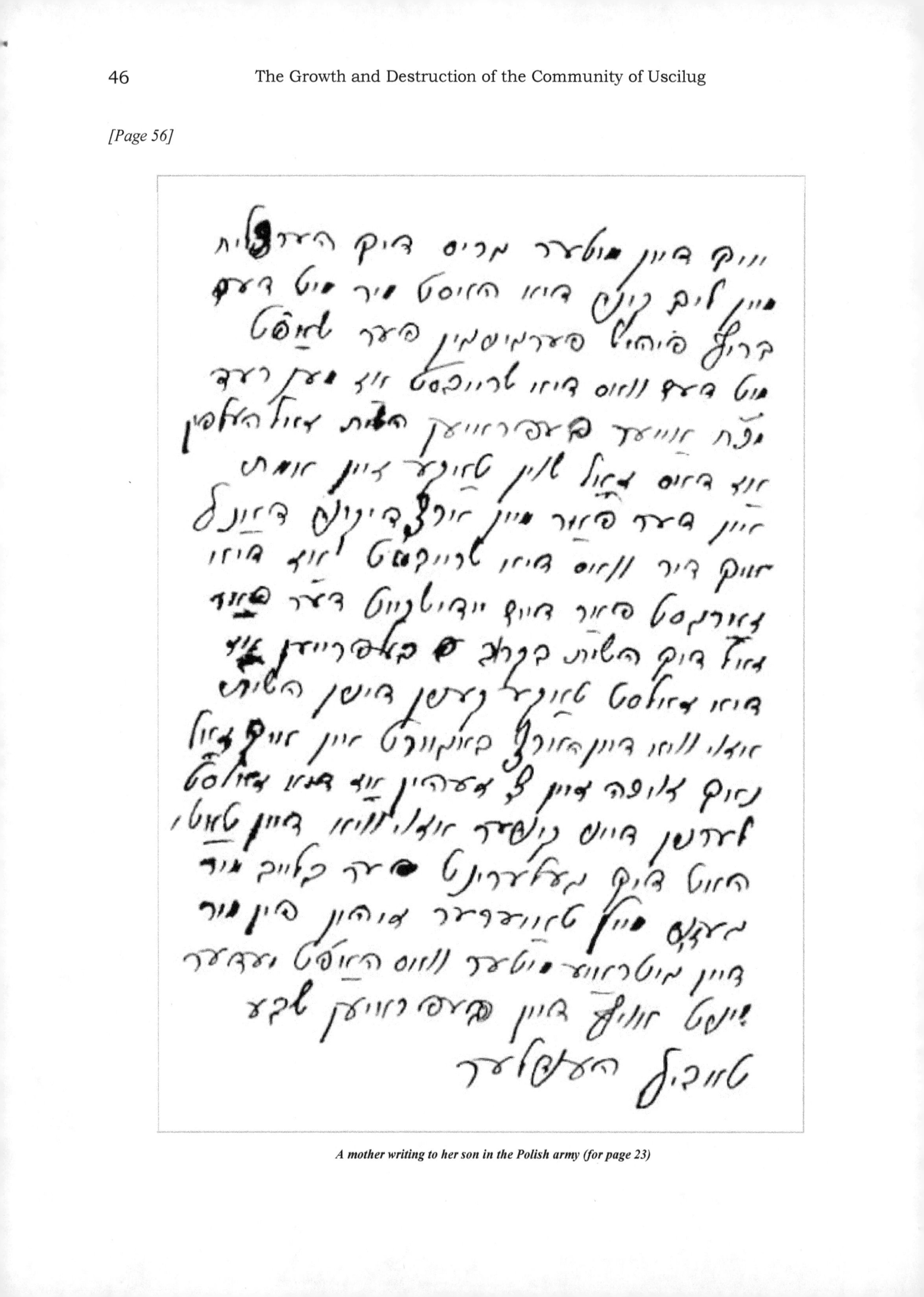

[Page 56]

A mother writing to her son in the Polish army (for page 23)

[Page 57]

In Light of Memories

by Elyhau Schlachter

Translated by Ala Gamulka

A. My town - a general look

My town Ustiluh- you stand in front of my eyes as if you were alive. Years have passed since I left you, but you are etched in my heart. I cannot forget you.

The Bug river streamed through the western part of town. It formed a natural border between Volyn and Congress Poland. The bridge on the river connected the districts of Ludomir and Hrobishov. Transportation used this route.

Earlier, the town was called Little Danzig. On a hill on the shore of the river stood two wooden warehouses. Wheat from nearby villages and lumber from the surrounding forests were placed on shelves inside. They were then taken by steamboat to Danzig.

When was this town founded? The residents were not really interested. Only the faded letters on ancient gravestones were proof that Jews had lived there for several generations.

The area of the town was small. It was surrounded by villages, forests and fruit orchards. The population was about 4000 and 90% were Jews.

In the center of town there was a large market place. It was filled with stores. Several small streets branched off it. The streets were: Ludomir, Danche, Bathhouse, Winehouses. Shlakhtse street was where my parents lived. Their house was encircled by a garden and cherry trees. Most of the neighbors were gentiles. Not far away were two government schools. Most of the Jewish youth attended them.

Most of the houses were built with wood. Only a few buildings had two stories. In the center there was a well. Water was drawn from it and carried in pails on a pole. There were also people who worked at drawing the water and delivering it. I remember Yankel Katchke (Duck) the water drawer and Baruch the Water Carrier.

There were two factories for making soda water: that of Reuven "Sodovnik" and the Shtimer family. The production was done in a primitive way: a large wheel was turned to start the engine and the needed gas was produced. In the hot summer days, people enjoyed drinking cool soda water. There were also 4 plants producing oil. They belonged to the Boim family. The mills for grinding the seeds were run by the help of a horse whose eyes were covered or who was blind. It would turn a huge wooden wheel. The ground seeds were drained in a large steamroller.

[Page 58]

On the other side of the Bug river there were around 20 Jewish families. They earned their living mainly from fishing and dairy. They would bring the milk daily to the store of Falik Khaznonlad in the town center. There was a large green meadow that served to feed their farm animals. These people from "the other side" were strong and brave. They were also excellent swimmers. It happened often that they were called to rescue someone drowning in the river. They came quickly in their boats to help out. In the beginning of spring the entire area was flooded with water. Sometimes their houses were in the water up to the roof. There was a danger of destruction as well as drowning. Even the big wooden bridge was in danger. Soldiers used to blast the frozen ice.

Later in the spring, the area became a place to walk and a soccer field. There were other pretty nooks in town: the fruit orchard of Bieliankin, his palace and the fields, the neighboring forest, Konstantin's hill, There was a small flour mill on the street of the Gentiles, lying among the green mountains that made our hearts happy.

On the Sabbath and holidays there were walks individually and in groups. Our young hearts were beginning to feel love and these pretty nooks kept our secrets. When the fruit was ripe, we would go into the garden to taste the apples and plums. We would sit in the shadow of the trees, sing and tell jokes. Before nightfall on the Sabbath, the entire community would walk on Ludomir street. It was the street for the walkers.

B. On weekdays and on the Sabbath

During the week, life was difficult. Light and shadow were intermingled. The marketplace was the source of income. Most of the stores were there and also the commerce with the gentiles from the nearby villages. The Jews would go to the marketplace early in the morning to see if they could find a bargain.

Sunday was the day of rest for the gentiles. The Polish authorities did not permit the opening of stores. However, the need to make a living forced the Jews to transgress. As soon as the police officer left and went to another street, customers would be sneaked inside through the back door.

All day, church bells would be heard. The church stood on Ludomir street. It was a large, tall building with its crosses piercing the skies. We were overcome by fear as we passed by it and we would murmur:" Let us be quiet so we are not harmed". A wall and tall trees circled the building. In the yard there were fruit trees. The priest leased the trees to Jews. Among them was Shmerl Lipinski who now lives in Israel. Another was Peretz Gurevitch. They used to stand in the marketplace selling various kinds of apples and pears.

Wednesday was market day and the sleepy town would awaken. The stores were filled with customers, mainly from nearby villages. Vendors in the marketplace would sell their wares. There was give and take, much noise and many people.

[Page 59]

The taverns belonging to Pinchas Berkes, Yenta Printsches and Esther Manises were filled with gentiles. They drank liquor and ate bread with herring. Yenta was a woman of valor and she kept everything in order. She listened to their arguments and prevented fights. When they became tipsy, she took them outside and said good-bye in a nice way.

On Thursdays, the women of Ustiluh would get up early. My mother also ran to the marketplace to buy meat and fish for the Sabbath.

On Friday mornings, before daylight, mother would fire the oven in order to bake Challot and bread for the entire week. My sisters, Esther, Hannah and Riza would also get up and begin to help. They would clean the rooms and iron clothes for the Sabbath. We studied in the Heder until noon. We then went to the bathhouse near the river bank. It was dangerous to go up and down in the winter since there was snow and ice. My brother Berel and Yossel, son of Tile, the shoemaker, went from door to door to collect Challot and loaves of bread for the poor.

At nightfall mother blessed the candles. We went to synagogue. It was clean and shiny inside. At the eastern wall sat Jews with beards. After services we returned home. Father would bring a guest. We said "Shalom Aleichem" and make kiddush. We washed our hands and ate the sumptuous Sabbath meal. Every course is accompanied with chants. The next morning Father walked through the room and recited the morning blessing. We got up and took the chicory drink, with milk, from the stove. We drank and went to synagogue. Jews would congregate and put on their prayer shawls. Yankel, "the yellow one", led the morning services. The Torah scroll was taken out and placed on the table. The synagogue director gave out the Aliyot. Moshe Yudel read the Torah. We prayed the supplemental portion. We greeted each other with “a good Sabbath” and we went home to eat the second meal. There was delicious food, especially Cholent and Kugel.

C. Holidays and festivals

Memories of Hanukah in the Heder with the dreidels spinning are etched in my memory. At Purim we worked hard to prepare masks and graggers. The Megillah was read in the synagogue and great noise was made when the name of Haman was mentioned. Presents of food- couples came to the doors and Father always donated generously.

I will describe in detail the preparations for Pessach: the women of the town worked hard to whitewash the dwellings and to clean everywhere beforehand. In our home the women did the painting themselves or they hired Motel Sofer, the painter. The house looked like a battlefield. Tables and chairs were moved with other items piled on top. Slowly, order returned. The house was all white inside. Everything was washed and scrubbed. In a special room stood a large basket with Matzos, covered with a white sheet.

[Page 60]

At dawn on the 14th day of Nissan, Father checked for Hametz. I held a candle and Father, had a feather in his right hand and a wooden spoon in the left one. We went from window to window and one piece of furniture to another. Father collected crumbs of chametz, prepared by Mother, into his spoon.

On the eve of Pessach, we would get up early. Father went to synagogue and from there to the slaughterhouse. There were long lines of men, women and children holding chickens to be properly slaughtered. At home, the last preparations are being made for the holiday. My sisters are working hard. They clean the windows, change the curtains and wash the wooden floors. At 10 the last chametz meal is eaten. Father burns the chametz in the small stove. We fire the stoves with high heat. According to the rules, the stove must glow.

The day passes. We have already dunked the dishes. We brought down, from the attic, the Pessach dishes. Mother gives me the honor of grinding matzos in a wooden mortar. This is hard work, but there is no choice. She makes me feel better by offering me pocket money to buy nuts.

After a festive prayer in the synagogue, we return home for the Seder. Father sits at the head of the table leaning on pillows. His face is pale. Mother is sad and tears are flowing from her eyes. She remembers her four sons Herschel, Nahum, Shlomo and Leibush who are not with us. They are in foreign lands. I am wearing a suit and new shoes. Everything in the house is clean and shiny. The wine in the glasses entices me. I ask the Four Questions and we read from the Haggadah. We drink wine and eat special food. My mother and sisters are tired and are dozing.

The first days of Pessach pass. On Hol HaMoed the weather is still cool. Everyone is wearing holiday clothes. People visit each other. Some go to the train station to welcome guests. The station is full of travellers, coming and going. There is excitement and the heart is happy and full of hope.

Rosh Hashana. The synagogue is completely full. Jews are wearing white kitels which are covered with talits. Their faces are full of dread and self examination. Father leads the morning services. When he begins the special tune for the Days of Awe, he starts to read from the prayer book. The crowd is silent. The Torah is read and the Shofar is blown. Everyone is together, listening to the entreaties of the prayer leader who raises his arms towards heaven as his voice becomes louder. I understood the meaning of the prayers. To this day I feel the sense of fear of that moment.

The eve of Yom Kippur. The afternoon prayer is done earlier. It is amusing to see grown men prostrating themselves on the floor like young boys. Moshe Yudel, the teacher, hits them with a belt to atone for their sins. We eat the last meal when the sun is still high in the sky. Father changes his clothes. My sisters wash the dishes. Mother blesses the candles in a tearful voice and wishes everyone a good verdict.

[Page 61]

We go to synagogue. One hears women crying from all the houses as everyone rushes to synagogue. Our synagogue is filled. The men wear kitels and talits and wish each other a good year. On the tables and in every corner, there are crates filled with sand. Inside are large wax candles. The floor is covered with aromatic hay. People step on it wearing slippers or socks.

The cantor and his assistants begin with Kol Nidrei. Everyone is standing and chanting with trepidation. This prayer reminds us of the forced conversions in the middle ages. After services, some elderly men remain in the synagogue. Some of them study the daily portion and others recite Psalms.

The next morning everyone comes back for morning prayers. Some do so in whispers and others move fervently and cry loudly. The Torah is read and the supplementary prayer follows. During Al Het (my sin) they beat their left side and confess to any sins which they did or did not commit. The "Unetaneh Tokef" is then said. Everyone is uptight during this heart-rending prayer. I still remember the feeling of that day. Sounds of crying are heard from the women's section. Sometimes a woman faints, weak from fasting. She is revived with a strong perfume that some of the attendees have. During Neilah, the final prayer, excitement grows. It is time for the final signature and everyone is fearful. When the prayers are over, everyone feels livelier and hopeful for the coming new year. The evening prayer is said quickly. Everyone is rushing home holding bits of lit candles. The elderly men stay to bless the moon.

The signature of Yom Kippur requires final approval and Hoshana Raba serves that purpose. The elderly men sit in synagogue all night. They read Torah and recite Psalms. All this to obtain a good result.

Simchat Torah. The synagogue is lit up. Boys and girls holding flags. The cantor says "You have shown us" and the large crowd replies with enthusiasm. Hakafot around the platform are done holding the Torah scrolls. After every circling, Hassidic chants are sung. I, too, circle the platform holding a small Torah. The next day, after prayers and a special kiddush in the synagogue, we go to visit many homes. There we eat potato pancakes with meat. The children chase the "drunks" and yell -" Holy herd- Meee!"

D. Childhood and War

After the holidays, life goes back to normal and to daily worries. The children, laden with books, return to the Heder to learn Torah. I was studying with the children's tutor Haim Wolf. He was a kind and honest man. He never beat his students. He treated me with patience. He showed me large letters of the alphabet using his pointer.

[Page 62]

He lived a life of dire poverty. He only ate potatoes and kugel made from the leftover pieces of bread of the students. He used to stir it with beer.

My brother, Leibush, studied with Yossel "the emperor". He was stern. On Thursdays, anyone who did not prove to him that he knew the portion of the week with Rashi commentary, would be lifted up by his ears. I saw my brother sitting behind the house, crying. He was afraid to go back.

This interesting time passes in front of my eyes like a film.

When WWI broke out in 1914, I was six years old, but I remember everything as if it were today. The Jewish residents were afraid of what was to come. Father dug a hole under the floor and hid clothes and valuables. This was in case there was a fire or we had to flee. There were rumors of losses by the Russian army and that the front was moving close to our town. Since we lived in a gentile area, my parents decided to move to the center of town- to the large inn of Pinchas Berkes. We packed bundles of clothes and food and we moved to the new place. We slept on the floor, in our clothes. At night, there was total darkness. On the streets there were Cossack guards. Early the next morning we woke up to the sounds of bombings. The Russians bombed the bridge on the Bug. The Germans shelled the town. There was great consternation and people began to flee the town. Some went by cart and others on foot, carrying their bundles on their backs. We fled in the direction of Ludomir. After we walked for several hours, we noticed it was completely quiet and before nightfall we returned to town. Everyone was anxiously waiting for the Germans to enter town. As they conquered the town, they did not harm the residents. The Ukrainian population fled to Russia and left its homes and land. The Germans took the men to work in digging and fortification. After a short time, the town management was transferred to the Austrians.

Illnesses and epidemics erupted, such as Cholera and Typhus. Hundreds of people died. There was hunger.

The Austrians established government schools and opened medical clinics. Every resident was inoculated against infectious diseases. There was free medical help. Bridges and roads were built with lumber from the forests. A small railroad was erected. Food was distributed (less and less eventually). Education was compulsory. I was registered in Grade One. My teachers were Moshe Kornfeld, Mentze Barak and Shmerl Sokoler. The principal was officer Kimmel. We learned Hebrew and German. I still remember the Austrian national anthem.

The Jewish youth began to organize and meet in the military shack of Leib Gut. It became a place to present plays. Once, during a play, fire broke out. The ceiling caught fire from a lantern. The entire audience tried to leave through the only exit. It took a long time to empty the hall. I was taken out through a window. The fire was quickly put out, but there were some injuries.

Four years passed and the war continued. Suddenly, it became known that there were revolutions in three rival states in Russia. The powerful Tsar Nikolai was thrown out and the same happened in Germany and Austria.

[Page 63]

The officers and soldiers who were staying in Beliankin's palace took off their insignia. They threw away their guns and embraced each other with happiness. The prisoner camp near our house was emptied of guards. The barbed wire fence was destroyed and the prisoners were freed. All the roads were filled with soldiers and refugees returning to their homes and their families. The Jewish soldiers who returned organized a self-defence group. There was news of pogroms on the Jews of Russia and Ukraine. Gangs of killers were roaming the forests. They attacked and took Jewish belongings. Among the members of the defence group in our town I remember Yitzhak Goldberg, Mordechai Fleisher, Kalman Blatt, Yerucham Zweig and a few more young men whose names I do not remember. Near the palace of Bieliankin there were large stores of food, cattle, horses and lumber. Everyone took what he wanted.

E. Poland is revived

There was a short period of relative calm. Nothing special happened and life continued. On Friday night, in the synagogue, I heard someone tell that a military troop came into town and stayed in the house of Pofelis. All day, on the Sabbath, there were military guards who went around and did not allow any gatherings. On Sunday, there were searches for arms. On the weekly market day there were fights between Jews and soldiers. The latter wanted to confiscate the carts and horses of Jews. They, in turn, opposed it.

The residents of the town did not know that the Polish people were coming back to life. They were surprised to hear the guests were representatives of the new regime. A meeting was called in the Great House of Study and it was decided to ask the commander of the troop to stop the confiscations and to behave properly towards the Jewish population. In the morning there was a parade going to the house of Pofelis. The people were shouting and shooting in the air. The commander and his soldiers were scared and began to fire a machine gun. Some people in the crowd were hurt and the others fled in many directions. The soldiers killed anyone they met on the street. Around 12 people were killed and many were injured. The next day, 10 town leaders, including, Bentzi the Dayan (judge), were imprisoned in the House of Study. They were heavily guarded. A group fine was imposed on the town. There was a threat of killing the hostages if the fine was not paid within 24 hours. After strenuous efforts, the fine was paid. Some of the defense team were freed. A committee was sent by the Polish parliament to investigate. The entire episode was erased.

F. Between Bolsheviks and Poles

In 1920, the war between the Poles and the Bolsheviks broke out. Trenches were dug and fortifications were built. The Polish soldiers from Poznan abused the Jews and cut off their beards. They especially performed these activities on the Sabbath. They took Jews out of synagogues and forced them to work on the Sabbath.

[Page 64]

I saw, with my own eyes, how a soldier caught Yehuda Fleisher and tried to straighten out his crooked finger. His screams filled the air.

The front approached our town. The Poles retreated and bombed and burned all the bridges. The Bolsheviks entered the next day. They were shoeless, wore torn clothes, and looked really miserable. The commissar called for a meeting and chose a local committee to run the town. The economic situation worsened. There was absolutely no commerce. They did supply propaganda material. There were newspapers in Russian and a lot of entertainment-concerts and plays. After six weeks, on the eve of Rosh Hashana, the Bolshevik army retreated from town and the Poles took possession again, after heavy bombing. Several people were injured and some houses were damaged.

G. National-public reawakening

Slowly, conditions began to ameliorate. Commerce began to develop. Schools were reopened. There were elections to the Polish parliament. I took part in the elections. All the Jews voted for A'. The village obtained the status of town. Most of the town councillors were Jews.

Michael Krakower, first chairman of the Jewish community with his grandson Leibele

[Page 65]

Branch of the scouts on Memorial Day for Herzl, 1924

[Page 66]

Teacher Shlomo Kent was elected as vice mayor. Michael Krakower was chosen as the chairman of the Jewish community. He was followed by Yeshayahu Eksmit. They were devoted civil leaders and fulfilled their positions with loyalty.

I returned to school. In the Polish school we were greatly annoyed by the gentile students and I left the school. I had private tutors: Yankel Zipper and Moshe Shpirer. The local youth was reorganized. A drama group was founded and was headed by my brother, Leibush, Moshe Burlyant and Haim Terner. The younger ones established a Hebrew library which had 750 books and another one for Yiddish. Plays were presented and the income was dedicated to the acquisition of books. We obtained a nice apartment with two rooms. From time to time, lecturers came to speak about various topics. The youth participated fully. Various political parties were organized- Zionist, Poalei Zion, Mizrahi Hechalutz, Hashomer Hatzair and Beitar. Hebrew evening classes were offered. We had discussions about Eretz Israel, Histadrut and their institutions. We celebrated, in grand style, the inauguration of the Hebrew University on Mount Scopus. We held memorial assemblies for Herzl and Trumpeldor. The speakers were Fishel Eisenberg, Yankel Yokhenzon and Yitzhak Yeshayahu Eksmit. Their speeches excited the listeners. Some young people were fortunate to make Aliyah.

H. Bloody events and crisis in Eretz Israel- depression in the Diaspora

News of bloody events in Eretz Israel- attacks by Arabs on Jewish settlements reached us. A protest meeting was held in the House of Study. There was resentment in the Jewish community about the exploitation of the Jewish workers by the orchard owner in the settlements.

In 1924 I was one of the first volunteers for kibbutz training. It was meant to accustom us to physical work according to the norms in Eretz Israel and to communal life. To my great sorrow, I could not withstand the work and I returned home after a short time. At that time there was a great depression in Eretz Israel, right after an increase in Aliyah. Some immigrants came back- Michel Shafran, Mordechai Vogenfeld and others. There was a feeling of depression and disappointment. Activities for Keren Hayesod and Jewish National Fund waned. The public stopped donating. The youth in town began to search for different methods to establish themselves and started to roam to countries across the ocean. My brother Leibush immigrated to Mexico.

In the meantime, the Jews of Poland were under heavy clouds. Anti-Semitism reared its head. The Nazi movement in Germany, like a plague, infected most of the gentile population of Poland.

I. My Aliyah- bloody events

The Jewish youth, with its healthy sense, predicted, for a long time, that the economic base was being taken away from the Jews. Another dry goods store will not resolve the issue. The worry about what was to come strengthened the need for a new life. In spite of the fact that my economic situation was sound, I went again to the training kibbutz. Other youths followed in my footsteps.

[Page 67]

After 3 years of work and suffering I was fortunate to make Aliyah in 1936. There were many good-bye parties. Several friends made Aliyah with me.

In the absorption center in Haifa, we were welcomed by all the friends who had made Aliyah before us. Each one chose his own settlement. At the same time, there were bloody events between the Arabs and the Jews. There were victims on a daily basis. Among them was our dear friend Yaakov Cohen. Avner Goldhaber was injured. There was high unemployment in the country. The Mandate government cut the number of permits for Aliyah. Many friends left the kibbutzim and settled in towns and moshavot.

J. Second World War- Holocaust

In 1939, the big war broke out with all its terrible events and destruction. I was working then as a plumber in the construction of the oil refinery near Haifa. Since my town of birth was conquered by the Red Army, I was fired from my job. Ominous news began to arrive. The town was completely burned. Leibele, my sister Rizaa's son, was killed by shrapnel. The house was burned and they were left with nothing. Here, too, we began to feel the war. The Italians bombed the oil tanks near Haifa. My dear friend, Yehuda Fleisher, was killed. I lived in Kiryat Haim, not far from the airport and we felt the bombardment quite often. For several years we had no reliable news of what was happening outside of the country. Here and there, we heard some rumors, that the Nazis were exterminating all the Jews. Without exception, no one wanted to believe that the "enlightened" German people would be capable of such deeds. Ships of illegal immigrants began to arrive in the country, especially after the State of Israel was established by a fiery war, and the few survivors from our destroyed town came. The bitter truth was confirmed by them. The Jews of Ustiluh were exterminated and no one was left from my cherished family. May their souls be bound in the bonds of life.

K. Election of Rabbis

I cannot end my reminiscences without mentioning a public event from my youth that left a mark in the town for some time. It created a state of celebration and great interest.

Rabbi Yossel Wertheim left town when WWI broke out and wandered eastward until bad times will have passed. The supervision of religious interests: marriages, divorces, kashrut, Torah laws, etc. was left on the shoulders of two Dayanim (judges)- Bentzi Reider and Reuven Zack. At the end of the war, he did not return to Ustiluh, but became the rabbi in Hrobishov. For several years, out town did not have a chief rabbi. Then, the rabbi from Beltz offered his son-in-law, Rabbi Pinhas (Piniele) Tversky for the position of Rabbi of Ustiluh. The Beltz rabbi wanted this to happen because our town was famous for its former rabbis who were truly righteous.

[Page 68]

Ustiluh also wished for this to happen as it wanted to be connected to a rabbi with thousands of followers. So, everyone agreed and there was a grand ceremony.

The Beltz rabbi was well accepted by the Polish authorities because of his civic loyalty. (He ordered his followers to vote for the party in power). For that reason, a special train was assigned to him and hundreds of followers came with him to Ustiluh for the crowning of Rabbi Piniele. The entire town came out to meet them. The Vinehauser people decorated their horses with colorful papers and there was a unit of horsemen who rode in front of the wagon. It was said that when the train arrived and the rabbi was to descend from it, Yossel Tiles, the shoemaker, lay down on the ground to serve as a step. I remember that the day was rainy and the way from the station to town was full of mud. The followers and the rest of the crowd ran after the wagon with their feet full of slush. Near the Shtiebel "Ahava Raba" (Great love) (Kuzmir), there was huge open tent to serve for prayers and to set tables. Hassidim from everywhere in Poland streamed to our town. Even sick people were brought to ask for healing.

The Beltz rabbi stayed for a month. In the meantime, Rabbi Piniele was crowned as chief rabbi. However, the merger did not work out. Rabbi Piniele mainly was occupied with religious matters, but Ustiluh needed a leader like Rabbi Yossel Wertheim. He returned to Galicia after a few years.

Ustiluh again did not have a Rabbi. The question was who among the two Dayanim (the late Reuven was replaced by his son-in-law Yehoshua Shintop), would be the official rabbi, recognized by the authorities. Elections were held and there was great competition.

In spite of the fact that Bentzi was known as an outstanding scholar and was also older than his competitor, young Yehoshua obtained a majority. Bentzi felt greatly slighted. He became ill and never regained his strength.

Personalities and Activities

"It is better to have a good name than a good oil"
A good oil goes from one room to another, but a
Good name lasts throughout the world.
(Shemot Raba, 48)

[Page 70] blank [Page 71]

Kindness of Youth
(a bundle of memories)

by Tzila Fleischer

Translated by Ala Gamulka

A.

The first social activity I recall, in which I participated at a young age, was the public kitchen. It was founded by Dr. Feltz in 1915. Others in its management were: Toivtze Mandelker (later Terner), Batya Burlyant, Mentze Brik, Binyamin Terner and Haim Burlyant. The kitchen served, every day, a hot meal to the poor population. It was especially needed by the families whose husbands were drafted to fight in the war. The kitchen was financed by various initiatives.

The first event I was permitted to attend, under the watchful eye of my older sister Pessia, – one of the organizers– was a "Literary Musical Evening". It took place on Hanukah of that year. There was a good revenue for the kitchen.

The next event was the establishment of a drama group which presented "Mirele Efros". This very successful play also produced good proceeds for the kitchen.

During the same period of time, "Young Generation" was organized. I was also a member. Its purpose o was national–cultural. There was a difference of opinion among the active persons. The adults wanted activities that would help the population in a material way, while, we, the younger ones, supported cultural events. There was a division that followed. One group dedicated itself to helping, in a material way, those who were poor. The second group – did cultural and spiritual work. The latter group had many difficulties since their parents were against their efforts. The first group was well received by the parents and the general public. Four young women (Pessia Rosmarin, Bunia Shturm, Toivtze Mandelker, and Batya Burlyant) organized the baking of Matzos. They were distributed free to poor people. The supervision was done by Rebbetzin Hannale Wertheim, Z"L and was approved by her husband, the Rabbi. Flour was bought by proceeds from Maot Hitim (wheat money). All work was done voluntarily. They even made sure the matzos were brought to the homes of the needy.

I remember an interesting event from those days: the Rebbetzin made the following condition: young men were not allowed to visit the bakery. These young men declared that during the holiday of Passover, the young women were to stroll with rolling pins…

The situation in the cultural group was different. We had war at home and on the outside. In spite of all this, we managed to establish a drama group. Our first income was dedicated to starting a library.

[Page 72]

There were those who insisted on only Yiddish books because most people using the library did not know Hebrew. The Zionists wanted purely Hebrew books. In our town, Hebrew had been taught for many years. Lana, the daughter of Volf Yokhenzon, a rich man in town, and Menashe Kandiner, used to write for "Hatsfira" (Hebrew newspaper).

There was fear of another dispute, so we agreed to open two libraries in both languages, with Yiddish having a larger percentage. This situation was resolved, but, in general, the condition of the organization was dire. There was no space to house the library, parents did not stop from voicing their opposition and our struggles were great.

In the meantime, a wealthy resident of our town passed away. Yechiel Natz, Z"L, had no children and he left a large house. In his will he left part of the house to a Shtiebel (his second wife lived in the other part with her daughter from her first marriage). One night, our young men infiltrated the house and appropriated two large rooms. This is where all our cultural activities took place. The two libraries became, in due time, the glory of the town. We offered evening classes to the youth from poor families.

Kindergarten in 1926

[Page 73]

B.

Our Zionist activities actually began in 1917, after the Balfour Declaration. However, Zionist ideas had come to our town many years earlier. In our house there was a Jewish National Fund book and it contained a list of volunteers and donors.

It was the custom to stand on the eve of Yom Kippur, with a bowl, in all the houses of learning and shtiebels in order to collect money for Jewish National Fund. In the Trisker Shtiebel, my brother Aaron, (now in the United States), stood with the collection bowl. My sister Pessia did the same in the women's section. At the time it was great progress. The Balfour Declaration precipitated Zionist activity at a quick pace. In 1918, on 20 Tammuz, we "dared" to parade, carrying national flags and mourning flags, to the great House of Learning. It was to commemorate the death of Herzl 14 years earlier. The parade included youth and adults from all stratas of society. Elderly people stood in front of their homes or peeked from their windows with great curiosity.

When we returned home, my mother asked our maid, daughter of Hune the shoemaker, where she had been for such a long time. She simply replied:" Dr. Herzl was my relative just like Tzirel's". My father Z"L, answered: "Who knows? It is not written anywhere that the Messiah will come on a white donkey. Maybe it is the era of the Messiah and he came as Dr. Herzl".

I enjoyed this conversation for many reasons. One– my father– a Jew who had completed the study of the Mishna twice and was an ardent follower of the Rabbi from Trisk– began to understand our spirit. (See the article by my brother Dr. Aaron Rosmarin– "My town Ustiluh" for a description of our family's ardent following of the Rabbi from Trisk). Two– the advancement of our servants who were influenced by us.

Our happiness was incomplete. We had to struggle for a long time with zealots who interfered with our work. We often stood on guard at night fearing arson of the library. Here is an episode of our suffering in those times. It was true that our parents opposed our activities, but they were not zealots nor were they consistent. On the other hand, my older brother, Abba, Z"L, continually tried to incite our father against us, but he was unsuccessful. Once he thought he was successful against me. We presented "The Jewish King Lear" and my brother Aaron and I participated in the play. It was quite successful. Almost at the end, a fire broke out in the ceiling of the stage. There was great excitement. There were some serious injuries and some light ones. There was a doctor among us, but he did not arrive in time to provide the appropriate care. My older brother, who lived nearby, heard the shouting and the noise. He came and when he saw me, he slapped me twice. As I was screaming, my friends came to my aid.

[Page 74]

He went to wake our father up and told him that because he allows us to read books, we have sinned...

Eventually, I caught him in his "corruption". He read War and Peace by Tolstoy. When I said: "Is it possible?", he apologized by saying that he was only reading the historical parts of the book. We, supposedly, would read the story.

I later discovered that he read many books in classical Russian literature.

After the fire, the mayor, the Pole Shtravitsky, called us. He told us that since the production was so successful, the town would finance the renovation of the building. New doors would be included with a special exit. All that, if we put on the production again. We were delighted after we had been so despondent.

Orphanage

In the meantime, we had more members from the younger generation. There was the establishment of branches of Zeirei Zion, Poalei Zion, General Zionists and the Young Mizrachi. Zionist activities were developing. Jewish National Fund and Keren Hayesod became popular. We were so strong that the radicals accepted us and left us alone. Now that we had the freedom to plan activities, the town stood out in this area. When we received money from the Central office in Warsaw, we were able to triple it.

[Page 75]

Some time later, when the social and Zionist activities were regular, we undertook the new task of helping the needy. The previous group had dispersed. Many had left town and others had married and concentrated on their families and personal issues.

When a representative group from the Joint in Rovno came and wanted to open an orphanage, it found us prepared to help. The Joint contributed considerable sums of money, but this was insufficient. We, therefore, organized various activities. We established an orphanage for 20 children. They had no father or mother and needed a roof over their heads.

The situation worsened when the town changed from one regime to another. Young people were insecure and looked for ways to immigrate.

In the meantime, the Red Army came closer to town. Those who had the means escaped to the United States. Loyal Zionists sought a way to make Aliyah. It was very difficult because the British Mandate government restricted the number of certificates. Anyone who truly wished to make Aliyah, found a way. This is how many families were able to avoid the Holocaust. Among those who made Aliyah in time, am I, the author of this article, my husband Mordechai and our oldest son, Moshe. I wrote many letters to my friends, from Eretz Israel, begging them to make Aliyah. I do not know what stopped them from leaving this small, modest town. Yes, it was charming and pretty. I know others have already described the beauty of the town with its rivers, mountains, forests, etc. The palace of Bieliankin has been mentioned. I believe that one item has been forgotten – the castle of the composer Stravinsky, brother–in–law of Bieliankin. He was married to the daughter of Nusenko. These were good people and many Jews earned their keep working for them.

However, all this beauty was desecrated by the Nazi beasts who hunted the Jewish residents of the beloved town. The lovely rows of trees on both sides of the road to Ludomir served to accompany them to the huge common grave. May God avenge the blood of the thousands of our dear martyrs!

[illegible]

Shtrotenberg?
February 4 1930
Dear Mrs. Tz. Felsher
Ustiluh

Dear Madam,

Your kind words that you sent to congratulate me on my seventieth year made me very happy. I was always truly sorry that our sisters did not know our national language well. This stopped them from learning our language and our Torah. I found this to be the main reason for the forgetting of the Hebrew language within our people. I would say that out ancestors sinned and we suffered the consequences. This did not happen to other peoples. They managed to retain their language. Only, we, the people of Israel, were more guilty than others and our ancestors did not remember their language. This affected their children as well. Of course, there are some of our people who are striving to teach their daughters the Hebrew language, but, unfortunately, it is only done in a shallow way. I always remark that they do not speak Hebrew, they just babble in Hebrew. I read your words and I found in them Hebrew thinking. This made me very happy. It is impossible to have Hebrew expression without Hebrew thought. This can only be acquired by reading literature in Hebrew with understanding. I tell you, my dear lady: many girls have succeeded and you are above all of them. I received many congratulatory letters these days, but only a very few, yours among them, pleased me.

Please accept, my dear lady, my good wishes and my thanks for your kind words.

I close with greetings and with feelings of honour.

Shimon Bernfeld

[Page 76]

The historian and philosopher Prof. Shimon Bernfeld, Z"L, whose letter is being published above, was born in Stalislavov in 1860. He died in Berlin in 1940.

[Page 78]

Torah Va'avodah Movement in Ustiluh

by A. Ben–Dov

Translated by Ala Gamulka

The year was 1920 and these were bright summer days. In Jewish Poland there was an awakening of national–Zionist spirit. Ustiluh was swept up in the current. Various Zionist organizations sprung one after the other. However, the Religious–Zionist movement was still missing in Ustiluh. I was nineteen years old then, a graduate of the House of Learning. I was not indifferent to events in the Jewish world. In my mind, the following question arose: where is the religious Jewry and, especially, where is the religious youth? Do they not hear the "voices of God saying –make Aliyah!"? What is the purpose of this indifference?

I knew that in Congress Poland there was a Religious–Zionist movement called Mizrachi. However, here, in Volyn, it had not yet arrived.

One day I met David Stav (Dunya) and we came up with the thought that it was about time that the religious youth in Ustiluh were to organize itself in a Religious–Nationalist movement, i.e., Mizrachi. We immediately went to work.

We first went to the two judges (dayanim), Ben Zion Reider and Reuven Zhak in order to obtain their approval and assistance. The latter held the tip of his long beard and asked: "Why specifically Mizrachi? Agudat Shlomei Emunei Israel is also a religious–nationalist movement. It recognizes the importance of rebuilding Eretz Israel and it will, no doubt, soon amalgamate with Mizrachi".

He showed us a ledger of contributions from members of Shlomei Emunei Israel where it was written, black on white, that the Agudah is striving to establish, in Eretz Israel, a Jewish settlement based on Torah and tradition.

We had not yet understood the difference between a Jewish settlement and political Zionism. We had come to have the Dayan join us and, instead, we were taken in by him.

We took our materials from Reuven and we went to find people who would join us.

This is how Agudat Zeirei Emunei Israel was established.

However, the agreement of the dayanim was not enough. It was necessary to capture the interest and support of the religious public. The way to do it was through the House of Learning.

Large posters were hung in all synagogues. On Shabbat, yours truly came, surrounded by other young people, to the Great House of Learning. I gave a speech in which I proved, quoting the Torah, Or Haim,

[Page 79]

and other holy texts, that, this time redemption will not come as a miracle, like the exodus from Egypt. It will come through nature, as predicted by Ezra and Nehemiah. The conclusion was, of course: join Shlomei Emunei Israel who are planning to rebuild Eretz Israel according to the Torah and tradition.

This is how the young Agudah became known. However, the attitude towards it in the Shtiebels was different: In the Radzin Shtiebel, some of the zealots ridiculed the "heretic" (the author of these lines) for diverting their young men from the proper way.

Committee of Zeirei Hechalutz and Mizrahi

On the other hand, the Kuzmir Shtiebel gave these young people the Women's section for a meeting place. In the synagogue itself, the Agudah opened a national–religious school. The teachers were, myself, Moshe Kandiner and others.

Soon, the leaders of Agudah discovered they had been misled or they were wrong. An article in the newspaper Der Yud informed us that monies collected for Keren Hayishuv (Funds for settlement) are simply lying unused. We checked and discovered our viewpoint and thoughts were not aligned with those of the publishers of the Yud. We simply waited for the right moment to make changes. An opportunity soon came.

[Page 80]

When the Bolsheviks entered Ustiluh that year, all national organizations were shut down. This meant the end of the Agudat Zeirei Emunei Israel.

A few months later, the Tora Veavoda movement arose. It included the youth of Zeirei Mizrachi, Hechalutz Hamizrachi and the women's group, Bruria.

The active members were the same, but this time, they were part of a real religious–Zionist movement. The group grew and two rooms were rented in the house of Yeshayah Goldhover, Z"L. There was great activity. Lecturers came from the central office and spoke to us in the clubhouse and in the Great House of Learning. We sent members to training and, in the end, they received certificates and were able to make Aliyah.

In the meantime, the author of this article left town, Dunya Stav immigrated to America, and there was no one left to dedicate himself whole–heartedly to the various activities. The movement slowed down, but soon the teacher Moshe Shpirer had returned to town and became its savior.

Quietly and carefully, he took matters in his own hands and led the movement in Ustiluh until the end. Vave Kreiner, Z"L, and other young people supported the work of Torah Veavoda in Ustiluh.

Other active members of the movement that should be particularly mentioned are Shalom Shpigel and Shlomo Tchil. They were also teachers in the school of Moshe Shpirer.

He, himself, always dreamed of making Aliyah when he could, but he did not make it. May God avenge his blood!

[Page 81]

Hechalutz Branch in Ustiluh

by Yitzhak Farber

Translated by Ala Gamulka

I am unable to write about Hechalutz in our town without mentioning three members who worked together with us and did not merit to reach their hoped–for purpose:

a. Moshe, son of Yaakov, Shroit

He was younger than us by a few years and was full of enthusiasm. He joined the movement full of energy and ready to act. He undertook any task needed and was prepared to contribute his own knowledge. It can be said that he was an intended Aliyah candidate, but cruel fate did not allow him to reach his goal. It was a hot day, one of those sweltering days in Tamuz. We were sitting together planning our activities for 20 Tamuz. During a break, Moshe went to the Bug River to swim and he did not return… Our loss was great and we could not get over it for a long time.

b. Shaul, son of Nahum, Stolar (Ritual slaughterer)

He did not grow up with us. He came from far away. His external appearance covered the heat inside. He quickly joined us and became one of us, as if we had grown up together. He was always alert and excited. He looked after his ailing mother, but he still found time to contribute, to plan a new activity. He even took part in a literary evening in the municipal library, named for I.L. Peretz.

He dedicated himself to two activities: 1. Hechalutz movement, 2. The library. He was an avid reader. He organized cultural evenings and was always one of those who were involved in all activities. Central Hechalutz wanted to establish a training kibbutz in our town. We were a little leery because there were some difficulties. Shaul did not hesitate for one second. He insisted that we give a positive answer and he immediately organized the food needed.

He loved all members with their attributes and deficits. He dreamed of fulfilling his dream, but he was unsuccessful.

c. Efraim, son David, Rubinshteyn

He acquired much knowledge from his father. He looked hurt, but he always kept to a specific framework. His mother and sister barely made a living and his lot was to roam as an itinerant teacher in the villages. Still, he managed to enrich his spiritual knowledge during that time. It was not enough for him. He wished to make Aliyah and he came to us. He knew how to give to others what he knew. When we began to organize Hebrew classes, he was one of our instructors. He did his work quietly and modestly. His explanations were given in a low voice, but he made sure they were well absorbed.

[Page 82]]

For family reasons, he still lived at home. Time ran away from him and he was killed in the Holocaust.

As a result of the situation in Eretz Israel, the movement in the Diaspora had highs and lows. Those who went through these times always had hope. There were days when we left everything else and dedicated ourselves to the good of the people. This gave us enormous personal satisfaction.

A visit by an emissary from Eretz Israel became a special experience that took us out of the humdrum days in which we were immersed. The emissary would give us tasks to accomplish, but he also brought fresh ideas. We could hope for a great future. We soared far away…

The commemoration of the Balfour Declaration, 20 Tamuz, was celebrated by us with parades, speeches and fund raising.

Hechalutz organization in 1931

[Page 83]

We celebrated Lag B'Omer in nature, in the nearby forest. It was a special day, full of singing and dancing– until nighttime. We returned in a parade of groups carrying torches and dancing a stormy hora–until we had no strength left!

The movement had highs and lows. It always depended on events in Eretz Israel. This deeply influenced every branch. I recall that, in 1925, days before the 14th Zionist Congress, there were several Zionist movements in town. The activities of two of them were especially evident: Hechalutz and Hechalutz Hamizrachi. The former was led by Yehuda Fleisher and Yaakov Yokhenzon, Z"L while the latter was supervised by the teacher Moshe Shpirer, Z"L. He was then a delegate to the congress. There was competition in raising funds and we reached a height that, for many years, we could not surpass. It must be said that the first pioneer from town to make Aliyah was a member of Hechalutz Hamizrahi and this fact influenced greatly the movement. Aharon Sholev, Z"L was the first one to fulfill the dream. He paved the way and received, with open arms, all those who followed and wished to be with him. May his memory be a blessing!

Several families left town and there was less activity. We were aroused again to new plans in Av 1929 when there were attacks in Eretz Israel. From that time on, until our town was destroyed by the murderers, we were quite successful. The dedication was sincere and heartfelt. There were those who laughed at us while others thought we were mad. We continued, tirelessly, to reach our goals.

It is understandable that there were arguments among our members. We were always confronted by locked gates. The movement grew, but it was not enough. Some of our members spent 3–4 years in training, but, still, they continued on. Life around us went on and although we lived there, our thoughts were far away.

Our activities were varied: felling trees to pay for a hall and paying taxes by holding cultural evenings, Hebrew lessons and other events.

In town there were two public places in which youth were concentrated– the library and Hechalutz. It is inevitable that there was a connection between them.

We always had the library for our use and we were able to obtain materials existing in it.

When I remember the library, I cannot forget those who, for many years, worked tirelessly for the benefit of the Hebrew library.

I visualize the library shelves, especially the Hebrew section. I can see Bluma Kornfracht, Tema Tish, Hinda Shinerman, Yaakov Yokhenzon and, still with us, the sisters Beila and Breindel Eichenboim. They performed their duties with sanctity– not to be compensated. It is due to them that we had evenings for Bialik, Brenner, Lamdan, etc. These drew large crowds and influenced many people.

[Page 84]

We reached heights in the years 1935–6. Many young people joined and were included in all ongoing events. The older ones attended training kibbutzim throughout Poland, in the hope of fulfilling their dream. Some made Aliyah and remained in touch with us. This was a good influence. There were young people from various social classes who joined. The events of 1936, with their difficult results, did not weaken the movement. The slogan was: "We will make Aliyah in spite of everything!" I, too, made Aliyah in 1936. When I look back on the Hechalutz movement, with all its struggles, I see it as a ray of sunshine within our gray lives in our town and other towns in Poland. The Hechalutz branch was full of excitement and was sensitive to all that was happening. Mainly, it had hope for the future.

Das Vort (the Word) – a daily newspaper of labour Zionists, Heatid (the Future) of Hechalutz, Hashomer Hatzair paper, Haolam (he World) during congress times– they all enriched our knowledge in all Zionist matters. They actually brought us into a different life cycle– one we yearned to reach. Only a few of us were successful and the rest were lost together with everything that was dear to us. The only thing left now are memories.

Just before the Aliyah of Yitzhak Farber in 1936

[Page 85]

Hashomer Hatzair and Other Youth Movements in Ustiluh

by Zvi Hadari (Pomerantz)

Translated by Ala Gamulka

The Holocaust ended 21 years ago. Often, I remember my town. It stands in front of my eyes, as if I had only seen it yesterday.

I also see its streets, the wooden houses and the fences peeking here and there. The famous boulevard leading to the beautiful, abandoned palace. We, the youth, used to visit it often when we went for evening walks.

I remember its Jews who struggled all week for their existence. On Shabbat, after a week of hard work and worry, the main street was filled with people. Groups would stand on street corners, holding excited discussions on all world problems. The majority of them were young people, each one with his own heated pointed of view.

I wish to write, on paper, my recollections of the youth and its activities in our town. I was a member of Hashomer Hatzair and I am still its member in one of its kibbutzim to this day.

After WWI, when the battles subsided, there was increased activity among the Jewish youth. It was mainly Zionist. Under the influence of Poalei Zion and Hechalutz, there were many groups, such as drama and advanced study. The large library opened many horizons and brought the youth closer to literature and knowledge. It was a time of cultural blossoming in town. In the early 192os, several members of Hechalutz made Aliyah.

Some time in 1926–27, a new group arose among the Zionist youth. It was Hashomer Hatzair, founded by a group of students in the high school in Ludomir. They began to organize children and youth under Hashomer Hatzair. At first, it was just scouting, but after a short while, we became a Zionist youth movement–socialist and pioneering– with the aim of making Aliyah.

During the blooming period of the branch, the number of members reached 150. The branch was an important part of the life of the youth in town. The best young people joined us. We appeared in celebratory parades, such as La B'Omer, dressed in uniform and carrying flags.

[Page 86]

The branch was quite active in collecting funds for Jewish National Fund and was involved in all that was happening.

The parents of the members were also interested in the activities in the branch and it seemed that they appreciated our work.

Hashomer Hatzair branch in 1934

The internal newspaper of the branch gave expression to all that was happening among us. We nurtured, in the children, a love of our people, our country and the labor movement. We participated actively in Zionist academies, sports activities, choirs, etc.

The graduating group of our branch was active in Hechalutz.

There were other Zionist movements in town: Beitar and Hashomer Haleumi. It seems that the majority of young people were involved in a movement. They had their own political views and there were arguments among them.

There were non–Zionist groups as well– the Communist Party attracted many Jewish young people. This, in spite of the fact that it had to be done in secret with the threat of imprisonment.

An important contribution to the existence of our movement and Hechalutz was the visit of Yehuda Fleisher, Z"L. We, the young people, had heard much about his activities within Hechalutz before he made Aliyah, as well his work there. He seemed to us to personify the image of working pioneer– a symbol of dedication to the ideals and of personal realization. During his visit in our town,

[Page 87]

Members of Poalei Zion before the Aliyah of Yehuda Fleisher

[Page 88]

Yehuda came to discussions at the branch and meetings of Hechalutz. He expressed his personal fulfillment. He wanted to eliminate the old and to start a new life in Eretz Israel. The appearance of Yehuda left an indelible mark on all those who came into contact with him. He was tall, “taller than everyone”, drawing respect. The youth were charmed by him. Yehuda made a great contribution to elevating the status of the pioneering movement within the youth. After his visit, there was an increase in the numbers of those going to training. Many of us went to training and soon made Aliyah. During WWII, he was killed in a bombing of the Haifa refinery, where he worked. It was a heavy loss.

Today we can only have memories of days past. It is difficult to describe the magnitude of the catastrophe that befell the Jewish world in general and our town and its Jews in particular. Entire families were cut down by these beasts. Everyone lost his cherished people and very few survived. We were unable to help. We did not even know the extent of the terrible events. We can only remember and never to forget what Amalek did to us. To remember and not to forget!!

We will tell our children and their children about the town of Ustiluh, its Jews, its Jewish youth. It existed once and is no longer here…

Hashomer Hatzair– older section (1927)

[Page 89]

Leaders of Beitar 1929

The Eagles in Ustiluh: 1 Adar 1935

[Page 90]

The Cultural Center in Ustiluh

by Sima Rutenberg (Goldberg)

Translated by Ala Gamulka

I would like to describe one house, in particular. It was the house of Ichel Natz. He was rumored to be a wealthy man, but during WWI he lost everything. He died too early, due to depression and sadness. He left a wife and an adopted daughter. He had no children. The house was large and occupied half a block. After the owners died, many poor families occupied the house. A part was taken over by some young people of the town intelligentsia. They turned it into a cultural center. There was a large library with thousands of excellent books. There were also a reading room and a games room. About two thirds of the local youth were members and twice a week there was a book exchange. Anyone who wished to meet good companions and spend a few hours having interesting conversations on various topics, playing chess or just talking, would find what they were looking for in this house. There was joy and happiness in these rooms. From time to time, lecturers were invited to speak on various topics. There were even emissaries from Eretz Israel. In this house, people from different classes would meet and listen hungrily to the emissary from Eretz Israel.

Library in memory of the thinker, Yehuda Fleisher

[Page 91]

The Hebrew Library

There was a literary group and I, the writer of this article, belonged to it. We would read aloud a story by one of the classical authors, mostly I.L. Peretz. We would discuss it, each one according to his ability and his world view. Last, but not least, the drama group in which I took an active part. It was the height of spirit. Mainly, the rehearsals helped to forget our daily troubles. I remember an interesting story– the library became a theater. It began with the fact that we would obtain the hall of the Polish school– with payment– before every performance. Once, a week before the scheduled performance, our young men went to rent the hall and were refused. Perhaps it was Anti–Semitism, already felt in our town.

[Page 92]

Or it may have been another reason. In any case, we were quite upset. We decided that we had to put on the play, no matter what. Overnight, the two rooms became one large one. Benches and chairs were brought from homes close and far. The play was presented at the scheduled time. Soon the rumour that the Poles were mean to us made the rounds. The people of the town came in crowds to see our play. They were amazed at the fact what a few young people were able, in days, to achieve. This was our youth…

There was no Aliyah for some time, but, soon, Menachem Kessel and I were the first to do so. We traveled to the Maccabia in Tel Aviv in 1932. As soon as I arrived, I discovered that many of my friends went into training. Some of them managed to make Aliyah before the war broke out, some came on Aliyah Bet. To our great sorrow, the majority of them did not manage to do it. Either they did not believe that there would be such destruction or because they could not afford to do so. They were killed together with the rest of the community in the great Holocaust.

[Page 93]

Figures

by E. Schlechter

Translated by Jerrold Landau

Donated by Christophe Philipon

I am now closing my eyes in order to bring to my memory the dear personalities who lived and functioned in our city of Ustilag. They appear before my eyes one after another like a movie in a theater. Each of them had their own appearance reminiscent of their activities and deeds, and the chapters of their lives and the life of the community as a whole.

First and foremost, my parents of blessed memory appear before my eyes. My father Reb Avraham was a dear man, knowledgeable in Torah, a *shochet* [ritual slaughterer], a *mohel* [ritual circumcisor], and the prayer leader in the *shtibel*. At times of need, he would go to one of the villages on the High Holidays to serve as a prayer leader without expectation of payment. He would beloved and acceptable to people because of his calm, deliberate demeanor. He related with patience to us, his children, who did not follow his path, even though the Hassidim sneered at him over this, and he certainly suffered from this… His home was open to every passer-by, for a warm meal and a place to sleep. Of course, this must be attributed to the merit of my mother, of blessed memory.

Reb Avraham the Shochet (Schlechter) and his wife Pesia

Friends and acquaintances would gather in our house on Saturday nights and weekday evenings to discuss words of Torah and world news over a cup of tea. Father would read to them from the Jewish newspapers current events of the country and the world in general. At times, he would sit with his family members in the evening and discuss bygone days, wonderful works of *Tzadikim*, the decrees of Czar Nikolay I, the snatching of children to the army, the Beilis blood libel trial, and other such topics. We would sit around him next to the warm oven on long winter evenings and listen attentively to his stories…

When the sons grew up, and he saw no future in Poland on the horizon, he did not oppose their emigration. Hershel, Shlomo, and Nachum immigrated to America. Lebish went to Mexico, and the writer of these lines made *aliya* to the Land of Israel. The only one to remain at home was my oldest brother Berl, a watchmaker by profession and a communal activist. During the years 1936-1939, years of crisis and bloody revolts in the Land, he would write me words of encouragement and ask me to maintain my stand and not despair. In September 1939, when the town was captured by the Red Army, the government allowed him to work in the "*shechita* trade" under their regulations, but he earned his livelihood with difficulty. Within two years, the town was conquered by the Germans, may their names be blotted out, and we lost connection forever.

[Page 94]

My mother Pesia of blessed memory, was also pious and good-hearted. She was always prepared to offer assistance at a time of difficulty. When she found out about a poor neighbor who did not have provisions for the Sabbath or who was sick and had no money for a physician or medicine, she would immediately turn to her neighbor the *rebbetzin*, the wife of the rabbinical judge Reb Bentzi. They would go together from door to door to collect the needed sum. She would distribute a portion of the meat that Father brought home from the slaughterhouse to the poor on Sabbath eves. She especially took care of her neighbor the wife of Yeshayahu the shoemaker, who was always sick and bedridden, and whose children were hungry and neglected. On the Sabbath, she would hasten to be first in the women's section, and at home she would study the Yiddish holy books of *Tzena Urena* and *Kav Hayashar*[1].

I recall the many preparations for the weddings of her sons and daughters, Hershel, Nachum Esther, Chana, and Roiza. How much energy did she impart into these preparations! One month before the wedding, the seamstress sat in our house to prepare the bride's clothes. Then the "*sarverke*" Ethel came to prepare the biscuits and foods for the wedding, etc.

My mother died of a protracted illness in 1939, approximately a month before the outbreak of the terrible storm. She left father to his grief and his bitter fate that was to overtake him a within a few years…

Young Activists

Yehuda Fliszer

He was the son of an honorable family, a relative of the famous Yochanson family. He was tall, full of energy, always serious, and modest in is actions. He loved simplicity and distanced himself from pride and bragging. He was pleasant with his fellowman. He was a central figure in our town in all organizational and political activities during the period following the First World War. During that time, a new spirit passed through our town, the spirit of *haskalah* and national renaissance, which penetrated deeply into the hearts of the Jewish youth. The desire for the historical homeland grew from day to day. Yehuda was among the choicest activists in the Socialist-Zionist movement. I recall the splendid parade that he organized along with his friends on the day of the Balfour Declaration. They decorated the city with flags. Lads rode on horses with the flag of the nation in their hands. A youth choir followed them, singing, "Wake up, my People, take your flag in the hand and march toward your Fatherland…" The enthusiasm was great. The parade left a strong impression at that time also on our gentile neighbors. Hearts were opened. Many donations of money and valuables flowed in for the redemption of the Land.

[Page 95]

Yehuda worked to spread the Zionist idea among the various strata of the city. He was among the founders of the Young Zion chapter. He was very active for the national funds and the Workers' Fund. He was one of the founders of the dramatic club that became famous in all the nearby cities. He was one of the founders of the Hebrew and Yiddish libraries.

In 1923, a chapter of Hechalutz and Young Hechalutz was founded, and he taught the youth Hebrew during the evening hours. On Sabbaths, he would arrange excursions to Biliankin Boulevard or the nearby forest. Discussions were conducted on the role of the pioneer [*chalutz*] in the upbuilding of the homeland, the value of the Histadrut[2], its institutions and activities. As a result of these activities, the youth began to stream to the *hachshara* depot in Klosowa and Grochow. A number of members succeeded in making *aliya* to the Land. Despite the crisis that afflicted the Land after the mass *aliya* from Poland during the Grabowski era, Yehuda made *aliya* in 1925. He worked at all types of difficult labors, and maintained his stand. He eventually worked in the Rotenberg Electric Company of Naharayim.

Bloody disturbances broke out in the Land in the year 5689 (1929). Yehuda was among the activists of the Haganah. He stood guard and protected the property and honor of the settlement. After the Land quieted down, he returned to his native city for a brief period. His presence in the town infused the Zionist movement with a living spirit. He participated in all the meetings and monetary campaigns for the Land of Israel. It was a special treat to see him strolling through the streets of the town wearing a white suit, with his camera in his hand. He returned to the Land after approximately a half a year. A few years later, he brought his fiancée D. L. on *aliya*. He settled in Haifa and was accepted as an official in the Shell Company. He hoped to attain a situation of peace. However, the Second World Wars suddenly broke out. Our land was also caught up in the bloody maelstrom. Italian airplanes bombarded the Shell oil refineries in May 1940, and a bomb hit his workplace. Yehuda was mortally wounded.

He was taken from us at a young age, leaving behind a wife and a child. All the natives of Ustilag in the Land and the Diaspora wept over his untimely death. May his memory be a blessing.

Yankel Yochanson

He was the son of Yedidya, the brother of the wealthy Reb Wolf Yochanson. Yaakov was among the activists of Tzeirei Zion and the founders of Hechalutz and Hechalutz Hatzair. He was one of the founders of the library. He was a fine orator, speaking with good taste and enthusiasm. His appearances at meetings left a strong impression on his entire audience. He decided to go on *hachshara* to Grochow, and from there to make *aliya*, however he was suddenly called up to the Polish Army. After he finished his army service, he took on the responsibility for sustaining the family. He worked in the lumber business. He was handsome. Everyone loved him and appreciated him. He perished along with his family. He left behind a brother Menashe and relatives in the Land.

[Page 96]

Fishel Eisenberg

He was the son of Reb Lipche the teacher. His house was at the edge of the town next to the bridge over the Lug River (the Stav) that led to the village of Zloza and the forest. This place was well known to the local youth from the many hikes during the summer. In the spring, at the time of the melting of the snow, when the entire area was covered with water, they would sail on barges to distant places. His house served as a rest stop for the youth as they returned to town from their long journeys. During his younger days, Fishel was a teacher in one of the small villages of Volhynia. He was always sure of his own abilities, and was immersed in reading books. He played an active role in communal institutions. He had a serious, content oriented way of thinking, so everyone took his opinion into account. I remember the first Hebrew orator who spoke in the Large *Beis Midrash* on the 20th of *Tammuz* in memory of Dr. Herzl of blessed memory. He was among the best orators in town. He would speak primarily about literary topics. He would speak words of anger toward the Communist opponents of Zionism, but his words were convincing, and he always had the upper hand during debates with them. He married Bluma Elbaum. He worked in commerce. During my conversations with him, he always pointed out that heavy clouds were covering the skies of Poland, and he foresaw serious dangers awaiting Polish Jewry. His prophesy was fulfilled before he managed to find a refuge, and he was swept up in the bloodbath along with his family on the day of the Holocaust.

Yaakov Sheinerman

He was the son of Yechezkel Sheinerman. He lived not far from our house. We were friends from the time that we studied in school together. He was a thin, short youth with red hair, blue eyes, and freckles on his face. He was intelligent, with a precious character. He was diligent in his studies in an exemplary fashion. He was orderly and meticulous. Not even a tiny smudge could be found on his books and notebooks. At home, he was constantly involved in preparing for his classes. He did not permit himself go outside for a stroll to enjoy the fresh air during summer evenings. His favorite subject was natural science. He derived special enjoyment from walking between the trees and bushes with a tin can in his hand to collect bees, insects and butterflies, and to collect wildflowers for drying.

When he finished his course of studies in primary school, he wished to study in the final grade for an additional year. He was fluent in the Polish Language. His handwriting was calligraphic, his style was witty, and he made a name for himself in the town. People began to ask his advice on various matters connected with government relations. He wrote requests for leniency and reductions of taxes. The Jewish middle class and tradesmen suffered a great crisis at that time.

[Page 97]

Grabowski, the Polish minister of the treasury, imposed unbearably heavy taxes on the Jewish population over and above the civic taxes. Yaakov acted to the best of his ability to help them. He worked for some time at the merchants' organization. He refused to accept payment for helping the poor residents. After a brief period, he was hired as an official in the Ustilag town council. He fulfilled his role with faithfulness and dedication. He helped anyone in need of assistance. The Polish officials looked at him with an evil eye and attempted to trip him up from time to time. I found out in the Land that they fired him from his work despite the fact that he was the only Jewish official in the town council of a town that had a decisive Jewish majority. At that time, the Poles were acting in accordance of the spirit of the times. He began to work in business, and was considered to be one of the wealthy youths of the city. His intention was to liquidate his business and to make *aliya* to the Land as a wealthy man. Suddenly the Second World War broke out. He perished along with his family at the hands of the Germans, may their names be blotted out.

I was a frequent visitor in his home. I knew his parents, brothers and sisters. Of them all, only his brother Eliezer succeeded in escaping. He lives in the United States today.

Yaakov was a faithful friend of mine. He helped me a great deal before I made *aliya.* He was active in communal institutions. He was a faithful Zionist and he worked on behalf of the funds. His pure blood screams out from the soil of the town on behalf of which he worked so hard to develop.

Shaul Stolar

When Reb Leibchi the *Shochet* (from the Shinman family) died, the community accepted one of his relatives, Reb Nachum Stolar of Turczyn, to replace him. From among the children of Reb Nachum the *Shochet,* his eldest son Shaul stood out. He studied Hebrew from the teacher Shalom Spiegel and began to draw near to the pioneering youth. At first, he was a bit shy, but he slowly gained self-confidence and began to play an active role in communal life in our town.

He was a member of the pioneering movement, and a librarian in the Yiddish library. He participated in all political and literary debates. He was always in a good mood, and he was accepted by the group. He worked in commerce and dreamed of making *aliya* as a wealthy man. In the meantime he married the member Geula Elbaum and established a family. His two brothers succeeded in making *aliya*, but he perished along with his family.

His beloved countenance will never be forgotten from my memory!

The Berliant Family

The head of the family Reb Moshe was a *maskil* and a faithful Jew. He was fluent in the languages that were spoken in Western Volhynia – Russian, Polish, and Ukrainian. He was appointed as the *Starosta* of Ustilag (a form of mayor) by the Czarist authorities. In this role, he was known as a fighter for justice and protector of the persecuted.

When the First World War broke out and the front approached our town, it was necessary to provide the Russian authorities with manpower to work on fortifications, fixing roads, and guarding the telephone lines. Since all of this implied certain sacrifices by the population, he gained many enemies. However, with the passage of time, everyone learned to value his honesty and true concern for the wellbeing of the town.

[Page 98]

It was told that the liquor distillery of the landowner Biliankin that was abandoned with the escape of its owners was a thorn in the side of the Jews, who were afraid that Russian soldiers would get drunk, do as they pleased, pillage, and perpetrate disturbances. Moshe Berliant and other activists rose up and hired several brave gentiles who poured out the liquor stock into the fields.

Even after the war, the work in the liquor distillery was not restarted. Its skeleton, along with its tall chimney that could be seen from afar, remained standing until I made *aliya* to the Land.

During the time of the Austrian occupation, Moshe Berliant served as vice mayor to the mayor Shmuel Izraeli. A Polish mayor was chosen after the town passed to Polish rule, even though the Jews formed the decisive majority. Reb Moshe was then appointed as the secretary of the town council, and served as the official spokesman of the community. During the brief period of Bolshevik occupation, Moshe Berliant served once again as the representative of the town to the authorities and the director of civic affairs after the Polish mayor fled for his life.

When the Poles returned, Moshe Berliant returned to his senior position in the town council. However, when the anti-Semitic winds began to blow through government circles and penetrated the town council as well, Reb Moshe was fired. He then founded the merchants' bank, in which he and his son Shmuel worked as accountants.

I recall one incident from 1925. I found out that a speech would be taking place in the yard of the Polish church. I and several other youths entered, and were shaken up to see the large gathering of Poles from all strata applauding every statement of the speaker that was directed against the Jews. A picture of a snake with a Jewish head was hanging from the church door… We immediately went to tell Reb Moshe Berliant, who wrote a complaint to the district captain. My friends and I signed as witnesses. We also informed the Jewish Sejm[3] representatives about this incident.

Reb Moshe Berliant had a large family: five sons and three daughters. They were all active in communal life, and the Berliant house was a center for all social happenings in the town.

The head of the family passed away after a long illness. The youngest daughter also became ill and died. Four sons Chaim, Yosef, Nachman, and Aharon and their eldest sister Sheindel immigrated to America before the Holocaust. The mother, the second daughter Batya and her family, and Shmuel and his family perished during the days of fury.

The children continued with their communal work in America. Nachman was the secretary and living spirit of the help organization of Ustilag natives. To our sorrow, the sad news had just reached us that Yosel and Nachman Berliant passed away this year. May their memories be a blessing.

Translator's Footnotes:

1. See http://en.wikipedia.org/wiki/Tseno_Ureno and http://en.wikipedia.org/wiki/Kav_ha-Yashar.
2. Zionist workers' organization.
3. The Polish parliament.

[Page 99]

In Memory of Moshe Shpirer

by Yakov Biterman

Translated by Ala Gamulka

It was during the winter in the 1930s. The municipality clerks and collectors spread in town like thieves. They confiscated everything in their way in order to increase the income of city hall. There was an atmosphere of confusion in town. No one was used to such an undisciplined method of tax collecting. Everyone was angry and was cursing. There was great resentment, but there was no practical way of reacting. One day, I was visiting my teacher, Moshe Shpirer. His face was serious and resentful and in a quiet voice he asked me if we, too, had been visited by the tax collectors. "Yes," I replied. "They took our wall clock". I added, with resentment, "They poured the water from our neighbors' metal barrel and took it away. The people cried with pain and embarrassment". He replied:" I want to do something about it. I wish to stop this thievery. It is good that you came here now". I wondered, "How can I, a young boy, help him in this task?" He immediately explained: he would send an anonymous letter to the mayor to warn him about his illegal deeds and to threaten him about a complaint to higher authorities if it did not stop". Since his handwriting was recognizable, he asked me to copy the letter in my script. I was very happy to fulfill his request and I immediately began to write. It was a long letter. It began by appealing to conscience and ended with a warning. It was signed: "citizens of Ustiluh who want justice". He put the letter in an envelope and handed it to me, with shaking hands, so I would place it in the mailbox. The next day, the collectors went out on their usual route, but they were suddenly recalled and the activity ceased.

The letter fulfilled its purpose...

He was a modest man in all he did. I knew him for 13 years, first as a student and later as a good friend. He captured my heart in his devotion to any task. He was one of the founders of the Hebrew school and he taught many students. They learned Hebrew and appreciated and loved him.

WWII broke out. The Soviets came to town and his house stood exactly on the border, next to the barbed wire. All Zionist activities were not permitted and any visit to his house, especially at night, was actually dangerous. I then felt empty and longed for the past. I knew all our hopes for realization were gone. Very difficult and somber days followed. The majority of the youth were drafted into the Red Army, I among them.

[Page 100]

It was one early evening when I went to say good–bye to him. I arrived at his house and knocked on the door. His wife peeked from behind the window curtain. When she saw me, she immediately drew me inside the house. I found him near a pile of books and notebooks, throwing most of them into the lit fireplace. I saw how difficult it was for him to do it. He looked at them as if he wanted to enjoy them one more time. I sat down next to him and I looked at every book he intended to burn. I found an album from the Zionist congress, beautifully bound (I believe it was the 14th congress to which he was a delegate). The pictures were beautiful. I was unable to throw it into the fire. I looked at all the pages and I found in it a message from Zionist prisoners in Russia. They were seeking help from the world, to free them. I wanted to take it with me, but Moshe did not allow it. "I am afraid that if you forget to destroy it and they will find it, we will all be in danger"– he told me with tearful eyes. I read it a few more times and then I threw it into the fire. I said good–bye to him and his family. As I stood on the threshold, I saw the burning books. I felt I was saying good–bye not only to my teacher, my friend, but also to the past that was now going up in smoke.

[Page 101]

Leibale Helfman

by Yehudit Sapir–Chen (Helfman)

Translated by Ala Gamulka

Leibale's life was not paved with roses. He was born in 1907 to a poor family. His father was sickly and he was exhausted by his work. His mother helped the father to earn a living by managing the wheat store. The boy was educated like all other Jewish children – in a Heder where he learned Torah and Talmud. He had special talents and he stood out among his classmates, so he was sent to the government elementary school in Ludomir. He graduated with distinction.

WWI broke out and Leibale wrote about the war and his conclusions: attacks by Cossacks on the Jews in villages, etc. He then determined that he wished to make Aliyah.

When he graduated from elementary school, he began to work as a bookkeeper in one of the guilds of the wheat merchants. He was self–taught in bookkeeping, as he was in other subjects: languages, geography, history– what he had not learned in elementary school.

He worked in the daytime and studied at night. He brought his earnings home. He became well–known for his honesty in his town and outside it.

He had a friend by the name of Yerucham Tzigel. He was an only child to his father who was well educated. The son, like the father, was studious and capable and was a good friend to Leibale. They had both passed the external matriculation exams, for which they had prepared by studying in the attic. Leibale said to Yerucham:" I don't have the opportunity to study at the university as I have to help my family, but you, an only child, should continue in your studies. Let me worry about the money you will need" … Leibale, together with a few friends, began to collect funds for his friend's education. He deposited the money with a neighbor and he obliged her to keep the secret. However, like other good Jewish women, she could not control herself and told Leibale's mother the secret. The news was spread through town, to Leibale's disappointment. He was modest and did not want publicity.

A second story had to do with the wife of a farmer who was buying wheat and forgot her purse in the store. When Leibale noticed, he immediately followed her cart and retuned the purse to the woman. The woman came the next day to the store and praised the young man.

[Page 102]

If he had not returned the purse to her, her husband would have beaten her to death. This story made the rounds in town. It was a wonder…

In addition to studying and self–educating, he was also active in the Zionist movement. He organized classes for studying the Hebrew language and the geography of Eretz Israel, in his home.

He was taken from us at a young age. He fell ill with dysentery and passed away in 1928.

During the funeral, Mendel Lipsky, a high school teacher in Ludomir, said the following to principal Starer:" I doubt that there is another genius like him in all of Ludomir". The principal replied: "Perhaps in all of Volyn it is difficult to find someone like him". The following saying referred to Leibale: "What God loves he takes to him".

[Page 103]

Two Figures– Two Destinies

by A. Ben–Dov

Translated by Ala Gamulka

a. David "the investigator"

Among those who prayed in the Shtiebel, the one who especially drew my attention was David Tzigel, nicknamed "the investigator". What really interested me was his brow. In particular, the top part of his brow was pale and shone with its whiteness, in comparison to the rest of his face which was dark and tanned. He had a black beard. It was as if this part of his brow announced:" this is where my brain resides and I do not want to darken it".

His life style was modest and I believe it was like that of a young boy. It was as if there was additional testimony that this person had more wisdom.

The store of David the investigator was in the row of wooden, narrow and low shops. He would use a hand grinder for the preparation of groats. The back door led to his living space– as wide as the store, but longer. There, stood a "train" of two beds, a couch, a large bookcase, a smaller wardrobe, an iron chest for clothes and linens, a small table and a few chairs. It was impossible to go across the room without touching the wall. It was true that David's eternal, brown robe was usually dirty with plaster…

Every time my mother sent me to get fresh groats from David the investigator, I would return thinking of his way of life with his little wife. She had a strange–looking eye. His little son, the quiet and bright Yerucham was also there. I decided that this man deserved my trust. Why should there be a question of trust? It is because David the investigator showed an interest in me. He used to ask me questions about my studies and test my knowledge.

I discovered that there was a secret friendship between him and my father. They would study Or Haim (the light of life) together. After studying they would speak to each other in an intimate way. This connection between a Hasid and an investigator surprised me.

Once there was a discussion in the Shtiebel about honors that Israeli (the son of Shifra) felt he was not given. David said, nicely: "You are a fool!". Israeli replied with anger:" you are a heretic!"

I pictured a heretic to look differently than David and I asked my father: “Father, is he really a heretic?” “No, my son” father laughed, “I believe he is a good Jew even if he is not a Hasid”.

[Page 104]

Indeed, I knew many Jews who were not Hasidim, such as my grandfather and other men, but I understood my father did not refer to them.

“If so” I said “he must be a Misnaged!” (an opposer of Hasidism). Father smiled and replied: “Perhaps”. Perhaps? – is it to be doubted. if so, what is he? In any case, he is a good Jew and a scholar who is neither a Hasid nor a Misnaged. He is a special person who is a thinker.

One early evening, when I was already 13 years old, I was in the Shtiebel with David the investigator. As usual, he asked me questions about what I was learning with my father. Finally, he asked a new question: do I read Hebrew literature?

In those days I was already reading secular literature, but not in Hebrew. These were books, mainly novels, that my sister would obtain in the public library. My father, Z”L, would sometimes scan the contents of such a book, for censoring purposes, and he would belittle it completely: “It is all nonsense, a waste of time, that's all!”

We also had other books, such as one dealing with Genesis according to the Darwin Theory. If father would have read it, he would have had a different reaction. However, I did not consider ideas in books written in Yiddish to be important. I certainly was not influenced by these ideas expressed by a gentile.

I did not reveal to David the investigator the fact that I read in Yiddish. I answered his question simply: “No, I do not have any books”.

“Oh, you could actually obtain books in the “Young Generation”, but your father would not be pleased about it. Why don't you come to me? For now, my library will be enough”.

This is how I began to read Hebrew literature.

In spite of the friendly relationship with David, my father was not so trusting. At the beginning, he checked the content of every book. What could be suspicious of an innocent topic such as “The History of Russia” by Mandelkorn? The first books that followed were of the same type. Then came “History of the People of Israel” by Gratz, translated by S.P.R. Aha! Here there were thoughts about the Talmud, the Zohar, messianism, Hassidism, etc. These ideas could shake the beliefs of such an innocent youngster as I was. Then came more books, collections and compilations, filled with “heavy material”: biblical criticisms and discussions of “Traitors of the Light”. These were ideas that were ancient, but they were new to me. They shook me deeply.

This was such a large amount of explosive material that it could destroy my inner world. David the investigator dealt with me in a manner that seemed appropriate to my well–being. After many “negative” books, he found me some “positive” ones.

[Page 105]

These were the writings of Dr. Kaminka, Zev Yaabetz, and others. From these books I learned that the previous group of books were not the final decision makers when it came to belief and thoughts.

David the investigator's method was, therefore:” Don't just follow. Study and read everything and use your brains to decide what is right”.

b. Simcha Shovalev

Among those who came to the Shtiebel, I noticed one outstanding person– Simcha Shovalev. He, too, was a scholar, but so different from David the investigator.

The main difference between them was the expression in their eyes. David the investigator's dark eyes looked at the world as a philosopher and a skeptic, Simcha Shovalev"S blue eyes were filled with clarification: "Slow down, you don't have to take everything so seriously…"

They were also very different in their external appearance. David the investigator was dressed like a Hassid, but Simcha wore a shorter garment than usual. He had a "semi modern" hat. In contrast to David the investigator, his clothes were always neat and ironed. It was only when it came to the beard that he outdid David. His beard remains in my memory for the following reason:

A short time before WWI broke out, my father sent me to secular lessons with Simcha Shovalev. At the time, he was also teaching the sons of Haim Bortnoyer, who were wild and dense. Once, during a lesson, the teacher dozed with his head on his arm and the tip of the beard lying on the table. What did these ruffians do? They brought scissors and were ready to cut the beard. I took my life in my hands (I was scared of them), I used a ruler and I hit the hand of the cutter. The teacher woke up and the beard was saved. (I, too, came out intact).

The differences related above are understandable as they are either external or by impression. However, the real differences that was characteristic to these two men was that David the investigator would always talk about his ideas, but Simcha was modest and shy. He always preferred to listen rather than speak. If you did not know that he taught Torah and language to grown youths, you would never know that he was a scholar. It was only one time that he broke his silence: when there was opposition in the Shtiebel to Jewish National Fund as the Zionists were considered as heretics. Simcha shouted: "I like these heretics better than any of your beautiful Jews!"

It was also interesting to see the reaction of the two to the legends that some people in the Shtiebel would tell. David the investigator would listen quietly as if he was interested. When he was asked for an opinion he would say, with sorrow, "I have nothing to do with legends!'

[Page 106]

On the other hand, Simcha would giggle and reply tersely:" Nonsense!".

All his years in the Diaspora, Simcha lived in sadness and poverty. His wife, Tzartel, was knowledgeable, genteel. She was pious, but never melancholy. Their economic situation was probably the reason. Perhaps, there was another reason. She died, in middle age, from cholera. Simcha was left with two sons, Aaron and Yehoshua. The latter died during the war. The older children had left home a long time earlier.

The father and son bought a rickety shack on the shore of the Bug. They renovated it and lived there, somehow. Aaron worked in carpentry and other jobs. He was injured in his leg and suffered greatly. There was only one hope for the two: to make Aliyah.

They merited to do so. Aaron came in 1924 and soon brought his fiancée Leah. Four years later his father joined him. They parted ways: the son went north while the father lived in Tel Avid until his death.

c. The fate of the family of David the investigator

One of the Holocaust survivors wrote me:

"In reply to your postcard about the fate of the family of David Tzigel and his son Yerucham– I know they died together with the rest of our townspeople during the Holocaust.

Yerucham Tzigel, before WWII, was an elementary school teacher. In 1939, when the Russians came, he became a principal. He was well respected in this position until the murderers came. They could not differentiate between good and evil and his fate was the same as the rest of the members of our community. Yerucham was married in 1933 and his wife, too, was a teacher. David the investigator was happy with them and they supported him. He lived comfortably"

d. Simcha Shovalev in Eretz Israel

When I made Aliyah in 1936, he was the first of our townspeople to visit me. His face showed the happiness he felt at seeing me here. I later visited his "apartment" in Tel Aviv. It was a container in the Yemenite quarters. It was very clean and neat.

I met him, a few times. in the Great Synagogue on Allenby Street. I saw indeed that he found his place there. He was dressed in clean black clothing. His beard was now gray and his face shining with happiness. He reminded me of the "Jews of Shabbat and Holidays" of I.L. Peretz. Here he was able to do good deeds. I know that he once collected funds and sent them to an orphaned family in Ustiluh. He was the only one of his generation of Ustiluh to be fortunate to see the establishment of the State of Israel.

[Page 107]

Simcha Shovalev in Eretz Israel

Late in life, he joined his son Aaron in Kiryat Haim (he had refused earlier to do it for religious reasons). He died there a few years before his son. He was 85. May his memory be a blessing.

[Page 108]

Three Who dared to Protest

By Moshe Zemel

Translated by Ala Gamulka

It is difficult to accept the fact that the Jews of Ustiluh, as most of the Jews of Poland, were brought to their graves as lambs to slaughter. As if they did not show any opposition to the murderers.

Whenever I think of it, the phrase "How the heroes have fallen!" comes to mind. (Samuel 2:19). I ask myself if it was so because cowardice was not characteristic of the Jews of Poland. The events in Pshitik, Minsk Mazovitzk, etc. are well remembered.

There were at least three cases of opposition to the rioters that are well etched in my memory and I wish to relate them here.

a.

It was a Shabbat in the summer of 1931. As was the custom, people would go for a stroll in the marketplace in the afternoon. The police station was located across from the walled home of Vegenfeld and Eichenboim.

Hersh Haim Fleisher, z"l

[Page 109]

We were a group of young men walking with our renowned friend Yehuda Fleisher, Z"L, who was visiting from Eretz Israel. We ran into a drunken gentile, a liberated legionnaire, a settler with military medals. He began to curse and insult Yehuda. "Why are you insulting me?" asked Yehuda. The drunkard replied by slapping him. There was no use fighting back– we thought– because soon other gentiles surrounded us and the police always takes their side. We pleaded with Yehuda to give in. The story reached his father, Hersh, an elderly man. He could not accept the evil that had been done to us.

Some time later we saw Hersh quietly approaching a group of gentiles standing near the drunkard and praising him. The old man approached the "hero" and slapped him twice. Soon groups of Jews and gentiles were gathered, but the police dispersed everyone and the event was stopped.

This event was a topic of conversation for a long time in the town. It served us as a source of encouragement and strength and raised our honor in the eyes of the gentiles…

b.

It was a Friday evening in the spring. I do not remember the year. A few carts arrived carrying intoxicated young farmers, after they had enlisted in the army in Ludomir.

It was an annual tradition for the young gentiles that, on their way to enlisting and back, they would "have fun" with the Jews. This time they bothered some elderly Jews, hurrying to the bath house, as they were passing the house of Esther Manises. Michael Shafran, the brilliant and educated man, lived nearby. He saw what was happening and could not stand the fact that it was permissible to attack elderly Jews who could not fight back. He approached the young men and began to hit them right and left. The dozens of young men ran away as they came and never showed their might.

c.

The third event happened on Motzaei Shabbat in 1937. A few friends were preparing to make Aliyah. There was a good–bye party in the Hechalutz branch, at the home of Yehoshua Hersh Kritz, Z"L. In the middle of the dancing a few well–known gentile youths appeared and began to disrupt the event. We invited them to join us in the party, but nothing helped. They began to bother us and the young women. Our member Nissan Schlachter lost his temper and hit them. The "heroes" ran away and we continued with our party.

I do not know how the old man, Zvi Fleisher, died, but we know exactly what happened to Michael Shafran.

Witnesses told us that he was the first to climb into the vehicle that took the victims to the big gravesite in Piatidan. There he gave a speech. He said there was no choice but to die the way the killers wished. When I remember Michael Shafran, who had routed dozens of evil young people, I must come to the conclusion that we cannot judge the ways of our martyrs who had been killed by the Nazi Amalek.

[Page 110]

In contrast with the deep pain that hurts our hearts as we remember the bitter end of the victims of the Holocaust, we recall with great happiness those who were fortunate to make Aliyah and who fought with us to free our country from oppressors. Among them– our dear friend, Nissan Schlachter– the third one to slap. Hurray!

[Page 111]

Concealed Lights

by Mina Sheinman

Translated by Ala Gamulka

The High Holidays are upon us– as we called them– and I find letters from home written 24 years ago. I read with sacred anxiety. This is what I do every year at this time– Sacred and Great, as my parents would say. Each time I remember anew these wonderful personalities, innocent and proper, who were slaughtered so cruelly by the Nazi beasts who pretended to be humans.

Here is one of the letters from my father, Z"L:

"My dear daughter Mindele. There are still two more hours in this holy and sacred night where God signs the fate of humans. I am full of dread and I wonder if, in your young heart, there is a feeling of shame for sins, in order to redeem the pure soul and not to dirty it with blotches. Mindele, these are days in which one must pray and ask for forgiveness and also to forgive others and to make peace. Please forgive me for the difficulties I caused you on your way to Aliyah. These are bloody days and the youth do not walk in the proper path. How could I agree to a way that was separate from the family? I do not usually speak much. However, my dear daughter, you must know that since you left us, I cannot find rest. I hold the newspaper daily with shaking hands and a beating hear. May the Almighty guard you and all other people and give you happiness and good health. May you continue on the straight path.

Your father who wishes you a good and holy year".

I continue to read the letters– there are very many– and there is a common theme in them: wishes for happiness, longings, preaching to keep the faith, to continue on the straight path, to love people, to forgive and to absolve, etc.

In front of my eyes, I see in a clear and wonderful light the image of a modest man, a shy Torah expert. He was short, but stood above everyone.

There was also a loving brother. His first letter after I made Aliyah said the following:

"I will never forget, my dear sister, the day we said good–bye to each other. Who knows until when? When you left, a large part of my life also left. Your image will always be in front of me. It feels as if I am still with you in the home of our late mother. My heart aches with your departure.

[Page 112]

I do not wish to mourn your leaving, but to congratulate you. You wish to find happiness and you are hoping for an ideal life, full of meaning. You had enough of the life of emptiness and idleness and you wish to improve it, to give it some beauty. Then, my dear sister, may you be blessed. May your star that has just begun to shine continue to do so in your life.

Your brother who misses you so much,

Binyamin"

His second letter:

"My eldest sister. Today is Hol HaMoed Pessach. I received your letter yesterday. Yes, my dear sister, it is the first Pessach that you are not with us at the traditional Seder of our family. I sit next to our dear father and he pours wine into the cups. He filled your cup instinctively. I look at your full cup and there is no one to drink the wine. My heart aches and many thoughts go through my head. Father is waiting for me to ask the Four Questions and I do not pay attention. I think of our saintly mother who was taken from us and then my eldest sister prepared for the holiday. Yes, my sister, how I would love to be a child again in my good mother's arms. Then I would not feel what is now in my sad heart. I understand, my dear sister, that you are also occupied with the holiday. I see you with a kerchief on your head, cleaning and organizing your narrow room, preparing the Seder together with your friends– the Hagadah and maybe even the kneidlach. The Four Questions are asked and really "How is this …different"? There are other questions in the air and not all of them can be answered. I do understand you. We must fill the empty space for the sake of tradition. My sister, do not forget your past, your homeland and your family. Do not give in to imagined liberty and anarchy. Life is rooted in the past and anyone who rebels against it will lose his future.

Your brother who is longing for his dear sister,

Binyamin"

Hidden lights, modest like Shabbat candles in the home of mother and father, are shining from these letters. You are my dear ones who lit them. Sacred is your memory. I will remember you for the rest of my life.

Afek, Tishrei, 1959

[Page 113]

Grandfather's Home

by Menashe Secharbrot

Translated by Ala Gamulka

The old, modest house stood near the Stav and the Bug in Ustiluh. It was not an ordinary family home, like the others, because it served as an educational institution for young boys, and even older ones. Grandfather Liptche (Isenberg) was an excellent teacher and educator, using the methods of those days. In addition, he was an outstanding prayer leader with a pleasant voice. He was active among the Hassidim of Neskhiz.

I was still very young when I left town in 1933. Still, I knew to value the traits and spirit of grandfather. He was an honest man, modest and gentle. He was a Torah scholar and a follower of commandments, but he had patience and did not tell others what to do. The following is a story I remember well:

I was in elementary school. I returned home from a lesson on the globe and the solar system. I asked grandfather his opinion. He, with great patience and control, replied that there are two systems of philosophy. This shows that he was a dear and intelligent man and far away from religious fanaticism.

[Page 114]

Grandmother Leah was a personality in her own right. She was bright and had an unusual sense of humor, in spite of the fact that she was bedridden for many years. She knew how to joke and even laugh at herself.

Once she called for grandfather to bring her something. He was involved in his studies and he did not hear her. She then turned to him, with irony: "Enough, already, studying the Gmara. My place in Gan Eden is guaranteed already, even though the chair is broken and it will fall over".

Last, but not least: my uncle Fishel Isenberg, His image stands in front of my eyes from many years ago, when I was a young child. I could not really judge people and appreciate them. Everyone says he was a many–faceted, talented person, even in sports– not too popular at the time in town. He was involved in political and social circles. I remember that in the bitter days when Hitler became the leader of Germany, my uncle, even then, predicted the future. At one of the large assemblies he warned about the danger of Nazism to the Jewish nation.

In the meantime, I left Poland. However, Fishel, his dear wife Bluma, their two daughters and my aunt Ethel with her son Yaakov stayed. They were all killed together with the rest of the community. My heart aches. Our dear ones will not return.

[Page 115]

Fillins – Institutions and Organizations

by M.K.A.

Translated by Ala Gamulka

a. Local authorities

Until WWI, Ustiluh was not considered a city. The Starosta (mayor), appointed by the district authorities would take care of the census. He also was the liaison between the local population and the authorities in all matters that were under the central offices.

There was very little attention paid by the authorities to municipal matters. It was confined to road repair (what repairs!) and sidewalks (wooden) and the cleanliness of the town.

The master of the town was the officer who was appointed to keep the peace with the help of a few policemen.

The conquering Austrians organized the town well, but it was actually a military rule.

During Polish times, a local council was established. The Jews were in the majority, but they still could only be represented by a vice–mayor. It was the teacher Shlomo Kant.

There were elections for the executive of the Jewish community. It was to deal with all religious matters. The chairman of the executive was Michael Krakower. He was unaffiliated. In the next elections, Yitzhak Yeshaya Eksmit of the general Zionists was chosen.

b. Economic organizations and institutions

There were two economic organizations in town: the guild of the Jewish merchants and the association of the Jewish craftsmen. Two banks, managed by capable hands, were attached to these groups. They were most useful for the members. There was also a Benevolent Society that gave loans without interest. In addition, there were several small societies in various circles.

c. Charitable institutions

The Orphans committee took care of all their needs. Funds were received from outside and from within. When the community was established, there was an assistance committee that looked after poor families and all the needy.

[Page 116]

Earlier, there were several general charity collectors: Yossel Tiles the shoemaker, Berl Schlachter, son of Avraham the ritual slaughterer, Haim Wolf, the teacher and several women in the community. The population trusted them and always helped them to look after the needy in the community.

In addition, next to every Shtiebel or House of Learning, there were public figures who look after these matters.

Synagogues and Schools
The Great House of Learning
The Danche House of Learning
The Rabbi's House of Learning
The Dveinhauser House of Learning
The Tailors' House of Learning
The Trisk Shtiebel
The Rozhin Shtiebel (Tsurtkov, Hosiatin, Sadigura and Boyan)
The Nesekhizh Shtiebel {Steppan)
The Kuzmir Shtiebel (Great Love)
The Beltz Shtiebel
The Radzin Shtiebel
The prayer group of the General Zionists
A few more small prayer groups

d. Educational and cultural institutions

There were three elementary schools in Ustiluh: government–Polish; Tarbut–Hebrew and national–religious–Yavne. The latter had Moshe Shpirer, the excellent educator, as its principal. (As to other teachers, read the article by B. Goldberg)

There were also private Heders where famous educators taught Torah: Mendele Fanik, Liptche Isenberg, Ber Tabakhandler, etc.

The two libraries, Hebrew and Yiddish, had thousands of books. The readers, mainly young, read much and were interested in all kinds of literature.

e. Political organizations

General Zionist Organization
Mizrachi and Young Mizrachi
Revisionists and Beitar

[Page 117]

Zeirei Zion and Poalei Zion
Hechalutz and Hechalutz Hatzair
Hashomer Hatzair
Organization of trade unions (Communists?)
All this was erased from our land.

It is only the lonely building of the Great House of Learning that still remained. Its windows were broken and the building looked deserted, like an unfortunate old man whose family, relatives and acquaintances were slaughtered by murderers. In the end, even his eyes were gouged. It stands alone, deaf and dumb, unable to express its sadness and pain.

However, if one happens to go there, one would hear the voices of 4 000 people crying from underground.

Our land, do not cover our blood!

Cemetery in 1933

[Page 118]

Figures from the Pre–Holocaust Generation

Translated by Ala Gamulka

Akhiezer Goldschmidt, town cantor

[Page 119]

Shalom Sofer (SH"TZ) and his wife

[Page 120]

Volf Yokhenzon and his wife Sheindel

Left to right: Yedidya Yokhenzon, Hinda Fleisher (nee Yokhenzon), Pinhas Yokhenzon

[Page 121]

Baruch Goldhaber (Liziner)

Yosef Rosmarin and his wife Hadas)

[Page 122] Blank [Page 123]

In Fire and in Blood

Translated by Ala Gamulka

"And ye shall perish among the heathen and the land of your enemies shall eat you up" (Leviticus 26:38)

"In the morning thou shalt say, Would God it were evening! And in the evening, thou shalt say, Would God it were morning! For the fear of thine heart wherewith thou shalt fear, and for the sight of thine eyes which thou shalt see." (Deuteronomy 28:67)

"And gleanings shall be left of him, as in the shaking of the olive tree, two or three berries in the top of the uppermost bough" (Isaiah 17:6)

"But I will leave a few men of them from the sword, from the famine, and from the pestilence" (Ezekiel 12:16)

[Page 124] Blank [Page 125]

On the Ruins of Our Town

by Yeshayahu Meltzman

Translated by Ala Gamulka

The following details I know from eye witnesses, as I lived in Ludomir during the Holocaust. We had moved there from Ustiluh when our house was burned down at the outbreak of the war. It was on the even of Rosh Hashana 1940. A large part of our town burned down at that time. There were many deaths.

On June 22, 1941, when the Germans attacked the borders of the Soviet Union– in our town the border was the Bug River–about 80% of the houses were burned. The only thing left was Danche Street and a few single homes on other streets.

On the first day of the German conquest, people were taken to rebuild the bridge over the Bug. Later, a few hundred more men were also taken. During working hours, these poor souls were beaten and some were killed. These are the names of the martyrs:

Avraham Erlich, son–in–law of Aharon Moshe Pofelis
Zev Mel, son of Alter Moshkis
Moshe Shinerman, son of Eliyahu
Zusia Katsav
Meir, son of Moshe Aharon Zelgs
Yosef Mamet, principal of the school, son of Shmuel Mamet
Rabbi Yehoshua Shintop, son–in–law of Reuvale Dayan, z" l, was crushed by a collapse due to a bomb. Binyamin Fenik, son of Mendele, was taken to load ammunition in the Ludomir train station. He worked until noon.

As he was unaccustomed to such hard work, one of the Germans put a sign on his back with white chalk. During lunch recess, the German pulled out his pistol and killed him in front of everyone.

As a result of these atrocious deeds, the Jews were afraid to go outside. They hid in cellars and anywhere else they could.

The German authorities, the police and the town commander proclaimed: the Jews were to organize a committee– Judenrat– to bring the citizens back to a normal life.

The committee was chosen with Michel Shafran as its chairman. There were negotiations with the Germans and they came to an agreement. Everything the Germans demanded from the Jews would be the responsibility of the committee. This is how the Germans, may their names be erased, began to rob the town in an organized and methodical manner. It was done through the committee.

[Page 126]

They demanded a monetary contribution and it was done. They wanted workers for various tasks in town– it was done. They requested winter clothing for men and women (furs)– all good items owned by Jews were handed over. The Jews remained with nothing. The murderers did not stop. They ordered the villagers not to sell us any food items or wood for heating. There was a ration on bread, but the Jews did not receive anything.

They also began to grab Jews and send them elsewhere, to work out of town, supposedly. However, these Jews disappeared and never returned to their families.

In March 1942, all the Jews in town were organized into a ghetto on Danche Street. There were twenty people in one room. As a result of these conditions, Typhus was rampant. The Germans used to send their helpers, the Ukrainian militia, to remove anyone with high fever and to kill him/her.

This was the life in the ghetto until the Jews finished preparing their own graves in the Piatidan fields. In these graves were buried the Jews of Ludomir and Ustiluh– 8 000 souls. The Germans told the Judenrat that since the front with the Russians was coming closer there was a need to dig these pits to prepare underground fuel depots.

I remember that I was working with Haim Yitzhak Myerson in the digging of these pits. He said to me, plainly:" It is not true that there will be fuel depots here. These pits are for us…"

Several weeks passed before the digging was completed. During the time we were working, many laborers slept in place. They were tired and worn out from the hard work. On the last day before the pogrom, the Germans arrived with more police and made all the workers sleep in the ghetto. We then knew that the great catastrophe was approaching. On the next day, 19 Elul, at 5:00 am, a unit of police and Germans came to the ghetto. They removed men, women and children, put them on trucks and brought them to the pits. The poor souls had to hand over to the killers anything they had on them. There were large milk containers standing and they were filled with money and gold, watches and jewellery. The second order was to get undressed completely. Rows of police and Gestapo stood like walls on all sides. They pushed these poor people into the pits. Machine guns sprayed them. This is how the lives of the Jews of Ustiluh ended on the Piatidan.

Michel Shafran, who was the first to climb on the truck, announced: "You see we have no choice. We cannot save ourselves. We must go on the path these sadists are demanding from us."

A small part of the Jews of Ustiluh who were hiding in the homes of the "good" gentiles, may their names be erased, were all killed. At first, they were taken in for their belongings, but soon they were killed or denounced to the Germans who came to remove them.

[Page 127]

I know the story of the family of Leahtche Topoler. She escaped with her three daughters to a gentile acquaintance of hers. She gave him all her belongings. He hid them for a few days. Once, he came to them in the middle of the night and said the place was too dangerous and he wanted to transfer them to another location, 2 kilometers away. He and some of his cronies, his partners in crime, put them in a cart near the Bug. There, the killers chased them into the river. Only the youngest daughter, who knew how to swim, was saved. That night she escaped, naked, to her home in Ustiluh. After that she stayed with Lipinski, the mayor of Ustiluh during Nazi times.

Dr. Muzikansky, with his wife and three–year–old child spent a few months with their friend in Stiziritch. When all the Jews in town were murdered and the killers had a list of names, from the census bureau, it was known that Dr. Muzikansky was still alive. The killers did not rest until, with the help of a denouncer, they found his hiding place. Through the window, the doctor saw the Ukrainian police and Germans coming close to the house. He did not wait for them and he gave poison to his wife and child as well to himself. When the killers entered, they were all dead.

With the cleansing of the refugees in the villages, the history of the Jews of Ustiluh ended.

*My body felt it and my eyes saw it...

As mentioned above, a large part of Ustiluh was burned when war broke out. Many of those who lost their homes moved to Ludomir, as did our family.

Fate punished them, too. Many were taken to the common grave of Ludomir and Ustiluh in Piatidan. The rest were tortured and killed in various ways. Among the first victims of the Nazis in Ludomir were Haim Leitsis, son–in–law of David Bliander, and family. The day the Nazis conquered Ludomir, they organized a blood bath on Kowalski Street. They went from house to house, took out the men and slaughtered them. When they came to Haim's home, his wife Rivka began to shout and to beg them to leave him alone. In reply, they shot her first, then they killed Haim and their oldest son, 15–year old Shlomiele. Only the 4–year old remained alive. He saw them lying on the floor and he begged them to get up... Finally, he went to Haim's sister, Feiga Leitsis and told her his father and mother are sleeping on the floor and not getting up. The bright child soon knew that even his aunt cannot wake up his parents and his brother and he began to cry.

The Yokhenzon family was also killed that day in the yard of their flour mill. Who can describe the fear and trepidation of the Jews? For several days no one ventured out.

[Page 128]

There was no contact between families. My sister, for example, lived on the next street and we did not know the fate of the family. Finally, children 7–8 years old were sent to reconnoitre the area and find out what was the situation. The news they brought back was terrible and frightening. It was exactly as is written in "Nesane Tokef" (Yom Kippur prayer).

Five days later, posters were hung telling all residents to register in the labor department. Anyone not doing so would be punished. People began to stream to the labor department and they received assignments. I, too, was sent to work in a vegetable garden five kilometers out of town. We walked to work every day and we returned home in the evening. I was pleased with this work because the supervisor was a gardener from the town hall, not a German. In the places supervised by Germans, there were victims on a daily basis. We worked like this for a month. During that time the Gestapo caught 800 Jews and put them in prison. They said they were taking them to work out of town, but these people never returned. They were killed in prison with rifle handles. They were buried there.

We were 40 Jews working in the vegetable garden. We left town before daybreak in order not to run into Germans. We returned in the darkness of night for the same reason. One morning, when we arrived at the garden, we saw some Germans circling the house. They came close to us and asked us who was the supervisor. One of us, a well–known member of the Judenrat, informed them he was the supervisor. One of the killers lifted a heavy picket and hit the Jew, in the head, several times.

At that moment all the workers fled. My brother–in–law, David Vopaniarsky, and I escaped in the direction of the main road Ludomir–Lutsk. The road was being repaired by Polish gentiles. When they saw Jews running away, they began to chase us. They caught us and gave us over to the Germans. The latter were occupied with flirting with young women and did not wish to stop. We told our chasers to bring us back to work in the garden. A half hour later, the Germans came and began to beat us. My brother–in–law David was badly hurt. I did not believe he would live after such a cruel beating. He was bleeding everywhere and they still continued to kick him in the groin. He fell down and was writhing in pain. He could not breathe. A few minutes later he caught his breath and asked for water. I was afraid and I continued to work. Who can understand the mind of a killer? The killer must have been upset by this. He ordered me to lie down on the ground and began to hit me with the picket. I will never forget this beating. My back was black with injuries. When they were finished with us, they realized that all the other laborers were missing. According to the young women, some Jews escaped into the nearby forest. The killers took their rifles and ran into the forest. This is when my brother–in–law and I ran away. We walked though wheat fields and we reached the edge of town. We met a woman we knew. "Where are you going?" and she added "The Gestapo is back in town and they are rounding up Jews!". We went to a friend's house and hid in his cellar. We waited until evening and we went back home. The next day we went to the doctor of the Judenrat.

[Page 129]

He gave us permission to be off work for a week. We never returned to the same job. We were sent to work in an ammunition warehouse in the barracks on Kowalski Street. We worked there for a few days– we were not beaten. One early evening, after work, we were told by the German supervisor to come, on the next day, straight to the train station. We were to travel to Vinnitsa (about 20 kilometers away). We did not pay attention to what he said and came back to the warehouse, as usual. We were afraid to go to the station in case we would not be brought back…

We arrived at the warehouse and found it locked. Not one of the Germans was there. After waiting for an hour, with no one coming, we decided to go to the train station and travel to Vinnitsa. The German was waiting for us at the station, very angry. He ran towards us armed with a thick stick and he began to beat us non–stop. He promised to punish us because we did not come on time. We went to Vinnitsa. In the station we found several crates filled with heavy ammunition. Each one of us carried, on his shoulders, a piece of artillery and in the other hand– an iron crate. The Germans were on horseback and made us go two kilometers into the forest. Anyone who tried to shift the heavy load from one hand to the other was beaten. We walked through a marsh. They dismounted and walked behind us prodding us with their sticks. We thought our end was near. I do not know how we were saved and managed to return home.

After that, we stopped working in the ammunition warehouse and we looked for work that would not put us under the supervision of the Germans, may their names be erased. We found work in digging peat for heating–about 4 kilometers from town. We spent three months there. During this time there were many problems in town. The Gestapo came three times to catch Jews, supposedly for work. My father and my father–in–law, Raphael Budenstein, were caught. We did not know their fate for several months. Finally, we discovered they had been slaughtered together with all the others who had been caught, in prison, on 6 Elul, 1941. A month later the Gestapo came for the third time. It was the eve of Yom Kippur– nicknamed Bloody Monday. That day, 1,500 Jews were captured. They were collected from various work places around town, from military camps and agricultural farms. They were put in prison and they never returned home. That day, we did not come home because my sister, Malka, came to tell us the news. We continued working on the sacred day, but we prayed in the fields and we cried over the great catastrophe.

That day, many people were buried alive. Among them was David Boxer from Ludomir. He begged the killers to shoot him, but they laughed at him. There was no shooting that day, only various methods of torture. After the bloodbath there was no family in Ludomir that was not affected by the "Public sacrifices".

Those who remained alive were in dire economic straits. They were afraid to leave town as the yellow star announced that they were Jews. When a Jew was caught without this sign, he would be immediately eliminated. In addition, the Gestapo people would come, from time to time, to visit the town to see if there were still Jews roaming the streets, how they were subsisting and what else could be taken from them. They came to the Judenrat and demanded money and valuables. All was given to them. Then they came and said that Jews should not be scattered throughout the town. A ghetto must be designated. They put barbed wire around a few streets. The moving day into the ghetto was designated as the last day of Pesach. The Jews moved into the ghetto, including my family. It was terribly overcrowded– 15 people to a room. News reaching us from other towns was even worse. It was said that in many towns the Jews were taken out of the ghetto and transferred to concentration camps.

[Page 130]

In July 1942 we found out that the district commander was on leave for two months and left a replacement. It turned out that he went on a special course in one of the concentration camps– to learn methods of eliminating Jews.

Indeed, he came back with a satanic plan. He informed the Judenrat that, since the Russians had reconquered Kiev and the front was coming closer to us, there was a need to prepare underground fuel depots. They would be protected when attacked from the air. The Judenrat was to provide 1,000 workers for digging the pits. The work was done under the direction of Jewish engineers. There were three pits dug. Each one was 100 meters in length, 50 meters in width and 4 meters in depth. During the time the work was being done, the workers received, daily, meat meals. These poor souls were happy that the Germans were feeding them meat while, in town, bread was being rationed– only to gentiles.

At that time, a new order was given: to assemble all craftsmen on a specific street, so the Germans would find them easily. Those who did not have a trade understood quickly that they would be slaughtered. That is why the craftsmen' ghetto was called the "live" ghetto, while the other was the "dead" one. In essence, anyone who had money paid it to the Judenrat and received a craftsman card. In the end, the Judenrat gave a list of 400 craftsmen to the district commander and they moved to the "live" ghetto. I and my brother–in–law David were not craftsmen at all. We also did not have any money. We remained in the ghetto with our families and awaited our fate. My other brother–in–law, husband of my younger sister, obtained a craftsman card and moved to the "live" ghetto with his wife and three–year–old child. Their fate was worse than ours.

As soon as we moved into the ghetto, we began to build a hiding space. We had two, one safer than the other (so we believed). The second was less safe. On the final evening, when we felt the angel of death coming closer, we moved the women and children to the "safe" hiding place. David and I hid in the second place. The next day, 18 Elul 1942, at 5 am, the killers removed the fence around the ghetto and began to capture people. They put them on trucks and brought them to the "fuel depots" in Piatidan. The next day the killers came to the hiding place of our mother and other neighbors.

[Page 131]

The Germans began to shoot and the children were scared and began to cry and shout. The sounds reached the killers and they immediately demolished a wall in the building. At that moment, my sister Malka escaped with her children to the second hiding place where David and I were situated. My wife, Tova, the children, my mother and the rest of the women and children were taken to Piatidan. I was in mourning and lay for 11 days in the hiding place together with my sister and her family. During all that time death was raging wildly on the outside.

From our hiding place we could observe what was happening on the street. We saw people being taken out of their hiding places, placed on trucks and taken to their death. On the twelfth day we heard Jews roaming our house, for a long time. I slowly opened the entrance to the cellar and I saw Jews collecting items from our house. I asked them if the bloodbath was over. "No"– they said– "people are still being taken out of their hiding places". They told us that there were about 50 workers who were given a temporary permit to collect belongings of the Jews and to bring them to the warehouses. They told me I could join them and so I did. I helped to pack the items and I went out with them, for a few hours, into the ghetto. I returned the next day to rescue my brother–in–law, David.

We left our sister and her children to God's mercy as we could not take them with us. It was a difficult decision. However, after giving it some thought we decided that we had to rescue whoever could be rescued.

The next day, the 14th day of the pogrom, the hunt was over and they came out of the hiding place.

During the killing days, about 14 000 Jews were buried in Piatidan.

After the slaughter, the district commander informed the Judenrat that Jews could come out of their hiding places because the Germans had fulfilled their quota. There would be no more killing.

We assembled about 3,000 people. A new ghetto was established in the stores of the Halles. Here, too, there was great crowding. We immediately began to dig a hiding place because we did not trust the killers' promises. We worked for several weeks. During the night we took out the earth and we straightened the area so as to obscure the construction. For an entire month we went to the previous ghetto every day to clear it. We lived on food products we found there.

When the district commander saw there were still about 3,000 people left, he gave new orders to the Judenrat. They were to, again, assemble the craftsmen and transfer them to a specific street. The Judenrat prepared a list of 800 craftsmen and gave it to the district commander so as to obtain cards with his signature. We knew, for certain, that a new bloodbath was being planned.

We were completely desperate and we almost accepted our lot. However, my sister Malka began to cry and said that we should learn a trade in the next few days in order to receive a craftsman's card.

[Page 132]

We thought about it, but we were unable to find a craft that can be learned in a few days. A few more days passed and there was great panic in the ghetto. The holders of craftsman's cards were leaving the ghetto and moving to the other street. Even the Judenrat moved there. My sister would not accept the situation. She thought we should go to the Judenrat and declare that we were craftsmen. We could manufacture shoe polish. We did as she suggested because we believed we had nothing to lose. The head of the Judenrat promised to give the district commander the list of two shoe polish manufacturers. Soon the head of the Judenrat called us and told us the commander wanted to see our product. We had begun this dangerous game, so we continued. We obtained two boxes of shoe polish, one black and the other white, from outside the ghetto. We put the shoe polish in ordinary boxes and gave them to the head of the Judenrat. We also added a list of ingredients used to prepare the shoe polish. With this subterfuge we managed to obtain two craftsman's cards. Malka and the children were registered as members of the family of the producers. We were given permission to move to the street of those "written for life", but we did not rush to move. The experience of the first group of craftsmen taught us not to trust –even with a member's card. At least, here in the ghetto, we had a safe hiding place. We stayed there for a month and a half until the second pogrom began. On the eve of the Sabbath, Vayerah portion, 1942, at 4:00 am, the killers surrounded the ghetto. They removed anyone they found and took them to Piatidan. When we heard screams, we immediately went to our hiding place. The next day, at 11:00 am, we heard Jews talking in the room above us. I went to the entrance and I saw an acquaintance collecting household goods. I asked him: "What is the situation?". He told me to immediately leave because if we were to be found, the craftsman's card would not help. We would be taken to Piatidan. David and I came out and mingled among the workers. David went to the Judenrat and informed them that his family was in hiding and he asked for permission to take them out of there. The head of the Judenrat said that he had to ask the head killer, the commander. He did so and brought back the authorization. The head killer, himself, stood on the road when Malka and the children came out so he could identify them. They showed him the craftsman's card and the transfer permit and he agreed. This is how we went to live in the third ghetto.

The next day, Sunday, we, the craftsmen, were taken to clear the ghetto of dead bodies. On the fourth floor of the Limonik restaurant there were several dead bodies. The Germans told us to break open the tin roof and to throw the bodies down to the street. We did not rush to obey. The Gestapo man took out his gun and threatened to kill us. I, and Abba, husband of Yocheved Halperin, picked up the tin slats and threw the bodies down. We were then told to take a stretcher and transfer the bodies to the prison. We walked under escort of a Ukrainian policeman.

In the prison we saw a horrific scene. I will never forget it– for the rest of my life.

[Page 133]

There were about 500 dead bodies in piles. In the courtyard there were laborers digging large burial places. We placed the body on one of the piles. The Ukrainian policeman said: "What do you want to do? Do you want to return to the ghetto to bring another body?". We replied "Yes" and we left the prison. We never returned to this kind of work.

On the way, we met several families that were taken out of hiding places and brought to the prison. All their pleading for mercy was in vain. They were brought to the prison and executed there.

The pogrom continued for two weeks. Daily, hiding places were discovered and the people were killed. When there were no more living people in the ghetto, the killers began to check among the craftsmen. This was to make sure there were no "illegals" among them. Thus, around 80 people were found. Among them was Abba Veverik, his wife and children and the wagon driver David Orils. They were with us for a month. Once, David Orils said to me: "Yeshayahu, you must remember the prophecy of the prophet Yekhezkel about the dry bones. What period of time did God mean when he asked "will these bones live? – now I know that it meant the destruction of Jewry in our time".

This is what this honest and innocent man said a day before he was massacred by the killers.

We were in the third ghetto, among the craftsmen, for an entire year. There were many difficulties during that time. We knew that in other towns not one Jew remained alive and we were certain one day our turn will come. One thought occupied us: where could we find a safe place outside the ghetto? I could not find such a place among any of my gentile acquaintances as I could not trust any of them not to denounce us to the Germans. Help came in a magical way. A woman we knew came to tell us that her family of three found a place with a good gentile. He was ready to accept another family. She was prepared to offer us this place if we would take care of her family until redemption comes. We agreed to the terms and we immediately went to that gentile. He did not ask for money, but he said: "If you will be lucky enough to save yourselves, you will repay me when you are free– whatever you can afford." We saw this as a sign from God, that an angel has been sent to redeem us. We immediately began to prepare our hiding place there. We completed the task in a few days and we began to prepare as much food as possible. This happened during the ten days of penance in 1943. Suddenly, there was a great fear in the third ghetto. We slept that night in our hiding place in the ghetto. We decided that if we survived that night, we would move to the place out of town (about 6 kilometers away). Actually, nothing happened that night. In the morning, the eve of Yom Kippur, we went to work, but we informed the new savior to come and get Malka and the children. He came that day and took them and the second family. David and I remained in the ghetto because we wanted to attend services on Yom Kippur. The following day I left the ghetto and went to join my sister. Only David remained in the ghetto because he could not abandon the "shoe polish factory". I stayed with my sister for a month and a half. We hid during the day and at night we went out for fresh air. In the meantime, I prepared a hiding place in reserve– a safer one. It was located 8 meters underground and air was conducted through an opening in well built with of cement. The savior brought us food in a pail, lowered into the well. David came to visit every Sunday and he would report on events outside. At the beginning of our seventh week there, David came to tell us there was a new order: all craftsmen were to undergo a new census by the S.S. Their office was outside the ghetto. I told him that it was probably a sign of a new liquidation. I did not want to sign up. David took my sister and they returned to the ghetto. They stayed there for two days until they were signed in. Malka returned and told me to do the same because she saw people, in the Judenrat, who were prepared to pay money to be added to the list of craftsmen. I vehemently objected and said I would not return to the ghetto. She began to cry and said that the head of the Judenrat sent her specially to come. He threatened that if I did not do so he would reveal my hiding place to the Gestapo.

[Page 134]

I could not stand this pressure and I returned to the ghetto. By then, the registration was completed, but I went into the Judenrat office and informed the director that I had come to register as he had demanded. He immediately ordered his police officers to lock me up in their jail. They held me there for two days and then I was called in for an inquiry. "Why did you run away from the ghetto?"– they asked. I replied that my sister cannot be alone with the children in that place. We also did not have the raw materials to produce the shoe polish for the Germans. I knew that once the materials arrived, my brother–in–law would inform me and I would return to work. I won!

On the next day, the Sabbath, I was sent to work in an army camp. When I returned in the evening, I met the daughter of Zalman Teitel. She told me that she had worked that day in digging ditches as the frontline was coming closer to us. The German supervisor told her that the following day the Jews will not be digging ditches.

We went together to the head of the Judenrat to tell him the story. He said: "Don't cause panic in the ghetto. Just as your lives are dear to you, so are mine and those of my family. I have a contact with the killers. If they want to annihilate us, I will know 48 hours earlier. I will then let the Jews know to leave the ghetto." We were calmed down with this news and we went home. David said to me: "Let us go visit Malka. We will return tomorrow". I told him I was ready to go as long as we did not have to return to the ghetto. He did not agree and he went by himself. I stayed in the ghetto.

The next day, Sunday, there was great consternation. The commander ordered the Judenrat to provide him with 30 Jews for work and they complied. In the evening, the people did not return and a delegation of the Judenrat went to the commander. He told them the people were sent, by train, to another place and he did not know when they would return. Panic ensued. That evening, my brother–in–law David returned.

[Page 135]

That was a night of fear and watchfulness. The women who had just lost their husbands were screaming and crying. There was a deathly fear in the ghetto. At 4:00 am, police officers from the Judenrat, knocked on doors to take people out to work. Suddenly, we heard shots from automatic rifles, coming from all sides. We immediately went into hiding. David and I sat there for a week. Now, he, too was ready to go to Malka and to not return to the ghetto. On the seventh night, we tried to leave the ghetto. However, the killers discovered us. They chased us and shot in the air. We managed to evade them and we returned to our hiding place. We stayed there for another week. We were 14 people without any food or water. Our bread had spoiled due to moisture. After four days, when our thirst was unbearable, we dug two meters down and we found, luckily, some water. It was not so clean, but we were happy not to spend another night without water. During those days we had no contact with the outside world. We did not know if hiding places were being searched. On day 14, in the afternoon, the killers came with search dogs. They rolled iron balls on the floor and discovered that there was a hiding place underneath. However, they did not find the entrance. They began to destroy the stove and sink. We were whispering our last prayers. We thought we would be discovered any minute. It was our luck that they did not manage to complete the destruction before nighttime. They stopped and left. They were probably certain that when they returned in the morning we would still be in the hiding place. We decided to leave the ghetto at midnight, even if they would chase us and shoot at us. At 11, groups of four began to leave. We crossed the fence in peace. We went through Bialoviez and crossed the road near the barracks on Ustiluh road. We walked through the fields. From far away we saw a lonely house and we came closer to it. I peeked in the window and I saw a woman– Polish–looking. She was sitting at a table reading a book. I knocked on the door and she asked: "Who is it?". I replied: "A Jew who escaped the ghetto". She opened the door and invited us in.

I entered with David and we told her all that had happened to us. We asked her to sell us a slice of bread. She brought a whole loaf. It was Christmas eve– 25th of December– and she refused our money. She added: "Perhaps we will meet again some day." We asked her for permission to stay there until 3 am when we would leave. She said it was not a good idea. The book she was reading was given to her by a German. She expected him to return that evening to take his book. She showed us a distant Polish settlement and suggested we go there to sleep. We walked in that direction. Suddenly, we heard: "Halt! Who is there?". They were right near us. It was a civil defense group of Poles – against Ukrainian killers. When they heard our story, they showed us a place to hide. It was too dangerous for us to roam at night as there were Germans and Ukrainians around. They could catch us. We stayed there until 3 am. We then left and began walking in the direction of Malka's hiding place. We had to go by a Ukrainian village. It was our luck that it was before daylight and they did not see us.

[Page 136]

We crossed the Ludomir–Kovel road and we saw, in the distance, some armed killers. We hid in a trench and waited for them to leave. We continued on our way and came to our hiding place. When our sister saw us, she fainted from excitement. She was certain we were no longer alive as we had not visited in a long time.

In those days, armed Ukrainians would attack, from time to time, Polish settlements. Our host was Polish and he was afraid. He left and went to live in town. My sister stayed alone with the children. Still, he came every two days to bring her food. When we reached her we found his 15–year–old son in the house. He immediately went to town to tell his father that we had escaped from the ghetto. Two hours later, our host and his wife came. They were ecstatic. He said: "I thought I would now have to look after a bereaved family. I thank God that he kept you alive. Now I do not have to worry about that."

We stayed "peacefully" for about a month in our hiding place. The good man would visit from time to time. He encouraged us by telling us the frontline was coming closer. Lutsk was already in the hands of the Russians and soon the Germans would leave. We truly believed we would be free in a few days. It was not so. The Germans received reinforcements and the frontline remained, for five months, near Kovel–Lutsk. All that time, Ukrainians would attack the Polish settlements in the area. Once, on a Sunday, the host came to bring us food for the week. He came down to our hiding place and discussed the situation with us. Suddenly, we heard submachine guns shooting. He left quickly and escaped on his cart. The shooting continued for two hours. We immediately blocked the entrance to the hiding place. We heard Ukrainians talking in the courtyard. They were mentioning our host, as they had seen him escape. We were lucky that day. The barn door was open and our entrance was inside. They had chased some Poles from the area, found them in the courtyard and killed them. We only found this out when our host returned the next day and told us to look at the dead bodies in the courtyard. There were seven. He said to us: "You must leave here. All the locals have left and are in town. I cannot come and endanger your lives. I have a proposition for you: in the village of Bielin, 8 kilometers away, there are Polish partisans. One of you can come with me to see if there are also Jews there. Perhaps you could move there". We agreed and David went with him. He was to return that evening, but he did not. Suddenly, we heard shots and Germans speaking. We did not know what happened to David. Maybe he returned and the killers noticed him? We decided that if David did not return by the next day, we would leave. Early the next day our host came. He was surprised that David had not returned, but he calmed us down by saying that perhaps David was afraid to use that road. He proposed that we move to Bielin. We agreed without any hesitation and we went with him. The road was dangerous, as we passed the village of Verba where there were many Ukrainian killers.

[Page 137]

Thank God, the Ukrainians did not see us and passed in peace. We reached Bielin and we found David. It was true that he did not come back because he was afraid of the Ukrainian and German killers on the road. We discovered there were some Jews in Bielin, but they were not joining the Polish partisans. There, we met Avraham Tsuker, son–in–law of Leib Sheinborn. A few days later, a Pole who had worked for him before the war came and took him out of the village. He killed him there.

We were not too certain of the safety of our location. There was much crowding because many Poles from different parts of the area streamed to the partisans. There was no place for us. With great difficulty, I found a place in another settlement– about one and a half kilometers away from Bielin. We felt more secure, so to speak. The Germans would not come there and we did not have to hide. Soon, there was a change in the situation. The Germans suddenly attacked the partisans with tanks and canons. The partisans retaliated with anti–tank grenades. A few Germans were injured. The Germans retreated and left behind one of their injured. The partisans looked after him and returned him, the next day, to the Germans. They even sent a letter of apology for their retaliation. They thought– so they said– that Ukrainians were attacking them. They would not have attacked the Germans. They received a reply telling them they will be informed whether they have been forgiven or not. In the next two weeks there were reconnaissance airplanes that were photographing the area. At Easter, four military craft dropped bombs and shot from machine guns until they destroyed the village by fire. There were around 200 houses. Not one building survived. All the Poles residing in the area escaped, the next day, to the other bank of the Bug. We also decided to go to the Russians for refuge. We began to walk towards the frontline. One time, the airplanes noticed us and began to fire. It was in a burned–out village. We scattered among the ruins and, once again, we were saved. The danger from airplanes made us deliberate whether to continue or to return. We decided to go forward and not to return to the killers, may their names be erased.

Towards evening, we reached a stream that had a destroyed bridge. Near the bridge we found an upended wagon with hay and a soldier's foot. The horses were cut into pieces. We had to travel about 6 kilometers from this bridge to the forest. We were told there were camps of Russian soldiers there. We walked in an open area and our hearts were beating fast with fear. Suddenly, we met two soldiers driving towards us. We were scared, but when they came closer, they calmed us down. They told us that their command post was at the entrance to the forest. We should ask for a soldier to take us through the forest since there were still some Ukrainian killers around. We went to the command post, but they refused to give us an escort. They said that the area was cleansed of gangs and Germans. We should not be afraid to go through the forest. After walking for about 4 kilometers, we met Russian guards every 200 meters. We passed through the forest and we reached a Ukrainian village.

[Page 138]

We were afraid again of running into the killers. We approached an officer and he assigned a soldier to escort us through the village, for about 3 kilometers. We continued on our way, feeling safe, because there were Russian soldiers everywhere. We walked about 25 kilometers that day and before night fell, we reached a village with many military groups. We stopped at one of the houses and asked to be put up for the night. A Soviet officer came out and invited us inside. He stayed with us until midnight and was interested in all that had happened to us and how we had managed to cross the frontline. Finally, he said to us: “After you managed to escape from the Germans and to remain alive, I advise you to not stay the night here. This is where we have our artillery and the enemy's artillery is only 6 kilometers from here. It is possible that at daybreak we will receive an order to attack. Therefore, I think you should leave now. I see you are very tired, but make the effort and reach 10 kilometers from this place”.

We listened to him and we walked for three more hours until daybreak. We found military transport and we were brought to a place called Holova. We found other Jews there. They had been liberated three months earlier. The local Jews immediately gave us a room to live in. We received food from the military kitchen. The next day, I went outside to speak to people who were already free. A police officer approached me for identification. I showed him my identity card from 1939. He took me to a mobilization office. A half an hour later, the office manager came to tell me that I was to come at 5:00 pm to be drafted. We would be leaving immediately. I told him: “Yesterday I was still under the Germans and I have just arrived. I need a delay of a few days.” He replied that he could not do it because the war has to be ended quickly.

I turned to the Jewish officer working there and told him everything I had gone through. They want to send me to the front? The officer replied: “I can tell you to get rid of the passport that was taken from you. Take the train to a location 50 kilometers from here. There you can change your name and find work”.

I took his advice and left that day together with David and his family. We went to Kivortza, near Lutsk. We found work the next day. We stayed there for 4 months until Ludomir was liberated and we returned there. We met a few people who had survived. The first thing we did was to go together to the common grave in Piatidan. We built a barbed wire fence around it and put up a gravestone.

May God avenge their blood and may their souls be gathered among the living.

[Page 139]

The Tale of Two Sisters

by Arie Avinadav

Translated by Ala Gamulka

We are sitting in the modest and serene home of the sisters Esther Kopit and Leah Tenerman, nee Vortzel (Yossel the Emperor). It is 16–19 years after the events. We are in the resort town of Tivon and we are trying to encourage them to share more details, in addition to what we already know. How can we skip known facts in order to obtain a complete picture?

The older sister, Esther, begins to speak. She becomes excited and her tears are flowing. It is difficult for her to speak. In addition, she is not quite certain about numbers and dates.

Leah continues the story. She, too, needs assistance to refresh her memory about continuity and details. They help each other out. Yaakov Lichtman, also a Holocaust survivor, adds some more and the story begins to take shape.

We are giving here a summary of the story, only omitting a few details that we feel are not to be mentioned, without trying to do a psychological analysis. We are not qualified to do it and it is better not to try.

a. The big fire and the Russians

When the war broke out at the beginning of September 1939, the Germans attacked the Poles near Ustiluh. A big fire burned and it consumed almost half of the town on the side of the Bug.

The urban Poles, always full of hate of the Jews, saw it as a good time to wage a pogrom on them. However, they did not succeed because the police chief was an honest man. He dispersed the gangs. Then came the Soviets. It cannot be said that the Jews were happy under their regime, but it was possible to exist. As far as the authorities were concerned, life was steady. Of course, the few wealthy people in town could not continue their comfortable life. The authorities often bothered them. In the end, they, too, got used to the situation. Obviously, under the Germans, life would be far worse.

The Soviets did not allow the refugees from the Nazis to stay in town. They were obliged to go further east. In addition, those whose houses had been burned down did not stay. They moved to Ludomir and surrounding settlements. There, they found a home and means to earn a living.

[Page 140]

b. Coming of the Nazis

On June 21, 1941 the Germans suddenly attacked the town with all their destructive might. Nearly all the houses in town were engulfed by fire. There were hundreds of people dead from shooting and debris.

The day the Nazis entered town, they assembled all the Jews near the bridge. They stayed there all day and all night and did not know what would come next. The next day they were brought to the square in front of the Polish school with the excuse that a German had been killed. Four Jews and a gentile friend of the Jews were killed. At the same time, the Jews were disrobed and a search was done. The women were freed, but the men were sent to work digging and other tasks. A month later, the Jewish committee, headed by Michel Shafran was established. There was also a Jewish–Ukrainian militia that was to execute any orders by the Nazis, under the supervision of the committee. With the help of the committee, every day, hundreds of people were taken to work. Each worker received 140 grams of bread daily, but non–workers only had 70 grams.

The workers and non–workers were placed under the arbitrariness of the Gestapo. Their lives were completely ruled by lawlessness. This is how were killed, during working hours the following: Zisha Melamed, Shlomo Melamed and others. However, Shmuel Shinerman was killed when he was driving his cart around town.

Efraim Vorik, a seventeen–year–old youth, was taken to load bombs on the train. He was weak and his work did not satisfy the task masters. They tortured him, cut off his ear and threw him into a toilet. He managed to hold on to the seat cover and his feet were in the dump. This is how he was hanging until he was released with the intervention of the Jewish committee. He lived with great pain until the first Aktion when he was freed from his suffering.

Here is another story that will break your heart:

The Gestapo people in Ludomir invented a game. They assembled hundreds of Jews into the courtyard of the prison. There were piles of sharp stones, broken dishes, glass, etc. They began to make the people run by sniping and shouting. The Jews fell on the piles and were bleeding. They were then all made to stand near the wall and about two thirds of them were shot to death. (Another source says that of 500 only 70 remained alive). Berl Krakower was killed then. Feivel Vortzel, the brother of Esther and Leah, survived and arrived in Ustiluh barely alive and bleeding.

c. The "Aktions"

The first pogrom began on September 1, 1942. Even before that, large groups were transported elsewhere. Their fate was unknown. Two months after the Jewish committee was established, the Gestapo demanded a list of the Jewish intelligentsia. About 80 people presented themselves, by order, and they were taken away.

[Page 141]

Later, the militia conducted a hunt on the town youth. Although they did not show up, many were caught and their fate was that of the others.

Esther Vortziner came and yelled in front of the Jewish committee. She told them she was hiding in the cemetery and saw how people were brought into a valley and shot. The members of the Jewish committee did not believe her. They said she was crazy and that they knew, for sure, that the people were transported to distant work places. Even when the digging of huge pits in Piatidan became suspicious, they still tried to calm everyone by saying the pits were meant for defense against aircraft.

On August 31, 1942, the Jewish committee announced, in the name of the Gestapo, that anyone who was out of town had to return by 6: 00 pm in the evening. They were to be moved to the Ludomir ghetto. Anyone who disobeyed would be shot to death.

At that time, the two sisters were in a village. Esther worked as a shepherd with a Ukrainian farmer in Khotiatchov. His name was Yarmul Liashuk. We must mention him as one of the Righteous of the Worlds. Leah worked for a Pole in Papdiokha.

When the order was brought to Esther's attention, she went to her sister for consultation. They decided to go back to town. On the way they met a farmer driving his cart. He told them he was on his way from Lutsk where there had been an Aktion. Suddenly, a flushed young man jumped out of the cart. They had not noticed him before. They were frightened at first, but what he said truly surprised them.

"Young ladies" – he said in Ukrainian– "I tell you not to go to town! I know, from a reliable source, that there will be an Aktion in three days".

They returned to Yarmul and asked him to go to town to their sister Pessel to tell her to come. The farmer went, but he did not enter town because he saw the Germans catching Jews and putting them on trucks. He understood that he could not save anyone and he was scared.

Yarmul advised them to hide in the nearby forest until the situation would calm down. They lay in the thicket of the forest, their hearts pounding. They heard sounds of movement coming closer to them. Their hearts almost stopped, but they saw two Jews from Ustiluh. They had been on a truck transporting them to the killing fields in Piatidan, but two fellows from the Saposov family cut the ropes. Everyone escaped. According to them they saw how the sisters' father was thrown into a truck. He had only one leg.

A brave deed, performed by someone from Ustiluh, only became known later:

Natan Vorik, 24, (brother of Efraim who had his ear cut off), was caught in Ludomir and was brought to an assembly point to be killed. Suddenly, he grabbed a gun from a German and hit the commander. Of course, he was immediately taken from there.

At the end of the great hunt that lasted ten days, only about 20% of the Jews of Ustiluh survived.

[Page 142]

Some had been in the ghetto where they worked in a clothing warehouse in the officers' school. The clothes were those of their dear friends and acquaintances who had been killed.

Very few people remained in Ustiluh and surrounding area. They lived in small groups or by themselves. Some worked in the military camp– considered a privilege. Those who did not, were dying of starvation.

Esther and Leah were fortunate in finding refuge in the hay loft or attic of Yarmul, the good man. He provided them with food and water for free. He even brought them a pail to serve as a toilet. He would empty it at night. Most people who were hiding in villages had different outcomes. One by one, they were discovered in their hiding places. Sometimes it was their hosts who denounced them and they were taken away and never seen again. Even Dr. Muzikansky, his wife and children, were captured at the home of their gentile acquaintance. They managed to swallow poison pills before they were taken and they died. They knew what awaited them in the hands of the killers and took care of their final moments.

d. the Ukrainian murderers

After the second pogrom in December that year, their brother Feivel came. He had been in the Ludomir ghetto. He hid with them for four months. Yarmul then told them that he suspected that their hiding place was known and they would need to find another one. Feivel went to Ustiluh and the sisters tried to find refuge with Leah's former Polish boss. He refused to take them in. That day, Yarmul went to Ustiluh and the sisters returned to his house, in the evening, to find out what happened to their brother. Yarmul did not know and, perhaps, he did not want to tell them. The next day, they, too, went to town because they could no longer stay with the farmer. This is how they learned the bitter truth, from an acquaintance, a farmer. The treacherous Ukrainians captured their brother who was carrying bread and a bottle of milk. They suspected he was a partisan and ordered him to disclose from whence he came and where he obtained the food. Since he did not want to denounce the good Yarmul, they killed him.

They spent a week in town. They wanted to enter the military camp, but the guards demanded a bribe– a parcel of food. Leah went to Yarmul to ask him for such a parcel. The good man advised her not to return to town. Even better, he went to town and came back with Esther. They returned to their hiding place in Yarmul's house. He had a struggle between his conscience and his fear. His wife was also a good person, but she could not stand the tension. She demanded that the two young women leave. He overcame everything and continued to endanger his life and that of his wife and daughter. In those days, the danger was multiplied because, in addition to the Gestapo, the Ukrainian partisans, Bandura's people, also wanted to get rid of the Jews.

Before the final pogrom, a terrible, shocking event happened: there were 5–6 young men from the Saposov family among the workers in the military camp. They managed to amass arms and ammunition and hid them in the village. They were waiting for an opportunity to join a unit of partisans.

[Page 143]

A Ukrainian go between helped the Saposov fellows and their cache to reach the partisans. However, these were Bandura's people. They took the cache and killed the young men.

e. The last pogrom

The Germans used the Roman strategy of "Divide and Conquer" to make trouble between the Poles and the Ukrainians. They incited the two opposing groups against the Jews. Therefore, the last pogrom in winter 1943 was easier. Its slogan was "Judenrein".

That day, Esther and Leah came to the military camp in order to get money from the military camp. They could not stand the cold in Yarmul's attic. When the hunt began, they fled and returned to the village. However, Yarmul's wife refused to take them in. They hid in a hay stack in the fields. Again, the good man overruled his wife and took them to the barn and to the attic.

The Benderovtzis came to the village. They even came to Yarmul's house. The sisters heard their voices and were petrified. The end of suffering was nearing.

In June 1944 the Russians came. This time, they really came as liberators and saviors.

[Page 144]

"Righteous art thou, O Lord,
When I plead with them: yet
Let me talk with this of my
Judgements"

(Jeremiah, 12:1)

Confession (An Elegy)
by A. Achi–Frida
Translated by Ala Gamulka

No, my God! I will talk with you of judgements,
Like that bitter person, the man from Anatot,
Who am I and what am I? Dust and ashes–
But, please, let me confess...
I will confess to you publicly,
You, God, interrogated me and you know–
That I will not find rest for years and years
I am unable to hold in what is in me,
Since the executioner stood over 6 million
The old and the infant, the parents
Our flesh and blood– torn from the living
How it hurts, woe to us!
On the day of remembrance, on a holiday,
In a house of prayer or in a fancy hall,
The cantor will stand and will trill with his voice,
Hearts will tremble and tears will flow,
"God of Mercy, dwelling in the skies

[page 145]

The judge over widows and the father of orphans..."
In front of my tearful eyes will appear
A row of figures, standing still;
Oh, Merciful God! There is Frida!
My widowed sister, my only sister;
Next to her stands Hinda, her daughter,
In her arms a young child;
There are Moshe and Berel in the row
And Mintzi–so big! A young woman!
And Fishel and Leibel and little Haimel,
Who did not even know his father, Natan,
At the end of the row is the second Frida
Daughter of my brother Fishel, she did not know him.
There are nine orphans and two widows,
God, look at them, God in heaven?
Woe is me, shame and disgrace!
They stand naked near the stage...
Look at their sad faces
Their frozen appearance rivets the hair,
And blood! Holy blood, black,
Look at them and see, Merciful father,
How great is their insult, it is deep.
It demands and shouts to the heavens,
It demands and shouts quietly:
"Why, dear God and why!?"

I knew, dear God, our ways are not yours,
I knew, our thoughts are not yours,
As was said by Yeshayahu, son of Amotz,
Our opinion is short and light like a chaff
Therefore, I will not speak of judgements with you–
Like that prophet and poor priest,

But I will justify you as he did– Oh God!
I cannot, forgive me, I cannot!

[page 146]

Frida, daughter of Fishel

[Page 147]

The Fate of One Family

by Bezalel Halperin

Translated by Ala Gamulka

Who of us, former residents of Ustiluh, does not remember the dry goods store of Nachman Halperin, z" l, and his wife Hannah? She was widowed at a young age and was left with six young children. She worked hard to raise and educate them. When Hitler and Stalin signed their pact and Ustiluh was given to the Russians, our townspeople thought redemption came. However, many new problems arose.

My younger brother Yaakov, was captured carrying a small piece of cloth–smaller than a baby's diaper.

Hannah Halperin

He was accused of owning a business. This was not permissible under the Soviet regime.

For that reason, the whole family was imprisoned, even my sister in Ludomir. She was married and had children. It is difficult to describe my mother's meeting with my sister. They were in prison through no fault of their own. In addition, pearls were found inside my mother's wig. She had treasured them because they were an engagement gift.

Much effort was put into saving and freeing them. One of "their" lawyers was brought from afar. He went over the charges and explained what he saw. It was clear that one of the prisoners had to stay. "So that people will see and hear!". Even 1000 defense lawyers would not have been able to annul the sentence– ordered before trial! It was mother's fate to be so chosen.

She was brought to a more secure location, in the interior of Russia. She walked to Kovel and fell without any strength left. She could not continue on her way. She was sent to the hospital. She escaped from there and returned home. It was, by them quite dangerous in town. She wanted to be with her children and grandchildren in her last days.

[Page 148]

One night, during the Nazi pogrom, she was captured together with her younger daughter Bluma and her son–in–law, David Spitzer and their little son Nachman. They were discovered in their bunker. The rest of the family survived because they were in a different bunker. The bitter tragedy did not end there. My younger brother did not want to stay there and he decided, with three other young men, to go to Lublin. It was a center for survivors. On the way, they were all killed by murderers, haters of Jews. May their names be erased.

May their pure blood be avenged.

Yaakov Halperin

[Page 149]

The Last Greetings

by Yitzhak Farber

Translated by Ala Gamulka

Matriarch of the family Yocheved, z" l

The letter was written in Russian. This was a testament to the fact that during the division, Ustiluh became part of the Soviet Union. I said: this, too, was good, the chasing of Jews, is not part of the official party line of the Soviet regime.

I was told that my younger sister, Mindel got married. My nephew David, son of Shifra, is named for my late father. He told me about Hinda's daughter, Yocheved. I knew her as she was born about a year before I made Aliyah. She was named after our late mother.

I was so happy to read the good news and I was remembering the olden days:

It was during WWI and our father had died (I almost do not remember him). Our mother was left alone with four small children. She was only 34 years old. She wandered and suffered until we returned to her town of birth, Ustiluh. Together with her mother Haya Rachel and her sister Gitel, she planned her new life. She had to devote herself to her children.

She worked hard for many years until we grew up and we began to help her. She never lost her cool. She suffered quietly in order to reach her goal. We, on our part, tried to lighten her load as much as possible. At the end, we did not allow her to work. These were her best days. We lived together for some time and managed well. She was happy and her eyes were smiling. But not for long! She became ill and her weakened body could not fight. She died after a few days. She left us forever.

Oh mother! It is not only Yizkor days that I remember you. It happens every day.

[Page 150]

I will never forget that terrible day on 27 Shevat 1933, the day you spoke to us for the last time. You had tears in your eyes when you said: "This is how I am leaving you". You closed your eyes for eternity.

Your lot on earth was not great. You dedicated your best years to your children. You did not merit to see them in the wide world. They, too, are gone. I am the only survivor.

Hinda, Haim and daughter Yocheved; Shifra, Zvi–Aryeh and son David; Mindel and Moshe–your days on earth were few and they were bad. You were cut down by cruel hands. I will not forget the days we continued together in our dear mother's tradition. We said good–bye in the hope of seeing each other again. My hope was proven to be a lie and everything was lost forever. Let these words be the markers on your unknown graves.

[Page 151]

From the Claws of Death (Memories From The War Years)

by Esther Goldman

Translated by Ala Gamulka

a. Before the Germans came

I was a young child of three, but I remember well our quiet home on Kovel Street in Ludomir. It was spacious and surrounded by a garden filled with flowers and fruit trees. Our family consisted of four people: my parents, myself and my sister Hela. She was seven years older. In addition to our family there was another small family: the Russian mayor and his wife. My father was a watchmaker and went daily to his store in the center of town. My mother supervised the house and my sister attended school. I would run around in the yard or on the street, playing.

This is how life was, until…

One morning, our Ukrainian neighbor (wife of Pansevitz) came in and gave my father a note that informed him he was to be drafted by the Red Army. I did not understand the depth of this calamity, but I sensed that my parents were in shock as a result of this pronouncement. My father went to a training camp near town. My mother used to take me to visit father and to bring him food. There were many Jews, Poles and Ukrainians training with him.

The draft deeply affected life in town. There was a great fear. All men of army age left their families and there was no one to take care of the families. Everyone felt something unexpected was coming, something terrible that no one could imagine. The fear was great as was the worry. Two months later the entire camp left town.

I remember how we all stood– mother, Hela, I and some other people– on the main road. We waved to the soldiers passing in tanks and trucks. The feeling was ominous. Would we ever see them back alive? What would happen to us, mothers and children?

At that time, our tenant, the mayor, tried to convince my mother that we should all run away with him to Russia in his truck. He explained that those who remain in the hands of the Germans will not have many chances to remain alive. My mother was afraid to leave home and to wander to the unknown with two little girls. She also believed that when father returned, he would not find anyone there. That was also a deterrent.

So, we said good–bye to the nice couple with our tears flowing. From that day one, we never heard from them again. They may have been killed on the way on mined roads or in bombings. Perhaps they remained alive. Let us hope so.

[Page 152]

b. In the hands of the murderers

A few days after the Russian army left, the Germans arrived. They immediately established a ghetto. At first, they forced the Jews, with threats, to bring valuables: radios, expensive clothes, jewelry, etc. The petrified Jews brought the items believing that they could save themselves by doing so. They did not yet know– they did not even imagine– what they could do to us. The ghetto was in the center of town and all the local Jews and from nearby villages were assembled there. Our house was outside the ghetto. Before we moved, my mother asked our neighbor to safeguard the house with its furniture and clothing. If we survived, that would be great, but if we perished– he should keep everything. During that time, my mother received news of my father from a Pole who managed to return to town. He told us that he was with my father when the unit was taken prisoner. At first, they were made to dig trenches and they did various jobs. Then, the Poles and Ukrainians were liberated. A day after he was freed, he found out that all the Jews in the unit were burned by the Germans. One can imagine how this news affected us.

We entered the ghetto a few days after Pessach 1941. We were five families in one room. I was the youngest among the children in that room. We slept on wooden crates. My mother managed to find work outside the ghetto. The work was exhausting: cleaning houses, carrying stones, laundry, etc. She would come back totally spent. Her hands and feet were swollen. However, she was able to bring back some food. Of course, the crowding was impossible and the dirt was unbearable.

Five months passed. The first pogrom– on the town Jews– began. There was great worry in the ghetto. The Germans captured Jews– men, women and children– and put them on trucks. The Jews did not really understand why they were captured. Still, anyone who could, escaped and hid. We moved to a different house and we hid in a large cellar. There were forty of us. The cellar was dark and the odor was fierce. We stayed there for two days, holding on to each other. We heard women shouting and children bawling on the outside.

Among us was an elderly woman who had lost her entire family. They were murdered in front of her. She, somehow, had managed to escape. She could not stop crying and yelling. The other people were unhappy because our hiding place could be discovered. They suggested to strangle the old woman. No one could really do it. There was also a five–year–old boy who cried constantly and asked for his father. His mother tried to silence him with sugar cubes and candy, but to no avail. The owner of the house assembled his friends and relatives– we were among them– and suggested

we escape to a small attic in the house. We were 14 people in this group. One night we began to climb up quietly so the others would not notice. My aunt was among us. She was fat and weak. It was difficult for her to climb. She gave up and said that if she felt danger approaching, she would then climb up. Three days later, the murderers discovered the cellar and took out its inhabitants, including my aunt.

[Page 153]

She was the only one who knew our hiding place. She died with the secret. We heard the screaming and the crying. The little boy, previously mentioned, cried bitter tears and his mother comforted him by saying: "Don't cry, my dear son, you are going to your father– the one you so wished to see". "Where is my father?" asked the boy. The mother replied: "Ask these cursed murderers and they will tell you"

This is how the mother and child talked a few hours before they were killed.

In general, people still trusted the Germans, that they were taking them to work. It was easier to believe it.

We peeked through the cracks of the attic and we saw how our cellar neighbors were being put on trucks and driven away. Our hearts were breaking. We were fortunate to find a new hiding place, but these poor people had their fate already determined. Would we be successful in hiding for a long time? We lay crowded together. It was not even possible to lift one's head. I lay on top of my mother. We spent six days in that place.

c. Outside there are ruins and inside there is fear

After we came out of that place, we found out that all the Jews from Ludomir and area were brought to a big forest nearby. They were murdered there. Some people managed, somehow, to return from the killing fields. Among them was a young girl from our town. After liberation she told us the story of what happened. The Jews that were murdered had dug the pits and trenches before hand. There were machine guns near the pits. The Jews were arranged in a row along the trenches and were shot. Some were ordered to lie down in the trenches and the Germans then shot them with guns and artillery. That young girl lay on top of her dead mother. Early in the morning, the Ukrainians came to cover the trenches with earth. At the same time, they also robbed the victims of their clothes and any other items they had brought. Suddenly they saw a frightening scene: a naked young girl, bleeding, rises from the pile of murdered bodies… One elderly Ukrainian woman had pity on the young girl. She dressed her and took her to her house. She stayed there until liberation.

I will return to the frightening day. When the Germans discovered the cellar, they took the people out. The Germans continued to search in the rest of the house– looking for Jews. We, in the attic, heard well their movements. We were lying without moving, without any food or water. After 24 hours my mother tried her luck and came down from the attic to the cellar. She then went into the house in search of food. She was fortunate to find, in the pantry, some food and water. On the way, some of the water spilled because her hands were shaking with fear. The same day, the Germans returned to the house and found the puddles of spilled water. This fact made them guard the house in the evening. We were in great danger. We were very hungry. The position in which we were lying and the crowding were difficult. All this was forcing us to run away from there. This is what we decided to do. However, we postponed the departure for midnight.

[Page 154]

A German came to visit his friend, the guard and brought vodka. In addition, he had good advice: "why are you guarding a Jewish house like a dog watching his master's house? Tomorrow we can burn the house down. If we find Jews here, they, too, will burn. Do not worry, they will not run away until morning. Now, let us enjoy our dinner to our hearts' content". It became quiet. We knew they had left the house. Without giving it much thought, we came down from the attic. It was dark and the descent was difficult, especially after having been immobile and eating very little. A person's will to live is great and one can overcome difficulties– as if they are more than the suffering. Finally, we came down in peace and we hurried to the neighbor's house not knowing what awaited us there. The house was empty. First, we searched for food. Anything edible that was found there disappeared quickly. We were fourteen hungry and weak people. We hid in that house in a large attic for 15 days until the end of the first Aktion. It had lasted three weeks. Interesting, there were Jews hiding in that attic before we came. They made themselves at home as if they had been there for many years. At night they went to find food and water. In comparison to the previous place, this was a most comfortable location. It was larger and had more air. There were fairly large cracks to peek outside and to see all the atrocities. We saw Jews transported forcibly by the Germans. Sometimes there were dead bodies lying in the street. Jews came with stretchers and collected them to bring them to a grave. The Germans accompanied them and prodded them. At first, I was not allowed to look outside, but then it was evident they could not stop me and I was left alone.

There was a store in that house. It had bolts of material. At night, we would go down the ladder and bring back scraps of material that were left over. The ladder was immediately pulled back up. The cloth was divided among all. Those who needed clothes were able to sew a garment. Others just kept the cloth.

Two weeks after we arrived in that attic, it was quiet on the streets. Slowly, Jews emerged from their hiding places. We, too, came out. We discovered that many Jews had been killed. We did not have numbers and we could not even imagine.

d. Between hope and desperation

At the end of the pogrom, the surviving Jews were allotted twenty houses. There were four families in each room. Again, there was crowding and great fear. My mother tried to go to work (as a rule, women with small children did not do it). At first, she worked inside the ghetto. There were various jobs: clearing destroyed houses, laundry for the Germans, etc. She then received permission to work outside the ghetto. It was a great gain because it was then possible to smuggle in some food, even though it was dangerous to do it. Nevertheless, there were many who endangered their lives and managed to bring, through the gate guarded by the Germans, a loaf of bread, some potatoes, butter or eggs.

[Page 155]

An additional difficulty was the spread of Typhus in the ghetto. I became ill, but it was a light case. I was able to get up within a few days. My sister got sick after me and her case was more serious. She had high fever and stomach pains. My mother went to work every morning and she returned in the evening. There was no one to take care of us. It was possible to call a doctor, but they avoided doing so. Sick patients would be transferred to the hospital. There, they would be given an injection, so as to stop the spread of the disease. From time to time, the Germans would comb the houses to discover sick people.

After I had recovered, I took care of my sister. I really did not wish to do it. I was angry at her for being ill and I found her to be a burden. During that time, mother tried to bring something home– at a great risk.

One day, mother returned from work looking somewhat happy. She told us that she had begun to work with a Polish family in their vegetable garden near the Old Peoples' Home, about 3 kilometers out of town. My mother became friends with the head of the family and he promised to hide her and her children in case there would be another Aktion. This fact gave us hope that perhaps we would be able to escape from the ghetto. My mother later discovered that the mayor of the village where the Old Peoples' Home was situated, was our Ukrainian neighbor, Pansevitz. She managed to meet him during her work day and he promised to help. He told her he did not know where she was and what happened to her, or if she even was still alive. Since then, from time to time, he brought my mother food to the ghetto gate. My mother was allowed to take it from him. Our life was a little easier now. We ate a slice of bread every day. It was possible to cook some potatoes and even an egg. The "euphoria" did not last long. One Friday evening, my mother returned from work upset and angry. She told everyone the ghetto was restless. Jews were standing in the streets talking about the catastrophe that was imminent. She suggested we try to escape, but no one believed her and they laughed at her. The residents of the apartment prepared for the Sabbath. They lit candles and prayed. My mother did not abandon her plan. She packed our belongings in a small package and we planned to leave. My sister had recuperated from her illness, but she was still weak. I should now tell you about a family relative, a young man of 14. His name was Moshele– he arrived in the ghetto and found us. We put him up in our room. The poor fellow became ill with Typhus. It was a difficult case and he could not move. My mother planned to transfer me and my sister and to return the next day for Moshele. The residents of the apartment promised to look after him. They convinced mother not to take him. How could she drag a boy sick with a fever of over 40 degrees? With a broken heart, we left Moshele lying with high fever. We went out of the house, feeling scared. Mother was leading and the two of us followed her towards the gate. Our bad luck materialized– a German policeman was guarding the gate. Mother gave him a watch and a gold ring. Not saying a word, he opened the gate. We breathed a sigh of relief. We were going to towards the Old Peoples' Home. Mother knew the area, but at night it was difficult to orient ourselves. We wandered all night in fields and hidden paths to avoid unpleasant encounters.

[Page 156]

It was very dark at night. From time to time, a rocket illuminated the skies. We immediately threw ourselves down on the ground. We walked fast, but we could not find our way. I suddenly felt that one of my shoes had fallen, but I could not find it. We did not want to be delayed. I continued to walk with one shoe only. Finally, we decided to rest and wait for dawn. We sat down on the cold ground and we tried to close our eyes. The sounds of constant shooting and the barking of dogs did not let us fall asleep. At dawn, we recognized where we were and we quickly continued on our way. We entered the village. Everyone was still asleep. We feared the dogs –that they would be barking at us. They would alert those who were not our friends. We hurried into the nearby hay stack. Mother hid me under the straw and went with my sister to the house of her Polish friend. An hour later, the Pole came with a wheelbarrow to the hay stack. He put me inside, covered me with straw and brought me to his house. I was scared and frozen. I found my mother and sister lying in bed, covered in blankets. I joined them immediately and I felt better.

e. For the good of charitable people

We were received warmly and with friendship. My mother could not have imagined that we would be so received. A bed and a warm blanket after a night of wandering revived us.

Mother asked the Pole, Agrontchik, to go to town to find out what was going on there. He did go, but he returned quickly with bad news: the roads were closed, the Germans were roaming. He found out from some farmers that the second pogrom had begun.

What luck we had that we were saved! How sad that our neighbors did not listen to mother's warning. Poor Moshele…our hearts were bursting with pain.

We had refuge in this house for 18 months. We spent days and nights in the little kitchen from which it was possible to climb into the attic. There was an entrance to the house in this kitchen, but it was camouflaged with clothes hanging on it. We could peek through the boards on the door to see who came into the house. Many times, we held our breath as one of the Polish villagers came into the house. Inside the kitchen there was a large stove that served as our bed. In addition, Agrontchik made us a bed out of planks as well as some shelves. For a year and a half, we spent our days and nights lying on these beds. Zusha, his wife, gave us food. They performed a great charitable act. They endangered themselves by hiding us. They were repaid for their efforts. Mother gave them gold and the village mayor, the Ukrainian Pansevitz, gave them flour, potatoes, etc. for us. There was a public Old Peoples' Home in the village and the fields belonged to the government. A few families worked the land as lessees. Agrontchik was in charge of the laborers, but during the war he had to do the work by himself.

[Page 157]

A few weeks after we began to stay there, Pansevitz came to visit us. He described the situation in the ghetto and on the front. The stories were not encouraging, but it was worse not to know anything. He came to visit from time to time.

On cold nights, Zusha would bring us into their warm beds. It was crowded, but at least it was warm. In the morning we returned to our cold kitchen.

We had many "friends" in our hiding place. The first were mice. They got used to us and we to them. We even played with them. Lice were also our friends, but they were not so pleasant. They roamed freely over our bodies, our clothing and anything else in the kitchen. The was a tiny window in the kitchen that was hidden on the outside with straw. We never turned on lights at night. We sat in the dark. I cannot remember how my sister and I occupied ourselves during those long days and nights. My mother found a job. She knitted socks and gloves for Zusha and her children. Our life was not always so" idyllic". We often had to climb into the attic and hide there for hours, sometimes even days. Guests would come to see Zusha. We did not starve, but Zusha could not bring us food.

Zusha had a sister in a nearby village. Her husband was a soldier. One day, before Christmas, she came with her children to visit. We immediately had to go up to the attic and we stayed there for three days without any food. When they left, Zusha came to apologize to us. She was sorry that she could not look after us during those days. She was afraid to tell her sister that she was hiding Jews. With great fear, she told us her sister invited her to visit and she could not find an excuse to say no.

Zusha prepared for the trip. Since the road was difficult, she decided to leave her baby daughter at home. She invited my sister Hela to join her. At first, mother was against it, but Zusha managed to convince her that nothing bad could happen. It would be good for her to be out in fresh air and in sunshine. They left on the trip. A few days later we received a letter from her. She was being well treated by the sisters. Zusha presented her as an orphaned Polish girl. Everyone believed it. They did not mention returning home.

Zusha sent her elderly mother to take care of the children. The old lady was a shrew. Zusha told her that we are the Jews hiding in her house and that she should look after us, too. She did do it, but she had to be paid. My mother gave her, from time to time, earrings or a ring with a precious stone or a gold chain.

f. Fire in the villages

At that time the frontline came closer and the partisans began to appear in our area. The thick forest served them as an excellent cover. They made contact with the farmers.

They obtained food and arms and found out about the movements of the enemy. The first chance they had, they attacked a German unit. They killed 18 and injured others. The news of this event was circulated in the area and the villagers were afraid. They knew the Germans would not accept it quietly. Their revenge would be great. The reaction came soon afterwards. At first, the Germans searched houses looking for arms. Then, they burned village after village and expelled the residents. When they found Jews hidden by farmers, all were executed.

We peeked through the small window and we saw fire everywhere. We were afraid. We felt they would reach us any day. However, since our village was a little farther from the forest, a few days passed before the Germans arrived. They ordered all furniture to be removed. They waited patiently and then they lit the houses on fire. They came to Zusha's house. Mother came out of hiding and pretended to be part of the family. She began to help the old lady to empty the house. Later, mother told me that the old lady had asked her to give me to her in case the Germans would burn the house down. My mother could not agree that the day would come when she would lose her entire family. She already knew about father's fate (in her heart she did want to believe it). She did not know what was happening to Hela. She did not agree to separate.

While she was moving freely in the house and in the yard, mother ordered me not to leave the hiding place. I was quite curious and I peeked from the slit in the wall. I saw my mother covered in a large shawl, carrying mattresses and other household goods. The old lady was barely able to drag anything. The children were crying. There was much noise and tumult. I felt very hot and I did not know the reason. I began to get undressed. Suddenly, I heard loud banging on the kitchen door. It had been discovered after the rags had been taken off. I was scared to open and I began to cry. When the banging became louder, I opened the door to an unfamiliar person. The man spoke to me, but I did not understand a word. I was confused and embarrassed because I was naked. I quickly began to get dressed and he disappeared. In a moment, I saw my mother near the window. She motioned me to come out. I did not understand and I did not do so. She was afraid, for some reason, to come inside. The house was on fire.

The German to whom I had earlier opened the door told my mother to take me out. My mother managed to do it at the last minute. The walls were crumbling. She even took my clothes and my shoes. After 18 months of sitting in an enclosed space, it seemed strange to me to step on the ground, to see so many people crying and yelling, running around and dragging sobbing children. Cows were trampling through the snow, without purpose and the Germans were standing and watching this "interesting scene", fire and smoke, collapsing houses. They were enjoying themselves and laughing at their own work.

[Page 159]

g. The flight

Mother was afraid that one of the locals would recognize her and would denounce her to the Germans. The old lady also thought so and advised her to quickly hide in the haystack at the end of the village until the Germans left. She again repeated her wish to look after me. Even in this moment of despair, my mother did not want to be separated from me.

As soon as we began to walk away, we heard: "Halt! If you don't stop, I will shoot!". My mother did not stop and quickened her steps, pulling me with her. We ran as fast as we could until we reached the haystack. Mother hid me under the bales of straw and ordered me to be quiet. "If they kill me"–she said–"If they will not find you, you can stay with the old lady until the end of the war. You will then look for Hela". I was shaking with cold and fear and I listened to mother. I was not even 5 years old, but I understood the situation. I knew I had to do as I was told. Mother kissed me and went to close the doors. From outside we heard the voices of Germans passing by the haystack. A few minutes later, the door was burst open and a German asked my mother: "Are you the woman who ran away with a little girl?" "Yes" – answered my mother–"I am the one. Do what you want with me, but do not torture me. My children are dead, my husband is dead. My whole family is dead. I have no relatives left".

"I promise you that we will not do anything bad to you as long as you tell us the truth"– said the German. "Tell me, where did you hide your daughter?" – "I told you, all my children are dead, I have no more children". The German began to search the haystack with the sharp end of his gun. He found me crying and shaking. He brought me to my mother and asked: "Is this your daughter?" Mother burst out crying and hugged me. "Are you Jewish?"– he asked– "Yes!", replied my mother. "Tell me, do you know anything about the partisans? Where have they been hiding until now?" My mother told him that we had only arrived in the village a few days ago. She had no idea what was going on here.

It seems the German believed her. He took out a picture from his pocket and showed it to my mother. "Do you see this woman? These are my wife and children who were taken prisoner by the Russians. Who knows if they are still alive? Now, hurry and find a place to hide until after Passover that is coming soon. Then you can go to the nearby village and join the Poles".

We stood as if glued to the ground. We could not believe our ears. I still remember the German. He was tall, with glasses. It seemed he was the commander of the unit that had done the burning. My mother thanked him and I bowed and kissed his hand. We said good–bye with this "ceremony". He ordered his soldiers to leave and we were able to continue on our way. We reached a house that stood further away from the village. My mother knew the owners. Fortunately, that house was not burned down. Perhaps because the lady of the house was very ill and lying in her bed.

[Page 160]

Mother asked for permission to stay for a few days until the Germans would leave the area. They agreed. We left after three days. The roads were covered with melting snow. We sunk in it up to our knees, but we continued to the nearby Polish village. On the way we met a peasant woman and we asked if the village still existed. She told us there was no purpose to going there as there were no people left. Still, we continued in that direction. We came to a crossroad and we did not know which way to go. Suddenly, we heard people speaking German. We immediately threw ourselves on the ground until the voices became fainter. When we got up, we saw three Germans walking leisurely in one direction. We decided to go the other way. We reached a settlement, but we discovered that most of the farmers had left the village. We joined the families leaving.

h. Wandering

We walked a great distance from there to Rozhishets. We wandered many days and nights. We walked on foot most of the time. If we were lucky, we had a ride on a cart. We were cold and hungry. Months went by. I do not remember the names of the villages we passed. Some villages were totally destroyed and some only partly. There was a thick forest with cleared areas where there was a deep pit in the middle. It seemed there had been a bomb there. I vaguely remember all of this. It is as if there was a thick fog, in a dream. The travelling was exhausting and the stops, mainly at night, were short. There were horses and other animals, but mainly horses. However, they were not always available to us.

On the way we came close to a bridge that the Germans had tried, for several days, to bomb. Everyone moved quickly, with one cart trying to overcome the other. Suddenly, the sound of the airplanes was louder and the bombing began. After we managed to cross the bridge, we found out from those who were closest to us that the bridge had collapsed. All the people who were not able to pass fell into the water, were killed or taken prisoner.

For a few days we traveled with gypsies. It was a family: husband, wife and a small child. They had two horses. Their cow had died on the way and there was no milk for the child. A few times, my mother bought milk for the child and, in return, they transported us in their cart. Finally, they got tired, for some reason, and asked us to get off. Again, we had to walk. I could not walk far and, at times, my mother had to carry me in her arms. She felt courageous and asked a young Polish woman carrying a baby if I could sit in their cart. The Polish woman agreed, but wanted to be paid. Mother gave her a gold ring and, in exchange, I lay down in the cart. I sighed in relief. Mother was still waiting to see the response as the woman had to consult with her husband. Soon a man, around 25 years old, came over and pointed to me. The woman quickly explained to him the situation and showed him the ring. He forcibly took away the ring from her finger.

[Page 161]

He returned the ring to my mother and said: "Get out of here, you stinking Jewess and take your daughter. If not– you will have a bitter end".

My mother was scared and she took me off the cart. She felt helpless. Soon, she recovered and asked another peasant woman for a ride for me. The woman had no husband, only a young daughter. Her cart was packed with belongings and was pulled by two horses. My mother promised to lead her cow. We finally found someone who had pity on us. I remember name– Kozlovska. She treated us very nicely. We ate and slept together as we wandered. One night, we were in the forest, the wind was howling and it began to rain. All the families had prepared tents. Kozlovska joined one of them, but no one invited us. We slept in the cart. We were soaked through and through. That night I developed a cold and I had small sores, full of pus, on my hands. They hurt, but I cried quietly. There was no ointment and there was fear I had scabies. It was not a dangerous illness, but quite infectious. The Polish woman drove to Rozhishets, already in the hands of the Russians, and she brought me an ointment for scabies. It did not help me. The sores became larger and hurt me terribly. They wrapped my hands with rags. Everyone looked at me with evil eyes.

The families began to go to liberated Rozhishets. Our Polish lady agreed to take us there. We said good–bye to her with friendliness. She helped us to find a medical clinic so we could get an ointment for my hands.

i. "I don't want to be Jewish"

I walked out of the medical clinic with my hands bandaged. I had a strange feeling. The nurse in the clinic had asked me what my origins were. I confidently told her I was Polish. Even after mother told her we were both Jewish, I stubbornly insisted that I was not Jewish. (The nurse wondered: why would I deny it?)

This feeling, not wanting to be Jewish or the question why I had to be Jewish and suffer so much awakened in me during our wandering. As we distanced ourselves from danger, this feeling became an open rebellion. This is what happened:

When we stopped in one of the forests, my mother found out that there were Jews in the area. She wanted to contact them. She told me she was going to speak to some Jews and would soon return. In that forest there was a pond surrounded by bushes. I told my mother that if she did not return immediately, I would drown myself. My mother left and I descended from the cart and went to wash up. As I was washing my feet, I fell into the pond. I do not remember if I did it intentionally or if it was an accident. My good fortune was that our gentile friend noticed it. She rushed and quickly took me out by pulling my hair. I turned out the pond was not very deep, but I still could have easily drowned. The woman undressed me

[Page 162]

and changed my clothes. I lay back on the cart feeling victorious. When my mother returned and the woman told her what had happened, she began to cry. I was giving her so much trouble. I told her: What business do you have with Jews? Why was she going to them? Poor Mother! Is it not enough that so much has happened to her because Jews were so disliked? Now she had her own "anti–Semitic" event.

Truthfully, time, which healed my scabies and obliterated my memory of the terrible events, also cleansed me of this "hatred".

j. Going home with Hela

We had not heard from Hela since the day we said good–bye. Mother did not stop speaking about her. Who knew if she was still alive? Suddenly, Hela arrived in Rozhishets, went straight to the market and found Mother. I was not present when they met, but I know Mother was deeply shaken. She was quite ill afterwards. I did not get too excited. I almost did not recognize her as she had improved so much. She told us about the hardship she had suffered.

She hid in the forest with the partisans. She then came to Ludomir where she hid with a Ukrainian peasant woman. She was not actually hiding, but she worked for her. The woman did not know she was Jewish. She attended church and wore a cross on her neck. She did everything, suffered quietly in order to remain alive. After liberation Pansevitz took her to him and told her that if she did not find her mother, he would adopt her. My sister did not stop looking. She went to the Jews who came back to town to ask if they had, by chance, met Mother. One woman told her that Mother and I were in Rozhishets. She decided to immediately go to search for us. It was dangerous and difficult to do so. The trains were full of injured soldiers returning from the front and the roads had dangerous people milling about. In spite of her young age (13), she overcame all the difficulties and came to us.

A few days later we decided to return to Ludomir. Our house was still standing. Our good neighbor Pansevitz guarded the belongings that we had left when we went into the ghetto. We had beds, a table and dishes, but we had no way of subsisting. Mother did not have any gold items left–she had used them up during the war to pay our way. Here, as in Rozhishets, the main way of earning a living was in the market, buying and selling food items and other things. For that, one had to obtain a permit from the police.

After much trying, Mother received a permit to sell bread rolls. She would buy flour, bake the bread rolls at night and sell them in the morning. Later, she also sold writing implements and other items.

Life was very hard. In spite of everything, we were pleased that we had withstood all our troubles and that we merited to see the end of the war and to start a new life.

Hela attended a Russian school– there was no Jewish school. I was still at home because I had not yet turned seven. I did not have any shoes, but my turn came to go to school. At the beginning of the winter, I started school. We were two Jewish girls in the class. Even in the other grades there were very few Jews. At first, it was difficult for me to learn. Soon I learned to read and write and I studied with great pleasure.

Although we got used to our new life, we did not wish to remain with gentiles. The few Jews who survived returned to Ludomir and Ustiluh, but they began to leave and work in other countries. Most of them went to Poland. Poland became an intermediate stop on their way to Eretz Israel or America. We also decided to leave our town of birth.

k. Safe harbor

In Summer 1945 we left Ludomir and traveled to Poland. We did not know what to expect, but our wish to live among Jews was strong. We had heard that in Poland there were large concentrations of Jews.

We lived in Bytom. There we found a large Jewish population and we saw the activities of various organizations. There was talk of making Aliyah. There were also Jews who went to Germany, to France and to America. Mother had a brother in Canada and another one in Eretz Israel. She did not know where to go, but, we, the girls, wanted to go on Aliyah. We knew nothing about life there and how we would manage. The decision was made and our wanderings began.

The first stop was in Austria. We spent a few months in a special camp. It had been a concentration camp during the war. It was difficult. People were still reliving their war experiences. Here they were brought to a former concentration camp where the ovens for burning bodies were still standing. There were also other signs. Near the camp there was a village of Austrian peasants. They told horrific tales about the extermination.

From Austria we went to Italy. There, we were received by a relative, Haim Stolar. He had served in the Red Army during the war and he was active in the Aliyah movement. He helped us to go to Ostia, a village near Rome. Life here was free and happy. There was no need to worry about making a living because we received everything, money, clothes and food, from the Joint and UNWRA. The happy Italians were very nice. I learned to speak Italian and we visited Rome and other places. These were very interesting trips.

My sister Hela belonged to Hashomer Hatzair and they were planning Aliyah. Mother became ill and underwent a serious operation in a hospital in Rome. Hela decided to stay until we could go on Aliyah when our turn would come. She was lucky, because the ship her friends had boarded was captured by the British and was brought to Cyprus.

[Page 164]

We left a month later. We took a small boat –with the help of Haim– that was bringing glue to Eretz Israel. We were only 10 people, carrying documents of returning residents who had left before the war and were unable to return.

We passed Cyprus and our hearts were beating fast. We were afraid to be discovered, but all went well.

On a summer night, 22.7.1947, we docked in Haifa. We stayed in port and the ship was rocking back and forth. Lights were flickering in the distance. Had we really arrived at our destination? Will our wanderings stop here? The lights of Haifa charmed us. We stood on deck and watched all night. The next day we were taken on a motor boat. We were checked and questioned. We then booked a hotel near the port. This was the first time I met Arab women. They were singing, but it seemed to me like crying. I was surprised they did not have tears in their eyes.

Mother telephoned my uncle in Kibbutz Mishmar Hayam. My aunt and uncle appeared a few hours later. The meeting was very exciting. We took our belongings and went to Kibbutz Mishmar Hayam. We were finally in safe harbor.

[Page 165]

Flowers and Tears

At the Mass Grave of Ustiluh
From her orphaned children around the world

[Page 166]

Explanation

The articles by the late brothers Yossel and Nachman Burlyant, as well as the one by Rabbi Aharon Wertheim(May he live long), are taken from the publication "In memorial of the Holocaust in Ustiluh", published in New York in January 1948.

These articles have been reprinted in our book in the same old, but mixed layout. Other articles in Yiddish, published in an enhanced method, are printed in the original style of the authors.

Editorial Board

[Page 167]

Ustiluh – Its Rich Past

by Rabbi Dr. Aharon Wertheim, Brooklyn, New York

Translated by Ala Gamulka

Many names of Jewish shtetls in Ukraine and Poland have been perpetuated in the spiritual life of our people. They have entered, never to be forgotten, the world of Jewish literature. It is in part due to the Hassidic leaders and Rabbis who were identified with them. Such shtetls as Meziritch, Kotsk, Ger, Psishkhe, d.g., would never have become famous in the wider world. They would have been long forgotten if not for the Meziritch Maggid, the Kotsker Rebbe, the Psishkher, etc. They produced history in their time and they perpetuated the names of their shtetls.

Our beloved shtetl Ustiluh has been entered forever in the history of our people because of the important rabbis who resided there. Their names are tied to that of the shtetl.

I do not know if among our Ustiluh brethren there are many who can recall the names of their 6th great grandparents who are connected to our shtetl. If there are such people, they must be few in number. I am one of them. My father, the Great Rabbi, as well as my grandfather, Eliezer, were both rabbis in Ustiluh. Even my grandfather's great grandfather was also a rabbi in Ustiluh. He was well–known as the great righteous Yossele, the rabbi of Ustiluh. He was the son of the Neskhitzer Rabbi, Mordekhai.

The great wedding in Ustiluh, part of the history of the Hassidic movement, occurred when the elder rabbi of Ustiluh married his offspring to that of the Rabbi from Opler. There were, at the wedding, "70 white points", i.e. 70 righteous men who followed the customs of those days of wearing white silk robes.

When the famous Yiddish writer and researcher Sh. Ansky passed through Ustiluh in 1913, he was pestered by these stories about the Great Wedding in Ustiluh. It was the old, 100–year–old Shimon Cohen who told him the story. He, himself, had attended the wedding and saw everything with his own eyes. Ansky recorded the stories and used some of them in his writings.

[Page 168]

In later years, even in our generation, religious life in our shtetl Ustiluh was far from being monotonous. It was always colorful. Ustiluh had, in addition to the Town House of Learning, Danoch's House of Learning, the Old Rabbi's House of Learning, many small shtibels. These were the Trotsker, Vlodovker, Rizshiner, Stepaner, Rodziner and Belzer.

There were also minyans in the Vinehauser and "on the other side of the river". There was also the small Tailors synagogue.

Every Hassidic shtiebel had its own specific customs with their own holidays and memorial days with special meals and tunes. Still, religious life was full and harmonious.

In all the Houses of Learning and shtiebels there were less people than in the big synagogues in Borough Park on Rosh Hashanah and Yom Kippur, but how drab religious life seems in an American synagogue the rest of the year. During the week we are frightened by its emptiness. It even feels like that on Shabbat and Holidays. In our shtetl, religious life was definitely colorful.

In every House of Learning there were young people learning Torah. Even our enlightened Hebrew scholars never studied anywhere else. They did not graduate from other "universities "– only from our Houses of Learning.

Ustiluh stood out with its students and teachers. The son of the Trisker rabbi, the rabbi from Zshurik, Poland, hired, for his children, a teacher from Ustiluh , Abush, z"l. The Tshartkover rabbi sent a teacher to one of his followers, a wealthy man from Odessa, Reuven Grinberg. He was Reuven Zak, son of Hersh–David. He was later the Dayan, replacing his father. Also, my grandfather, the rabbi from Bendery, imported erudite teachers from Ustiluh to Bessarabia.

[Page 169]

There were teachers such as Liptche and Mendelee Fanik who educated their students as did the greatest pedagogues in the world. They earned the love and respect of their students.

Ustiluh was truly known as a fine Jewish community. The famous Belzer Rebbe chose it as the first rabbinical post for his son–in–law, the great, righteous scholar Pinele Twersky. Twersky stayed there until he was recruited by the big city of Pzemishil. My father , the Great Rabbi, after his time in Ustiluh, served in important rabbinic towns such as Ostrava, Hrubeshov and Bendery. However, the title of the Ustiluh Rabbi was always dear to him for the rest of his life. Very strong feelings of love kept him attached to Ustiluh and its inhabitants. He even left these feelings as an inheritance to his children.

I was only 12 years old when our family left Ustiluh, at the beginning of WWI. My mother, may she live a long life, made sure my memories are etched deep in my heart. The more I think of the town and its people, the more I feel the sorrow of the unspeakable Holocaust.

There were once generations that included important people and holy righteous ones, but that one small shtetl should have, in one generation, 4000 martyrs! Who can overcome this? Who can stand it?

It is so sad to think about those who are lost, but not forgotten.

[Page 170]

My Town – Ustiluh

by Dr. Aharon Rosmarin, New York

Translated by Ala Gamulka

The name Ustiluh is a combination of two Slavic words meaning shores and lawns. From a geographic point of view it is a tiny island. On the west side is the Bug river. Its source is in the Carpathian river and it leads into the Wiessel river. On the other side is the Staff which passes between green shores and flows with strength into the Bug. Its rushing current passes by flour mills. On the third side is the modest, barely moving little Vinehauser river. On the fourth side, near the village of Piatidin, runs the small river crowned by a water mill.

The southern side of the Bug

[Page 171]

The shtetl was surrounded by endless green fields, heavy with Ukrainian wheat, numerous forests sporting berries.

The air was always fresh. It was quieter than quiet and it calmed the nerves and cleared the moods.

The entire space touched the soul. Our hearts were proud that the world–famous, today the biggest composer, Igor Stravinsky, used to spend his summer vacations in Ustiluh. He wrote some of his great compositions there.

In the shtetl, a few hundred families led a Torah–centered life. One never heard the word Kosher. One could eat in the home of the water carrier, the store clerk, the artisan, as well as the one of the wealthy ones . There was never a sermon about keeping the Sabbath. No one ever desecrated the Sabbath. (except maybe the usual "pharmacist" in all towns).

What a concert could be heard from the students, singing on their way home from Heder, in the freezing winter evenings! What weekday nights in the world could compete with the summer Saturday night celebrations. Those walks through the corn and wheat fields to the Sosnow forest! One could study a chapter on the porch. What drinks could compete with a glass that had homemade jam. It was prepared "in case of need". What fruit could compare with the traditional Sabbath evening roasted apples?

The east European shtetl is well described in Yiddish and Hebrew literature– poetry and prose. In general, all of these shtetls were painted with same brush: Houses of Learning, Heders (sometimes in one location), a ritual slaughterer or several, wealthy owners, shopkeepers, artisans, water carriers, a bath house with a Mikveh , a sanctuary and sometimes even a town fool.

[Page 172]

In the main, Ustiluh was a shtetl like all others. Everyone loves his hometown with its mud and sunshine, its negative and positive sides. My shtetl Ustiluh is not an exception.

B.

It is now over forty years since I left the most serene and calm place on earth. I came to a noisy, excited city with a population of 8.5 million people and 4 million vehicles. It is the boiler room of the world. Still, one cannot forget certain peculiar types, even if one wanted to!

Shprintze the dealer. She was a small, skinny woman with a wrinkled body, a descendant of a Righteous person. She never left town, her whole life. Every Friday she spent the day going from house to house with a sack on her hunched shoulders. She collected challahs for the sanctuary. Her small, yellowed face shone with inner happiness. Her sunken, exhausted, fermented cheeks were suddenly refreshed. One could see how happy she was with the gift of freshly baked loaves. Poor people will celebrate the Sabbath with fresh challah. How wonderful!

Haim Volf: a teacher of young children. He had a large room with a kitchen in one corner. In another corner was the dining area. In the third corner was the bedroom and in the fourth– a Heder, a classroom. In the middle, on clay benches, sat young children– 3, 4, 5 years old with their slates. These were the infants of the school or, as our ancestors described them, Guardians of the Town. From 8 am until late at night, one could hear Aleph A, Aleph O… His face was drawn, darkened and worried. As well as his students repeated the lessons, the more he demanded. Torah has no limit. Another worry for him: it is already Wednesday afternoon and he did not yet receive the four guilden he needs for the Sabbath. His small, patched purse is empty like his stomach or vice versa!

[Page 173]

However, on Friday afternoon, free from the little ones, you see Haim going from house to house, carrying a sack on his shoulders. He collects challahs, pieces of challahs, for the poor. His face is smiling with contentment. Every portion of challah that he places in his sack makes him happy. Poor people will celebrate the Sabbath with fresh challah. The fuller his sack the happier he becomes. He spends 12 hours a day, every day of the week, week after week, summer and winter, even on Hol Hamoed, teaching old and new students. Poverty is everywhere. His only "vacation " is the hours he spends on Friday afternoons collecting challahs for the poor.

Yehoshua Bok. This is what this plain, observant, poor and honest painter was called. I know 10 Hebrew words to describe poor and they all could be used to speak about him. In spite of this,he was an excellent host. I doubt if he knew the phrase: “Good hosts become holy”. If he did it as a Mitzvah or because he had pity on people, he was still noble.

He was poor and could really not afford to have guests for the Sabbath, but this nice man came up with a solution. In general, visiting poor people were invited for a meal only. He offered them a place to sleep and even a hot drink. He believed what Israel Salanter said– that instead of worrying about one's body and another's soul, it is better to think of one's soul and the other's body. This quiet, modest man, Yehoshua Bok, did not speak badly of others. He practiced, day in and day out, this worthy custom.

Yehoshua Bok was a God–fearing man among poor folks. Envy is one of the 3 sins that remove a person from this world. From childhood, I never saw even a touch of envy in him. He was called Yehoshua Bok and he was admired by all.

[Page 174]

Bentzi Dayan: he was often called the young Dayan (judge). The shtetl barely appreciated him.

On the Sabbath, in the Trisker shtibel, he could not sit still on the eastern or western wall. He walked back and forth. He seemed deep in thought, not a sound on his lips. Others whispered that the Dayan was not praying. On summer days, wearing a yarmulke, he would jump over heaps of scraps, walking from his house, deep in thought. What was the Dayan thinking about? No one knew what bothered him. No one could figure it out. If someone actually noticed something, it was not complimentary. When the Dayan tried to answer a complicated Rambam question, no one was surprised. They then knew what a brilliant, studious man existed in Ustiluh.

During my school days in Berlin, I was translating Rashi into English and contributing to the Encyclopedia Judaica. I often visited the home of the famous genius, Haim Heller. He died in New York on the last eve of Passover. The second part of his “For the Study of Laws” was published and I sent it to the Dayan. The Dayan wrote a letter to Haim telling him he had an issue with an abandoned wife. He was in contact with many scholars in Poland and Lithuania. However, in “For the Study of Laws” he saw the work of a great scholar. He needed to be told what to do. The Dayan also added commentary to the book. When Haim saw the commentary, he declared:”your Dayan is a genius!” Ustiluh had a genius, but no one knew about it. These were the modest, righteous men and women who lived in the shtetl of Ustiluh.

C.

I, personally, did not experience our great national devastation. Understandably, I cannot describe these experiences. I will restrict myself to a few chronological comments.

Ustiluh was a Hassidic shtetl. In addition to the Great House of Learning, the Tailors' shtiebl and Danche's House of Learning , all the other shtiebls were Hassidic. These were: Trisker, Belzer, Stepaner.

[Page 175]

Rizshiner, Great Love (Blodavker), Radziner. The shtetl was under the influence of Trisk.

The Radziner rebbe, Gershon Henikh, the Blue one, only came once to visit us. He stayed with my parents. However, the Radziner followers destroyed any evidence of the Trisker Magid found in our house (as in other houses of Trisker followers). He was immediately asked to leave the shtetl.

I have something interesting to add, but it goes with a different topic. The Stepaner rebbe seldom came. When he did, he stayed in the Stepaner shtiebl. Food was brought to him. Also, a couch came from the house of Moshe Shmayes (Veidere).

The Trisker rebbe, Yaakov Leibeniu, used to come every year. He would arrive, after Shavuot, on a Friday. He was accompanied by his entourage. He had no difficulty staying in my parents' house. His companions slept in my uncle Yosef's house. He always left on the following Thursday. This is a story in itself, but for another occasion.

It could also be useful to speak of the Ludomir girl. Ludomir (Vladimir Volynsk) lies 10 viorsts from us. A girl lived there. Her name was Hannah Rachel and she was the daughter of Munisl Verbenmacher.

She was the daughter of a rabbi. Not only Hassidic, but other people used to come to her. She put on tfilin. She divorced her husband of 40 years and left for Eretz Israel. There, she tried to practice Rabbinics.

When the rabbi of Ustiluh, Yossel (the first), son of the Nikhizsher rabbi, heard that the Lubliner "seer" will be spending a few days in Ustiluh, he was eager to host him. He knew that when the "seer" sleeps in an unfamiliar bed, he sometimes yells:" it's bothering me!" Yossel invited an observant carpenter to build a new bed. He ordered him to first go to the Mikva and to build the bed with clear intentions. When the carpenter heard that he was to build a bed for a saintly person, he worked with great trepidation and holy intentions.

[Page 176]

The rabbi, put the bed in another room and placed new linens on it. When the "seer" arrived, the rabbi took him home. He showed him the room and the bed specially built for him by a God–fearing man. He asked him to lie down and rest after his long trip. As soon as he lay down, he began to yell "It's bothering me!"

When the rabbi heard this, he was frightened and invited the "seer" to go back to bed. He did so and immediately fell asleep. When the "seer" woke up, the rabbi reminded him that the bed was built by a God–fearing man. The "seer " replied: " the bed is kosher, but it thrives on black bile because it was built during the nine days!" Since the carpenter is a God–fearing man, he would make the bed mourn the destruction of the Temple.

The murderous German killers came and with brutal cruelty performed bestial atrocities and annihilated my shtetl Ustiluh. They burned homes and buried people alive. These were simple, honest, observant Jews, children and the elderly.

May God avenge their blood.

Among the martyrs were my brother, sister and their children and grandchildren, many friends and relatives.

I wrote the following with my bloody tears flowing:

In memory of the martyrs killed, slaughtered, burned, drowned and suffocated on the holy of holies, by the Germans, May their names and memories be erased.

God of Mercy, God of the Heavens, may they be remembered with other righteous people of the world.

May their spilled blood be avenged!

[Page 177]

The School System and Children's Education in Ustiluh at the Beginning of the Current Century

by Baruch Goldberg (Buzie Haddasses), Buenos Aires

Translated by Zvi Kaniel

The following translations were commissioned by Avigail Frij, whose maternal grandparents were from Ustilug (Kopp and Kultin Families)

When we bring up memories of the social life in our tragic, destroyed, beloved town, I believe that it will not be an exaggeration to look back 50 to 60 years from now, how the school system looked then, what and how children and youth studied. I think that everyone who remembers those times would agree that those at the top were the teachers of religious studies: the written or Oral Torah, and all their offshoots, which were being taught in dozens of chadarim, from [primary level to advanced Gmara and Tosfos [commentaries], as well as those who studied on their own in the Study Halls. But all would agree that although at that time there were no modern educational systems in the schools, the chadarim and Study Halls were not the only learning institutions. An entire line of self–taught teachers gave lessons in Hebrew, Russian, math, etc., to individuals or groups of students. Understandably, however, the "luxury" of having an instructor, aside from the teacher, was only possible for those who could afford it. The result was that the majority of children from poorer families remained illiterate even in Jewish subjects, let alone in Hebrew or Russian. In particular, the helplessness of the people became apparent when they had to write a Russian or Latin address. Every "knowledgeable person" (literate) often had to write an address to husbands in America or to sons in the military – and often even the actual letters themselves, although these were written in Yiddish. I would like to describe one of those people who performed such favors: the warm, dear, Baruch Feiga – who worked for the marquis and who perished in the Holocaust. May his memory be blessed.

A relatively small number of the town's youth studied in the Ludomir "Hebrew School."

[Page 178]

That was a special government school in which Russian was the language of instruction. Among others, those who were enrolled there were Moshe Burlyant's children: Yossel, Bashe, Chaim, and Nachman (the younger two brothers, Shmulik and Aharon, already belonged to the post–war youth of 1918).

It is also worth mentioning that four children born to two Ustiluh families studied in high school and ended up marrying into the families of the so–called "free professionals." These were the brothers Berl and Sholom Yokhenzon, and the brothers Yudel and Zalman Yevilevitch, grandsons of Frumet Sheva's, who ran the local tailor shop. All the Yokeanzons were murdered by the Nazis. The Yevilevitch brothers emigrated to *Eretz Yisrael.*

Evening courses in the years 1915–1917

Summing up my description of Ustiluh up to the end of World War I, I would like to mention an incident connected to me. It was when a group of the abovementioned "self–taught" teachers opened the first modern school under the name of "*Beit Sefer*". This had a negative impact on the conservative fathers who considered this type of school to be a deviation from the traditional ways and inappropriate gender mixing.

[Page 179]

Even though I was already 13 years old at the time, an age that could be considered too late to begin studying, I was very interested in the "*Beit Sefer*" with the modern facilities and the methods of instruction, including recesses. In particular, I liked the pedagogical style that emphasized teacher –student interaction. I decided to ask my father to enroll me in the "*Beit Sefer.*" He answered me, "As long as I live, you will not attend a school where they don't cover their heads ...." As you can imagine, my father was not the only one who opposed the aspirations of the younger generation in this manner.

Finally, I feel obliged to mention the names of the first teachers who wrote in a beautiful, descriptive page of history about the intellectual – educational efforts in our town. I remember the following people:

Simcha Schwalb, Shmerl Sokoler, Shlomo Kanat, Moishe Kornfeld, Montzia Brik, Avraham Tzigel, Moishe Shpirer, Yankel Grinberg, and two Bokser brothers who later left Ustiluh to become teachers in Ludomir.

Of all these mentioned, Moishe Kornfeld was the only one who survived the Holocaust. May the memory of all the others be blessed.

[Page 180]

The Teacher and His Circle

by Yaakov Zipper (Montreal, Canada)

Translated by Zvi Kaniel

This story is a chapter from Y. Zipper's book "On the Other Side of the Bug [River]." Anyone from Ustiluh will recognize that Berel Taub is the pseudonym for the beloved teacher Shmerl Sokoler, may his memory be blessed.

– The editors

On Shabbos afternoon, Shternberg and Leibel went to the teacher Berel Taub, who lived on the train street. His house was small, low–ceilinged, half caved in, that he inherited from his parents. The roof was overgrown with mold and strange wild growth, closed in with boards positioned at an angle on all four sides. It seemed that the roof would soon slide down to the nearby field that was filled with wild grass, and would leave the curved walls of the house exposed to the elements.

In bygone days, this house had a fence around it and a foot path that led from the small gate straight to the large, heavy front door, that had a massive, gnawed out window frame of oak wood. These days, the gate was broken. Only the rotten wooden posts remained, and from every angle you could reach the damaged door, that, without the frame, looked like a crown without a head. But once inside, you could not recognize any aging. The curved walls are hidden under large frames, from which older Jews looked out with their wide, wavy beards and hard caps on their heads, and also Jewish women with light headscarves and smoothly combed bonnets. Paned cupboards packed with religious books hid all the cracks in the corners. The house always exuded a festive calmness, featuring a long table in the middle of the room that was always covered with a flowered, holiday tablecloth.

[Page 181]

"Berel is our gem," Leibel said. "There are not many like him."

The entire town called Berel by his first name and he was praised like a bottle of fine wine. You just had to remember that Berel said such and such, and it was already enough, so that everyone should listen to him. Even those religious ones had respect for his honesty and sincerity. They were not really very pleased with his manner of study, but they knew that he knew a lot, and meant everything for the sake of Heaven. He taught poor children at no charge, and in the freezing winter months when many of his students could not come to school because their boots were torn, he went to the various houses until late at night and learned with these children by candlelight, at the fathers' work table. He did this with such simplicity, that everyone in town already considered this to be totally natural behavior. It seemed normal that in the heavy frost, his few wealthier students knew not to wait for Berel in their homes, but to go find him in school before he strode through the back streets to the other, poorer students' homes.

"The poor do not have a choice," he explained simply to those who could not stand it.

From his Hebrew–Yiddish school, which was founded during the war at the time of the Austrian occupation, not everyone supported him, but no one would openly dare say a bad word about him. They all knew that only Berel had the strength to maintain the school in those difficult times, and that his students were among the best in town. At a meeting of the American Aid Committee, when the issue of giving assistance to the school came up, some religious people tried to inject a word, that the American Jews were not interested in providing assistance to a school in which the students learned without a head covering. The aged religious judge (Dayan) silenced them by declaring, "People, do not touch Berel. Those like him are meritorious for a town." The Dayan explained to the bewildered citizens: "People, what do you not understand?"

[Page 182]

"Maybe he really studies with his head uncovered, Heaven help us! and he will have to answer for that, may Hashem help him, but we cannot punish him. You know that his love for the Jewish people is limitless."

After the Austrians left, the teachers, mainly from Galicia, disappeared from town in a hurry. In the chaos, no one thought of the school. Even the teachers who remained had preferred worrying about other matters. Only Berel Taub, even in those days when it was dangerous to go out into the streets, continued going to the school.

"Just because the Austrians left, does that mean we should stop learning with Jewish children?" he argued with his Leiba who begged him to stay home. "Have the religious Jews stopped praying and studying a page of Gmara? Do you mean to say that my portion of Chumash is worth less, or that since the Austrians have left and the Poles have not yet set themselves up, I can pause and not learn with Jewish children a chapter of Yitzchak Leibish Peretz, or a verse by Chaim Nachman Bialik? Do you think that our grandfather Reb Mendele would do differently? She had nothing to say in response. And Leiba, a fine, petite woman, always a worrier, coming from great poverty with which it was difficult for her to deal, already knew that if Reb Berel would take Reb Mendele as a witness, you were stuck. True, every writer holds the title of "rebbe," but he could not manage to utter the name in its simple form. He only rarely mentioned the name Reb Mendele. He was satisfied with the title "zeide" ["grandfather"], and only in exceptional situations did he use the title "the zeide Reb Mendele." He uttered it with such great piety that it would have been pointless to question it – Reb Mendele himself wanted it that way.

She no longer tried to stop him. She knew she could not change him. So, she quietly told him that if he was going out, that for Heaven's sake, remember to give a few classes to the children from the wealthier households as well. This way, he'd earn some money for their family. The poorer children he taught for free.

"You are right, Leiba, very right," he promised her, as he positioned his short–sighted eyes on the cupboard. "It's good you reminded me."

[Page 183]

"I am looking for Motel of Pessie [novel by Sholom Aleichem], that's who I am looking for. I want to turn today into something of a holiday. The children are, so frightened, and they have no one to play with. I am the only one." He sighed as he quietly left the house.

Although the school was not far from his house, Berl did not go there directly, but headed to Garbarnia Street, near the river. From there, up the hill to the distilleries, where the tailors, shoemakers, tinsmiths and carpenters lived, along with the yarn spinners, wagon repairers. He walked slowly, and looked at the squat houses with the half–rotten straw roofs. He knew the houses well, and they were easy to recognize by their signs that were flapping on the broken fences, and by the broken tools that were scattered in front of the houses

He looked around without saying a word. It seemed that he was looking at a rusty barrel at the wagon maker's house, and at the broken wheel in front of the yarn spinner's door, but everyone understood well what he was doing there.

"Teacher Berel just passed by!" one said with excitement to the other.

"Our leader and teacher," the older students called after him, and by the time he came to the school, the hallway was already filled with children who welcomed him with sincere affection.

"Why are you all so quiet, you pranksters?" He took them all into the largest classroom. "Today we will read something beautiful. Sit down and we will hear how Motel of Pessie, the *cantor*'s son became a very big name in America."

"Oh," the group clapped their small hands and Berl's eyes moistened with his heart filled with delight.

As they watched him, the other teachers also returned, which was how they kept the school running during those difficult times.

Shternberg became acquainted with Berel at a meeting in the library. It seemed to be a regular staff meeting. In the darkened library room, there were dozens of young boys and girls, most of whom were standing, quietly listening to the secretary's report.

[Page 184]

On the table lay the official report book along with permission to hold the meeting and was signed by the director himself. From that meeting, it seemed that the number of members was increasing and it became necessary to buy books. Someone would have to travel to Warsaw to buy them because in the nearby city center you could not get anything. They would also need to arrange a literary evening to raise money for purchasing the books. During the discussion, a middle–aged young man with a winding, black beard circling his pale face, almost fell into the room.

"Why are you sitting in the dark?" He closed the door adding, "You know, we will soon be having guests from Ludomir. Some have suggested that this summer we send a few young people as pioneers to *Eretz Yisrael*, so we have to prepare. Oh, are you in the middle of something?" He quickly caught himself and replied, "I am running without catching my breath. I have a plan for building a kibbutz, but I have to get a plot of land." He uncommonly bowed his head, and with the short–sighted eyes looked into the puzzled faces.

"Come closer, our dear teacher," the chairman respectfully invited him to the table, and he asked him, "Perhaps the students did not have to come here. The permit is really for conducting the library meeting. We are not allowed to interfere."

"And not everyone is interested," someone from those standing interjected.

"So, not interested," Berel caught the interferer. "What's the matter, Chaim? Do you think you always have to live in fear of tomorrow, wait for the Messiah as we wallow in the mud?"

"God forbid," the other person argued back. "You have to dry off the mud, and really do it here and now. We are preparing to build here."

"Forgive me," the chairman pleaded. "This is not the place for this [discussion]."

"What do you mean, not the place for this?" The teacher removed his glasses, looking at everyone present with his soft eyes. "Everywhere that Jews are gathered is the right place. You mean that getting the piece of paper from the director was to alert the books in the bookcases? I say, that this is the place to discuss everything, and they," he said pointing to the bookcase,

[Page 185]

"and they teach us that way too. If they waited until the right time and place, nothing would be left of us."

Those present threw glances at each other and could not understand why the teacher, who was always so careful with his words not to offend anyone, was suddenly now so agitated that he was barely looking into their eyes. His pale face was strangely mottled red and he was continuously twitching.

"You need to understand that you are among the first who merit preparing your own redemption." The teacher did not notice how the others were looking at one another.

"Not everyone wants to leave here." Chaim once again could not contain himself. "We want to create our own liberation here, and that time is not so far off as you might think."

"Certainly not," Berel interjected into the other's words. "Who is saying that? We need pioneers here too. You forget that the same kibbutz will be ready for anything, for work and for self–defense," he finally confessed, counting his words. "So, I say, who then, if not you? You have to prepare. Everything you do," he said, lowering his tone, "is also prepared for you. How do we know what will happen to us.? So, I say: Children, prepare yourselves for all possibilities."

The room became uncomfortably quiet. The darkness thickened as if the group of boys and girls were completely swallowed up. The teacher put his glasses back on and smiled in good humor.

"Do not be upset with me. I did not, God forbid, mean to frighten you. I think that you yourselves know well where things are with us. So, I will not disturb you anymore. We will speak about this again," he moved away from the table, "tomorrow at my house."

Not knowing what to do next, the chairman closed the meeting with the suggestion that everyone should leave as quickly as possible, because it was already quite late and the permit allowed them to be out of their homes only until ten at night.

On the way out, Berel went over to Shternberg extending his hand as if he knew him for a long time.

[Page 186]

"I've heard about you."

"I'm very happy," Shternberg replied. "A good group, your students."

"Don't tell them. They'll become arrogant."

"That's not so bad. You ought to be proud of them."

"Why me?" Berel did not release Shternberg's hand. "There is good earth here and a decent cemetery … You can visit there sometime, and you will see how many prestigious names this community has produced. In the 15th century, this community was already called "a city and mother of Israel." Poland and Volyn collaborated and built the town right on banks of the Bug River. It did not just fall from heaven by itself, my friend," he explained with a smile, not without some pride. "The old ancestors in this cemetery have a large share in this room here."

"But they know only you," Shternberg persisted.

"As a teacher, you know that we are only mediators. By the way, do you plan to stay here?" He took Shternberg's arm and veered him outside. "Come to me on Shabbos and we'll talk a little. It might be that I could help you with getting lectures."

"I do not know yet. I would prefer to get a position in a village for the summer," Shternberg said and immediately felt that he had made this decision just that very moment, not knowing exactly why. "I've never been in a village over the summer."

"Are you preparing to study agriculture?"

"I dream of going to *Eretz Yisrael*."

"Very good, so then I am not the only so–called crazy person among the teachers," he added and began to walk quickly, pulling Shternberg along with him. "You know it pains me very much in my heart for these little streets that will be empty when we all leave here. They will not need new houses. The fertile earth will not raise a new generation. It simply will not be. And the old earth will remain infertile. Only in the old cemetery will the great ancestors' roots embrace the old earth with the bittersweet dream, that wherever Jews live is holy land."

"What did you mean before when you said that we need pioneers here too?" Shternberg asked cautiously.

[Page 187]

"You know," Berel suddenly stopped, "do you think that you can let something huge turn to nothing without feeling anything? But there is no choice. I feel that with each moment our strength for living here is weakening, as if we were standing at a crossroad and feel that we are at the edge. From this point on, this is how it is: Either we go on a new route, or we will drown here without a trace. You understand that every time I look into their eyes, I feel like saying: Children, you see the situation. Prepare yourselves for the journey. And I am just looking for a little food for the journey for them."

"Do you intend to stay here?" The question slid off Shternberg's tongue.

"What should I tell you," Berel replied with an unusual sadness as if to himself. "I do not have the strength to start all over, and people will still be needed here. You know maybe I am already too old and can just hold onto an old dream. I think I completely belong here."

"Forgive me for saying this," Shternberg had a feeling that Berel wanted to hear this, "is that why you were so agitated when you were talking about preparing to go to *Eretz Yisrael*?"

"Probably," Berel's voice rang with a fearful sadness and gruesomeness. "What will they protect here? And what can they expect here? These last few years have broken us. Only possessing our own homes will be able to straighten that out." He suddenly put out his hand to say goodbye. "What do you say, Shternberg, will you come on Shabbos? It might be that I will have a place for you in a village. I will ask my friend the village Jew about it. Actually, it is not far from here. Good night!"

"Berel, don't rush off!" the town's "lunatic" appeared from nowhere. "You won't be able to catch Mashiach anyway." He placed himself in the middle of the road, threw his head back, and screamed in an uncanny voice, and with the melody of a selichos song [from the High Holidays]: "Who is the greatest Tzaddik [righteous person] of the generation? Berel Taub! Who will be led to the Akeida ["binding" of Isaac by his father Abraham; also refers to concept of "slaughter"]? Berel Taub!"

The lunatic's voice carried gruesomely into the surrounding moonlit silence.

[Page 188]

It was white everywhere. On the roofs and the small staircases lay slabs of cool moonlight that seemed to lament along with him. "Who will they drag by their ear locks to watch all this? Moshe Motel the madman and the Messiah himself…"

Silently, Shternberg and Berel rushed home, with the madman's laments trailing after them, along with a hateful questioning from the city's night guard and an alarm sounding from the police posts in the middle of the market.

Finally, when Motel the hunchback told everyone that the teacher had a new magazine, many of Berel's former students gathered together on Shabbos afternoon, students from the club "*Hador Hatzair*" ["the young generation"], spending time in discussion and readings. Often, they stayed over until late at night, and in many houses in town they already knew that on Berel's table there now was a large urn, seething with boiling water. Leiba "the Rebbetzin," as the group called her, stood by the dish cabinet, speaking in Hebrew with great passion, and spreading thin slices of bread with American marmalade, which Motel the Hunchback brought as a gift for Shabbos.

Leiba would not allow anyone else to do her work. This is her *mitzvah* and her *nachas* [pride] – that Berel raised such dear, Jewish children. She did not have any children of her own, so Berel filled her house with large groups of children. "Master of the World," she prayed from the depths of her heart. "May there be no Evil Eye on them, the younger generation.

"No, no," she chases them away when they offer to help her. "This is my responsibility as the woman of the house."

"What are we, guests?" the group argues, knowing from the start that they could not win. They did it because they enjoyed arguing with her and giving her the opportunity to speak Hebrew, counting each word as if it were a gold coin.

"True, you are not guests, but one also serves one's own children.... It's as if you really are coming home, but in a respectable home, expressing her deep dissatisfaction with the constant poverty, "you give Shabbos fruit to good children, and here what? A little water, no more...."

[Page 189]

The group did not allow her to continue because they knew that soon she would ask them why each one of them had brought along something decent. One brought a little water, another brought tea. Motel the Huntchback, who was circulating among the group, felt quite at home, since here he was like all the others, having brought some American marmalade.

"Let it be like that, but we are allowed to bring a few things." They wanted to win this argument. "You don't have to serve us even with the food at the table."

"Foolish children," she finally laughed, and her pale face began to flush. "What else should I do, learn with you? Go in good health to the Rabbi's table."

The group understood this look and they left the kitchen. They knew that Berel was unhappy if anyone sneaked out from under the table in the middle of a reading.

The afternoon passed quickly in Berel's house. Shternberg could not read enough of the new magazine that he found there. He was too wrapped up in his readings to notice what was going on around him. He did not hear the discussions, and missed hearing the new story that was read from the new issue of "Zukunft" ["Future"] that arrived that week. He did not see how the group actually inhaled a piece of America with the new story, and did not feel their shudder with the story's tragic ending. He was preoccupied with himself and forgot everything else. Only when it was time for tea and a bite to eat did the hostess manage to draw him away from the magazine.

"He was so attracted, sadly, like a thirsty person is to water," she politely said. "Do something for the sinning body, for the throat, I mean, Mr. Shternberg. Your palate must be dry by now. I shouldn't have to beg you."

"Take something in your mouth," Berel said, now cheerful as always when his students were around him, supporting the homemaker, so to speak, and he pushed an article from the newspaper in front of Shternberg. "You see, here you have a story by Bergelson, describing a town that is emptying itself.

[Page 190]

"He clearly saw the doom, but failed to hear the sadness of the destruction that remained. It even gave him some strength."

"Bergelson's town leaves for America," one of the students interjected. "They leave one at a time, and don't have the vision of building something new. They are simply running away from poverty."

"So, what can be learned from this, Yehuda?" Berel stared with his soft eyes at a young boy with strong shoulders and a stubborn, pointy chin.

"I think," Yehuda shook his ear locks and nervously moved in his chair, "I think they are running away and the town is completely falling apart. Those who remain are simply lazy."

"I still do not understand." Berel was still looking at him, and the student was becoming even more nervous under Berel's gaze, and could not sit calmly on the chair.

"It's hard for me to explain. But I feel that when we will leave with the group to *Eretz Yisrael* we will empty out the town here. But those who will remain here will continue living with our hope."

"Do you think that the loneliness will be easy here?"

"Is there any other way?" said Chayale, the *Dayan's* daughter, her face changing with excitement. "Lately, I don't understand you, our Teacher," she struggled to hold back her words. "Why should we care about the ruins that will remain? The faster they fall apart, the better. They should not be left as witnesses to our departure. Every little street and mountain of trash is filled with the fear and dejection of all of us."

"You are still young, Chayale." Berel stood up from his chair and began to race around the dark room, and his long, dark shadow followed him around the curved walls. "And precisely because of that, the fear and dejection are here with us in every corner. But there is also in every corner, our dream and truth, body and life. If you tear it up, then blood runs."

"But do we have a choice here? Where?" Chayale followed him angrily.

"A choice?" A hoarse shout came from behind them, and everyone went right back to the corner, where the very large Boruch'ke was sitting– a quiet young man whose eyes spoke more than his dulled lips. Generally, he sat among the group for hours and did not open his mouth, but sometimes it happened that he woke up and words poured out from him, hot and furious, as if he was on fire. His black eyes sparkled with an eerie sheen and his closely shorn head of hair spiked up like a porcupine. You had to hear him out completely and not interrupt. Everyone heard his words, his pale lips became sharp, and you could have thought that not he was speaking, but all of his limbs were expressing themselves.

[Page 191]

"Of all the options, you chose to leave everything behind, and you want to convince yourself that this is right by polishing it with nice words and beautiful figures of speech," as if spewing lightning all around with his black eyes. "I also think that we have to organize ourselves, but not only to leave. We have to chase away the black devils from here, and who should do this, if not us?"

"How do you think this should be done, Boruch'ke?" Berel tried to calm him down.

"We have to organize ourselves and not be frightened," Boruch'ke remarked to his teacher, "and give back beating for beating. You hear? Strike back. Do not allow ourselves to be trampled upon like worms. They are beating only us. They are choking the farmer and punishing him." He grew short of breath and started choking on his words. "There will be a big change this summer. Things will not stay the way they are now."

"By the time we resolve this, our souls will have left us," Chaya said standing opposite him. "And even our good friends do not want us here any longer. There comes a time when a Jewish settlement has to uproot itself regardless if "they" want to or not. Now it's our turn, Boruch'ke," she burst out at once. "And the great fortunes of the 'other side' we've also seen." She laughed bitterly, intimating at Boruch'ke's connection to the more radical "leftist movements."

"A little calmer, children." Berel realized that the discussion had gone too far and he approached Boruch'ke.

"Chaya, I think," Boruch'ke did not allow himself to be put off; "I think that we are standing along with everyone else. Not everyone is able to flee."

[Page 192]

"And I believe in building your own home. You are just dragging yourself after others," Chaya shouted over Berel who was standing between them.

"Of course, you believe, and meanwhile you are seeing the ruins and running away from them."

"And you don't see that it could be possible that everyone should stay, but we will all be eventually destroyed…"

"Both of you mean well, children," Leiba mixed in. "One could think that you are lifelong enemies, the way you jump on each other."

"It seems that you have forgotten that nowadays walls have ears," someone tossed out to both sides.

"They believe both sides." Berel gave a bitter smile and spoke as if to himself and then he sat down. "That's how it is with all discussions. You start from one point but you wander off to unknown realms. What do you have to say, Shternberg?" He was lost and turned to Shternberg as if saying to him: "Do you see what is going on here?"

"Is it like this only today?" Shternberg wanted to shift the discussion to another subject. "I am sure that when it will be necessary, both sides will do what they have to."

"Which means…? Berel was curious.

"Fight here when you can, and flee when you have to."

"But we want to build!"

"There is no building without a fight!" The discussion heated up once again, but this time Leiba mixed in without any niceties:

"And meanwhile none of you has tasted anything. And have not even sung a song. Our guest might think that it is always so heated here, always jumping at each other. You should be ashamed of yourselves, children."

"That's fair, Leiba, we will yet see *nachas* from all of them." Berel recovered his equilibrium, and with a smile, looked into everyone's eyes. "Have a bite everyone, and stop looking like angry chickens. Somewhere I read about two important people who fought each other all their lives and could not even look into each other's eyes. Only when they got older and met at some festive occasion, one stretched out his hand to the other and they kissed. So, someone later told this story about them.

[Page 193]

"In their younger years, they both went out to dig a tunnel that would connect their nation to the world, but each one dug from another side. So, they did not see one another's work, and thus became each other's enemy. Only now, at the end of their lives, they met in the middle of the tunnel and saw each other in their true light…"

"Listen here, children," an excited Leiba began again in elegant Hebrew, "and learn from this example here. When the tunnel will be ready you will meet and stretch out your hands, like they did."

"They can stretch out their hands even now." Motel the Huntchback felt that the time had come to put in a good joke. So, he lifted up his humps and danced over to Boruch'ke and jerked him out of his corner: "Go over, you animal, and ask for forgiveness of the future mother of your children," he said loudly that which everyone already knew, that the two were not indifferent to each other. The group roared with laughter and the heavy mood suddenly lightened up. Someone began singing a happy melody, and slowly the dark room filled with quiet song, and the now happy, youthful gathering made them forget everything around them.

"So, what do you say? Will we ever be proud of them?" Berel Taub asked Shternberg almost secretly as they were about to part for the evening.

"You mean that you are already proud of them."

"You are making a mistake, my friend. My heart trembles with fear for what awaits them."

"But they have what it takes to survive in the world."

"If only that were true," Berel, thought to himself, squeezing Shternberg's hand. "And did you really decide to take on a position in the village? You could also set yourself up here."

"But I already promised."

"That's too bad. We could really have used you here."

"It's not far from here. I can come to the city often. I enjoy walking."

[Page 194]

"Fine, so be it. Don't forget us when you get to the city."

"Thank you so much. It's a pleasure." Shternberg squeezed his hand with sincere gratitude.

He did not leave right away, but rather stood there a while watching the teacher with his last few students in a quiet conversation, leaning on one of the house's support columns. An unusual feeling of sadness overcame him. He was nearly certain that he was seeing them for the last time, which evoked painful longings.

"Come, friend Shternberg." Leibel pulled him over. "Our Berel has created a fine group. I `am so jealous of him for that. We will yet hear about them in the future."

"Certainly." Shternberg was still preoccupied with the nagging feeling of sadness. "A fine youth was raised, sadly, a really fine youth."

"What do you mean 'sadly,' friend Shternberg?" Leibel shivered.

"I don't know myself. It just came out [of my mouth]. Don't take it to heart. I am always the one to be gloomy. I'm sure it will all turn out well."

"And I think the exact opposite." Leibel thought he knew what was bothering Shternberg. "You have to be proud of this kind of youth. They will accomplish great things. Right?"

"That depends on them. The problem with us is that we think it depends on us and we act as if we could be in charge of that thing."

"Does that mean that we are being pulled with the tide?"

"And we think that we swim alone..." Shternberg just blurted out those words.

"But it could be that our generation will succeed in gaining control over our lives..." Leibel explained himself.

"Let us hope, my friend, that we are still bosses over ourselves." Shternberg began to take leave. "Thank you for everything, Leibel."

"Go safely, and let's hear from you!" They embraced like brothers.

[Page 195]

The Phenomenal *Matmid*[1]

by Baruch Goldberg

Translated by Zvi Kaniel

The following translations were commissioned by Avigail Frij, whose maternal grandparents were from Ustilug (Kopp and Kultin Families)

Tear for Moshe Shpirer, may his blood be avenged.

Of all the positive figures mentioned in my previous article, I particularly got to know the phenomenal student Moshe Shpirer. My first experience with him came about in the following manner: In my childhood years, since they used to bring us all kinds of craft works from the Betzalel school in *Eretz Yisrael*, my favorite was a small siddur with small panels of hard wood that were decorated with a Magen David, upon which was written "*Zion*" and "*Yerushalayim*." I could have made the panels myself, but could not have printed the words. My father took me to Moshe Yankel Geillis (as he was known at that time) in the Blodovker *Shtiebel*, where we prayed together, and then he drew the letters for me. From that time on, we remained close until the bitter end.

I knew Moshe so well, because he was my teacher and served as a role model on how to avoid wasting time with useless things. For this reason, I consider it my right and obligation to write some of the events in his life as a memorial to him and for future generations. It is important to know what valuable people our town possessed, people who were slain in a horrific manner by the Nazi murderers.

Moshe was born – according to my calculation – in the year 1894. His father, Shmuel, who came from Dubyenka, was a grain producer. His mother, Gelle, was the daughter of Yankel Geillis, who would not speak any mundane "weekday" words on Shabbat. Until 1914, they lived in the village of Treszczanko, but Moshe always lived in Ustiluh at his grandfather's home, learned in the local Heders. He was, however, under the constant supervision of his uncle, the enlightened person] and teacher Shloime Kanat.

[Page 196]

Moshe's tourist status quickly ended, and he soon received his own visitor's card [permit]. He became a teacher, like his Uncle Shloime.

Together with some other teachers, they opened the first modern school in Ustiluh where the young Moshe had the opportunity to demonstrate his considerable teaching skills. Moshe taught others while at the same time educated himself. He devoured all the Hebrew books from the Shtiebel submissions, along with all the original Russian classics. At one point, he decided to become a literary expert. He threw himself into this endeavor with all his study skills and with the added assistance of correspondence lectures from St. Peterburg. He once offered me the opportunity to study with him. But I could not accept his offer. First, I was far below Moshe's level of general knowledge, and of Russian language in particular. Second, my father decided to send me to Warsaw under the supervision of my older brother Yitzchak, to learn a trade. I left for the capital city. When, after two years, I returned home, I found Moshe a changed person.

For various reasons, he had to terminate his correspondence with St. Petersburg, but meanwhile, he had memorized the contents of the book she read.

This came to good use for him in the "*Beit Hasefer*" as well as in private lectures.

The young teacher maintained his modest lifestyle for fifteen years. During WWI, when the Austrian army took over our town, economic life broke down. This also brought the closure of the *Beit Hasefer*. Along with the rest of the population, Moshe, his parents and sister, endured much hunger. Furthermore, the Austrians pressed people into forced labor, while some were conscripted into the army. Others fled to wherever they could. Some in the village, some in Beliankin's yard, or simply in the forests, where they used to weave fences for the military. Yisrael, the son of Yossel Kiser and I, left for Ludomir, and worked as carpenters in Wolf Yokenzon's warehouse. But Moshe was nowhere to be found. He hid in his grandfather's attic, only coming into contact with his family. But this turned out well for him. He diligently studied the German language that he was later able to put to good use. When the town slowly began to get involved with wartime conditions, people were looking to acquire some merchandise to satisfy at least to some degree, the town's needs.

[Page 197]

This was impossible without obtaining a permit from the military official in charge of the city, to move about in town, except to the edges of town. Suddenly, knowing how to write in German became a vital necessity. Until now, the official "petition" writers were not so well skilled. Now, Moshe Shpirer's German writing skills were in high demand.

Although he wrote for individuals, he mainly wrote to advance community interests. And what writing it was! A high–level literary style that evoked amazement from the new "businessmen." They invited him to meet them so they could get to know him personally, but Moshe did not go. He was a skilled writer, but not such a good conversationalist. Other than that Moshe suffered from a physical problem: He was a bit deaf and he feared they might laugh at him or make light of him. For that reason, he strove to remain in the background, often avoiding unknown company. I remember a certain lieutenant, who lived at the home of Moshe Frishberg (metal dealer), who, after visiting him, highly praised his writing talent.

Sometime later, a Polish priest found out about Shpirer, the one who knew German, and offered him a teaching exchange: Moshe would teach him German, and the priest would teach Moshe Polish. Moshe accepted the deal.

I don't know how well the priest advanced in his German studies, but Moshe certainly learned Polish well. Many people attested to his later Polish language writings during the time of the government uprising.

In 1919, Moshe published a one–time newspaper (handwritten) containing several important articles that he had written. He convinced me to contribute something as well, and I did. My article, of a humorous nature, was entitled "An Overheard Discussion." The newspaper was passed around from hand to hand, and when Nachman Burlyant traveled to North America, he took the newspaper with him.

For a short time, he worked in the Polish congress (I believe in Lublin), where he had successful surgery on his ears. After recovering, he stepped up his social life. In particular, he became the director of the Mizrachi movement that had just recently opened in town.

[Page 198]

Thanks to him, this movement was largely accepted in the Chassidic circles, to which Moshe, as a deeply religious person, felt a strong loyalty. As strange as it seems, we must understand that Moshe was a different type of intellectual than typical irreligious types they knew. He did not shave with a razor [in accordance with Jewish law] but used an electric shaver. His clothing and his overall deportment followed Orthodox customs. He did not scorn Jewish religious practices, like most of the non–religious General Zionists, let alone the leftist Zionist parties.

At that time, the *Beit Sefer* was reopened by a group of teachers, among whom Moshe held the most prominent position. Even though the Polish government sent a supervisor to the school, the educational program followed a Jewish national spirit, and over the years, the number of young people who had both Jewish and general knowledge increased.

In 1929, when I left for the second time to Argentina, we parted very warmly. Even though we followed different paths in life, we continued to correspond occasionally.

In his last letter to me, he asked me to speak to a particular family, and remind them that they owed Moshe for some writing he did for them that assisted them in immigrating to Argentina. Then the family was unable to pay him, and now they would pay off the debt ten–fold. Except that now, there was no one to deal with the debt, because Moshe and his family along with most of the Jews of Ustiluh had been so horrifically murdered.

In conclusion, I would like to say a few words that emanate from depths of my heart:

Dear teacher and friend Moshe! I don't know where your physical remains are, so let these few written words about you be the memorial that will remain for eternity.

Translator's Footnote:

1. Diligent Yeshiva student

[Page 199]

Nachman Burlyant, Z"L
In memory of a *Landsman*, Friend, and Cousin

by Tzila Fleisher

Translated by Zvi Kaniel

Nachman was born in 1895 in Ustiluh. His father – an educated Jew, was, for a long time acted as the town mayor. Later, he became the head bookkeeper, in effect, the director of the People's Bank.

Their home was more elegant than many of the others. Their children were well educated, even attending the high school in the nearby city of Ludomir, which, before WWI, was an unusual feat. Young Nachman could not attend the gymnasium because the World War had broken out, which upended normal life for the children, along with everyone else. But Nachman studied with special effort on his own, and thus kept up with his studies. In addition, Nachman was an extraordinarily good–natured person who was always ready to help the sick and the needy.

[Page 200]

I remember during our childhood years, when, on the way home after school, the children would sometimes get into fights. Nachman always stood up for the weaker one. In later years, once on a Shabbos evening, we went to accompany a friend home. She lived on the other side of the Stav River Bridge. Suddenly, we were attacked by boys from Danches Street. Nachman, walking with friends on the hill, heard our shouts, and ran over to help us. When we got older, and began to occupy ourselves with societal activities, the difference between the "cultural" and "material" was made. Nachman was of the "material" ones. That does not mean that he did not appreciate culture, but he argued that "if there is no bread, there is no Torah." First you have to help the poor people and only afterwards can you build libraries and other cultural associations. He was, in fact, active in the drama section and in all other societal activities in the city.

In 1920, when the mass exit of the youth began, Nachman and his brother also left Ustiluh, heading to the United States. He returned after a few years and married Sarah Yokhenzon and had a child. Nachman, however, could no longer live in Poland. Growing anti–Semitism was in the streets and in the government and this forced Nachman back to the United States. After a while, he succeeded in bringing over his wife and child.

In the United States, Nachman replanted his social activities and became one of the leaders of the Ustiluh relief committees.

At the beginning of 1945, we received a letter from Nachman, that we should connect with Ustiluh survivors wherever they were. The committee would send them aid because it was easier to contact them from Israel. Their son Pinchas was also interested in the fate of his compatriots. “The actions of the fathers are a symbol for the children” [Book of Genesis]. I heard a lot about this when I was their guest in the United States.

In his last years, Nachman suffered from heart disease, but he ignored it, refusing to abandon his activities.

On July 19, 1960, after a heart attack, his good, refined heart stopped beating.

May his memory be honored and blessed!

[Page 201]

For God and For People

by Malka Chometzki (Reiz), Brazil

Translated by Zvi Kaniel

Our place of birth, the town of Ustiluh was destroyed by the Nazi savages and by local Ukrainian murderers. Yet it always stands before my eyes with its beloved Jews, and the beautiful, intelligent youth, with whom I spent my younger years.

I well remember the hard work and difficult conditions in which they were raised. I can never forget that in my family, paying tuition fees for my brothers' education was more important than food on the table. My dear, beloved father, Shalom Chazzan, of blessed memory, earned just a few rubles, changed it for a golden ten [coin], and put it away to pay the tuition fees. And if, Heaven forbid, no other income would be earned to make Shabbos, we would be without meat and fish… as the Shalom Aleichem saying goes, you can make something tasty even from an onion.

I remember, once on a Friday night, a fire broke out in which dozens of houses burned down and hundreds of souls were left without a roof over their heads. Friends and relatives came forward to gather the homeless into their homes. Our family went to Moshe Burlyant, the mayor of the town.

At the Shabbos table, my father sang the Shabbos songs as usual. Eidel, the wife of Moshe Burlyant, a relative of my father, while she served the food, asked, “How can a Jew sing so joyfully when he just lost all his belongings?” My father answered, “That's exactly why I am happy. Because my entire fortune is sitting here around the table.” That meant that he left behind all his worries for the weekdays and not for Shabbat.

Simple, warm friendship marked the relationship between Ustiluh's Jewish residents.

[Page 202]

I remember in particular the Rosmarin family. One day our dear friend Brontzia had not seen even one person from our family. In the middle of her chores, she locked her door and came over to see if, Heaven forbid, someone was sick.

I could describe many memories of my dear town Ustiluh, but I am sure others will do so with greater skill. So, may I be permitted, in my simple words, to express my great pain and deep anguish about the horrifying deaths of our martyrs, among whom are: my brother Avram'ke and his wife and three children, my sister Faigie Perlmutter, her husband and three children, and so many other relatives of ours. Our large, extended family was murdered by the Nazis. May their blood be avenged.

Faigie and her family

[Page 203]

Avraham (Avrom'ke) Reiz
Founder and First Director of the Drama Circle

by Tzila

Translated by Zvi Kaniel

After his sister Malka has already given a brief character sketch of their father Reb Shalom Chazan, may he rest in peace, and his blessed optimism, all that is left for me to add is that this optimistic spirit was a feature of the entire Reiz household.

Their home was always bright and cheerful. You could not know if a rich man or a pauper lived there. The children were taught in the same way as the children of wealthier families and were dressed the same as the others.

Avram'ke, the oldest and brightest, left to the capital city Warsaw where he worked in a dry goods store. In his free time, he devoted himself to cultural and scientific studies.

[Page 204]

He attended musical and literary evenings and made acquaintances in all the various literary circles.

He would come back to Ustiluh for the holidays when he would share his impressions of the big city with his friends.

During the First World War, after he came home for one of the holidays, he was unable to return to Warsaw. Then his cultural activities began to flourish in town.

"The Wild Man"

He first created a cultural group that held literary and musical evenings. The income from those gathering was used to fund other cultural activities. Later, he organized a drama club. The first piece that they performed under his direction was "Mirele Efros". After that, they performed many other plays by Yaakov Gordin, Peretz Hirschbein, Shalom Aleichem, and so on.

[Page 205]

After his marriage, Avram'ke lived in Kharkov, where he built himself a beautiful home. There, too, he continued with cultural activities until the horrible end. Avram'ke and his family were massacred together with the rest of the community.

דראמאטישע סעקציע אוסטילה

מוצאי שבועות דען 5 יוני 1919

דער איינטראג איז בעשטימט פאר די ארימע

פ ר א ג ר א ם

I.

חאשע די יתומה

א דראמע אין 4 אקטען פון י ע ק ב ג א ר ד י ן

פ ע ר ז א נ ע ן :

יואיל טראכטינבערג איין רייכער קויפמאן — ה״ים בארליאנט

פריידע זיין ווייב — — — — — — עטיל קוואסעוויצער

וולאדימיר זייער זוהן — — — — — נחמן בארליאנט

קאראלינע זייער טאכטער — — — — שרה יוהענזאהן

מאטיע שטרייבעל. פריידעס א שוואגער א דארפס יוד — נחמיה קאלטאן

חאשע זיין טאכטער א יתומה — — — — טויבה סטאוו

מארק קאראלינעס חתן — — — — — שלמה שלעכטער

פאשא א קאמערמעדיל ב״י טראכטינבערגין — בליומה שיינבראן

יונגע לייט, מאמזעלין

ע ס ק י מ ט פ א ר א י ן י ע ק א ט ע ר י נ א ס ל א ו.

סאפליאר מ ש ה ב ר י ף.

II.

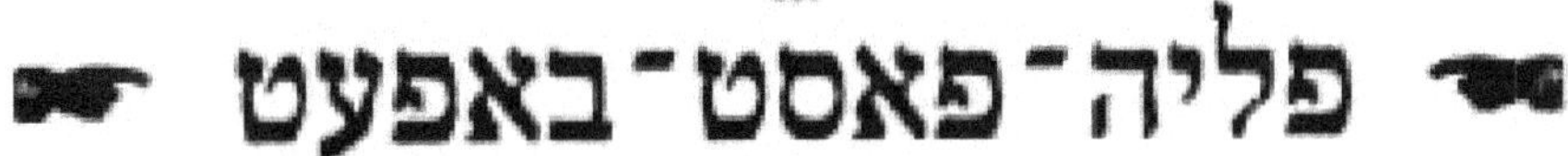

Ustiluh Drama Group

Translated by Ala Gamulka

End of Shavuot, June 5, 1919
All proceeds dedicated to the Poor

Program

I.

Chashe the Orphan

A drama in 4 acts, by Yaakov Gordin

Cast:

Yoel Trachtenberg, a wealthy businessman	Haim Burlyant
Freida, his wife	Etel Kvassevitzer
Vladimir, their son	Nachman Burlyant
Carolina, their daughter	Sarah Yokhenzon
Motya Shtreibel, Frieda's brother–in–law, a village Jew	Nechemia Koltun
Chashe, his orphaned daughter	Toybe Stav
Mark, Carolina's fiancée	Shlomo Schlachter
Fasha, Trachtenberg maid	Bluma Sheinborn

Young boys and girls

Performed in Ekaterinoslav

Arranged by Moshe Brif

II. Discrimination–Post–Buffet

Program: Chashe, the Orphan 1919

[Page 206]

אמאטארען־אבענד

אויסגעפיהרט דורך דער יוגענד אין אוסטילע.
ערשטע נאכט חוה"מ פסח תר"פ 4/IV 1920

דער איינטראג איז בעשטימט פיר קולטור

פראגראם

I.

דער ווילדער מענש

א לעבענסבילד אין 5 אקטען און 1 פערוואנדלונג
פון יעקב גארדין

פערזאנען:

שמואל לייבליך, א רייכער וויצהענדלער	פישעל אייזענבערג
ליזא, א האלב־ענטוויקעלט מיידעל	טויבע סטאוו
זימאן, גימנאזיסט	יעקב גרינבערג
אלכסנדר, גלאט א נאר־ניש	מרדכי פליישער
למך, אידיאט	פישעל נידערבערג
שפרה, א דינסט	רבקה בלאנדער
זעלדע, זיין צווייטע פרוי	בתיה בורליאנט
וולאדימיר וואראביישיק, זעלדעס געליעבטער	נחמן בורליאנט
פייוועל גאלדשטיין, ליזעס געליעבטער	שלמה שיינערמאן

זשוליקעס, סטודענטען
ארט דער האנדלונג — אדעס
סופליאר — חיים בורליאנט

II.

מוזיק, כאר, פליה־פאסט, בופעט.

[Page 207]

"The Wild Man"

Translated by Ala Gamulka

Organized by the youth of Ustiluh

First evening of Hol HaMoed Pessach, 4/1920

Proceeds dedicated to cultural activities

Program

The Wild Man

A life story in 5 acts and 1 transformation

By Yaakov Gordin

Cast:

Shmuel Leiblich, a wealthy merchant	Fishel Eisenberg
Liza, his semi–retarded daughter	Toybe Stav
Ziman, his son, a high school student	Yaakov Grinberg
Alexander, his son, a nothing	Mordechai Fleisher
Lemach, his son, the idiot	Fishel Giderberg
Shifra, a maid	Rivka Blander
Zelda, his second wife	Batya Burlyant
Vladimir Voroveitchik, Zelda's love	Nachman Burlyant
Feivel Goldshteyn, Liza's lover	Shlomo Shinerman

Rascals, students

Stage manager– Odes

Organizer–Haim Burlyant

II.

Music, Choir, Buffet

A Vanished Dream
(from a letter to friends and former neighbors)

by Eliezer Reiz, Brazil

Translated by Zvi Kaniel

… As a vanished dream I wish to describe those sweet times. My memories carry myself back to our small home town of Ustiluh, a town like many other towns in Volyn –Ukraine, whose Jews were merchants, shopkeepers, craftsmen, village peddlers, along with those who worked in religious occupations. They struggled to earn a living, but were always filled with faith and trust in Hashem. Even under the most difficult economic situations, they did not lose strength, and stubbornly faced the future. They carried the heavy yoke of the exile with the hope for Mashiach and the return to Zion. Life was sweet despite their poverty.

I remember the beautiful Shabbos and the holidays: "The heartfelt sounds of praying and learning that were heard from the synagogues, Shtiebels, and Study Halls. The prayers, melodies, and Shabbos and holiday songs that used to fill the streets brought the Jews a sense of pride, a connection to Hashem and their own souls. I well remember the large Study Hall where my father Shalom, the *cantor*, led the morning prayers on the High Holidays. My older brother Avram'ke and I were his choir, and my mother Bayle– or Shlom'ke, as she was called – would gaze from the balcony of the women's section, melting with pride.

I remember the narrow, small shul and its congregants – simple, hardworking Jews, and how my father sang the Rosh Hashana and Yom Kippur Musaf prayers. My brother Avram'ke, who, with his sweet tenor voice, would sing out loud the "*haben yakir li Efraim*" ["my precious son Efraim"], and "*ve'al hamedinot bo ye'amer,*" and the holy silence that reigned among these devout people; the love and gratitude that shone from their eyes towards the exceptionally talented young boy.

My brother Avram'ke! He sang in the Warsaw Hazamir choir, was a bookkeeper in a store. When he came home for Pesach he usually brought along some new songs, sayings, and happenings. These fresh ideas reinvigorated the town, making her more joyful and festive during the holidays.

[Page 208]

And who could forget my sister Faigie, the pretty face and genteel manners and enormous will to study!

I remember the first *Beit Hasefer* [school] that was created. Despite the fact that my father was the city's *cantor* and a Trisker Chassid, I was one of the first children who registered in the school. This was despite the desire of many teachers who wanted to scare off the religious parents because of their modern (often "heretical" views). With particular respect, I want to mention the teachers Shloime Kanat, Shmerl Sekular, and Moshe Kornfeld, who lived in Milwaukee. Shloime Kanat, the genius in town, and Shmerl Sekular, and Moshe Kornfeld, now in Milwaukee. Shlomo Kanat was the genius of the town and Shmerl Sekular, fully devoted to Hashem. He was a studious learner who was willing to go hungry so that he could buy a new religious book and then sit all night studying it.

Shlomo Kanat with his daughter Mindel and grandson

[Page 209]

Today, before my eyes, there stand the scholars of the Trisk *Shtiebel*, the ritual slaughterers Leibtzi and Avrom'ele, our modern and shining Rav, Reb Yossel Wertheim; the city patron Wolf Yokhenzon, would come to the *siyum*[1] carrying his *Maseches Brachot*[2], and his wife Sheindel, a very charitable woman. She gave charity discretely, helped brides marry, and gave charity for all kinds of communal needs; our good friend Moshe Yekes and Brontzia, and their extended family; and all the wonderful neighbors. A shudder of horror passes through me when remembering that all this, along with thousands of other Jewish communities, are gone, so tragically destroyed by the Germans and their collaborators, may their memory be erased. We are not allowed to forget them. We have to try to continue their unfinished lives, and their images must always remain before us. May Hashem bless those who, through publishing these Yizkor books, create a permanent monument, a gravestone for future generations of what once was. Let the world know of the unspeakable crime that they endured. I am sure that one day, some great spiritual writer will find a way to express this great tragedy and the anger at the destruction of European Jewry.

Translator's Footnotes:

1. Celebration of completing a *masechet* (tractate) or the entire Shas.

2. The first tractate in the Shas.

[Page 210]

The Ustiluh Youth – From 1917 to 1922

by Chaim Weinshel, Milwaukee

Translated by Zvi Kaniel

I take to writing the memories of Ustiluh with a heavy heart. I look at a picture of a class in the Yiddish *Folkshule*. It is 1917 and the question is: Where are all those people who we see in the picture? Here another photo, a picture of "*Hador Hatzair*" ("The Young Generation"), 1919. How many of those in the picture were still alive after the war? That is the feeling with each picture from those times. The anger grows, permitting no rest. But you strengthen yourself to concentrate and continue writing.

I will not write about the physical attributes of the city. even Hashem was good to Ustiluh bestowing upon it two beautiful rivers – Lug and Bug – with lush forests around the city. But the anti–Semitic atmosphere created by the Polish–Ukrainian populace did not create any great love for all this.

I left Ustiluh and went to the United States in August 1922. So I will just describe the youth of those years of which I was a part. No doubt many of those who lived in Ustiluh will write about the earlier and later generations since they are naturally more familiar with those times.

In Ustiluh there lived a large intellectual group. One can say the same for the children and youth of that time. They were nationalistically inclined, proud, and knowledgeable in Jewish matters. One example that comes to mind is an incident that I feel is unequalled, and is worth describing. This happened some time in 1916–17. During World War One, when Ustiluh was under Austrian occupation, the Jewish *Folkshule* was headed by Captain Kimmel, who forced

[Page 211]

upon us students a great deal of German and Polish studies at the expense of Yiddish and Hebrew. Those of us in the highest grade – fourth, I believe – went on strike. When Captain Kimmel came into our classroom and began to study a certain subject with us, every single one of us refused to respond to his lecture. We told him that we would not study German and Polish subjects unless they would give us more time for Yiddish studies. And we won.

A class in the school in 1917

It was the same youth who, sometime later, founded "*Hador Hatzair*" and conducted Zionist activities in town. They participated in the "Flower Days" parade, marching through the streets on the day of Herzl's yahrzeit, along with other Zionist demonstrations, and went to every wedding to collect money for Keren Kayemet. They also founded a library, and anxiously awaited every new book that arrived from Warsaw, especially the publications of the publishing house *Shtiebel*. There were also readings and lectures on Shabbat afternoons

[Page 212]

Another incident, that even though it ended in tragedy, deserves mentioning. This happened toward the end of WWI when the German and Austrian revolutions[1] broke out and the occupying government collapsed and fled back to Austria. Ustiluh was left without a governing power, so the local Jews created a militia to maintain order in the city. In time, a small number of Polish soldiers took over the government and occupied the region for the Polish government. The occupying Austrian forces left behind many horses and other animals, and a great deal of food. Most of this was seized by the Polish gentiles, while only a few Jews managed to obtain some of these things. After some of the Polish soldiers had entered the city, the Polish gentiles told them that the Jews had taken everything. The Polish soldiers demanded a large sum of money from the Jews as compensation. The Jews argued that most of the merchandise was grabbed by the non–Jews; Jews only took only a few things. But the soldiers refused to budge and issued an ultimatum to the Jews requiring them to pay a large sum of money within a few days. They also arrested a number of important townspeople. There were not many Polish soldiers and the Jews had an armed militia. Many argued that they should not give in, but should resist this attempted extortion. Although the Jews did resist, unfortunately, they were ill–prepared for such a confrontation. The result was thirteen Jewish fatalities and many wounded.

Regarding the youth movements, the "*Hador Hatzair*" group later created a branch of *Zeirei Zion*. The entry requirements of this group were so strict that many in the group claimed they were older than they actually were in order to join the group. This branch was very active, and in a short time became the leading branch of Zeirei Zion in the area. The founders of the party would often send its leaders to visit the Ustiluh branch. E.g., Koltun, Shvalba and others.

[Page 213]

In Ustiluh in those times, 1918–1919, there was an exceptional drama group for adults. But we also wanted to perform in the theater. Although we were only 14–16 years old, we considered ourselves experienced adult performers who, in fact, used to perform in the *Folkshule* theater. So, we created our own youth drama circle. Over the years, we performed many plays. I remember only a few of them: "The Destruction of Jerusalem" by Yosef Lateiner, 1919; "Yeshiva Student" by Zlotorewski; "The Carcass" and "The Intellectual), by Peretz Hirschbein, 1922. The group had many talented actors. For instance, Schlachter, a very talented comic; Hinde Zak, a natural character performer; Bluma Sheinborn, a fine dramatic performer; along with several others. I am certain that under more favorable circumstances, part of the group would have contributed more to the Yiddish theater.

In 1920, part of the youth studied with the teacher Kloper, in preparation to advance to higher education. We went to Ludomir for the exams. Interestingly all of us Jews failed the exams, and all the non–Jews passed....

For the next few years, until my departure for America in 1922, we were active in two main areas. We performed in the theater, and worked diligently for the rebuilding of *Eretz Yisrael*. But, the anti–Semitic atmosphere in Poland at that time constantly put forward vast challenges to Jewish existence. We did not see a future for us in Poland. Whenever some opportunity arose, the Poles wrecked it. This is why part of that generation scattered to all corners of the earth, including Eretz Yisrael. The majority, however, remained in Poland, only to perish later at the hands of the German murderers.

[Page 214]

"Hador Hatzair" ["The Young Generation"], year 1919

Translator's Footnote:

1. The German Revolution was a civil conflict in the German Empire at the end of the First World War that resulted in the replacement of the German federal constitutional monarchy with a democratic parliamentary republic that later became known as the Weimar Republic. In Austria, there were mass strikes and mutinies after which the Habsburg monarchy collapsed.

[Page 215]

Links in a Chain
(Lines and memories)

by Bernard Ginsburg

Translated by Ala Gamulka

It was September 9, 1939, after Germany attacked Poland and after daily air bombardments on our new home- Zamshtat. There were many victims, physical destruction and economic chaos. We decided to return to Ustiluh. However, Ustiluh, only 70 kilometers out of Zamshtat, was not easy to reach. Our voyage took 5 days. We could only travel at night since the German airplanes were the absolute rulers. All the roads were controlled from the air and bombs were dumped everywhere.

The mood in Hrobishov was strained. It was full of activity. The military authorities had held back long rows of horses and wagons. There was difficulty, or even impossibility to reach Kovel through the Bug River. It was a hot day. The tongue was dry with thirst. The crying of the women and children was mixed with the neighing of the horses. The air was filled with a wild tumult, charged and empirical.

It was not easy for us to convince the military forces that we were returning home.

Not far from Ustiluh, on the dusty Khotiatchov road, we met a man from the Vinehauser family. He was happy to see us because he could talk to someone on his way home. He said to my father:

Oy. Mister Akiva. How are you? You are back from Zamshtat. Eh? How are things there? Here it is terrible. People are being caught and taken to work- to dig trenches. Yesterday, one of us was killed. A German airplane dropped a bomb not far from the men who were working near the railroad… God help us! You do not see any Polish airplanes to help us. What will be?

[Page 216]

"What will it really be?"- was the burning question asked by the simple Vinehauser man -to be answered by the world…
The streets of Ustiluh were empty. The population is worried. There is unrest and insecurity.

Truthfully, the Jews should have been on the side of Poland- naturally united against Hitler. However, years of anti-Semitic tradition, cultivated by Polish authorities almost until the last day, did not allow the Poles to see the facts. Is it a wonder, then, that the Jews felt the real danger from Hitler's Germany with acute sensitivity?

The naïve ones wondered: Is Germany really so brutal towards the Jews? Will they dare to apply their racist program? However, there is no danger in hiding your head in the sand. It is clear- this is not a happy situation.

The German army is advancing. The higher Polish officers run away to Romania and leave the people without leadership.

No matter what will happen – the situation for Jews is dire for another reason- the Ukrainians. Petliura and other Pogrom leaders, may their names be erased, are still fresh in the memories of older people. They know that the Ukrainians only wait for the opportunity of the German arrival. They are the truest collaborators of the Nazis.

For all these reasons, the Jews of Ustiluh tried not to be seen outside of their neighborhoods.

Our relatives in Ustiluh were happy with our arrival. My mother felt better, more cheerful. Her sisters, Beila, Tcharna and Ethel greeted her:

Oy Haike, sister of ours. We already thought that we would not see you again. Thank God. Tears were flowing from their eyes.
I believe that it is important to defend against attacks from the air. We need to be prepared in advance. I have an ax and I immediately want to attend to it by contacting the city administration. This, in spite of the protests of my parents.

In the Bieliankin yard, where the city administration is located, I go to Trizianovsky, the secretary. I meet him outside and he looks at me wondering:

-What are you doing here? You returned to Ustiluh with an ax? --he smiles- When did you come back?

[Page 217]

- I came back two hours ago. I could not find a shovel, only an ax. You do not have to be afraid. I have a good idea about how to use the ax to help with building trenches.

He praises my patriotism, but – he declares- since he does not have any specific orders, he does not know what to do.

Two days, more or less, pass without anything special happening. I even feel like seeing my friends and acquaintances.

Suddenly, on the third day, shooting is heard. It soon becomes a battle. The intensity of the shooting increases constantly- machine guns, bullet shooters; grenades, lit by artillery brilliance, fly in the air with hellish cacophony. The walls shake, the window panes are smashed by stray bullets. It is dangerous to stand up and, therefore, everyone sits on the floor. In a short while, a horde of Jews come to our house. They tell us that the houses parallel to the Bug River are on fire. Our house looks like a narrow, besieged nest. Even this ends suddenly. A loud thud outside shocks everyone. Someone yells: "They have hit our House of Learning. Look at the smoke." This was like a panic signal and everyone runs away- some to the outside cellars, some to the loft protection groove in the garden. I do not lose my equilibrium. From the stable can be heard a loud sound. My mother has tied a dog and a cow there. I decide that it is better to release them in case a fire breaks out. I accomplish my mission. Bullets penetrate the door; but some of the bullets from outside enter the house itself. Three cousins are with me, Ben Zion and Velvel Veinshel and Shaul Gold. I tell them to stay under the table. It would not be helpful if we are found immediately. But the heavy table would protect us if the ceiling collapses.

Suddenly, knocking is heard on the front door. I open it and in front of me stands a young neighbor, Feiga Katz. She is covered in blood and her hair is full of wooden splinters. We bandage her light wounds, but it is impossible to calm her and to find out what had happened when the roof of her house collapsed and she ran away in a panic.

[Page 218]

In the evening, the battle subsides. Everyone creeps out of their hiding places. One could still hear sporadic shooting from patrol activity. Near our house we meet a Jewish officer from the Polish army. His morale- excellent, his mood-fighting for security. He was expecting new activities in the morning and he anticipated that it would be better to abandon the town, towards the right, to Pozov. My parents did not want to roam again. They were extremely tired. However, they suggested that, we, the young ones, should go. Hopefully, the situation will improve and, if not, they will follow in the early morning.

My brother, cousins, some acquaintances and I, come to "Mindel from Pozov", during the night. There were already some people there from Ustiluh and surroundings. We are well received there. The big barn, covered in fresh smelling hay, becomes the guest house for the refugees.

We quickly felt remorse because we had left our parents and family. What would happen?

The heavy mood battled with physical weariness during the late-night hours in the darkened barn...

We had just fallen asleep when we were awakened by a movement and light from a flashlight. We were so happy to see our parents, my sisters Shifra and Rachel and my little brother Hershele. After we had left, they soon decided to follow us.

When the first rays of the sun illuminated the trees, we finally fell asleep. However, not for long. We heard about German tanks in the area, Ukrainians sharpening their knives and other disturbing news.

Mindel and her household (the only Jewish family in the village) advised us not to be seen outside in groups. As proof of the situation, very soon a few stones were thrown our way and hit people as they were washing up.

[Page 219]

My father had come back from seeing the school director, where he had gone to hear the news. He heard on Moscow radio about the German-Soviet Pact. Poland was to be divided. The Bug River was to be the border between Germany and Soviet Russia. Ustiluh was to be in the hands of the Soviets. The news sounded incredible. A sigh of relief could be heard: the Germans would not be coming here. The Ukrainian hooligans would have to put away their sharpened knives.

Back in Ustiluh, the mood is mixed. There was relief at the avoidance of a German danger, but fear of the Polish and Ukrainian antagonists. They have a common sentiment of hatred towards the Jews,

The air is filled with tension. Fighting between the Poles and the Ukrainians leaves many dead, with cut off hands and feet. They lie near the Bug River in a bloodbath. In town there is terror. The authorities have broken down. A Polish functionary declares a state of emergency. People feel they are cut off from the world, surrounded by hatred and danger. Any minute, a surprise can occur. There is knocking on the door. A Polish officer with a group of soldiers, wearing helmets, with bayonets on their rifles, grenades on their shoulder straps, enter and search. Who is here in the house? Together with us, is actually a Polish family from Czhentstechov with small children. We met them in Pozov and we felt sorry for the children. They came to stay with us, using up our provisions. It seemed that one of the women had whispered to the soldier

-to whom do the bicycles belong?

-My brother and I- I reply

-Requisition the bicycles- the officer tells the soldiers.

-You cannot take the bicycles. You have no right- I reply. My father and others near him are horrified and worried. The soldier pushes me away with his bayonet. His eyes are full of anger. It is clear to me that they will keep them for themselves and I say it to their faces.

My father wants to ward off danger and he gives the bicycles to them.

[Page 220]

He gives them to the soldiers who are armed to their teeth. I take mine back and declare, categorically: - you cannot take mine. I have other ideas for fighting in a war, and so on.

Oddly, they are satisfied with one bicycle. It is possible that the existence of the Polish family had them doubt my Jewishness (the whispers by the Polish woman were unclear). My aunt, Tcharna Eichenboim, overheard them as they were leaving the house: "He is not a Jew".

The Red Army is moving slowly. The waiting time is full of tension. It is felt that it is necessary to fill the existing lack of authority with a legalized order. If the situation will continue longer the current Polish-Ukrainian antagonism will explode. The result will be blood shedding and robberies.

The Polish police no longer exist. The latest military divisions have also disappeared. A citizens' militia is organized in order to maintain order and to protect the population.

In the building of the previous police force (owned by Moshe Kleiner) there is much activity. Not only the Communists (Jewish and Ukrainian), but also ordinary citizens and Jewish youths from the Zionist groups. There is not enough ammunition (a fact not widely known). The psychological effect of seeing young Jews patrolling the streets is to calm the Jewish population. People heave a sigh of relief...

The character of Ustiluh changed under Soviet occupation. The offices and institutions were filled with new elements. The veteran Communists, the old political prisoners (like Shmuel Boim, Motya the user) seemed to be ignored. There was no democratic, representative authority. All the positions of control remained in the hands of the Soviet party leaders. Private institutions were pushed aside without a satisfactory replacement. This caused a chronic lack of consumer products and reduced the level of daily life to a minimum.

[Page 221]

In general, all the changes in the social and economic structure remained primitive and provincial. There was no reason to remain in Ustiluh. I, therefore, took a job in Lutsk as a photo correspondent with the editor of the central Voliner newspaper "Rodzianska Volyn". I was thus in contact with people from various social strata everywhere in Volyn, and in Ustiluh.

Universal education was accessible under Soviet rule. Indeed, more youths, also in Ustiluh, seized on the opportunity. The curriculum, though, suffered from official Soviet guidelines- conforming in a dogmatic way.

Actually, this education was foreign, without traditional components.

Many young men were called to the military- to serve in the Red Army. Among those was my brother Avraham who was sent to Dnipropetrovsk.

My sister Shifra had attended a teachers' seminary in Ludomir and became a teacher. She was beloved by her students. My younger sister Rachel and my little brother Hershele (Yaakov Zvi) went to school. My father ran a photography studio.

Since Ustiluh was on the border, the regime was more strict and more limited. Many houses near the Bug River and in Zalush were evacuated. People who were always free to cross the river to the other side (the other's side), were suddenly unable to do it. Some people were even exiled from Ustiluh.

During my last visit in May 1941, I went to the school-located in Beliankin's building. From there one could see a broad panorama. One could see the Lug River as it flowed into the Bug on "the other side". It was now in German hands. I took some pictures of the teachers and, ironically, saw the Germans in the background. Yossel Mamet was the school principal and we stood together chatting on the steps outside. My little brother, Hershele, 12 years old at the time, stood a bit further- being respectful. There was a good, quiet bond between the brothers. I looked sideways at my brother and I noticed how he had changed, how he had grown. Yossel Mamet seemed to read my mind and said:

[Page 222]

-He is a good student. Very bright.

I did not know then that this last picture of my young brother, Hershele, on the slope of the school, would remain a memento of our last meeting...

On June 22, 1941, a heavy, long nightmarish night began. Nazi darkness reigned in the world...

My later travels in Cuba, Caucasus, central Asia are accompanied everywhere with the anxiety about the fate of my dear ones in Ustiluh and reminds me of the town:

Here is the small town of Ustiluh, surrounded by three rivers- Bug, Lug and Studianka. It is decorated with mountains and valleys. Nearby are green fields, moody forests and gorgeous countryside. Ustiluh, with its simple people, colorful appearance, sounds, echoes and unique charm.

I even remember Aisik the water carrier with his popular, refined sharpness... Pinchas Shtadlan in the silken coat and belt around his thick waist, visiting the Houses of Learning on Shabbat morning, announcing, from his reading table, the traditional tunes as decided by the Jewish community... I can hear the thunderous baritone of the old Nikolayev soldier, Buntche Shuster, calling his sons to free the cattle from the stable or to lock up the horses. His strong, hardened face with his yellowish beard reminds us of a patrician character. Even the bullying he uses to call his sons does not mask the warmth in his eyes...

I remember events, happenings and episodes:

It is Lag Baomer. Several hundred Jewish children are marching carrying blue and white flags; Hebrew songs are heard on the way to the forest.

Hashomer Hatzair, Hechalutz, Beitar conduct their own exits as part of a contest among the youths for their ideologies.

[Page 223]

The forest is full of the sounds of dance, singing, games and shooting by the children.

The evening ends with fiery sounds, but the memories remain for many years...

There was a literary evening enacting Shakespeare's "Merchant of Venice". The audience meets in the hall of the Jewish Public Library named for I.L. Peretz (I was the librarian). Some people come early to play chess or to read the "Literary Newspapers" before the event began.

The tribunal includes Fishel Eisenberg, Shaul Stolar, Yitzhak Farber, Avraham Tsuker and others. The fiery speeches of the prosecutor and the defense attorney fill the hall with emotional pathos. It is as if Shylock were there in person. The jury is caught up and I, the court clerk, am sorry that I do not know shorthand.

Another evening, in the Hechalutz premises, is intended to say good-bye to some members who are leaving for the Training Kibbutz. Our member Tevye from the central office takes part. The spirit is heightened; there is purpose. There is growing anti-Semitism in Poland and there is hope for a new life in Eretz Israel.

Here steps up a writer and dramatist, Leib Melech. He paints pictures of Jewish life in South America. He speaks of the life there and of Jewish types in various parts of the world. He also talks about the beauty of the Yiddish language of the Jewish women of the market (the gossipers). They have a colorful lexicon of swear words. For example: “A fire in his tongue will roast his liver”. ” May all his teeth be pulled out, leaving only one for a toothache”.

In a conversation with the writer, he tells me about my uncle Haim Veinshel (from Ustiluh) whom he had seen a few months earlier in Milwaukee (America). Haim is active in a Jewish dramatic circle. We are both pleased with the meeting and we both write to Haim about his old home in Ustiluh.

Here is another episode which happened in 1936:

[Page 224]

I stopped at the cinema theater to look at pictures advertising films. I noticed that the corner of a picture was cut off. It turned out that it was the Polish owner who had done this on purpose. He did it to remove the stamp of UFA, a German film studio run by a Nazi minister.

I immediately went inside to the see the owner to protest his deceptive effort to erase the German control and his support for German films at a time of Hitler's persecution of Jews and Poles. It was an insult to the intelligence and feelings of movie goers.

His answer was not satisfactory. I warned him that I would make it public.

It was afternoon, not much time remained before the premiere of the film. I decided to act quickly. Together with my brother Avraham and other young people I immediately prepared a poster. I went to the soda water business of Mordechai Fleisher (it was a well visited location). We had just hung the poster when the cinema operator came and angrily tore it down from the wall.

-It is really a pity- I declare- that you do not use your energy against the support of your employer of the German economy. Hitler is not only an enemy of the Jews, but also of the Poles. You joined voluntarily without a trace of reluctance. It is a pity my words were lost on you as you did not understand anything. I retain the right to later discuss your behavior. Now I am upset that I have to make new posters.

We immediately went home. Yonatan Veverik also applied himself. He took paper and paints and went to the Jewish library to make new posters.

On the way we meet a policeman. “Who is the older Ginsburg?”- he asks and states that I must immediately go with him to the station and bring all the materials with me.

-Mr. Ginsburg is at the disposal of the officer- he reports to the receptionist at the station.

[Page 225]

-You will have to wait in the other room until the commander will arrive- the policeman orders me.

-When do you expect the commander? I don't have time as I have to prepare the posters.

-I don't know. Maybe in an hour…

-If I have to wait so long, I would like to prepare the posters here. If you allow me to use a table.

-There is no empty table.

-In the other room- I don't let up.

He scratches his head, shakes it, but agrees.

I finished the first poster in Yiddish and Polish. I began to work on the second one. Suddenly, he comes in, looks at it and reads aloud the Polish text:

"How long will Germany persecute our fellow Jews? Boycott all German goods".

"This is brought to general attention- the film "The porter of the Atlantic Hotel", now screening in the city cinema, is a German production by the studio UFA. The studio is under the direction of Hugenberg, a minister in Hitler's cabinet. Emil Jennings, who plays the leading role, is also a member of the Nazi party. "Polish citizens, and especially Jews, are being called to be in solidarity with the boycott, as a protest against the barbaric exclusions campaign of the Nazis. Do not see the film!"

-Hhm, boycott! - comments the policeman.

I don't waste time and I continue to paint. Suddenly we hear heavy steps. The commander is finally here. He is not in a good mood. He is breathing hard and is sweaty having climbed the steps (the police headquarters was in another building, on the second floor of the wagon garage). He heard the story of the event.

He immediately began to shout at me.

-You will conduct a boycott and disturb the public calm. I will not allow it! Look what is happening! The cinema hall is worth money!
[Page 226]

This is serious business! I will use the strictest measures against such agitation!

When he saw the posters, his eyes became bloody. He screamed with froth on his lips. His fat, heavy body became convulsed.

I address him:

-But, Mr. Commander, I see, on your desk, the newspaper I.K.Z. A few days ago, this newspaper had an article about the Jewish boycott of Germany. It said it was an action that deserves a follow-up.

- We also read newspapers- he screams- don't tell me stories!

-It seems you only read certain news.

-Enough. I will not tolerate an upset of the public calm and order. Write a report- he tells the sergeant- and put the posters into it. Everything should be in evidence.

When I came out of the police station, many people already knew what had happened. This helped, to a great extent, to popularize the boycott of the film.

However, in order for the action to be complete, we stood on the sidewalk near Yokhenzon's. We warned every passer by about the film. All the Jews, and even some Poles, turned back. The hall was almost empty. I don't remember if the cinema later showed other German films.

In my wanderings in the hot Uzbekistan, Tajikistan and Kirghiz, the memories of Ustiluh filled me with special nostalgia.

In September 1942, I received a telegram from my brother Avraham. This was the first sign of life. I had searched for him for 15 long months. He was in Askar-Ala (between Gorky and Kazan). I was in Leninabad (Tajikistan). What a happy moment this was! It was the happiest event since the war had broken out. I also found out that several young men from Ustiluh who had been with me in the Red Army, were not far away from him. These are the names: Haim Stolar, Avraham Stelnik, Moshe Shpeizer and L. Shinerman.

[Page 227]

In 1944, the successful offensive of the Red Army on the long front lines had evoked hope and impatience to hear news from home. The news about the liberated areas did not live up to those hopes. Suddenly, the horrible, bloody catastrophe was discovered. Hundreds of Jewish settlements, despite the long history of lawlessness, persecutions and pogroms, had managed to build a many-sided history, much manufacturing activity, had demonstrated remarkable cultural and economic vitality. There was an effervescent reservoir of Yiddish and Hebrew writers, thinkers, leaders; A rich source of Jews who were enthusiastic about Judaism in many lands; It was an eastern European Jewery with an extended network of schools, political parties, Yiddish and Hebrew press and social institutions, an idealistic Zionist youth with creative energy and a rich tradition. A people- parents, sisters, brothers- so brutally were we cut down.

Finally, the first letter from Ludomir, from my brother Avraham- January 11, 1945: "...with me are Haim Stolar and Shinerman. We stopped here, where Hitler and the Ukrainian collaborators murdered our dear ones- our parents, sisters, little brother and relatives.

It is impossible for me to describe what I see and hear. Ludomir is ruined, burned- entire streets are eliminated. However, more tragic is that out of several thousand Jews, only 35 have survived.

The Ludomir and Ustiluh Jews were transported to Piatidan. There they were shot and fell into previously prepared graves. From Ustiluh, there are only about twenty people left: Rachel Miller, Motel Topoler, Eliezer Garbatch, Yehoshua Kleiner, Esther Teitel and her sister, Vopaniarsky with his wife and children, Yeshaya Maltzman, Velvel and Yankel Halperin, Lishtchinker (from Vinehauser), Breindel Danziger, Ita and Breindel Eichenboim, Mendel Gobel, Kh. Freizinger, Hava Krigsher and young brother, Sh. Dimant, Sosya Teig and sister. Miraculously, these people of Ustiluh defied death. No one survived in our family. Not in Trisk, not in Ludomir, not in Ustiluh. I write these words and I cannot believe that what I see here is the truth.

[Page 228]

I visited the graves of our dear parents, sisters, little brother and all those dear to us. The martyrs lie in a mass grave- 12,000 Jews. All victims from Ustiluh are together. Since the trench was not completely filled up, Jewish bodies from Ludomir were added to it.

To describe to you what we see is not for anyone to read. I cannot cry anymore.

Even in Jewish history there is no such tragedy. The descriptions in the press and on the radio represent only a fragment."

In a second letter from Ludomir, dated 25 January 1945:

"...yesterday I went to Ustiluh with my friends. What I saw there, my eyes could not believe. The town is completely destroyed. There are no houses, no street leading to our house, where I lived and where I left my parents and my dear ones in 1940. That is when I joined the army.

I found a path to a single remaining house. I looked around on all sides and my eyes were filled with tears. A deep wound opened in my heart. I felt my throat close and I was unable to make a sound. My memories returned to the past. It was not so long ago, but it seemed to me that hundreds of years had gone by. Our house is gone, but most of all, gone are our beloved parents, sister, brother and relatives.

I retraced my steps, searching for our house. I only found the skinny, drooping bushes in our garden. I felt like asking them about our beloved family, but they stayed silent about everything that had happened.

We had a big tree in our garden, which, as children, we always climbed. It, too, stood. It is impossible to recognize that, once, a garden existed there. The entire town looks like a sobbing cemetery.

I entered the house of the Kaminsky family. They are gone.

[Page 229]
An old woman recognized me. I wanted to ask her something, to speak, but I could not do it. I sat down. She began to tell me about various events. I did not even ask her about our parents. I already knew all too well.

I looked again everywhere. I cried a great deal and blessed the place for eternity."

January 1945. Munich. In the town where lunatics, dark rogues, degenerates and murderers wove their cruel plans about world domination. Munich, which gave birth to the monstrous Nazi beast- which later plunged the world into a cataclysm. Munich, in the broken nest of the world's undertakers- a monumental symbol of the eternity of the Jewish people. Here, the remnants of European jewery assemble. The Congress of the freed Jews gives an expression to the deepest and holiest feelings. Courage was not broken by the cruel catastrophe- the eternal light was not extinguished. The historic light emanates from every delegate. The bloody experience underscores the necessity for a Jewish state in Eretz Israel.

Ben Gurion greets the assembled delegates. His words- "No power in the world will break the Jewish spirit"- are healing and are applauded.

The old Jewish community in Eastern Europe has vanished. Ustiluh has become a mass grave.

In a special newspaper interview, which I conducted with Ben Gurion, he sends a message to the surviving Jews. In retrospect, his words take on a deeper meaning, like those of a prophet:

"In spite of everything, of all the pitfalls- the country will be ours and you will be the builders."

Chicago, August 1960

[Page 230]

The Tear That Was Not Shed

by Bella Eichenboim-Terner, Cuba

Translated by Ala Gamulka

In memory of my dear ones

"Man is like a tree in the fields". My family was a large, well-defined clan- many- branched. I was still young then, when I was torn away by the storm of those days. I was swept away on ocean waves to distant places.

I went to foreign places far away from home. Places we dreamed about in childhood, in those crazy young and tender days. The sun would shine in the blue and white sky. We looked at the eastern horizon. There it was, far, far away beyond the green meadows, fields and gardens spread on both sides of the river. Distant green spaces stretched with blue skies. We always dreamed of the east, but our destiny sent us west.

I received this note from Israel: "Only your house, of all buildings, remains standing. It stands erect over the town". From my parents' home, from my dear family, from our friendly neighbors, from our townsfolk, from the dearly beloved town of Ustiluh, only one building remained after the catastrophe. This one building was once my home. Alone, it stands desolate and silent. Who knows if its silence is not a sign from above? It could be that it hovers over its burned walls, doors and windows. The red bricks remind us of the fire. It was not always a plain building. It remembers, perhaps, the happy life in it.

[Page 231]

It was one of the most beautiful homes in town. Perhaps the building misses its former glory. It is possible that its empty rooms echo the sounds of its previous occupants. I remember that it was a nice summer day and all four windows in the hall, on the top floor, were open. Tcharna Meir Feniks and Toivtze Heinischs were leading the graduation of the first Kindergarten in town. The hall was filled with guests and all the windows were densely occupied. It was a happy celebratory atmosphere. Small children, boys and girls danced in a long row and young sweet voices, like young birds, sang: "Beautiful bird, beautiful bird, a black cat came to the house. A black cat saw the bird". The blond, sunny girl who portrayed the bird in the graduation of the kindergarten, flew away like a swallow before a storm. The chubby, sweet boy who was the black cat who killed the bird, was Hershele Pomerantz, may he live a long life. He now lives on a kibbutz in Israel. The good child who fractured his hands and who almost burst out crying in sorrow- was my beautiful, dear, only brother, Efraim Fishel. He is no longer with us. The same is true for many of the beautiful children from the first kindergarten- they were young when they were murdered by the Nazi killers, may their names be erased.

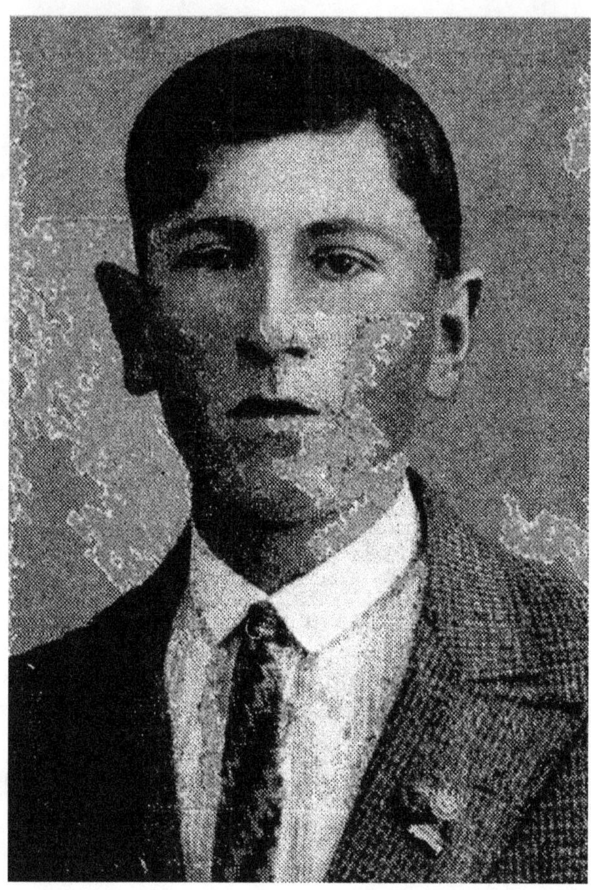

Fishel Eichenboim, the martyr

[Page 232]

I remember the happiness when you, my only brother, were born. My three sisters and I were in school when we were given the happy news that we now had a little brother. I remember the beautiful celebration of your bris and the wonderful party for your Bar Mitzvah. Often, when I think of the terrible tragedy, I see you from the day you were born. My memories accompany your sunny being, my only brother. I remember when you studied with Liptche Eisenberg. I see in front of me a childhood figure when you crossed the street, on Shabbat, to visit Haim Eidelshteyn so he would listen to you recite Gmara. I see the lovely faces of our father and mother and their pleasure when they were complimented on your scholarship. I hear your sweet voice when you chanted from the Torah. I see you bent at the table when you recited from the Scroll of Esther. I actually hear the sound of your voice. Some neighbors are in the house. We, the girls, are prepared to make noise at the sound of the word "Haman". Mother stands nearby with her arms folded across the chest. Her eyes are glistening and she swallows every word coming out of your mouth. Never, never, as long as I live, will I forget those minutes when you embraced me before my journey.

[Page 233]

Your bright eyes were misted over and they looked deep into mine. You did not say a single word to me. Your voice was not heard. The corners of your mouth twitched nervously, trying to control your sobbing. Your lips trembled when you bent down to kiss me. Who would have predicted then the storm that caused death and annihilation? Who would have thought there would be such a terrible end for everyone?

I remember: a Shabbat afternoon in the winter. Our parents slept soundly after eating Cholent. Many of my friends attended a Zeirei Zion meeting at the Hebrew Children's Library- there was also a library for the older ones

among us. We needed to elect a new administration so that elections could take place, but it was Shabbat and we could not write. Out friends came up with an idea: white and black beans. A white bean for this candidate and a black bean for the other. When the administration was finally elected, a few jokers stood in front of the losing candidate and sang: "How lonely sits the city. A black bean belongs to you".

I remember: the beautiful Shabbat and holidays. The lovely holiday of Pesach with the wonderful Seders. The days in between when the town was filled with visitors. There was a custom to visit in those days. The beauty of Shavuot, the happiness of receiving the Torah and the fresh, green decorations. The High Holy Days with all the special preparations. Rosh Hashana with the festive jewelry and footwear, when, we, the youth, accompanied our dressed-up family on our way to synagogue and back. Our town was small, tiny, but, in addition to the big town synagogue, there were many small Shtiblach. In the last few years, the young people prayed separately – they were called the Goshen Shtiebel because there were many unshaven "heretics".

[Page 234]

"In the Land of Goshen there was no hail" (play on words as Berd means beard in Yiddish.} However, especially there was the true happy atmosphere of dance and song.

I remember the special time before Kol Nidrei- many lights were lit. One could see the candles in every window. Men, women and children were streaming to the synagogues and Shtiblach. Their hearts were filled with reverence and prayer, planning to place themselves in front of the celestial council for judgement. After the High Holy Days came the happy days- building Succoth, followed by celebration of Simchat Torah. The Hassidim of Stepan used to come to us. They ate and drank and sang Hassidic happy tunes. They also danced. One bearded, belted man goes to the oven in search of kugels. The doors and windows were open and the street enjoys the happy Hassidic singing, accompanied by children's voices.

I also remember tragi-comic episodes which later had serious consequences: one Friday night there was a self-invited guest. He was a young, tall Polish inspector from Ludomir sent by the authorities. When he met my father, he told him he wanted to eat in the house of the "Jewish Rabbi". He licked his fingers with my mother's gefilte fish and could not have enough of the chalot. Jewish noodles in soup were an amazing food. It must have been difficult for my father to chant kiddush, sing Zmirot and recite grace after the meal that Friday night. Afterwards, we had to listen to the young man describe his knowledge of sports. He was quite drunk. He did not only drink the kiddush wine, because my father asked him if he wanted to partake in a bottle of whiskey. What a question! It was so easy for him.

A liter bottle of whiskey was placed on the floor and the gentile threw himself down with all his might. He spent a considerable time on the floor, not stopping for long. He lost his temper and left our house late at night. In the morning he returned and argued with father: this was a Jewish trick, that he should clean out the Jewish fish.

[Page 235]

The sitting on the floor attached to the bottle made him ache all over his body.

Some time later, I was told that this same inspector had written about the tax debts of my parents. In town, magistrates' posters were hung announcing the day of the auction. I was told that the inspector spoke to my father and he said that he would even sell his socks to repay the debts. Father attacked the gentile with a stick and the latter took out his pistol. Other people intervened.

This is the end of my memories of Polish taxes.

I remember; a small Shtiebel with one window and one door. One Friday night, I am sitting on the bank, under the window with Batya (Machel's) Shafran. She was telling me, with great nostalgia, about Jewish life in Eretz

Israel. She paints for me, with beautiful colors, summer nights in the Holy Land, the beauty of the sky. The Shafran family soon left for Eretz Israel, but they returned to Poland. They perished with all the other Jews.

Next to the large entrance gate to the bronze courtyard and above the gate are the densely grown lilac trees with magnificent blooms. The big house with its porch. In the second house lived the family of Yossel Yaikes. I see Ber Moshe (Shmayes) coming in from prayers. From the porch he calls the children playing somewhere on the street:" Sareniu! My love! Moshele, my love! Shmayanu, grampa! Sheva-Reyzele, grandma! Come inside, Come inside for dinner".

There are various memories of school life. Also, the plays presented by the senior classes in school. From childhood I often belonged to the choir and was part of the presentations. I even had a real part.

I remember: Moshele Glaz directed with us the three-act play- "The Abductors". Tcharna (Meir's) Feniks- then still Kornfeld- had translated it into Yiddish- so it was said. When all the roles had been cast, we were invited, on a Shabbat afternoon to Tcharna's house. She was already sick then and could not leave her bed. We put on "The Abductors" for her and she was very interested in the presentation. She sat in bed, her smile warm and her gorgeous eyes gleaming. She was quite taken by our play. She made several comments and recommendations. The presentation of the play was a great success.

[Page 236]

In general, in those years, there was always some theater. There were many theater lovers among the older generation. Tcharna once played the main role in "Mirele Efros". Other plays were "The Jewish King Lear", "The massacre"," Khassia the orphan". Zeirei Zion of that time also participated. They had great performances of "The Idler"', "Dvorale the Aristocrat", "The simple tavern". Later, the young people, I among them, presented, for the second time, "The Simple Tavern", "Shayna Sheindel from Yehupetz", "The Black Wedding Canopy", "Broken Heart", "Money, Love and Shame", "The Needy Young Man", "Where Are My Children?". There were some talented people. I can still see Shmuel Burlyant playing the roles of the old, needy Shachne and the old peasant. I have attended theater in the wide world with big artists and even film stars. I can say, with confidence, that even the most famous actor would not have portrayed the role better. It would not have been a better Shachne.

A theater presentation in town was a happy event. The hall was filled with young and old. Even Jews from surrounding villages would come to the theater. The young people from nearby Haradle never missed our presentations.

I will always remember the morning of March 5, 1930. It was my last morning in town. It was a Sunday. It was very cold. We ignored the cold and kept the door to our house open from early in the morning. Neighbors came to say good-bye. People came and went. I remember that I continuously went up and down the steps. I tried very hard not to cry. I did not want my parents to see my tears.

[Page 237]

Finally, we went into the two wagons standing in front of the door. People congregated around them. Jews came from synagogue carrying their tallit bags under their arms and stood on the sidewalk. The horses began to move and my heart moved, too.

"The Needy Young Man" – 1930

When the horses turned the corner, I waved my hand to say good-bye. We were already near the hut of Binyamin Meir Feniks. I had a second to turn my head back once more. One more look at my home that I was leaving and going somewhere far away. I would never see it again. But, no, I did not turn my head one more time. My mother was sitting across from me, her eyes swollen and red. We passed by Meir Feniks' long house and I am already scared. No! I can no longer see our house. It has disappeared. I feel a heaviness that hurts me. We drive on Ludomir street. There is the holy place- the cemetery. My mother speaks to her dead parents who are lying there peacefully, under snow-covered monuments. She asks them to look after me and to provide me with good luck.

[Page 238]

Who knew at that time that in only a few years would come the terrible catastrophe? That there would be a tragic end for so many people. That death and destruction would be the lot of all my dear ones, my extended family. Only a few survived. It was a tragic and appalling end for my friends, our neighbors with their families and for all the Jews in town.

It hurts, it really hurts that I said good-bye that morning to my home. The unshed tears are still in me and weigh on my heart with blood and stone.

It cannot be that it is enough to write a memorial book to remember all that existed, the world that we had. We are no longer there. Tears are not enough for the substance of a human being to mourn the tragic results- the murders of the families in our town.

The tiny town of Ustiluh was a small, sparkling fountain of Jewish life. If, for some reason, you went far away, you still carried in your heart the memory of the Jewish way of life. It was a small treasure that was sacred.

In our heart of hearts, until the last moments of life, we will not abandon the flame that is always like a memorial candle – to always remember and never forget our martyrs.

[Page 239]

The Destruction of Ustiluh

by Nachman Burlyant, New York

Translated by Zvi Kaniel

The following translations were commissioned by Avigail Frij, whose maternal grandparents were from Ustilug (Kopp and Kultin Families)

Our old home town Ustiluh had about 4,000 Jews, 15 Houses of Learning, a secular Hebrew school "Tarbut," a Talmud Torah, a Bikur Cholim [organization for caring of the sick], and a Yiddish library.

Economically, the Jews did not live badly, but the anti–Semitic politics of the Polish government had begun to push many Jews out of their secure economic positions, making their future precarious.

On September 1, 1939, when the Nazis suddenly invaded Poland, the Jews of Ustiluh were unaware of the goings on, and did not realize that their years were numbered.

And two weeks later, September 5, when the Russians slaughtered the Poles in Ustiluh, there was a tremendous fire where a quarter of the city was burned down. Namely, Meyer Vogenfeld's large fence in the middle of the market; three rows of houses of Bath Street, from Shaikel Goldhaber's house until Mechel Krakower's house. The fire cost 12 Jewish people their lives. On September 17, the Russians occupied Ustiluh, and life became somewhat more normal again. Even the economic situation was bearable.

For reasons unknown, the Russians deported about thirty families deep into the country. Many Jews moved to the nearby city of Ludomir due to the shortage of housing resulting from the fire. About 3,000 Jews remained in Ustiluh itself and continued to live with hope for their future.

All that continued until June 21, 1941. One beautiful early summer morning, at five AM, all the Ustiluh Jews were awoken by cannon fire, aerial bombardment, and the bark of machine gun fire.

[Page 240]

Tongues of fire shot up in the sky. All this mixed with people crying and screaming amidst the fire and blood, the agonies of death as the victims shrieked "*Shema Yisrael*!" The fires destroyed the entire town, from Yekhezkel Sheinerman's house down in the distilleries district, all the shops, the Ludomir road, Dan'kes Street, and so on. About 500 Jews lost their lives. Mothers lost their children, and families were torn apart. All this, and more, the ferocious Nazis achieved when they marched into Ustiluh. Mothers searched for the bones of their children in the mountains of ash in the midst of the destruction, men sought the remains of their wives, sisters their brothers, to bring them to the Jewish cemetery. And now the real inferno began for the Ustiluh Jews. Very soon, Jews were seized and sent to work. The frail, elderly or sick were shot on the spot. Jews went into hiding. But the murderous Germans soon created a "*Judenrat*," (Jewish Council) that had to make available to the Germans, every day, hundreds of workers who were taken away for work– of which ten percent less returned home every day. How did this ten percent die? The frail and sick, who could not work, were "liquidated."

It should be mentioned that the *Judenrat* in Ustiluh, with the chairman Mechel Shafran at its head, risked their lives to save Jews from death.

Jews were now living under terrible circumstances – hunger, death, freezing cold, and typhus were spreading. There were no doctors and no medicines. Hundreds of our beloved brothers and sisters died then, and in Ustiluh, no more than about 2,000 Jews remained.

This tragic situation dragged on until August 31, 1942, when the Gestapo arrived in Ustiluh. That same day, the SS troops issued an order that the following day, September 1, at six in the morning, all the Jews, their wives and children were to assemble in the market place near the pump, and those who go into hiding would be captured and shot. The Jews felt a great looming tragedy. There were no cries, no pleas that could help.

[Page 241]

When children asked their mothers why they were going to be shot, their mothers answered: "Don't cry, my child, it's nothing. We are going to a more beautiful and better world."

September 24, 1942, 28 Elul 5702, six o'clock in the morning, on a beautiful summer day, when the sun shone brightly, its warm rays enveloping Mother Earth, military trucks arrived. The Germans began loading the Jews onto it. The first to get on the truck was the chairman of the *Judenrat*, Mechel Shafran along with his family. The second, Benyomtze Meyer Fenix and his family, and so it went. They drove the trucks away behind the village Piatidan, across the bridge, and left to the Piwnik forest, on the road to Ludomir, where the Jews were sent to dig huge ditches. The Germans told them they were preparing hiding places for their airplanes. They stripped the Jews naked and sorted their clothing, shirt to shirt, shoes with shoes. They ordered the naked Jews to stand at the edge of the ditch, and groups of savage German Nazi and Ukrainian soldiers and policemen aimed their guns right at the hearts. After each volley of fire, dozens of Jews fell into the large ditches. The rich, black Ukrainian soil became red from all the blood that flowed. The sun shone that day as if nothing unusual had happened. How could the sun shine on such a dark day? Why did the sun not become dark like it was in the mass grave? The trucks drove quickly back into town with the clothing of the victims, and to bring back a fresh load of victims. This is how the *actzion* continued for ten straight days, until Ustiluh was Judenrein (free of Jews).

It is important to mention that many Jews fell into the ditches out of terror, still alive, but were subsequently buried alive. A very small number were able to crawl out of the mass grave and escape into the forest to the partisans. The others went to their slaughter with the last words, "*Shema Yisroel*!" and screamed out, "Whoever survives this should take revenge!" At the same time and place, they murdered 15,000 Ludomir Jews, including 1,000 Ustiluh Jews who had moved there. This was a total of about 17,000 Jews in one mass grave. The approximately 300 Jews who did not present themselves in the market place on that dark day, ran away into the forests, fought with the partisans, hiding in the ditches until the Russian Army liberated them.

[Page 242]

It is also important to mention that a few good Christian Poles risked their lives by hiding Jews until the liberation.

Until today, we have registered in our relief committee over two hundred Jews who lived in the camps in Europe, and with your help, we can support them with food and clothing every month. We help them get to America; we send them money so that they should be able to reach the Land of Israel. This is the tragic summary of our old home Ustiluh.

On a tall mountain surrounded on all four sides by flowing water on the Western Ukrainian side, on the Polish border, at the River Bug, there was once a calm beautiful Jewish town – Ustiluh. About 4,300 Jews lived together there and hoped to have a long happy life.

Ustiluh is no longer; it is wiped off the earth.

And our beloved dear Ustiluh Jews?

A mass grave of 4,000 martyrs, without tombstones, without even a low fence marking the cemetery…

We cry for you with tears mixed with blood!

We will never ever forget you!

Yitgadal V'yitkadash!

[Page 243] [Page 244] [Page 245]

The Massacre in Piatidan

by Kehat Kliger

Translated by Zvi Kaniel

The autumn trees were watching and were silent,
The Elul skies did not cry out to God

Autumn trees, why are you silent?
A. Elul skies, why are you not crying out?

My Jewish town, my twenty thousand Jews,
were slaughtered in the village Piatidan on the 19th of Elul

Woe to you, trees, from the town of Piatidan,
Woe to your skies, over the town of Piatidan

From infants to children, from women till the aged,
The blade sliced through from one to the other;

The blade sliced through, the knife cut
The bride, the groom, the rabbi.

From the main street to the *shul* court, from the poor to the wealthy,
The blade sliced through everyone equally.

My twenty thousand Jews – how many remained?
None remained, no one survived.

The autumn trees watched and were silent,
The Elul skies did not cry out to God.

At least tell me, skies, tell me, trees,
From the Piatidan slaughter days, woe is to me, woe is to me.

I know it, this town, the cottages, just one,
With the deficient, unpaved roads, with the dry plains;

I know this town, this Volyn, Piatidan,
Each poor farmer from the markets and the fairs;

I know each motion, each sound of the scythe.
In sunny spring, and the waves of the oceans,

Oh, tell me, heavens, tell me, trees,
About the Piatidan slaughter days, woe is me, woe is me!

The Rav Yaakov David, the gray–haired, refined person,
Did he really smile as his soul left him?

Hinda, wife of the *gabbai*, was she in her Shabbat headscarf?
Did she accept with love the brown murder?

Oh, tell me, heavens, tell me, trees,
About the Piatidan slaughter days, woe is me, woe is me!

Did the chazzan's wife, Pessia Gitel – my mother
Along with my sister – her only daughter –
Dance towards the slaughterer, singing:
Holy! Holy! – and take three steps [as is done during prayer?

Did Yitzchak Shlomo the *shochet* utter the blessing
When the evil person's blade slit his throat?

Did the pious water carrier – the quiet Srul,
Scream before his death: "God will pay them back"?

Was the cry of Nechemtze's child – one year and seven months
like a parched "Shema Yisrael," remaining hollow?

Woe to you, trees, you bloodied witness,
Why were you silent during the Piatidan slaughter?

I will inscribe it in my journal, upon my heart
So that it remains engraved in our memories for generations.

That while my town – the 20,000 Jews,
Were murdered on 19 Elul in the town of Piatidan,

The trees on the ground did not cry, did not shout,
And the heavens remained silent witness to the bloodshed.

From the book "The World Begs Me to Die"; Buenos Aires, 1950.

[Page 246]

A Stroll
Dedicated to My Home Town Ustiluh

by Yossel Burlyant, z"l, New York

Translated by Zvi Kaniel

On a tall mountain, sprinkled with fruit gardens, surrounded by green meadows and ponds, stood our town Ustiluh.

Strolling north from the middle of the marketplace: two lines of shops, a large, broad place known as Warsaw Street, with that name because of the beautiful houses belonging to the wealthy businessmen in Ustiluh.

Next, the strolls through the mountains, the Lug River and the good fish, with the large river ripples in the reed covering, the two mills with the locks [in the canal] which block the water from the Lug that flows into the Bug and provides energy to the mills so that they can run. The highway to Zeluzhe, the roads to Warczin, Widernitz, Stizhericz, and Krinitz, and the famous Sosnow forests.

Left: Back onto the mountain, and a look to the west, there's the Rabbi's house with the orchard. Way at the bottom, at the foot of the mountain, the Bug River flows calmly. From where? Somewhere from Galicia. Where to? Across Poliesa to Pinsk and into the Vistula. On the other side of the Bug, the large hay stacks.

Then to the right: The teachers' street. The Rizhiner and other small synagogues. Behind the mountain, near the river, the bath house, Bluma Ziske's small house with the straw roof. The frame slides back and forth. The houses on the other side, the city gate, the large chimney can be seen at a distance from the Striszow sugar warehouse.

Back to the city, a stroll to the south. The large House of Learning, the Trisker *Shtiebel*, the tailors' *Shtiebel*, which is about to fall into the ground as the sinkhole gets bigger and bigger, almost reaching the town council hall, and that might even cut the town in half.

[Page 247]

And noteworthy! As the ditch reaches a holy place, it moves off in another direction. Also, there was the mail that used to bring us the world's news four times a week, and of course, a letter from America.

Farther down, past the fence between two tall mountains, is the road to the distilleries. In fact, between the distillery buildings there are a few female deer, and [there's a place] where they produce oil in a primitive fashion. Then, another river flows there, the Rydzek River, which flows into the Bug. On the other side of the bridge, you can see the brickyard, the roads to Rossov, Izov, and so on. A little higher up to the left on the little mountain is Sokolov's large house, which was the school for over half a century. Around the river there are more green meadows with the fragrant hay of summer.

On the way back to the marketplace, there are another two rows of shops, no stores. In one shop, there is a barrel of herring; in another, a barrel of kerosene; in a third, two or three sacks of flour; and so on. A winding right to the east, and there are another two rows of shops, but these were already more "profitable." Here you are able to find material for a suit, a container of sardines, tobacco, sugar, iron, and so on. Continue right, and there is the large Russian church with the large fruit orchard. There's the Christian street with the straw roofs, and farther down is the road to Ludomir, the blacksmiths, the Polish church, the hospital where no Jewish foot has ever stepped, the empty park, but the pears and apples were the best, and right after World War One, a train station was built there and set up.

On the left, there are two long rows of chestnut trees, where, on Friday nights, both young and old would stroll to the Jewish cemetery because on the other side of the cemetery there is a small, narrow, hardly noticeable river that flows, with the erroneous name of "Bielebi," that flows north into the Rydzek near the priest's mill, with the wide meadows all around, where the youth would spend a happy and lively afternoon after their Shabbat meal. Towards the south, the Bielebi (real name is Bieli–Bug) flows into the Lug River. Further down, across the small river, between two rows of trees, is the wide highway to Ludomir, the city district where I received 75% of my education.

But, I shudder when I look there at the larger city.

Over there, where we say from where the sun rises and falls, and we use the words "I have set G–d before me always," there on the main road, just a few kilometers from Ustiluh is the village of Piwnik; now the "holy village." In that village is the mass grave of our martyrs. That is where the Nazi murderers killed our dear and loved ones: mothers, fathers, brothers, sisters, uncles, aunts, our relatives and friends, all who perished in sanctification of the name of G–d, with these words on their lips: "Do not forget us!" There were exactly 4,000 people, and only 200 managed to save themselves, spread right across Poland, Italy, Austria, and a few in Russia.

[Page 248]

No! I cannot continue. I run back to my town, but…! It's a disaster! Where am I? There is no town left here, no Ustiluh, only ruins, the houses destroyed, here and there only a remnant of a house, a chimney, no marketplace, no shops, no churches, but there is the 100–year–old large *Beit Midrash* [Study Hall], left standing tall and proud, as a symbol for the victims to show that we are a nation with a strong backbone. No one can destroy us! We survived the Pharaohs, the Amalekites, Torquemada, all kinds of pogroms, and Hitler, may his name and memory be erased, erased forever. No! We who survived will not be defeated!

The enemies will receive their punishment, and all of us together, without any political differences, will build a Jewish city in the Land of Israel, that will serve as an example for the entire world to learn tolerance and democracy.

[Page 249]

Ustiluh in the Old Days

by Tzirl

Translated by Ala Gamulka

Ustiluh in the old days,
With its muddy streets and lanes,
With its small, low houses,
From Vinehauser to the novice garden,
From Ludomir street to the big bath house.
It is all etched in my memories.

Ustiluh in the old days,
With rivers on all sides,
In the winter- choked as if in chains,
A slide, sisters, what happiness!
Summer- boats far and wide,
It is all etched in my memory.

Ustiluh in the old days,
Surrounded by green fields
And old, big pine forests.
On Shabbat and Lag Baomer,
The trees rejoiced with us.
It is all etched in my memory.

Ustiluh in the old days,
With its elderly Hassidic Jews,
And the youth, National-Jewish,
Sweet children, dearly beloved,
Naughty and naïve-
It is all etched in my memory.

Ustiluh in the old days,
With its several hundred families,
Merchants, clerks and craftsmen
Teachers, Tutors and simple learners,
Dealers, brokers and matchmakers-
It is all etched in my memory.

Ustiluh in the old days-
As I think of it,
Day and night.
Where are you all the Jews of Ustiluh,
Plain Jews, Hassidim and modern nationalistic ones
Thousands of innocents, blameless people-
Old, middle aged and small children
Were they really all killed?
So quickly- between day and night?

Memories can no longer give us more
About Ustiluh- only heartache remains.

[Page 250]

[Page 251]

The "Revenge" Battalion

Told by Shmuel Diamant

Translated by Ala Gamulka

If I speak about what I endured and saw during the Nazi invasion of Poland, a whole day and night would not be enough time. This is why a special book is being written. I must also limit myself to the confines of the Yizkor Book.

A.

It is not a secret for the people of Ustiluh who lived in the town at the beginning of WWII, that I was a follower of the Soviet regime. I truly believed in the possibility of international brotherhood. As an expression of this brotherhood, I saw the friendship of the Ukrainian Party members. Especially so with a certain young man called Gritchuk. He worked together with me as an official in city council. Avraham Hovel was the vice-chairman.

In May 1941, we were drafted into the Red Army to guard the border near Izov. We were told that it was only for 45 days- until regular soldiers would arrive.

We were not relieved by the expected time. In the meantime, the Nazi offensive caught us on June 22nd. The entire frontline fell like a decomposed flea. I, together with a young man called Yossel (I do not remember his family name), managed to cross the Bug River. We ran to Mikulicz where we were overtaken by the Nazis. There, about 6,000 people were brought to a field. There, I found Avraham Hovel and Gritchuk. When he saw us, Gritchuk went over to a German soldier and said- "Comrade commissars". Luckily, the German did not pay attention. It was clear to me that my life was in danger.

[Page 252]

A comment: I would like these words to reach the Jewish Communist leaders. They should understand how one cannot trust gentile "friends". I am certain that if there had been an Arab conquest (may they not live that long!), they would have been the first victims-at the hands of their so-called friends.

Therefore, when I saw how a Soviet officer behaves, I crawled on all fours. I was able to go some distance and I remembered to take Yossel with me. This is how we managed to escape.

I came to Ludomir where I ditched the military uniform. I returned to my people in the colony of Seliske. My family was in town and there were no other Jews in the colony. I sent a farmer to town to bring my family. I paid him by giving him a horse. He actually brought my family as well as some news: 1. All men were brought to the Polish synagogue, 2. They make them work hard and be tired out, 3. Communists are being sought.

After these items of news, I resolved to flee to the forest. I had hoped to meet some Soviet soldiers and to go with them wherever they went. However, I did not find them.

Near the colony there was a fort that had been confiscated by the Germans. The village magistrate had announced that all Jews in the area had to work in the fort. I worked with everyone else through the rest of the summer and the winter. In the meantime, there were rumors that Jews from the small towns were to be systematically annihilated.

I then searched for a well-known Soviet person who lived hidden somewhere in the village. Together, we organized a partisan unit. However, the Jews to whom I made the proposal, laughed at me. I got in touch with the famous family Spasov, but even they were not ready to join. In the meantime, the Gestapo found the Soviet person and shot him.

At that time, my father-in-law, Yossel Hallel's (Karsh) and mother-in-law came to me.

I continued to work at the fort, but I did not give up the idea of finding a way to rescue myself and my family.

[Page 253]

B.

I had an acquaintance- a famous Polish officer called Zachartchuk.

He once came from town with the news that the Germans are preparing for a slaughter. Graves are being prepared in Piatidan. This message hit me like a thunderclap. "What should I do?"- I asked him. "My advice is"- he replied- "that you should pretend to be sick, wrap up your face and go to alert your fellow Jews. The money they had prepared for the Germans would be better used to find arms and to create a resistance. When you begin to do it, we will come to help you. This is the only way you can save yourselves".

I immediately put a bag of wheat on the wagon and I went towards the water mill. I also tied a cloth around my teeth.

When I entered town, I went to Doctor Muzikansky and relayed the message from Zachartchuk. The Doctor immediately went to the Jewish Committee. He returned quickly, frightened, and told me to hide. The Jewish Committee people were upset that I was creating panic for no good reason. They would probably denounce me to the Gestapo.

I hid myself and only in the evening did I return to the village. In the morning, while I was working in the field, a gentile woman came and told me that the Jewish police came to my house and took everything out of it. I, together with my brother-in-law Elie Karsh, immediately ran home. There, the Jewish policemen Moshe Linder and Shimshon Garbatch, were waiting. They said I had to pay a contribution of 8,000 kabavanitzes. My blood was boiling. I picked up a broom and tried to hit Linder, but my brother-in-law restrained me.

Shimshon Garbatch came up with a compromise: I should give a few hundred kilos apples for a Gestapo banquet.

My reply was as follows:

"I understand that I will not eat the apples, but you also will not live to bite them".

The policemen left with nothing and my brother-in-law Elie and I left for the forest. We had prepared a bunker for the family there.

[Page 254]

C.

I again encountered Zachartchuk and we went together to Ludomir. I used the opportunity to bring a loaf of bread for my sister-in-law in the ghetto. For this "sin" they were called into the Jewish Committee for a hearing.

Having forgotten the happenings with the Jewish committee in Ustiluh, I went to the Ludomir committee at the suggestion of Zachartchuk.

Their reply was that the plan must be followed, but they would only speak to the one who made the suggestion. Zachartchuk came to them and repeated the plan. Several units of the Polish A.K.A were required to wait not far from the ghetto during the time when the Germans would come to gather the people in the market square. The ghetto had to be completely prepared with gasoline and other protection devices to greet the Germans. Then, the Polish units would attack the murderers from the outside.

Zachartchuk came back satisfied. It meant that the suggestion was well received.

On the evening of September 1, when the first pogrom began in Ludomir and Ustiluh, the A.K.A were waiting for a signal from the Ludomir ghetto. However, it did not happen. The Nazi beasts transported thousands of victims to Piatidan without any resistance. Eight days earlier there was an order to gather all the village Jews who were not working the land. This is when my brother-in-law Elie Karsh was caught together with Issachar Teig and they were taken into town.

A day before the pogrom I saw through my window two police officers on bicycles. I immediately sent the family to the forest to hide and I watched to see what the two were doing. One of them was the provocateur Gritchuk who had been freed by the Germans together with other gentiles.

The two policemen took some chickens from the coop and left.

When I arrived in the forest, I found the following: 17-year-old David Rothstein from Zabelity, two daughters of Elie Teig, Peshke Bitterman from Fizov, her husband and their two daughters. We spent 15 days together.

[Page 255]

We were then joined by the brothers Moshe and Yeshayahu Spasov and their cousin Moshe with two small children, a son of Yitzhak Tovel. Also, my brother-in-law Elie returned.

At the same time the Soviets were building, around Ustiluh, fortified tombs which I believed to be a weapon. I proposed to the Spasovs that we should take advantage of this, but they refused.

On September 15 (Fast of Gedaliah), I went home to the Colony in order to bring food products. Other people did the same. In the forest, I found only my family, my wife's parents and the husband of Peshke Bitterman.

On the road, we were suddenly shot at by Ukrainian hooligans. Everyone scattered in different directions. I, Elie Karsh and Moshe Tovel fled to the swamps.

About half an hour later- it was already dark- we heard shooting in the forest. During the middle of the night, we came back to the bunker in the forest- it had been burned down. There was no sign of any people there. Elie went to Colony to find out about the fate of those who had been in the bunker. In the meantime, we had decided to meet in a specific place. At dawn, we met with dishonesty.

All our dearly beloved had been murdered and our neighbors, Gostetsky and Markevitch had buried them 50 meters away from the burned- out bunker. (We had not noticed the freshly dug grave in the darkness).

We sat on the marshes. I was drawn to the grave and when I came to it. I ignored the danger and said Kaddish. I cried loudly and I swore to avenge their deaths. We could not tear ourselves away from there, until we had covered the bodies with earth. Elie banged his head in the earth.

In my great despair, I wanted to give myself up to the Germans. However, Elie said that we must fight to stop the Angel of Death.

That night, we returned to the Colony. We sat a day and a night on the floor on a straw mat. We then went to a Polish acquaintance, a miller called Branek. He received us nicely and brought us food and drink.

We stayed in Branek's barn for seven weeks.

[Page 256]

One day he came to us with the news that Jews are being sought. He suggested we dig up a bunker. We did so. We dug at night and we spread the earth in such a way that no one would notice.

Again, we sat there for seven weeks. One night we came out and went to someone called Tsingalovsky.

Isrolik Diamant

He lived near the forest. There awaited us good news: Elie Teig's daughter and Peshke Bitterman were alive and the Spasovs had escaped into town. Every night- so Tsingalovsky told us- they came to him for food.

To our delight, they did not have full confidence in Tsingalovsky and stopped coming. We went out to look for them.

Passing a pile of straw, we saw a basket full of potatoes and bread. I had a revolver at that time, which Branek had given me.

[Page 257]

Since I had already allowed myself to stop near the basket, we quickly found the frightened women hidden in the straw. Surprised by this happening, they fell on us, crying, and begged us to take them with us in our flight. But how can "guests" in our situation take along other "guests"? We obtained a bottle of whiskey and honey from Tsingalovsky. We came to Branek, drank up with him and told him, sobbing, about the women. "Go bring them"-he said- "It is the same risk for me."

I embraced and kissed this good man.

So, we brought them. They were torn, swollen and full of wounds. We found clothes for them. The wounds healed. Then they were sick with a stomach illness. In time, they became healthy again.

D.

The winter passed.

In the meantime, with Branek's help. I obtained a rifle. I felt freer to move in the area.

One March, 1943 Day, I saw, in the field, two men running. I stopped them. They were Jews from Ludomir who had been expelled, with their families, by their "do-gooder".

They were ready to pay well for a hiding place, for some space. I informed Branek and he agreed to take them in. It was a family of five people: an old woman and two daughters, a son-in-law and the bridegroom of the other daughter. They also brought a couple from Zmushets. The man's name was David. The latter had a child living with a gentile. He went to get the child, but he never returned. (All the others live now in America). Branek went to where they told him to go and he brought back a wagon full of goods.

We lived in the bunker for several months. The entrance to it was through a trough.

At that time, there was a Ukrainian band of hooligans in the area- Benderovtsky's people. They searched for Jews and Poles- even more than fight the Germans.

[Page 258]

Branek was afraid of a night raid, had left his house and only came to check from time to time.

This is how our situation was even more unsafe.

We had a radio appliance. We once heard an unclear bit of news. We went to Tsingalovsky, who also had a radio, to clarify the news. On this occasion, Tsingalovsky told us that David Rotenstein is with him, but he is afraid to keep him. We found him in a pile of straw, naked, shoeless and swollen with hunger. We immediately took him with us.

Another time, Branek came with the news that our hiding place has been discovered. Here we were: myself, Elie Karsh, Peshke, the two Teig sisters and David Rotenstein. We went to the Ukrainian magistrate. The others remained in place until Branek moved them to a different location.

In time, though, we returned to Branek. We had also begun to show ourselves in the Colony. The only people remaining there were not prepared to denounce us.

Once, sitting with Elie in the house, a neighboring young gentile yelled: "Vensky is coming!". Vensky was a German gendarme from the nearby police station.

We began to run away, but too late. Vensky stopped us. With him was David Rotenstein, who had pointed us out. The story went like this: the policeman had found David and the two girls at Branek's mill. They found my rifle there. When asked whose it was, the petrified young man had immediately given us up. We were surrounded by 40 Polish policemen, among them many acquaintances. Even the commander, Sondei was a good friend.

The acquaintances calmed us down and said they would not allow us to be killed. We maintained we did not know whose rifle it was and that we did not even know how to shoot. To our poor luck, they found, on Elie, a photograph of him standing wearing a military uniform. (Truthfully, he had been photographed in a uniform as a fantasy)

[Page 259]

The German became angry and slapped Elie in the face so hard that he was dripping blood. They then ordered him to show how he shoots -unsuccessfully.

We became hostile to David Rotenstein- as if we did not even know him.

We were taken to dig a pit. I turned my head and looked into commander Sondei's eyes.

The searing look had succeeded. Sondei ordered that we should be taken to the police station. He asked us if we knew where the partisans were situated. We replied "yes". We were therefore taken straight to the station.

I had a gold watch, a pair of new shoes and a coupon for merchandise. I immediately went to the German commandant Vensky and gave him everything.

The next morning, Vensky asked me to take him to the village where there were Ukrainian partisans.

That day, the police had caught and arrested many of them. They found arms and ammunition. They also burned down the village. It was my first revenge on the Ukrainian murderers.

We spent two weeks in the lock up in the station. Elie and I went with the police to search for Ukrainian bandits. The women and David Rotenstein worked in the kitchen.

One fine day, commandant Sondei came to tell us that we were to be transferred over to the Gestapo. What was his advice? Run away!

We did not stop to think and at night we waited, in the garden, for Sondei and some of his trusted people to say good-bye.

"Go in peace"-said Sondei- "We will follow you. Be careful and let us see each other again".

In the morning, when Vensky discovered that we had escaped, he went to the Colony and shot at a few places. Vensky then reported that he had caught the Jews and had shot them.

He told me about it some time later.

[Page 260]

E.

We again sat in the hiding place, but we were not idle. I acquired arms and I went again to the few remaining houses. My only aspiration and hope were to find out the murderers of my family. I had an idea who they were. I found one family of theirs and I burned their house down. I even burned the nearby houses. The Poles were very happy.

We slept a few nights in an empty house. We then returned to Branek, thinking no one would figure out we were there. We also found other families who had been hiding there the whole time.

We were sitting with Branek with the radio on quietly. Suddenly, Germans (we recognized the uniforms) came running in our direction. Everyone went to hide in the stable. The Germans were actually Poles, led by Sondei, who were looking for a way to join the Polish partisans.

When they noticed our escape, they beat Branek to find out where we were hiding. They began to destroy everything in the house.

They wanted to burn the stable. We came out and saw Sondei. The former policemen became excited when they saw us. They had beaten and destroyed the home of a "good Pole". I was really upset to hear Branek try to calm them down by saying: "We will fix things between us".

Sondei advised us to wait in place until an organized partisan unit came and we would join it.

We stayed in the house until nightfall. A unit of partisans came and wanted to shoot us. This time, it was David Rotenstein who saved us. "We are Jews!"- he shouted. The partisans put down their arms and continued on their way.

It was terrible to stay in that house. We went to the cellar of the Ukrainian magistrate. He had left his house.

[Page 261]

We spent two days and two nights there. On Shabbat, Polish partisans came and began to repair the house.

I went to my friends Markevitch and Bushka and I asked them to intervene on our behalf, so that we would be taken in by the partisans. We went together to the house. On the way, I met a gardener-Elie was petrified (such was his luck), but, suddenly, good fortune came upon us. It was our good friend Zachartchuk (he had planned the resistance in the ghetto). For us, he was the defender and we avoided problems.

F.

Zachartchuk recommended that I stay in the house to indicate the path and Elie would be in another place.

A new era had begun in my life. I had been a persecuted person, at best a pale imitation, eliciting pity from well-meaning people. I now again became a person. Truthfully, we had all lived in constant danger, but the present danger had a purpose. The fact that I had been a Communist, standing hand in hand with Polish reactionary elements, did not bother me. We had a common goal: to finish off the German and Ukrainian murderers.

In order to raise the morale which had fallen from time to time, I made them happy with various stories. They called me "our Schweik". Maybe it was an obvious honor, but I was not seeking a new title. One aspiration and hope dominated me- to live through these critical times and to take revenge for the innocent spilled blood of my wife and children, as well as all other Jewish fathers and mothers, brothers and sisters.

In my situation I knew I could only realize my expectation with the help of the Polish A.K.A units.

I knew well all the villages and roads in western Volyn. For that reason, I was sent, many times, to make contact between various units. Every action or change of base, I went ahead. Still, I did everything with fear and voluntary self-sacrifice.

Once I was sent to a pond near Libevone.

[Page 262]

There I met Naftali Leitzes in a partisan enclave. They did not know he was a Jew. He called himself Michael.

I did not understand, then, why he was hiding his identity. Only later, when my elders spoke to me about conversion, did I begin to understand the true situation of the few Jews among gentile partisans.

In the presence of the partisans, I gathered, in our colony around 150 Jews. They were all concentrated in one house. This did not last long. Two young men left the colony and were caught by the Germans. The village was then bombarded, as a result. The staff ordered the transfer of Jews to Vortshin. There were only a few laborers left in the colony.

G.

Together with my commander, Farotchnik Bialy, I moved to another village, to establish a new base. We quickly organized a battalion which was called, at my suggestion, "Zamsta" (revenge). It consisted of people who were the sole survivors of their families. The first base was the village of Pozov. We soon were called to a bigger action.

The villages of Stiziritsh and Mikutitsh were terrible nests of the Benderovtzis and our purpose was to get rid of them.

Following my advice, the viper nests were attacked from three sides and only a few were able to save themselves. We burned down all the others without showing any mercy, then our unit moved to Stiziritsh.

We were lying in defense trenches, when we saw German tanks arriving. We allowed them to come close. When they noticed us, two officers jumped down and came near us:

"We did not come to do war with you-they said-allow us to go through to Mosso, as the Soviet partisans shot down one of our airplanes".

"That is not within our jurisdiction- we replied- come into our base where you can speak with those who can decide"

[Page 263]

It is difficult to understand the thinking of these people. Suffice it to say that they allowed themselves to be caught.

As they came into the base, they were disarmed and were forced to write to their underlings: "We are prisoners. Put down your arms!". Without saying one word, 130 Germans put down their arms and like good little children allowed themselves to be arrested. They were sent to Astodole.

A priest arrived and told us that the Germans in Ludomir had taken hostage several partisan families, among them that of Farotchnik Bialy. We had no choice but to free the Germans-but without their arms.

The Germans had so quickly been disarmed. At that time there were only about 300 men in Ludomir. We were informed about it by the Soviet partisans. On the basis of that we decided to attack the barracks in Ludomir where they were located. Our decision was proven wrong. The Germans brought, by train, a large contingent of soldiers, aided by many airplanes. Under these circumstances, the partisans retreated to their previous locations in the forest. We did not rest for long.

There was a bridge close to the forests of Mikutitsh, watched by our people. We were suddenly informed that the Germans were coming closer. I was sent, on horseback, to bomb the bridge. However, the Germans were shooting so much that there was no way to reach the bridge on horseback. I climbed down and hid under some ruins. I was able to creep to the bridge. I met Zachartchuk there. He was overwhelmed when he saw me.

He did not believe that he would ever see me again alive.

The bridge had already been destroyed. The horse galloped to me. I climbed on him again and I returned to base.

The horse was foaming.

We returned to the forests.

[Page 264]

H.

We moved to the east, very close to the front. On the road between Kovel and Brisk we were told that a famous and important German general was coming through there. It was an opportunity to "eliminate" him.

Mines were placed on a certain bridge where he was to drive through. Eighteen men were hiding among nearby trees. The general came in an armored car, with guards in cars in front.

We allowed the guard cars to go through the bridge, but when the general's car went on, we blasted the mines. The bridge with the car were completely demolished.

Among our people, one was badly injured. We took him with us.

Another time we found 18 Germans and 9 locals. Two of the latter gave themselves up freely. It turns out that one of those two was a Jew. We obtained important information from these two.

I and a young Pole shot the Germans out of pity. The locals were allowed to live. Later, they fought with us against the Nazis.

We received special treatment in the Ukrainian villages. The Jewish doctor from Dubno who was in our camp told me angrily: "Shmuel, how long will you continue to agitate?"

The problem of supplies was complicated. We were often hungry. I undertook, early in the morning, to get food. I was given local currency and dollars to buy food. However, the farmers did not want to sell. I began to scream. Once we brought six cows and a wagon full of potatoes and tobacco. Hungarian soldiers shot at us, but we arrived safely.

Another time I went with a few people and brought back a horse and a wagon full of bread and other food items, together with the farmer.

[Page 265]

It went so far that there was envy of me and people in the villages feared me.

I.

In May 1944, we were bombed by the Germans. We left the place and moved to another forest.

A short time later- we were in the Pinsk swamps- we received an order to find our way to the front. In order to do so we had to go through a highway and railroad line.

The Germans received us with machine guns and cannons. We managed to get through, but many of us fell. About one hundred men were lost.

At that time, Tsuker, the dentist's brother, was wounded (he lives now in America). I carried him to the forest where I found a Soviet partisan unit. I gave them the wounded man.

In that forest I found my regiment in the previously decided place. As thanks they involved me in studying the maps for every outing (In the beginning I did not understand much).

After a few days in a forest near Ratno, we resumed our march to the front.

We prepared ourselves for the attack. At night we reached the Pripet River. With me were two Jews from Ustiluh: Leyzer Dina's (Ginzburg), his son and grandson. Not far from the river we ran into Germans who were in graves. They had run away scared leaving ringing telephones. We went into the graves. They quickly recovered and began to shoot at us. Even the Soviets shot at us in error.

Many of us tried to swim in the river, but they fell in the water. The older Ginzburg also died. I remained on the shore.

I suddenly saw a few boards on the river which I used to go across. I called others to do the same. We were shot again from both sides.

[Page 266]

I reached the Soviets. Many of them were naked.

From 600 people, only 280 remained.

A few days later, we were transferred to Kivortza where we were absorbed by the regular Polish army-reorganized in Russia.

The front was now in Tortchin and we were getting ready to liberate Ludomir. I became sick near Kovel and I was demobilized.

On July 23, 1944 Ludomir was liberated. I stayed there and worked in a military sausage factory.

I could not live in peace as long as I did not find the murderers of my family. Once I went to a village with a Polish soldier. I caught one of the murderers. We immediately "took care of him". I went back to the village two more times. On the third visit I fell into the hands of N.K.V.D. I had been denounced by one of the group of killers.

A few months later, I and my old commander, Farotchnik Bialy, were sentenced to death. The sentence was changed to ten years in prison. I was sent to the distant north where I spent three and a half years in a forced labor camp.

After many appeals to the highest court, I was freed knowing it was revenge.

On 19.3.48 I was sent back to Poland.

I arrived in Poland on 24.4.48, completely broken.

The will to live pulled me to Silesia where there were many survivors from various Jewish communities. There, I found Avraham Becker and under his influence I decided to move to our newly founded state. There I would meet former friends and acquaintances and I would tell them everything.

As you can see, I told my story.

Written by A. Avinadav

[Page 267]

Victims of the Shoah

Translated by Ala Gamulka

Yaakov Bir (Feivel's)

[Page 268]

Meir Terner (Fenik) and his family. Alive is Eliezer Terner.

Aharon Goldberg and his family

[Page269]

Haya Rachel Holtzer, her daughter Gitel, son-in-law Avraham Weiner and their family

Shlomo Goldschmidt, the cantor, and his family

[Page 270]

Hershel Goldhover and Yeshayahu, son of Gitel

Tcharna Goldhover and her family. Still living is Bluma.

[Page 271]

Michael Krakover and family

Krakover children. Still alive-Penina.

[Page 272]

Betzalel Eiger and family

[Page 273]

Victims of the Shoah (cont.)

Abba Rosmarin and family. Still alive-Tuvia.

Yokhenzon family. Still alive: Sarah, Paula and Tuvia.

[Page 274]

David Rosmarin and family

Tzirl Shtimer (nee Rotenberg)

Beila Kilm (nee Rosmarin) and family

Avigdor Rosmarin and family

[Page 275] [Page 276]

Yaakov, son of Michel, Shafran

Sheintzi, daughter of, Haim *No index entries found.No index entries found.*

[Page 277]

Yizkor

Translated by Ala Gamulka

Oh, that my head were waters, and my eyes a fountain of tears, that I might weep day and night for the slain of my daughter of my people!

(Jeremiah 8;23)

[Page278]

May God Remember

The pure souls, thousands of Jews, who were annihilated by cruel and profane enemies, the scum of the earth. It was a foreign world of desecration–

The refugees from the death lands who found a haven in foreign places, always yearning for their resurrected homeland. Their souls ascended from foreign lands–

The illegal immigrants–refugees, who came on rickety boats, suffering hunger and thirst. They waded through strong currents to reach safe shores. They were swept into the sea or were locked out of their homeland.

The builders and defenders of our country, men and women, elderly and young, who fell on the battlefield, on the roads and in towns, at work and in school. Their death paved the way for the living–

All those who dreamed and fought and were fortunate to reach their homeland, but still left us too early in turbulent times–

May God remember them for good and may their souls be bound among the living.

We will remember them reverently in our hearts, all our lives. We will speak of their deeds, to our descendants, to all generations.

[Page 279]

גל עד
לזכר עולם
בהר ציון
לקדושי קהלת
אושצילוג והלין
שהושמדו ברצחו ובשחטו
בשנות השואה תרצ"ט-תש"ה
ע"י הנאצים ימ"ש
זכרם לא ימוש מקרבנו לנצח עד סוף כל הדורות
יום הזכרון נקבע י"ט אלול
ת'נ'צ'ב'ה'
ארגון יוצאי אושצילוג והסביבה בישראל ובגולה
מגלת השמדה

On Mount Zion
In memory of the martyrs of

The Ustiluh Community, Volyn

They were annihilated, massacred and butchered
During the years of the Holocaust, by the Nazis
(May their names be erased)
Their memory will never leave us, for all generations
Yizkor (Memorial) Day was chosen as 19 Elul

May Their Souls Be Bound Up in the Bond of Everlasting Life

Association of Former Residents of Ustiluh and surroundings in Israel and the Diaspora

Scroll of Destruction

For death is come up to our windows, and is
Entered into our palaces, to cut off the children
From without, and the young men from the streets.

(Jeremiah, 9:20)

B"H

Tuesday, Netzavim–Vayelech portion, 19 Elul, 5719

Association of Former Residents of Ustiluh (Ustzilug) and surroundings in Israel and the Diaspora

[Page 280]

Remembrance Scroll

We, hereby commemorate the names of our dear friends and relatives who were massacred during the Holocaust. May this scroll serve as an eternal memorial on Mount Zion and may this gravestone be a reminder of all those who were murdered and not buried in a Jewish grave.

Memorial Day was chosen as 19 Elul. On this day we will reunite with all those who are no longer so they will not be forgotten

May their souls be bound up in the bond of everlasting life

Necrology

Translated by Shalom Bronstein

Alef	Bet	Gimel	Dalet	Hey	Vav	Zayin	Chet	Tet	Yod	Kaf
Lamed	Mem	Nun	Samech	Ayin	Peh	Tsadek	Kof	Resh	Shin	Tav

Family name(s)	First name(s)	Maiden name	Gender	Marital status	Father's name	Mother's name	Name of spouse	Additional family	Remarks	Page
ALEF										
IDELSTEIN	Tzipora		F		Nachum	Devorah				281
IDELSTEIN	Sheintzi		F			Tzipora				281
IDELSTEIN	Zvi		M			Tzipora				281
IDELSTEIN	Meir		M			Tzipora				281
IDELSTEIN	Ya'akov		M		Yosef					281
IDELSTEIN	Avraham		M	Married	Manos	Sheintzi	Gitel			281
IDELSTEIN	Gitel		F	Married			Avraham			281
IDELSTEIN	Yitzhak		M		Avraham	Gitel				281
ALBOIM	Meir		M		Simcha	Yenta		His family		281
ALBOIM	Yosef		M	Married			Zlata			281
ALBOIM	Zlata		F	Married			Yosef			281
ALBOIM	Yenta		F		Yosef	Zlata				281
EINIS	David		M	Married			Yehudit			281
EINIS	Yehudit		F	Married			David			281

EINIS	Bracha		F		David	Yehudit				281
EINIS	Zelda Meity		F		David	Yehudit				281
EINIS	Chana		F		David	Yehudit				281
EINIS	Avraham		M		David	Yehudit				281
EIGER	Bezalel		M	Married						281
EIGER	Bina		F	Married			Bezalel			281
EIGER	Moshe		M		Bezalel					281
EIGER	Shimon		M		Bezalel					281
EIGER	Vella		F		Bezalel					281
EICHENBOIM	Efraim		M	Married			Chana			281
EICHENBOIM	Chana		F	Married			Efraim			281
EICHENBOIM	Boni		M		Efraim	Chana				281
EICHENBOIM	Asher		M		Efraim	Chana				281
EICHENBOIM	Leah		F		Efraim	Chana				281
ORFIN	Alter		M	Married			Sarah			281
ORFIN	Sarah		F	Married			Alter			281
ORFIN	Aharon		M					His family		281
ORFIN	Shlomo David		M					His family		281
OPTOWSKY	Yitzhak		M	Married		Batsheva	Leah	Children, number not recorded		281
OPTOWSKY	Leah		F	Married			Yitzhak	Children, number not recorded		281
OPTOWSKY	Avraham		M			Batsheva		His family		281
OPTOWSKY	Batsheva		F						The mother of Avraham & Yitzhak OPTOWSKY	281
OVENTHAL	Avraham		M	Married			Rachel	Their daughters		281
OVENTHAL	Rachel	GLOZ	F	Married			Avraham	Their daughters		281
OVENTHAL	Ben-Zion		M	Married			Gitel	Children, number not recorded		281
OVENTHAL	Gitel	GLOZ	F	Married			Ben-Zion	Children, number not recorded		281
UNGER	Avraham David		M				Devorah			281
UNGER	Devorah		F				Avraham David			281
UNGER	Moshe		M		Avraham David	Devorah				281
UNGER	Chaim		M		Avraham David	Devorah				281
UNGER	Yekutiel		M		Avraham David	Devorah				281
UNGER			F		Avraham David	Devorah				281
UNGER	Aharon		M					His family		281

UNGER	Shimon Yehuda		M							281
UNGER	Chaim		M		Shimon Yehuda			His family		281
	Peril Toiba	UNGER	F		Shimon Yehuda			Her family		281
UNGER	Baila		F					Her family		281
UNGER	Chaya Ita		F							281
UNGER	Chaim		M			Chaya Ita				281
UNGER	Eliezer		M			Chaya Ita				281
UNGER	Vaveh		M			Chaya Ita				281
UNGER	Etti		F			Chaya Ita				281
UNGER	Sarah		F			Chaya Ita				281
UNGER			F			Chaya Ita				281
ILBOIM	Mordecai		M	Married			Perl	Children, number not recorded		281
ILBOIM	Perl		F	Married			Mordecai	Children, number not recorded		281
ADLERMAN	Simcha		M					Children, number not recorded		281
EICHENBOIM	Sarah		F							281
	Baila	EICHENBOIM	F			Sarah		Her family		281
EICHENBOIM	Yehoshua		M	Married			Charna			282
EICHENBOIM	Charna		F	Married			Yehoshua			282
EICHENBOIM	Yosef		M		Yehoshua	Charna				282
EICHENBOIM	Shimon		M		Yehoshua	Charna				282
EICHENBOIM	Binyamin		M	Married			Chaya Rachel			282
EICHENBOIM	Chaya Rachel		F	Married			Binyamin			282
EICHENBOIM	Fishel		M		Binyamin	Chaya Rachel				282
ANIS	Zisha		M	Married			Rachel			282
ANIS	Rachel		F	Married			Zisha			282
ANIS	Baila		F		Zisha	Rachel				282
APPLEBAUM	Mendel		M	Married			Chana			282
APPLEBAUM	Chana		F	Married			Mendel			282
APPLEBAUM	Pinchas		M	Married						282
APPLEBAUM			F	Married			Pinchas			282
APPLEBAUM	Elkana		M	Married						282
APPLEBAUM			F	Married			Elkana			282
APPLEBAUM	Rizel		F		Elkana					282
ALINIK	Rachel Leah		F					Her family		282
ALINIK	Moshe		M			Rachel Leah		His family		282
OCHSMUT	Yitzhak Yishayahu		M	Married			Miriam			282

OCHSMUT	Miriam		F	Married			Yitzhak Yishayahu			282
OCHSMUT	Simcha		M		Yitzhak Yishayahu	Miriam				282
OCHSMUT	Chava		F		Yitzhak Yishayahu	Miriam				282
ISENBERG	Liftzia		M	Married			Leah			282
ISENBERG	Leah		F	Married			Liftzia			282
ISENBERG	Etil		F		Liftzia	Leah				282
ISENBERG	Fishel		M	Married	Liftzia	Leah	Bluma			282
ISENBERG	Bluma		F	Married			Fishel			282
ISENBERG	Yenta		F		Fishel	Bluma				282
ISENBERG	Rachel		F		Fishel	Bluma				282
ATLAS	Moshe Yehuda Yudel		M							282
ATLAS	Chaim		M							282
ATLAS	Yissachar		M							282
IDELSTEIN	Shmuel		M	Married						282
IDELSTEIN			F	Married			Shmuel			282
IDELSTEIN			F		Shmuel					282
IDELSTEIN	Aharon		M		Shmuel					282
IDELSTEIN			F		Shmuel					282
IDELSTEIN			F		Shmuel					282
AGRAS	Riva		F					Her family		282
EIDEL	Baila		F							282
EICHENBOIM	Yehuda Meir		M	Married			Sarah			282
EICHENBOIM	Sarah		F	Married			Yehuda Meir			282
ABRAMOWITZ	Yitzhak		M	Married			Hinda			282
ABRAMOWITZ	Hinda		F	Married			Yitzhak			282
ISENBERG	Fishel		M			Freida				282
ISENBERG	Freida		F						The mother of Fishel ISENBERG	282
ABRAMOWITZ	Chaim		M					His family		282
ABRAMOWITZ			M					His family	The brother of Chaim ABRAMOWITZ	282
ABRAMOWITZ	Yona		M		Chaim					282
ABRAMOWITZ	Eliezer		M		Chaim					282
ABRAMOWITZ	Yenta		F		Chaim					282
EISENSTEIN	Chava		F							282
EISENSTEIN	Yosef		M					His family		282
EISENSTEIN	Adil		F					Her family		282

APPLEBAUM	Zvi		M					His family		282
APPLEBAUM	Moshe		M					His family		282
	Avraham		M					His family	His occupation is listed as butcher	282
	Avraham		M					His family		282
	Avraham		M			Sonia		His family		282
BET										
BOJM	Esther		F				Zvi			283
BOJM	Matityahu		M	Married			Ruchtzi			283
BOJM	Ruchtzi		F	Married			Matityahu			283
	Zelda	BOJM	F		Matityahu	Ruchtzi		Her husband		283
BOJM	Moshe		M	Married			Sarah	Children, number not recorded		283
BOJM	Sarah		F	Married			Moshe	Children, number not recorded		283
BOJM	Chaim		M	Married			Chaya Rachel	Children, number not recorded		283
BOJM	Chaya Rachel		F	Married			Chaim	Children, number not recorded		283
BOJM	Chaim		M	Married	Zvi		Sheindel			283
BOJM	Sheindel		F	Married			Chaim			283
BOJM	Moshe Zvi		M		Chaim	Sheindel				283
BOJM	Rachel		F		Chaim	Sheindel				283
BERGER	Sarah	BOJM	F					Children, number not recorded		283
BIER	Moshe		M	Married			Tzirel	Children, number not recorded		283
BIER	Tzirel		F	Married			Moshe	Children, number not recorded		283
BIER	Ya'akov		M							283
BIER	Moshe		M		Ya'akov					283
BIER	Shamai		M		Ya'akov					283
BIER	Gitel		F		Ya'akov					283
BIER			F		Ya'akov					283
BITERMAN	Pinchas		M	Married	Ya'akov		Chava			283
BITERMAN	Chava		F	Married	Tuvia		Pinchas			283
BITERMAN	Bluma		F		Pinchas	Chava				283
BITERMAN	Chana Rachel		F		Pinchas	Chava				283
BITERMAN	Tuvia		M		Pinchas	Chava				283
BITERMAN	Yissachar Dov		M		Pinchas	Chava				283

BECKER	Eliezer		M	Married			Esther			283
BECKER	Esther		F	Married			Eliezer			283
BECKER	Moshe		M		Eliezer	Esther				283
BECKER	Yosef		M		Eliezer	Esther				283
BECKER	Baruch Chisha		M		Eliezer	Esther				283
BECKER	Freida		F		Eliezer	Esther				283
BECKER	Arieh		M	Married			Mentzi			283
BECKER	Mentzi		F	Married			Arieh			283
BECKER	Yitzhak		M		Arieh	Mentzi				283
BECKER	Batya		F		Arieh	Mentzi				283
BECKER	Simcha		M							283
BECKER	Yosef		M		Simcha					283
BECKER	Chaya		F		Simcha					283
BECKER	Motel				Simcha					283
BERGER	Batsheva		F						The niece of Shprintza BERGER	283
BERGER	Feiga		F			Batsheva				283
	Shprintza		F						The aunt of Batsheva BERGER	283
BYKSENHOLCZ	Rachel Leah		F							283
BANIS	Yosef		M							283
BANIS	Chaya		F							283
BANIS	Esther		F							283
BANIS	Tamar		F							283
BANIS	Moshe		M							283
BANIS	Simcha									283
BELTZER	Shalom		M	Married		Shprintza	Batya			283
BELTZER	Batya		F	Married			Shalom			283
BELTZER	Shprintza		F						The mother of Shalom BELTZER	283
BURLYANT	Shmuel		M	Married			Batya	Children, number not recorded		283
BURLYANT	Batya		F	Married			Shmuel	Children, number not recorded		283
BICHER	Yehuda		M	Married			Batsheva	Children, number not recorded		283
BICHER	Batsheva	REIF	F	Married			Yehuda	Children, number not recorded		283
BLATT	Mendel		M	Married			Breindel	Their daughters, number not recorded		283

BLATT	Breindel		F	Married			Mendel	Their daughters, number not recorded		283
BLATT	Kalman		M					His family		283
BRIK	Chana		F							283
BRIK	Eliyahu		M			Chana				283
BRIK	Etil		F			Chana				283
BOIGEL	Chaim		M	Married			Esther			283
BOIGEL	Esther		F	Married			Chaim			283
BOIGEL	Sarah		F		Chaim	Esther				283
BOIGEL	Pinchas		M		Chaim	Esther				283
BOIGEL	Bluma		F		Chaim	Esther				283
BOIGEL	Leah		F		Chaim	Esther				283
BLATT	Hinda Roiza		F							283
BURLYANT	Eidel		F							283
	Batya	BURLYANT	F			Eidel		Her family		283
BROIT	Yosef		M					His family		283
BERNSTEIN	Hinda		F							283
BERNSTEIN			F			Hinda				283
BRENNER	Breindel		F							283
BLIANDER	David		M	Married			Chana			283
BLIANDER	Chana		F	Married			David			283
BLIANDER	Sheindel		F		David	Chana				283
BLIANDER	Devorah		F		David	Chana				283
BLIANDER	Charna		F		David	Chana				283
BENO	Yehoshua		M	Married			Chana	Children, number not recorded		284
BENO	Chana	GOLDHOVER	F	Married			Yehoshua	Children, number not recorded		284
BORG	Dovidtshe		M					His family		284
BOKSER	Ya'akov		M							284
BOKSER			F						The mother of Ya'akov BOKSER	284
BOKSER			M						The brother of Ya'akov BOKSER	284
BLATT	Ya'akov		M	Married			Bluma			284
BLATT	Bluma		F	Married			Ya'akov			284
BLATT	Feiga		F		Ya'akov	Bluma				284
BLATT	Tzirel		F		Ya'akov	Bluma				284
BLATT			M		Ya'akov	Bluma				284

BANIS	Simcha		M					His family		284
BICHER	Zalman		M	Married			Chava	Children, number not recorded		284
BICHER	Chava	KRAKOVER	F	Married			Zalman	Children, number not recorded		284
	Baruch		M	Married				His wife	His occupation is listed as barber; his wife was the daughter of Golda the midwife	284
	Bunim		M					His family	His occupation is listed as carpenter	284
	Baruch		M					His family	His occupation is listed as shoemaker	284
BODENSTEIN	Refael		M							284
BODENSTEIN	Zvi Arieh		M	Married	Refael		Golda			284
BODENSTEIN	Golda	WAPNIARSKI	F	Married			Zvi Arieh			284
BODENSTEIN	Mendel		M		Zvi Arieh	Golda				284
BODENSTEIN	Sheindel		F		Zvi Arieh	Golda				284
BODENSTEIN	Hinda		F		Zvi Arieh	Golda				284
BREE	Shamai		M					His family	The brother of Riva [BREE]	284
	Riva	BREE	F					Her family	The sister of Shamai BREE	284
No index entries found	Binyamin		M	Married			Baila	Children, number not recorded		284
BLEY	Baila	COHEN	F	Married			Binyamin	Children, number not recorded		284
	Baruch		M					His family	His occupation is listed as a tinsmith	284
	Ber		M		Chaim				The son of Chaim the chimney sweep	284
	Berish		M	Married			Tovah Treina		His occupation is listed as carpenter; Tovah 'the deaf one' was his relative	284
	Tovah Treina		F	Married			Berish			284

	Tovah		F					Her family	Known as Tovah 'the deaf one,' she was related to Berish the carpenter	284
	Bluma		F		Ber Nachums			Her son, her daughter & their families		284
GIMEL										
GREENBERG	Bunim		M					His family	His occupation is listed as a teacher of young children (melamed)	284
GOLDBERG	Feiga	BOJM	F							284
GOLDBERG	Ya'akov Moshe		M	Married		Feiga		Children, number not recorded		284
GOLDBERG			F	Married			Ya'akov Moshe	Children, number not recorded		284
GOLDBERG	Freida	TABAKHENDLER	F							284
GOLDBERG	Hinda		F			Freida				284
GOLDBERG	Moshe		M			Freida				284
GOLDBERG	Berel		M			Freida				284
GOLDBERG	Mintzi					Freida				284
GOLDBERG	Fishel Leibel		M			Freida				284
GOLDBERG	Chaim		M			Freida				284
GREENBERG	Avigdor		M	Married			Anya			284
GREENBERG	Anya		F	Married			Avigdor			284
GREENBERG	Ya'akov		M		Avigdor	Anya				284
GREENBERG	Tovah		F		Avigdor	Anya				284
GURVATZ	Sheindel		F		Arieh					284
GURVATZ	Esther		F		Eliezer					284
GOLDHABER	Shlomo		M	Married			Leah			285
GOLDHABER	Leah		F	Married			Shlomo			285
GOLDHABER	Yitzhak Abba		M		Shlomo					285
GOLDHABER	Shamai		M		Shlomo					285
TZELNIK	Sarah		F			Leah			The daughter of Leah GOLDHABER	285
TZELNIK	Ya'akov		M			Leah			The son of Leah GOLDHABER	285
GOLDSCHMIDT	Shlomo		M	Married			Esther	4 children	His profession is listed as cantor	285

GOLDSCHMIDT	Esther		F	Married			Shlomo	4 children		285
GOLDSCHMIDT	Efraim Yitzhak		M	Married			Rivkah	Children, number not recorded		285
GOLDSCHMIDT	Rivkah		F	Married			Efraim Yitzhak	Children, number not recorded		285
GOLDSCHMIDT	Yisrael		M	Married			Gitel	Children, number not recorded		285
GOLDSCHMIDT	Gitel		F	Married			Yisrael	Children, number not recorded		285
GOVAL	Ya'akov		M					His family		285
GOVAL	Pinchas		M	Married			Leah			285
GOVAL	Leah		F	Married			Pinchas			285
GOVAL	Avraham		M		Pinchas	Leah				285
GOVAL	Chana		F		Pinchas	Leah				285
GOVAL	Yissachar		M		Pinchas	Leah				285
GOVAL	Yosef		M		Pinchas	Leah				285
GOVAL	Chaya		F		Pinchas	Leah				285
GINSBURG	Akiva		M	Married			Chava			285
GINSBURG	Chava		F	Married			Akiva			285
GINSBURG	Zvi		M		Akiva	Chava				285
GINSBURG	Shifra		F		Akiva	Chava				285
GINSBURG	Rachel		F		Akiva	Chava				285
GOLD	Etil		F							285
GOLD	Moshe		M			Etil				285
GOLD	Feiga		F			Etil				285
GOLD	Rachel		F			Etil				285
GOLD	Malka		F			Etil				285
GOLD	Shaul		M			Etil				285
GOLD	Arieh		M			Etil				285
GOLDHOVER	Charna		F							285
GOLDHOVER	Zvi		M			Charna				285
GOLDHOVER	Rachel		F			Charna				285
GLAZER			M					His family	His 2 brothers & their families also perished	285
GLAZER			M					His family	His 2 brothers & their families also perished	285

GLAZER			M					His family	His 2 brothers & their families also perished	285
GOVAL	Freida		F							285
GOVAL	Reizel		F			Freida				285
GOVAL	Natan		M			Freida				285
GOVAL	Gitel		F			Freida				285
GOLDBERG	Yitzhak		M	Married	Avraham		Sarka			285
GOLDBERG	Sarka		F	Married			Yitzhak			285
GOLDBERG	Ya'akov		M		Yitzhak	Sarka				285
GOLDBERG	Gitel		F		Yitzhak	Sarka				285
GOLDBERG	Sheindel		F		Yitzhak	Sarka				285
GOLDBERG	Temma		F		Yitzhak	Sarka				285
GOLDBERG	Shlomo		M		Yitzhak	Sarka				285
GOLDBERG	Aharon		M	Married			Doba			285
GOLDBERG	Doba		F	Married			Aharon			285
GOLDBERG	Gitel		F		Aharon	Doba				285
GOLDBERG	Chaim Shalom		M		Aharon	Doba				285
GOLDBERG	Toiya				Aharon	Doba				285
GOLDBERG	Golda		F		Aharon	Doba				285
GOLDBERG	Hadassah		F		Aharon	Doba				285
GOLDHOVER	Risha		F							285
GREENBERG	Ben-Zion		M	Married			Chana Chava			285
GREENBERG	Chana Chava		F	Married			Ben-Zion			285
GREENBERG	Yosef		M		Ben-Zion	Chana Chava				285
GREENBERG	Shmuel		M		Ben-Zion	Chana Chava				285
GREENBERG	Yitzhak		M		Ben-Zion	Chana Chava				285
GINSBURG	Leib		M	Married			Mirla			285
GINSBURG	Mirla		F	Married			Leib			285
GINSBURG	Esther		F		Leib	Mirla				285
GINSBURG	Dreizel		F		Leib	Mirla				285
GREENBERG	Yitzhak		M					His family		285
GREIZ	Bluma		F							285
GREIZ	Isser		M							285
GREIZ	Ya'akov		M							285
GREIZ	Chentzi									285
GREIZ	Motel		M							285
GRUBER	Nota		M	Married			Chaya Sarah			285

GRUBER	Chaya Sarah	KARSH	F	Married			Nota			285
GRUBER	Hillel		M		Nota	Chaya Sarah				285
GRUBER	Reizel		F		Nota	Chaya Sarah				285
GARSTENBLIT	Moshe		M							285
GARSTENBLIT	Esther		F							285
GARSTENBLIT	Chaim		M							285
GARSTENBLIT	Shabtai		M							285
GREENBOIM REICHMAN	Glickel		F						Her sisters were Zlatka & Mali	285
GREENBOIM REICHMAN			M				Glickel			285
	Zlatka		F						She is the sister of Glickel GREENBOIM REICHMAN & Mali	285
	Mali		F						She is the sister of Glickel GREENBOIM REICHMAN & Zlatka	285
GLOZ	Chava	TERNER	F		Meir					285
GOLDFEDER	Pinchas		M					His family		285
GOLDFEDER	Hersh		M					His family		285
GLIZER	David		M					His family		285
GOLDZEMER	Mordecai		M					His family		285
GOLDZEMER			M	Married					He is the father of Mordecai GOLDZEMER	285
GOLDZEMER			F	Married					She is the mother of Mordecai GOLDZEMER	285
GORVATCH	Ichel		M					Children, number not recorded		285
GORVATCH			F						She is the mother of Ichel GORVATCH	285
GREENBERG	Ya'akov		M	Married				Children, number not recorded		285
GREENBERG	Tovah	ROFF	F	Married				Children, number not recorded		285
GORVATCH	Shimshon		M					His family		286

GLAZER	Temma		F					Her family, mother, brother and sisters		286
GINSBURG	Risel		F					Her family		286
GLAZER	Pesach		M		Izik			His family		286
GOLDHOVER	Etia		F							286
GOLDHOVER	Mendel		M			Etia				286
GOLDHOVER	Moshe		M			Etia				286
GORVATCH	Avraham		M					His family		286
GORVATCH	Peretz		M					His family		286
GOLDBERG	Mendel		M						His occupation is listed as bathhouse keeper	286
GORGAL	Mordecai		M							286
GOLDZEMER	Toiba		F							286
GOLDZEMER	Motel		M			Toiba				286
GOLDZEMER			F			Toiba				286
GLAZER	Yishayahu		M					His family		286
GLAZER	Yitzhak		M					His family		286
GARBER	Chaim Eliyahu		M	Married				Children, number not recorded		286
GARBER			F	Married			Chaim Eliyahu	Children, number not recorded		286
GRUBER	Moshe		M		Aharon Zelig			His family		286
GRUBER	Meir		M		Moshe			His family		286
GRUBER	Hersh		M		Moshe			His family		286
GOVAL	Natan		M					His family		286
GREENBERG	Bunim		M					His family		286
GOVAL	Yisrael		M	Married			Ita	Children, number not recorded		286
GOVAL	Ita		F	Married			Yisrael	Children, number not recorded		286
GREENBERG	Moshe		M					His family		286
GRABER	Shabtai		M							286
DALET										
DIAMANT	Moshe		M							286
DIAMANT	Devorah		F							286
DIAMANT	Yochanan		M							286
DIAMANT	Baruch		M							286
DIAMANT	Chaya Rachel		F							286
DIAMANT	Batsheva		F							286

DIAMANT	Yisrael		M			Batsheva				286
DIAMANT	Esther		F			Batsheva				286
DIMENTSTEIN	Moshe		M	Married			Devorah	Children, number not recorded		286
DIMENTSTEIN	Devorah		F	Married			Moshe	Children, number not recorded		286
DANZIGER	Pinchas		M	Married			Tovah	Children, number not recorded		286
DANZIGER	Tovah	LEVERTOV	F	Married			Pinchas	Children, number not recorded		286
DRUKER	Yitzhak		M					His family		286
DARTVA	Iver		M					His family		286
DIAMANT	Nachman		M	Married			Rachel	6 children		286
DIAMANT	Rachel		F	Married			Nachman	6 children		286
DIAMANT	Elkana		M	Married			Miriam			287
DIAMANT	Miriam		F	Married			Elkana			287
DIAMANT	Gershon		M		Elkana	Miriam				287
DIAMANT	Yochanan		M		Elkana	Miriam				287
DIAMANT	Elkana		M		Elkana	Miriam				287
DIAMANT	Mali		F		Elkana	Miriam				287
DIAMANT	Yochanan		M	Married			Tzipora			287
DIAMANT	Tzipora		F	Married			Yochanan			287
DIAMANT	Avraham		M		Yochanan	Tzipora				287
DRUKER	Chaim Hersh		M					His family		287
HEY										
HALPERIN	Chana		F							287
HALPERIN	Ya'akov		M			Chana				287
HUBEL	Binyamin		M							287
HUBEL	Chana Sarah		F							287
HUBEL	Pinchas		M							287
HUBEL	Leah		F							287
HUBEL	Yissachar		M							287
HUBEL	Sarka									287
HUBEL	Yosef Dov		M							287
HUBEL	Chaika		F							287
HUBEL	Chana Gitel		F							287
HUBEL	Yosef Mendel		M							287
HUBEL	Zvi		M					His family		287
HUBEL	Chaim		M					His family		287
HUBEL	Ya'akov		M	Married			Chana	2 children		287

HUBEL	Chana		F	Married			Ya'akov	2 children		287
HUBEL	Moshe		M	Married			Freida	Children, number not recorded		287
HUBEL	Freida	SPEISER	F	Married			Moshe	Children, number not recorded		287
HUBEL	Arieh		M	Married			Chaya Gitel	Children, number not recorded		287
HUBEL	Chaya Gitel		F	Married			Arieh	Children, number not recorded		287
HELFMAN	Natan		M	Married			Sarah			287
HELFMAN	Sarah		F	Married			Natan			287
HELFMAN	Chaya		F		Natan	Sarah				287
HALPERIN	Moshe		M	Married			Nechama			287
HALPERIN	Nechama		F	Married			Moshe			287
HALPERIN			F		Moshe	Nechama				287
HALPERIN			F		Moshe	Nechama				287
HALPERIN			F		Moshe	Nechama				287
HERING	Mindel		F							287
HERING	Moshe		M			Mindel				287
HERING			F			Mindel				287
HOLTZ	Yosef		M	Married			Sheindel	Their family		287
HOLTZ	Sheindel		F	Married			Yosef	Their family		287
HERBST	Yosef		M	Married			Devorah			287
HERBST	Devorah		F	Married			Yosef			287
HERBST	Gitel		F		Yosef	Devorah				287
HERBST	Riva		F		Yosef	Devorah				287
HERBST			M		Yosef	Devorah				287
HERING	Tiltza		F							287
HERING	Moshe		M							287
HERING	Baruch		M							287
HERING	Mendel		M							287
HON	Gershon		M					His family		287
HUBEL	Yitzhak		M					His family		287
HORNSTEIN	Esther		F							287
HORNSTEIN	Sarah		F			Esther				287
HORNSTEIN	Golda		F			Esther				287
HORNSTEIN	Ya'akov		M			Esther				287
BOIMEL	Yechiel		M						He is the grandson of Esther HORNSTEIN	287
HAMMER	Batsheva		F							287

HAMMER	Chana Malka		F							287
HOICHMAN	Yosef		M	Married			Malka	Children, number not recorded		287
HOICHMAN	Malka		F	Married			Yosef	Children, number not recorded		287
HERLICH	Avraham		M	Married			Chava	Children, number not recorded		287
HERLICH	Chava	POPLIS	F	Married			Avraham	Children, number not recorded		287
HOAR	Mendel		M	Married			Chinka			287
HOAR	Chinka		F	Married			Mendel			287
HOAR	Gitel		F		Mendel	Chinka				287
HOAR	Roiza		F		Mendel	Chinka				287
HOAR			M		Mendel	Chinka				287
HECHT	Ya'akov		M	Married				9 children		287
HECHT			F	Married			Ya'akov	9 children		287
HERBST	Eliyahu		M	Married			Adel			288
HERBST	Adel		F	Married			Eliyahu			288
HERBST	Moshe		M	Married	Eliyahu	Adel	Hinda Devorah	Children, number not recorded		288
HERBST	Hinda Devorah		F	Married			Moshe	Children, number not recorded		288
HERBST	Yechiel		M		Eliyahu	Adel		His family		288
HERBST	Henich		M		Eliyahu	Adel		His family		288
HERBST	Hersh		M		Eliyahu	Adel		His family		288
HECHT			M		Ya'akov			His family		288
HUBEL	Avraham		M							288
HON	Ben-Zion		M					His family		288
HON	Yechiel		M	Married	Ben-Zion		Breindel	Children, number not recorded		288
HON	Breindel		F	Married			Yechiel	Children, number not recorded		288
HOLTZ	Moshe		M					His family		288
HOLTZ	Ezra		M					His family		288
HOIVAN	Batsheva		F							288
HOIVAN	Avraham		M	Married		Batsheva	Esther			288
HOIVAN	Esther		F	Married			Avraham			288
HOIVAN	Ya'akov		M			Batsheva				288
HIMBER	Shalom		M	Married			Sheindel	Children, number not recorded		288
HIMBER	Sheindel	POPLIS	F	Married			Shalom	Children, number not recorded		288
HERING	Hersh		M					His family		288

HUBEL	Mordecai		M	Married			Hinda	Children, number not recorded		288
HUBEL	Hinda	ZACK	F	Married			Mordecai	Children, number not recorded		288
HUBEL	Yisrael		M							288
HUBEL	Devorah		F		Yisrael					288
HUBEL	Yitzhak		M		Yisrael					288
HOLTZER	Chaya Rachel	TABAKHENDLER	F							288
HOROWITZ	David		M					His family		288
HUBEL	Yitzhak		M					His family		288
	Hersh Eliezer		M					His family		288
HOIVAN	Moshe		M	Married			Masha	Children, number not recorded		288
HOIVAN	Masha		F	Married			Moshe	Children, number not recorded		288
VAV										
WEINER	Pinchas		M	Married			Yenta			288
WEINER	Yenta		F	Married			Pinchas			288
WEINER	Sheindel		F		Pinchas	Yenta				288
WEINER	Moshe		M	Married			Etil			288
WEINER	Etil		F	Married			Moshe			288
WEINER	Yudel		M		Moshe	Etil				288
WEINER	Pinchas		M	Married	Moshe	Etil				288
WEINER			F	Married			Pinchas			288
WEINER	Ben-Zion		M		Moshe	Etil				288
WEINER	Yehezkel		M		Moshe	Etil				288
VEIGER	Avraham Yitzhak		M	Married	Yisrael		Gitel		The son of Rabbi Avraham	288
VEIGER	Gitel	HOLTZER	F	Married			Avraham Yitzhak			288
VEIGER	Asher Zelig		M		Avraham Yitzhak	Gitel				288
VEIGER	David Dov		M		Avraham Yitzhak	Gitel				288
VEIGER	Chana Leah		F		Avraham Yitzhak	Gitel				288
VEIGER	Yisrael Chaim		M		Avraham Yitzhak	Gitel				288
VEIGER	Amalia		F		Zvi					288
VEIGER	Zvi		M		Moshe					288
WEINSHEL	Ya'akov		M	Married			Baila			288
WEINSHEL	Baila		F	Married			Ya'akov			288
WEINSHEL	Yitzhak		M	Married	Ya'akov		Chaya			288
WEINSHEL	Chaya	HOLTZ	F	Married			Yitzhak			288

WEINSHEL	Arieh		M	Married	Ya'akov		Rivkah	2 children		289
WEINSHEL	Rivkah	POPLIS	F	Married			Arieh	2 children		289
WEINSHEL	Ben-Zion		M							289
VERTZAL	Yosef		M	Married			Rigal			289
VERTZAL	Rigal		F	Married			Yosef			289
VERTZAL	Feivel		M		Yosef					289
VERTZAL	Pesia		F		Yosef					289
VIDRA	Dov		M	Married			Fradel			289
VIDRA	Fradel	ROSMARIN	F	Married			Dov			289
VIDRA	Moshe		M		Dov	Fradel				289
VIDRA	Shemaya		M		Dov	Fradel				289
VIDRA	Sheva Rizel		F		Dov	Fradel				289
VIDRA	Gershon		M	Married			Baila	Children, number not recorded		289
VIDRA	Baila		F	Married			Gershon	Children, number not recorded		289
VEVRIK	Sheindel		F							289
WEITZMAN	Eliezer		M	Married			Sarah	Children, number not recorded		289
WEITZMAN	Sarah		F	Married			Eliezer	Children, number not recorded		289
WEINRIB	Ya'akov		M	Married						289
WEINRIB			F	Married			Ya'akov			289
WEINRIB	Leah		F		Ya'akov					289
WEINRIB	Esther		F		Ya'akov					289
WEINRIB	Zelig		M		Ya'akov					289
WEINRIB	Nachum		M		Ya'akov					289
VEVRIK	Ya'akov		M	Married			Chana	Children, number not recorded		289
VEVRIK	Chana		F	Married			Ya'akov	Children, number not recorded		289
VEVRIK	Sosha		F							289
VEVRIK	Kalman		M			Sosha		His family		289
	Sheindel	VEVRIK	F	Married		Sosha	Pesach	Children, number not recorded		289
	Pesach		M	Married			Sheindel	Children, number not recorded		289
WAGONFELD	Elimelech		M	Married			Essi			289
WAGONFELD	Essi		F	Married			Elimelech			289
WAGONFELD			F		Elimelech	Essi				289
WAGONFELD			F		Elimelech	Essi				289
WAGONFELD			F		Elimelech	Essi				289

WAGONFELD	Sarah		F					Children, number not recorded		289
WAGONFELD	Meir		M							289
WAGONFELD	Mordecai		M					His family		289
WAGONFELD	Avraham		M	Married			Henya	Children, number not recorded		289
WAGONFELD	Henya		F	Married			Avraham	Children, number not recorded		289
VIDLER	Rivkah		F							289
WEITZMAN	Ya'akov		M	Married						289
WEITZMAN			F	Married			Ya'akov			289
WEITZMAN	Etti		F		Ya'akov					289
WEITZMAN	Leibel		M		Ya'akov					289
WEITZMAN	Hersh		M							289
WEISS	Yitzhak		M					His sisters & brothers		289
WEISS			F						The mother of Yitzhak WEISS	289
VEVRIK	Abba		M					His family		289
WASSERMAN	Nechemia		M					His family	Mali is his sister	289
	Mali	WASSERMAN	F						The sister of Nehemia WASSERMAN	289
VASLER	Berka		M					His family		289
WAPNER	Rachel Leah		F	Married			Avraham Meir	Their family		289
WAPNER	Avraham Meir		M	Married			Rachel Leah	Their family		289
WAPNIARSKI	Yisrael Chaim		M							289
WAPNIARSKI	Pesil		F		Yisrael Chaim					289
WAPNIARSKI	Avraham		M	Married			Rina			289
WAPNIARSKI	Rina		F	Married			Avraham			289
WAPNIARSKI	Ya'akov		M		Avraham	Rina				289
WAPNIARSKI	Pinchas		M		Avraham	Rina				289
WAPNIARSKI	Gitel		F		Avraham	Rina				289
WAPNIARSKI	Efraim		M		Avraham	Rina				289
WAPNIARSKI	Berel		M					His family		289
WAPNIARSKI	Mordecai		M					His family		289
WEINREB	Moshe		M					His family		289
WEINSHEL	Yosef		M	Married			Zehava			289
WEINSHEL	Zehava		F	Married			Yosef			289
WEINSHEL	Feiga		F		Yosef	Zehava				289
WEINSHEL	Shprintza		F		Yosef	Zehava				289

WEINSHEL	Baruch		M		Yosef	Zehava				289
WAPNER	Yitzhak		M							289
WAPNER	Bela		F							289
WAPNER	Chaim		M							289
WAPNER	Yehudit		F							289
WAPNER	Frayda		F							289
WASSERMAN	Chaim Leib		M					His family		290
WASSERMAN	Yosef		M					His family		290
WERBER	Abba		M					His family		290
	Wolf		M		Yosel			Their family	He is the son of Yosel the wagoneer	290
ZAYIN										
ZIGELBOIM	Moshe		M	Married			Etil			290
ZIGELBOIM	Etil		F	Married			Moshe			290
ZIGELBOIM	Nota				Moshe	Etil				290
ZIGELBOIM	Freida		F		Moshe	Etil				290
ZACK	Baruch		M	Married			Chaya	Children, number not recorded		290
ZACK	Chaya		F	Married			Baruch	Children, number not recorded		290
ZACK	Elazar		M	Married			Henya			290
ZACK	Henya		F	Married			Elazar			290
ZACK	Rachel		F		Elazar	Henya				290
ZACK	Tuvia		M		Elazar	Henya				290
ZEMEL	Chaya Bluma		F						The family of the late Avraham ZEMEL	290
ZEMEL	Miriam		F						The family of the late Avraham ZEMEL	290
ZEMEL	Feiga		F						The family of the late Avraham ZEMEL	290
ZEMEL	Gitel		F						The family of the late Avraham ZEMEL	290
ZEMEL	Tamar		F						The family of the late Avraham ZEMEL	290

ZEMEL	Ayzik		M						The family of the late Avraham ZEMEL	290
ZEMEL	Batsheva		F						The family of the late Avraham ZEMEL	290
ZEMEL	Shlomo		M						The family of the late Avraham ZEMEL	290
SINGER	Mirel		F							290
ZEMEL	Ya'akov Mordecai		M					His family		290
ZEMEL	David		M					His family		290
ZEMEL	Moshe		M					His family		290
ZEMEL	Chava		F					Children, number not recorded		290
ZEMEL	Yudel		M					His family		290
ZYLBER	Shosha		F							290
ZONSHINE	Zvi		M					His family		290
ZONSHINE	Yoel		M	Married			Chava	Their family & his mother		290
ZONSHINE	Chava		F	Married			Yoel	Their family & her husband's mother		290
ZONSHINE	Efraim		M	Married			Tovah	Children, number not recorded		290
ZONSHINE	Tovah		F	Married			Efraim	Children, number not recorded		290
ZONSHINE	Reuven		M							290
ZONSHINE	Gitel		F							290
ZONSHINE	Mordecai		M					His family		290
ZUBERMAN	Hersh		M	Married			Michal			290
ZUBERMAN	Michal		F	Married			Hersh			290
ZUBERMAN	Gitel		F		Hersh	Michal				290
ZUBERMAN	Yosef		M		Hersh	Michal				290
ZEIDEL	Chava Sarah	BRENNER	F							290
ZISKIND	Pinchas		M					His family		290
ZISKIND	Mali		F							290
ZISKIND	Chaim		M							290
ZYLBER	Matityahu		M	Married						290
ZYLBER			F	Married			Matityahu			290
ZYLBER			M		Matityahu					290
ZYLBER			M		Matityahu					290

ZYLBER	Avraham		M					His family		290
ZALTZ	Moshe		M	Married			Mindel			291
ZALTZ	Mindel	FARBER	F	Married			Moshe			291
	Zanvil				Moshe Yona					291
	Chava		F		Moshe Yona					291
ZILBERSTEIN	Yehuda		M					His family		291
CHET										
CHAZANWALD	Falik		M	Married	Tuvia		Tzina			291
CHAZANWALD	Tzina		F	Married	Dov		Falik			291
CHREIN	Menashe		M	Married			Chaya			291
CHREIN	Chaya		F	Married			Menashe			291
CHREIN	Chana		F		Menashe	Chaya				291
CHREIN	Leah		F		Menashe	Chaya				291
CHREIN	Freida		F		Menashe	Chaya				291
CHREIN	Avraham		M		Menashe	Chaya				291
CHREIN			M					His family	He perished with his brothers	291
CHREIN			M					His family	He perished with his brothers	291
CHASID	Boniya		F							291
CHASID	Shimon		M			Boniya				291
CHASID	Shlomo		M					His family		291
	Chanan		M					His family	His occupation is listed as shoemaker	291
	Chanan		M					His family	His occupation is listed as water drawer	291
	Chana		F						Known as "the white girl'	291
	Chanina		M					His family	His occupation is listed as a tinsmith	291
	Chaim Elia		M					His family	His occupation is listed as shoemaker	291
	Chaya Etya		F					Her family		291
TET										
TOPOLER	Gedalia		M	Married			Chaya Baila			291
TOPOLER	Chaya Baila		F	Married			Gedalia			291

TOPOLER	Pinchas		M		Gedalia	Chaya Baila				291
TOPOLER	Motel				Gedalia	Chaya Baila				291
TOPOLER	Sarah		F		Gedalia	Chaya Baila				291
TOPOLER	Arieh		M		Gedalia	Chaya Baila				291
TOPOLER	Ya'akov		M		Gedalia	Chaya Baila				291
TOPOLER	Moshe		M	Married	Gedalia		Mindel	Children, number not recorded		291
TOPOLER	Mindel		F	Married			Moshe	Children, number not recorded		291
TOPOLER	Pinchas		M	Married			Leahtch			291
TOPOLER	Leahtch		F	Married			Pinchas			291
TOPOLER	Sheindel		F		Pinchas	Leahtch				291
TOPOLER	Sarah		F		Pinchas	Leahtch				291
TEIG	Aharon		M	Married			Perl	Children, number not recorded		291
TEIG	Perl		F	Married			Aharon	Children, number not recorded		291
TEIG	Shmuel		M		Aharon	Perl				291
TISCH	Zelig		M	Married			Baila			291
TISCH	Baila		F	Married			Zelig			291
TISCH	Hodel		F		Zelig	Baila				291
TISCH	Temma		F		Zelig	Baila				291
TISCH	Ruchtzi		F		Zelig	Baila				291
TISCH	Moshe		M		Zelig	Baila				291
TISCH	Yehuda		M		Zelig	Baila				291
TERNER	Binyamin		M	Married	Meir		Batya			291
TERNER	Batya		F	Married	Shlomo		Binyamin			291
TERNER	Rizel		F		Binyamin	Batya				291
TERNER	Rachel		F		Binyamin	Batya				291
TERNER	Chaim		M			Rachel				291
TEITEL	Toiba	TZIMERING	F							291
TEITEL	Nachum		M			Toiba				291
TEITEL	Zalman		M					His family		291
TEITEL	Ber		M	Married						292
TEITEL			F	Married			Ber			292
TUBAL	Yitzhak		M							292
TUBAL	Sheindel		F							292
TUBAL	Moshe Abba		M							292
TUBAL	Aharon		M							292
TUBAL	Chaim Leib		M					His family		292

TESHEL	Feiga		F							292
TESHEL	Shlomo		M			Feiga				292
TESHEL	Chanina		M			Feiga				292
TESHEL	Gitel		F			Feiga				292
TESHEL	Chana		F			Feiga				292
TESHEL	Freida		F			Feiga				292
TANERMAN	Henya		F							292
TANERMAN	Zvi		M	Married		Henya	Pesia			292
TANERMAN	Pesia		F	Married			Zvi			292
TANERMAN	Nena		F		Zvi	Pesia				292
TANERMAN	Yenta		F		Zvi	Pesia				292
TANERMAN	Shlomo		M	Married			Elka			292
TANERMAN	Elka		F	Married			Shlomo			292
TANERMAN	Nota				Shlomo	Elka				292
TANERMAN	Rivkah		F		Shlomo	Elka				292
TABAKHENDLER	Freida		F		Fishel					292
TESLER	Ben-Zion		M	Married			Chava			292
TESLER	Chava		F	Married			Ben-Zion			292
TESLER	Efraim		M		Ben-Zion	Chava				292
TESLER	Ita		F		Ben-Zion	Chava				292
TESLER	Zelda		F		Ben-Zion	Chava				292
TESLER	Yehoshua		M		Ben-Zion	Chava				292
TOYER	Shmuel Leib		M					His family		292
TOYER	Yosef		M	Married			Mindel			292
TOYER	Mindel		F	Married			Yosef			292
TOYER	Breindel		F		Yosef	Mindel				292
TOYER	Esther		F		Yosef	Mindel				292
TOYER	Tzirel		F						The sister of Yishayahu TOYER & Rachel	292
	Yishayahu		M						The brother of Tzirel TOYER	292
	Rachel		F					Her family	The sister of Tzirel TOYER	292
TEFER	Mordecai		M					His family		292
		TEFER	F					Her family		292
		TEFER	F					Her family		292
TOYER	Moshe		M					His family		292
TOYER	David		M					His family		292
TOYER	Malka	EISENSTEIN	F					Her family		292

TEITELBAUM	Matityahu		M	Married			Tzirel	Children, number not recorded	The brother of Manya	292
TEITELBAUM	Tzirel	COHEN	F	Married			Matityahu	Children, number not recorded		292
	Manya	TEITELBAUM	F					Her family	The sister of Matityahu TEITELBAUM	292
TUREM	Mordecai		M	Married			Meika			292
TUREM	Meika	KRAKOVER	F	Married			Mordecai			292
TUREM	Leibele		M		Mordecai	Meika				292
TEIG	Eliyahu		M					His family		292
TEIG	Yissachar		M					His family		292
TANENBAUM	Moshe		M					His family		292
	Tovah	KRIMER	F		Arieh			Her hasband & 3 children		292
YOD										
JOCHENSON	Yedidia		M	Married			Baila			292
JOCHENSON	Baila		F	Married			Yedidia			292
	Keila	JOCHENSON	F		Yedidia	Baila		Her family		292
JOCHENSON	Ya'akov		M		Yedidia	Baila				292
JOCHENSON	Yehuda		M		Yedidia	Baila				292
JOCHENSON	Ben-Zion		M		Yedidia	Baila				292
JOCHENSON	Avraham		M		Yedidia	Baila				292
JOCHENSON	Mali		F							292
	Lena	JOCHENSON	F			Mali		Her family		292
JOCHENSON	Lipa		M	Married		Mali	Bracha			292
JOCHENSON	Bracha		F	Married			Lipa			292
JOCHENSON	Yisrael		M		Lipa	Bracha				292
JOCHENSON	Esther		F		Lipa	Bracha				292
JOCHENSON	Ben-Zion		M			Mali		His family		292
YELLEN	Yosef		M					His family		293
	Yishayahu		M					His family	His occupation is listed as shoemaker	293
	Yitzhak		M					His family	His occupation is listed as wagoneer	293
	Yosef		M					His family	His nickname was "Yoshnaki	293
	Yoel		M			Etia		His family	The son of Etia TILIS	293
	Ya'akov		M					His family		293
YOCHT	Tovah		F					Her family		293

YELLEN	Zvi Yosef		M	Married				Children, number not recorded		293
YELLEN			F	Married			Zvi Yosef	Children, number not recorded		293
	Yosef		M					His family	His occupation is listed as a plasterer	293
	Yosef		M					His family		293
	Yishayahu		M					His family	His occupation is listed as a tinsmith	293
KAF										
KATZ	Yisrael		M	Married			Rachel			293
KATZ	Rachel		F	Married			Yisrael			293
KATZ	Yosef		M		Yisrael	Rachel				293
KATZ	Yishayahu		M		Yisrael	Rachel				293
KATZ	Breindel				Yisrael	Rachel				293
COHEN	Batsheva		F							293
	Bluma	COHEN	F			Batsheva		Her family		293
COHEN	Moshe		M			Batsheva		His family		293
KATZ	Kehat		M	Married						293
KATZ			F	Married			Kehat			293
COHEN	Mendel		M	Married			Chana			293
COHEN	Chana		F	Married			Mendel			293
COHEN	Hinda		F		Mendel	Chana				293
COHEN			M		Mendel	Chana				293
COHEN			M		Mendel	Chana				293
KATZ	Mordecai		M	Married				3 children		293
KATZ		SHROIT	F	Married			Mordecai	3 children		293
KATZ	Yitzhak		M					His family		293
LAMED										
LISHCHINKER	Avraham		M	Married			Batsheva			293
LISHCHINKER	Batsheva		F	Married			Avraham			293
LISHCHINKER	Yitzhak		M	Married			Breindel			293
LISHCHINKER	Breindel		F	Married			Yitzhak			293
LISHCHINKER	Yosef		M		Yitzhak	Breindel				293
LISHCHINKER	Tzviah		F		Yitzhak	Breindel				293
LISHCHINKER	Nachum		M		Yitzhak	Breindel				293
LISHCHINKER	Mordecai		M		Yitzhak	Breindel				293
LISHCHINKER	Chaya	LERNER	F							293

LISHCHINKER	Moshe		M			Chaya				293
LISHCHINKER	Bracha		F			Chaya				293
LISHCHINKER	Chana		F			Chaya				293
LISHCHINKER	Avraham Moshe		M	Married			Shoshana			293
LISHCHINKER	Shoshana		F	Married			Avraham Moshe			293
LISHCHINKER	Mordecai		M		Avraham Moshe	Shoshana				293
LISHCHINKER	Shprintza		F		Avraham Moshe	Shoshana				293
LISHCHINKER	Sheindel		F		Avraham Moshe	Shoshana				293
LISHCHINKER	Slava				Avraham Moshe	Shoshana				293
LISHCHINKER	David		M	Married			Chaya			293
LISHCHINKER	Chaya		F	Married			David			293
LISHCHINKER	Gitel		F		David	Chaya				293
LISHCHINKER	Yitzhak		M		David	Chaya				293
LISHCHINKER	Tzipora		F		David	Chaya				293
LISHCHINKER	Shalom Yoel		M	Married			Baila			293
LISHCHINKER	Baila		F	Married			Shalom Yoel			293
LISHCHINKER	Beni		M		Shalom	Baila				293
LISHCHINKER	Aharon		M		Shalom Yoel	Baila				293
LISHCHINKER	Dov		M		Shalom Yoel	Baila				293
LISHCHINKER	Freida		F		Shalom Yoel	Baila				293
LISHCHINKER	Yosef Mordecai		M	Married			Leah			293
LISHCHINKER	Leah		F	Married			Yosef Mordecai			293
LISHCHINKER	Binyamin		M		Yosef Mordecai	Leah				293
LISHCHINKER	Zev		M		Yosef Mordecai	Leah				293
LISHCHINKER	Moshe		M	Married			Esther	Children, number not recorded		294
LISHCHINKER	Esther		F	Married			Moshe	Children, number not recorded		294
LISHCHINKER	Shalom Kalman		M	Married			Baila	Children, number not recorded		294
LISHCHINKER	Baila		F	Married			Shalom Kalman	Children, number not recorded		294
LISHCHINKER	Zvi		M	Married			Shosha	Children, number not recorded		294
LISHCHINKER	Shosha		F	Married			Zvi	Children, number not recorded		294
LICHTMAN	Necha		F		Yosef		Pinchas			294
LICHTMAN	Mordecai		M	Married	Pinchas		Chaya			294
LICHTMAN	Chaya		F	Married	Godel	Bracha	Mordecai			294
LICHTMAN	Charna		F		Mordecai	Chaya				294

LICHTMAN	Bila		F		Mordecai	Chaya				294
LICHTMAN	Hinda		F		Mordecai	Chaya				294
LICHTMAN	Moshe		M		Mordecai	Chaya				294
LICHTMAN	Yitzhak		M		Mordecai	Chaya				294
	Bracha		F				Godel			294
	Devorah		F		Godel	Bracha				294
	Mirel				Godel	Bracha				294
	Menachem		M		Godel	Bracha				294
	Ben-Zion		M		Godel	Bracha				294
	Zvi Shmaryahu		M		Godel	Bracha				294
	Dov		M		Godel	Bracha				294
	Chaya		F		Mendel					294
LILKA	Moshe		M					His family		294
LEVERTOV	Yosef		M					His family		294
	Rivkah	LEVERTOV	F					Her family		294
LAKRITZ	Yehoshua Zvi		M	Married			Breindel			294
LAKRITZ	Breindel		F	Married			Yehoshua Zvi			294
LAKRITZ	Roza		F		Yehoshua Zvi	Breindel				294
LAKRITZ	Manya		F		Yehoshua Zvi	Breindel				294
LAKRITZ	Shmuel		M		Yehoshua Zvi	Breindel				294
LAKRITZ	David		M					His family		294
LEBENSBOIM	Avraham		M					His family		294
LEDER	Eliyahu		M							294
LEDER	Shimon		M							294
LAROCH	Shimon		M	Married			Sonia			294
LAROCH	Sonia		F	Married			Shimon			294
LEITZIS	Sheindel		F							294
LEITZIS	Chaim		M	Married		Sheindel	Rivkah	Children, number not recorded		294
LEITZIS	Rivkah	BLIANDER	F	Married			Chaim	Children, number not recorded		294
LEITZIS	Dov		M			Sheindel		His family		294
	Feiga	LEITZIS	F					Her family		294
LEITZIS	Naftali		M							294
LISHCHINKER	Esther		F							294
LUTVAK	Avraham		M					His family		294
LERNER	Gavriel		M					His family		294
LANDSBERG	Miriam		F	Married				Her husband and 2 children	The sister of Essi WAGONFELD	294

LANDAU	Yosef		M					His family		294
LORBER	Avraham		M					His family		294
LUTVAK	Binyamin		M					His family		294
LACHMAN	Feiga		F							294
LACHMAN	Yosef		M	Married		Feiga	Henya			294
LACHMAN	Henya		F	Married			Yosef			294
LACHMAN	Gitel		F		Yosef	Henya				294
LACHMAN	Yehoshua		M			Feiga		His family		294
LARACH	Pinchas		M					His family		294
LANDAU	Yitzhak		M							294
LANDAU	Shprintza		F							294
LANDAU	Shlomo		M							294
LERER	Esther Bila		F							294
LERER	Rachel		F							294
LEV	Zev		M	Married			Yehudit	Children, number not recorded		294
LEV	Yehudit	KATZ	F	Married			Zev	Children, number not recorded		294
LEFEL	Nota		M	Married				Children, number not recorded		295
LEFEL			F	Married			Nota	Children, number not recorded		295
LICHTBOIM	Eliezer		M					His family		295
LIALTZUK	David		M					His family		295
MEM										
MAYERSON	Menachem Manos		M	Married			Miriam	Children, number not recorded		295
MAYERSON	Miriam		F	Married			Menachem Manos	Children, number not recorded		295
MAYERSON	Chaim Yitzhak		M	Married			Dina			295
MAYERSON	Dina		F	Married			Chaim Yitzhak			295
MAYERSON	Matil				Chaim Yitzhak	Dina				295
MAYERSON	Breindel				Chaim Yitzhak	Dina				295
	Zehava	MAYERSON	F	Married			Moshe	Children, number not recorded		295
	Moshe		M	Married			Zehava	Children, number not recorded		295
MANERDRON	Mordecai		M	Married			Rachel			295
MANERDRON	Rachel		F	Married			Mordecai			295
MANERDRON	Pinchas		M		Mordecai	Rachel				295
MANERDRON	Feivel		M		Mordecai	Rachel				295
MANERDRON	Sarah		F		Mordecai	Rachel				295

MANERDRON	Bracha		F		Mordecai	Rachel				295
MANERDRON	Shoshana		F		Mordecai	Rachel				295
MANDELBAUM	Chaim		M	Married			Rachel			295
MANDELBAUM	Rachel		F	Married			Chaim			295
MANDELBAUM	Avraham		M		Chaim	Rachel				295
MELTZMAN	Mordecai Meir		M	Married			Batsheva			295
MELTZMAN	Batsheva		F	Married			Mordecai Meir			295
MELTZMAN	Shamai		M		Mordecai Meir	Batsheva				295
MELTZMAN	Tovah	BODENSTEIN	F							295
MELTZMAN	Sarah		F			Tovah				295
MELTZMAN	Shimon		M			Tovah				295
MELAMED	Moshe		M	Married			Miriam			295
MELAMED	Miriam		F	Married			Moshe			295
MUZIKANSKI	Doctor		M					His family		295
MEHL	Moshe		M	Married			Sarah	Children, number not recorded		295
MEHL	Sarah	ROFF	F	Married			Moshe	Children, number not recorded		295
MEHL	Zev		M	Married			Breindel	Children, number not recorded		295
MEHL	Breindel	MELAMED	F	Married			Zev	Children, number not recorded		295
MAMET	Shmuel		M	Married						295
MAMET			F	Married			Shmuel			295
MAMET	Dontzi		F		Shmuel					295
MAMET	Avtzi		M		Shmuel					295
MAMET	Yosef		M					His family		295
MANDELYOK	Reuven		M	Married			Machli	Children, number not recorded		295
MANDELYOK	Machli	EISENSTEIN	F	Married			Reuven	Children, number not recorded		295
MANDELYOK	Shmuel Hersh		M	Married			Baila	Their 4 children & his wife's sister		295
MANDELYOK	Baila		F	Married			Shmuel Hersh	Their 4 children and her sister		295
MILGROIM	Menashe		M	Married			Dina			295
MILGROIM	Dina		F	Married			Menashe			295
MILGROIM			M		Menashe	Dina				295
MILGROIM			M		Menashe	Dina				295
MANDELKERN	Tzirel		F							295
	Sarah	MANDELKERN	F			Tzirel				295

	Shimon		M	Married		Sarah		Children, number not recorded		295
	Tila	SHAMS	F	Married			Shimon	Children, number not recorded		295
MANDELBAUM	Yisrael		M	Married						295
MANDELBAUM			F	Married			Yisrael			295
MANDELBAUM	David		M		Yisrael			His family		295
MANDELBAUM	Simcha		M		Yisrael			His family		295
MELAMED	Bracha		F					Her sons		295
MELAMED	Beniya									295
MELAMED	Bluma		F					Her family		295
MONTAG	Ya'akov		M			Sarah		His family		295
MONTAG	Sarah		F							295
MANDELBAUM	Yitzhak		M	Married						296
MANDELBAUM			F	Married			Yitzhak			296
SUTNIK								Family	In the book it states "MILLER the family of Hersh SUTNIK"	296
	Mordecai		M	Married			Chava	4 children		296
	Chava		F	Married			Mordecai	4 children		296
MANDELKERN	Meita	TISCH	F							296
MANDELKERN	Lipa		M	Married		Meita	Sarah	2 children		296
MANDELKERN	Sarah	SHTREIMAL	F	Married			Lipa	2 children		296
	Hodel	MANDELKERN	F	Married		Meita		Her husband & their children		296
MELAMED	Yehoshua		M	Married						296
MELAMED			F	Married			Yehoshua			296
MELAMED			M		Yehoshua					296
MELAMED			M		Yehoshua					296
MANDELBAUM	Michael		M					His family		296
MANDELBAUM	Yoel Ber		M	Married			Zelda			296
MANDELBAUM	Zelda		F	Married			Yoel Ber			296
MANDELBAUM			M		Yoel Ber	Zelda		His family		296
		MANDELBAUM	F		Yoel Ber	Zelda		Her family		296
MANDELYOK			F					Her sister		296
MANDELYOK			F					Her sister		296
MELAMED	Simcha		M					His family		296
MELAMED	Shosha									296
MELAMED	Zisha									296
MELAMED	Chaim		M							296

MELAMED	Henya		F							296
MELAMED	Ya'akov		M			Henya				296
MELAMED	Moshe		M			Henya				296
MELAMED	Yechiel		M			Henya				296
MELAMED	Yehuda		M	Married			Chaya	Children, number not recorded		296
MELAMED	Chaya		F	Married			Yehuda	Children, number not recorded		296
MASTENBAUM	Chaim Leib		M							296
	Mintzi	MASTENBAUM	F	Married			Eliezer			296
	Eliezer		M	Married			Mintzi			296
MASTENBAUM	Hinda		F							296
MASTENBAUM	Yosef		M			Hinda				296
MASTENBAUM	Efraim		M			Hinda				296
MASTENBAUM	Yenta		F			Hinda				296
MASTENBAUM	Arieh		M	Married			Tzviah			296
MASTENBAUM	Tzviah		F	Married			Arieh			296
MANDELBAUM	Ya'akov Leib		M					His family		296
MANERDRON	Ya'akov		M	Married			Keila			296
MANERDRON	Keila		F	Married			Ya'akov			296
KANDINER MANERDRON	Rechil		F						It is not clear in the book if the surname is KANDINER or MANERDRON	296
KANDINER MANERDRON	Chana		F						It is not clear in the book if the surname is KANDINER or MANERDRON	296
KANDINER MANERDRON	Moshe		M						It is not clear in the book if the surname is KANDINER or MANERDRON	296
MARKIZER	Baruch		M	Married						296
MARKIZER			F	Married			Baruch			296
MELAMED			M							296
MILLER	Baruch		M					His family		296
	Freida	MILLER	F		Baruch			Her family		296
MILSTEIN	Breindel		F					Her family		296

MASTENBAUM	Visaf Yosef		M					His family	Perhaps the Visof ???? that appears in the book is a typo	296
MANERDRON	Neitel Nota		M					His family		296
MAMET	Yishayahu		M	Married			Malka			296
MAMET	Malka		F	Married			Yishayahu			296
MELAMED	Eliezer		M					His family		296
MACHLOK	Levi		M					His family		296
	Moshe		M						The son of the person known as "the soldat - soldier"	296
MAMET	Yisrael		M					His family		296
MAMET	Benzion		M					His family		296
	Moshele		M					His family	His occupation is listed as a hatmaker	296
	Motiya		M					His family	His occupation is listed as a hatmaker	297
MAMET	Shalom		M	Married						297
MAMET			F	Married			Shalom			297
MAMET	Pesia		F		Shalom					297
MAMET	Chaya		F		Shalom					297
MAMET	Chana		F		Shalom					297
MILSTEIN	Yitzhak		M			Breindel		His family		297
MILTZ	Baila	IDELSTEIN	F		Shmuel			Her family		297
	Chaim		M	Married			Sarah			297
	Sarah		F	Married			Chaim			297
	Zisha				Chaim	Sarah				297
	Baruch		M		Chaim	Sarah				297
	Chanoch		M		Chaim	Sarah				297
	Chaika		F		Chaim	Sarah				297
NUN										
NIGAL	Yisrael		M		Chaim Zev					297
NIGAL	Golda		F							297
NIGAL	Etil		F		Yisrael					297

NADEL	Avraham		M						His occupation is listed as a teacher of young children (melamed)	297
NADEL			F		Avraham					297
NADEL			F		Avraham					297
NADEL			M		Avraham					297
	Moshe		M							297
	Noach		M		Pinchas			His family	The son of Pinchas the 'shtadlan'	297
	Tzina		F		Pinchas			Her family	The daughter of Pinchas the 'shtadlan'	297
			M	Married				His wife & 2 sons		297
SAMECH										
STOLER	Nachum		M	Married	Dov		Feiga		His occupation is listed as shochet (slaughterer of kosher meat)	297
STOLER	Feiga	MELAMED	F	Married			Nachum			297
STOLER	Shaul		M	Married	Nachum	Feiga	Margalit			297
STOLER	Margalit	ALBOIM	F	Married			Shaul			297
STOLER	Baruch		M		Nachum	Feiga				297
STOLER	Yisrael		M		Nachum	Feiga				297
STOLER	Yehoshua		M		Nachum	Feiga				297
STOLER	Moshe		M		Nachum	Feiga				297
SOBOL	Yehoshua		M	Married			Batya			297
SOBOL	Batya		F	Married			Yehoshua			297
SOBOL			M		Yehoshua	Batya				297
SOBOL			M		Yehoshua	Batya				297
SOBOL			M						The brother of Yehoshua of Piatidin	297
SOBOL			M						The brother of Yehoshua of Piatidin	297
SATALNIK	Dov Ber		M					His family		297
SATALNIK	Moshe		M	Married			Baila			297
SATALNIK	Baila		F	Married			Moshe			297
SATALNIK	Chana		F		Moshe	Baila				297
SATALNIK	Shimon		M		Moshe	Baila				297

SATALNIK	Yitzhak		M					His family		297
SPOSOV	Ben-Zion		M					His family		297
SASS	Ber		M	Married						297
SASS			F	Married			Ber			297
SASS	Malka		F		Ber					297
SASS	Ya'akov		M		Ber					297
KIRZCHNER	Sender		M					His family		297
SAPP	Chaya Ita		F					Her family		297
	Liba	SAPP	F			Chaya Ita		Her family		297
SMIYATITZKI	Yishayahu		M					His family		297
SMIYATITZKI	Nachman		M					His family		297
MOSHKAS	Sender		M					His family		298
	Sender		M					His family	His occupation is listed as a hatmaker	298
AYIN										
ENGLE	Yehuda		M					His family		298
ENGLE	Nachum		M					His family		298
ENGLE	Shefa		M	Married						298
ENGLE			F	Married			Shefa			298
ENGLE			M		Shefa					298
PEH										
POPLIS	Feivel		M					His family		298
POPLIS	Yona		M					His family		298
POPLIS	Hersh		M	Married			Boniya			298
POPLIS	Boniya	JOCHENSON	F	Married			Hersh			298
	Devorah	POPLIS	F		Hersh	Boniya		Her family		298
PATORITZ	Meir		M	Married			Yehudit			298
PATORITZ	Yehudit		F	Married	Zvi		Meir			298
PATORITZ	Zvi Yisrael		M		Meir	Yehudit				298
PATORITZ	Devorah		F		Meir	Yehudit				298
FARBER	David		M	Married	Yitzhak		Yocheved		They died at an early age and their graves were desecrated	298
FARBER	Yocheved		F	Married	Arieh		David		They died at an early age and their graves were desecrated	298
FANIK	Menachem Mendel		M	Married			Feiga			298

FANIK	Miriam		F		Menachem Mendel					298
FANIK	Binyamin		M	Married	Menachem Mendel		Feiga			298
FANIK	Feiga	ROFF	F	Married			Binyamin			298
POMERANTZ	Elkana		M	Married			Sima			298
POMERANTZ	Sima		F	Married			Elkana			298
POMERANTZ	Esther		F							298
POMERANTZ	Rachel	SHAMASH	F							298
POMERANTZ	Dan		M			Rachel				298
POMERANTZ	Dan		M	Married			Etil			298
POMERANTZ	Etil		F	Married			Dan			298
POMERANTZ	Mindel		F							298
POMERANTZ	Reizel		F			Mindel				298
POMERANTZ	Hodel		F			Mindel				298
FINGER	Eliezer		M	Married			Meiti	Children, number not recorded		298
FINGER	Meiti		F	Married			Eliezer	Children, number not recorded		298
FINGER	Heshil		M	Married			Batsheva	Children, number not recorded		298
FINGER	Batsheva		F	Married			Heshil	Children, number not recorded		298
PELTZ	Gedalia		M	Married			Miriam			298
PELTZ	Miriam		F	Married			Gedalia			298
PELTZ	Sarah		F		Gedalia	Miriam				298
PELTZ	Batsheva		F		Gedalia	Miriam				298
PELTZ	Avraham		M		Gedalia	Miriam				298
FLIM	Yisrael		M	Married			Devorah	Children, number not recorded		298
FLIM	Devorah	TERNER	F	Married			Yisrael	Children, number not recorded		298
FREIMAN	Mordecai		M	Married			Maya			298
FREIMAN	Maya		F	Married			Mordecai			298
FREIMAN			F		Mordecai	Maya				298
FRISHBERG	Perl		F							298
FRISHBERG	Ya'akov		M			Perl				298
FRISHBERG	Shmuel		M			Perl				298
FRISHBERG	Ita		F			Perl				298
FRISHBERG	Ben-Zion		M	Married		Perl	Bracha	Children, number not recorded		298
FRISHBERG	Bracha	GOLDHOVER	F	Married			Ben-Zion	Children, number not recorded		298

FRISHBERG	Eliezer		M		Ben-Zion	Bracha				298
FRISHBERG	Bluma		F		Ben-Zion	Bracha				298
FRISHBERG	Reuven		M	Married		Perl	Feiga			298
FRISHBERG	Feiga		F	Married			Reuven			298
FRISHBERG	Reizel		F		Reuven	Feiga				298
FRISHBERG	Mordecai		M		Reuven	Feiga				298
POTIKA	Mintchi		F							298
POTIKA	Freida		F			Mintchi				298
POTIKA	Ya'akov		M	Married		Mintchi	Liba			298
POTIKA	Liba		F	Married			Ya'akov			298
FADIM	Hersh Leib		M					His family		299
FEIN	Yehoshua		M							299
	Feiga	FEIN	F		Yehoshua			Her family		299
	Temma	FEIN	F		Yehoshua			Her family		299
	Freida	FEIN	F		Yehoshua			Her family		299
FEIN	Gershon		M		Yehoshua			His family		299
PLETZEL	Menashe		M	Married						299
PLETZEL			F	Married			Menashe			299
PLETZEL	Avraham		M		Menashe			His family		299
PLETZEL	Simcha		M		Menashe			His family		299
PLETZEL	Hersh		M		Menashe			His family		299
PERLMUTER	Shimon		M	Married			Necha	Their family		299
PERLMUTER	Necha		F	Married			Shimon	Their family		299
PLATNIK	Mordecai		M					His family		299
PERLMUTER	Yona		M					His family		299
FELDMAN	Menachem Mendel		M	Married						299
FELDMAN			F	Married			Menachem Mendel			299
PULKA	Hersh		M	Married				3 children		299
PULKA			F	Married			Hersh	3 children		299
PERLMUTER	Zvi		M					His family		299
FRANZAK	Rachel		F			Sheva		Her daughters	The listing states 'daughter of Sheva BERTZAS' - meaning uncertain	299
FISHMAN	Sarah	VIDRA	F							299
FISHMAN			F			Sarah				299
PREISINGER	Eliyahu		M					His family		299

FRANKFURT	Miriam		F					Her family		299
PALIS	Chana	KRONGOLD	F							299
PALIS	Sheindel		F			Chana				299
PALIS	David		M			Chana				299
PALIS	Esther		F			Chana				299
FELER	Leib		M					His family		299
PERLMAN	Sonia		F							299
POMP	Chava	WOLF	F							299
POMP	Tzila	TRAKELTOIB	F							299
PELTZ	Chaim Yosef		M					His family		299
FELDMAN	Mordecai		M					His family & his brothers		299
FELDMAN	Mendel		M					His family		299
PELTZ	Mordecai		M					His family		299
PELTZ	Yerachmiel		M					His family		299
POSH	David Hersh		M	Married			Miriam	Children, number not recorded		299
POSH	Miriam		F	Married			David Hersh	Children, number not recorded		299
PERLMUTER	Zlata	BOJM	F					Children, number not recorded		299
FINKELSTEIN	Shmuel		M	Married			Gitel	Children, number not recorded		299
FINKELSTEIN	Gitel	SHIFER	F	Married			Shmuel	Children, number not recorded		299
PRIVNER	Mordecai		M					His family		299
FRIEDMAN	Asher		M	Married			Sheindel			299
FRIEDMAN	Sheindel	MELTZMAN	F	Married			Asher			299
FRIEDMAN	Rivkah		F		Asher	Sheindel				299
FRUMER	Shmuel		M	Married			Tzeitel	Children, number not recorded		299
FRUMER	Tzeitel		F	Married			Shmuel	Children, number not recorded		299
PERLMUTER	Ya'akov Moshe		M					His family		300
PAPIR	Yehuda Leib		M					His family		300
PAPIR	Mordecai		M					His family		300
FADIM	Zvi		M							300
FADIM	Esther		F							300
FADIM	Arieh		M							300
	Pinchas		M		Yitzhak David			His family		300

	Pinchas		M					His family	His occupation is listed as shoemaker	300
	Frayda		F			Batya				300
	Feiga	REIZ	F	Married	Shalom Chazan			Her husband and 2 children		300
TSZADEK										
TZIMERING	Aharon		M					His family		300
TZIMERING	Baruch		M					His family		300
TZIMERING	Berka		M	Married			Roza			300
TZIMERING	Roza	SHLECHTER	F	Married			Berka			300
TZIMERING	Shneour		M		Berka	Roza				300
TZIMERING	Sarah		F							300
TZIMERING	Simcha		M	Married			Esther			300
TZIMERING	Esther		F	Married	Avraham		Simcha		The daughter of Avraham the shochet	300
TZIMERING	Fridel		F		Simcha	Esther				300
TZIMERING	Chana		F		Simcha	Esther				300
TZIMERING	Leibush		M		Simcha	Esther				300
TZUPERFINE	Nisan		M							300
TZUPERFINE	Henya		F							300
TZUPERFINE	Rachel		F							300
TZUPERFINE	Meir		M							300
TZITRIN	Efraim		M					His family		300
TZIGAL	Liber									300
TZIGAL	Reizel		F							300
TZIGAL	Moshe		M							300
TZIGAL	Yitzhak		M							300
TZIGAL	Shimon		M	Married				2 children		300
TZIGAL			F	Married			Shimon	2 children		300
TZIGAL	David		M	Married			Devorah			300
TZIGAL	Devorah		F	Married			David			300
TZIGAL	Yerucham		M		David	Devorah		His family		300
TZIGAL	Yosef		M	Married						300
TZIGAL			F	Married			Yosef			300
TZIGAL	Mindel		F		Yosef					300
ZWEIG	Yerucham		M	Married						300
ZWEIG			F	Married			Yerucham			300
ZUCKER	Yosef		M					His family		300

ZUCKER	Batya		F							300
ZUCKER	Mindel		F			Batya				300
KOF										
KRAKOVER	Michael		M							300
KRAKOVER	Yitzhak		M	Married	Michael		Chaya			300
KRAKOVER	Chaya	TZIMERING	F	Married			Yitzhak			300
KRAKOVER	Yisrael		M		Yitzhak	Chaya				300
KRAKOVER	Sally		F		Yitzhak	Chaya				300
KRAKOVER	Yosef		M	Married	Michael		Tovah			300
KRAKOVER	Tovah		F	Married			Yosef			300
KRAKOVER	Sally		F		Yosef	Tovah				300
KRAKOVER	Esther		F		Yosef	Tovah				300
KRAKOVER	Zelig		M		Michael					300
KRAKOVER	Dov		M	Married	Michael		Sarah	Children, number not recorded		300
KRAKOVER	Sarah		F	Married			Dov	Children, number not recorded		300
KRONGOLD	Shlomo		M	Married			Chava			301
KRONGOLD	Chava	EICHENBOIM	F	Married			Shlomo			301
KRONGOLD	Leah		F							301
KRONGOLD	Yosef		M	Married		Leah	Malka			301
KRONGOLD	Malka		F	Married			Yosef			301
KRONGOLD	Ratzi		F		Yosef	Malka				301
KRONGOLD	Chava		F		Yosef	Malka				301
KRONGOLD	Sarah		F		Yosef	Malka				301
KRONGOLD	Moshe		M	Married		Leah	Gitel	Children, number not recorded		301
KRONGOLD	Gitel		F	Married			Moshe	Children, number not recorded		301
KORNFRECHT	David Zvi		M	Married	Yosef Meir		Yenta			301
KORNFRECHT	Yenta		F	Married			David Zvi			301
KORNFRECHT	Chana		F		David Zvi	Yenta				301
KORNFRECHT	Shmuel		M		David Zvi	Yenta				301
	Baila Bluma	KORNFRECHT	F	Married				Her husband		301
	Leah		F			Baila Bluma				301
KARSH	Shimon		M							301
KARSH	Yissachar		M							301
KARSH	Mordecai		M							301
KARSH	Shabtai		M							301
KARSH	Sima		F							301

KARSH	Meir		M							301
KARSH	Yosef		M	Married			Feiga		The brother of Feiga & Reizel	301
KARSH	Feiga		F	Married			Yosef			301
	Feiga	KARSH	F	Married				Her husband & their children, number not recorded	The sister of Yosef KARSH	301
	Reizel	KARSH	F					Her family	The sister of Yosef KARSH	301
KAVSOVITZER	Reizel		F							301
KAVSOVITZER	Moshe		M			Reizel				301
KRIGSHER	Yehoshua		M	Married			Tovah			301
KRIGSHER	Tovah		F	Married			Yehoshua			301
KRIGSHER	Esther		F		Yehoshua	Tovah				301
KRIGSHER	Rachel		F		Yehoshua	Tovah				301
KARSH	Zvi		M							301
KARSH	Ita		F							301
KANDINER	Menashe		M	Married			Sarah			301
KANDINER	Sarah		F	Married			Menashe			301
KANDINER	Rivkah		F		Menashe	Sarah				301
KOLTON	Avraham		M							301
KOLTON	Bluma		F							301
KOLTON	Tzipora		F							301
KOLTON	Rachel		F							301
KOLTON	Pesach		M							301
KOLTON	Moshe Zvi		M							301
KOLTON	Ya'akov		M							301
KOLTON	Hinda		F							301
KLEINMAN	Moshe		M					His family		301
KENT	Shlomo		M	Married			Pesil			301
KENT	Pesil		F	Married			Shlomo			301
KENT	Akiva		M		Shlomo	Pesil				301
	Mindel	KENT	F		Shlomo	Pesil		Her family		301
KRISHTAL	Zev		M	Married			Sima			301
KRISHTAL	Sima	LACHMAN	F	Married			Zev			301
KRISHTAL	Avraham		M		Zev	Sima				301
KRISHTAL	Tzila		F		Zev	Sima				301
KRISHTAL	Moshe		M		Zev	Sima				301
KRISHTAL	Ya'akov		M		Zev	Sima				301
KRISHTAL	Roza		F		Zev	Sima				301

KVITEL	Yisrael		M					His family		301
KVITEL	Menashe		M					His family		301
KOPF	Yosef		M					His family		301
KELNER	Moshe		M	Married						301
KELNER			F	Married			Moshe			301
KELNER	Yishayahu		M		Moshe					301
KELNER	Rachel		F		Moshe					301
KORNFELD	Moshe		M	Married			Rachel	Children, number not recorded		301
KORNFELD	Rachel		F	Married			Moshe	Children, number not recorded		301
KORNFELD	Zelig Ya'akov		M		Moshe	Rachel				301
KORNFELD	Malka		F		Moshe	Rachel				301
KORNFELD	Feivel		M		Moshe	Rachel				301
KORNFELD	Shlomo		M		Moshe	Rachel				301
KORNFELD	Necha				Moshe	Rachel				301
KOLTON	Menachem Mendel		M	Married			Menucha			301
KOLTON	Menucha		F	Married	Achiezer Chazan		Menachem Mendel			301
KLEINMAN	Dov		M	Married			Sheindel			301
KLEINMAN	Sheindel		F	Married			Dov			301
KLEINMAN	Sarah		F		Dov	Sheindel				301
KLEINMAN	Doba		F		Dov	Sheindel				301
KOL	Chaim Yisrael		M					His family		301
KRAMER	Yehuda		M					His family		301
	Sarah	KRAMER	F					Her family	The sister of Yehuda KRAMER	301
KRAINER	Chava	GOLDHOVER	F							301
KRAINER	Refael		M			Chava				301
KRAINER	Shmuel		M			Chava				301
KRAINER	Moshe		M			Chava				301
KRAINER	Chaya Bluma		F			Chava				301
KRAINER	Zev		M			Chava				301
KROTCH	Ezra		M					His family		302
KARP	Avraham		M					His family		302
KRISHTAL	Moshe		M					His family		302
KRISHTAL			F						The mother of Moshe KRISHTAL	302
KORIS	Asher		M	Married			Zisel	Children, number not		302

								recorded		
KORIS	Zisel	BLATT	F	Married			Asher	Children, number not recorded		302
KASEL	Yitzhak Meir		M	Married			Feiga			302
KASEL	Feiga		F	Married			Yitzhak Meir			302
KASEL	Avraham		M		Yitzhak Meir	Feiga				302
KOLTON	Avraham		M	Married			Manya			302
KOLTON	Manya		F	Married			Avraham			302
KOLTON	Doba		F		Avraham	Manya				302
KLEINER	Ezra		M	Married			Leah	Children, number not recorded		302
KLEINER	Leah		F	Married			Ezra	Children, number not recorded		302
KRISHTAL	Gershon		M					His daughters, number not recorded		302
KRISHTAL	Reizel		F							302
	Boni	KRISHTAL	F			Reizel		Her family		302
KRAMER	Moshe		M					His family		302
KAFKA	Meir		M					His family		302
KITIKA	Shimon		M					His family		302
KITIKA	Ber		M					His family		302
KLEINER	Moshe		M	Married						302
KLEINER			F	Married			Moshe			302
KLEINER	Yosef		M		Moshe			His family		302
	Sonia	KLEINER	F		Moshe			Her family		302
	Malka	KLEINER	F		Moshe			Her family		302
KILIM	Simcha		M	Married			Baila			302
KILIM	Baila	ROSMARIN	F	Married			Simcha			302
KILIM	Yerucham		M		Simcha	Baila				302
KILIM	Mordecai		M		Simcha	Baila				302
KARSH	Hillel		M	Married			Gitel			302
KARSH	Gitel		F	Married			Hillel			302
KARSH	Avraham		M		Hillel	Gitel				302
KARSH	Moshe		M		Hillel	Gitel				302
KOTIKA	Yosef		M							302
KARSH	Shimshon		M	Married			Osnat	Children, number not recorded		302
KARSH	Osnat		F	Married			Shimshon	Children, number not recorded		302
KATZNER	Hinda	LODINER	F		Baruch					302

KATZNER	Aharon Moshe		M	Married		Hinda		Children, number not recorded		302
KATZNER			F	Married			Aharon Moshe	Children, number not recorded		302
	Rachel	KATZNER	F	Married		Hinda		Her husband & their children, number not recorded		302
	Sarah	KATZNER	F	Married		Hinda		Her husband & their children, number not recorded		302
	Devorah	KATZNER	F	Married		Hinda		Her husband and 2 children		302
	Susel	KATZNER	F	Married		Hinda		Her husband		302
KARSH	Meir		M					His family		302
KVITEL	Berel		M					His family		302
KITAI	Fradel		F							302
KITAI	Eidel		F			Fradel				302
COOPERSTEIN	Moshe		M	Married			Reizel	Children, number not recorded		302
COOPERSTEIN	Reizel	SHIFER	F	Married			Moshe	Children, number not recorded		302
KORNFELD	Shmuel		M	Married			Gitel	Children, number not recorded		302
KORNFELD	Gitel		F	Married			Shmuel	Children, number not recorded		302
KRAMER	Avraham		M							302
KRAMER	Pesia Malka		F							302
KRAMER	Yechiel		M							302
KRAMER	Nachum		M							302
KRAMER	Aharon		M							302
KRAMER	Moshe		M							302
KRAMER	Chana		F							302
KRAMER	Sarah		F							302
KRAMER	Nachman		M							302
KRAMER	Yehudit		F							302
KRAMER	Moshe		M							302
KRAMER	Batya		F							302
KRAMER	Zvi		M							302
KAUFMAN	Elchanan		M	Married			Breindel			303
KAUFMAN	Breindel	KATZ	F	Married			Elchanan			303
KAUFMAN	Sarah		F		Elchanan	Breindel				303
KAUFMAN	Feiga		F		Elchanan	Breindel				303

KORNFELD	Ben-Zion		M	Married			Chana	Children, number not recorded		303
KORNFELD	Chana	POTIKA	F	Married			Ben-Zion	Children, number not recorded		303
KOTZKI	Eliyahu Fishel		M	Married			Bela			303
KOTZKI	Bela		F	Married			Eliyahu Fishel			303
KOTZKI	Yehoshua		M	Married	Eliyahu Fishel	Bela				303
KOTZKI			F	Married			Yehoshua			303
KOTZKI			M		Yehoshua					303
KOTZKI			M		Yehoshua					303
	Puah	KOTZKI	F	Married	Eliyahu Fishel	Bela		Her husband & their daughter		303
	Bracha	KOTZKI	F	Married	Eliyahu Fishel	Bela		Her husband & their son		303
KRAMER	Avraham Moshe		M					His family		303
KATZER	Bunim		M					His family		303
KATZER	Zalman		M					His family		303
KONDAS	Ya'akov		M					His family		303
KONDAS	Yehuda		M					His family		303
KARP	Motel		M					His family		303
RESH										
ROSMARIN	Pesia		F						The sister of Mali JOCHENSON	303
RABIN	Michael		M					His family		303
RABIN	Chaim		M					His family		303
RABIN	Mordecai		M					His family		303
ROSENBERG	Ben-Zion		M	Married			Tovah	Children, number not recorded		303
ROSENBERG	Tovah		F	Married			Ben-Zion	Children, number not recorded		303
ROFF	Avigdor		M	Married			Matil			303
ROFF	Matil		F	Married			Avigdor			303
ROFF	David		M	Married	Avigdor	Matil	Baila	Children, number not recorded		303
ROFF	Baila		F	Married			David	Children, number not recorded		303
	Bluma	ROFF	F		Avigdor	Matil		Her family		303
	Feiga	ROFF	F		Avigdor	Matil		Her family		303
RUBINSTEIN	Perl		F			Rachel Leah				303
RUBINSTEIN	Efraim		M			Perl				303
RUBINSTEIN	Rivkah		F			Perl				303

	Rachel Leah		F						The mother of Perl RUBINSTEIN	303
REICHMAN	Arieh		M							303
REICHMAN	Pesia		F							303
RUTENBERG	Sarah		F							303
RUTENBERG	Meir		M			Sarah				303
RUTENBERG	Pinchas		M	Married		Sarah	Mindel			303
RUTENBERG	Mindel		F	Married			Pinchas			303
RABIN	Ya'akov		M							303
RABIN	Zalman		M		Ya'akov					303
RABIN	Shlomo		M		Ya'akov					303
RABIN	Chaim Eliyahu		M		Ya'akov					303
RABIN	Devorah		F		Ya'akov					303
ROSMARIN	Avraham Abba		M	Married	Moshe		Freida			303
ROSMARIN	Freida		F	Married			Avraham Abba			303
	Shifra	ROSMARIN	F	Married	Avraham Abba	Freida	Avraham	2 daughters		303
	Avraham		M	Married			Shifra	2 daughters		303
ROSMARIN	Avigdor		M	Married	Avraham Abba	Freida	Pesia			303
ROSMARIN	Pesia		F	Married			Avigdor			303
ROSMARIN			M		Avigdor	Pesia				303
ROSMARIN			M		Avigdor	Pesia				303
ROSMARIN	David		M	Married	Moshe		Breindel			304
ROSMARIN	Breindel		F	Married			David			304
ROSMARIN	Yitzhak		M	Married	David	Breindel	Chava			304
ROSMARIN	Chava		F	Married			Yitzhak			304
ROSMARIN	Leibele		M		Yitzhak	Chava				304
	Baila	ROSMARIN	F	Married	David	Breindel		Her husband		304
ROSMARIN	Sarah		F		David	Breindel				304
REIVER	Chaim		M	Married			Esther Rachel	Their sons, number not recorded		304
REIVER	Esther Rachel	OVENTHAL	F	Married			Chaim	Their sons, number not recorded		304
RECHTSHAFT	Moshe		M					His family		304
ROSENBERG	Natan		M					His family		304
ROSENBERG	Aharon		M		Natan			His family		304
RUTENBERG	Leahtchi		F					Her mother		304
RUTENBERG	Avigdor		M					His family		304
RUTENBERG	Bezalel		M					His family		304

RASLAS	Shalom		M	Married			Sarah			304
RASLAS	Sarah		F	Married			Shalom			304
RASLAS	Chava		F		Shalom	Sarah				304
RASLAS	Ita		F		Shalom	Sarah				304
RASLAS	Bluma		F		Shalom	Sarah				304
RASLAS	Chana Pesia		F		Shalom	Sarah				304
RASLAS	Devorah		F							304
RASLAS	Avraham		M							304
RASLAS	Shaul		M							304
RASLAS	Tovah		F							304
RASLAS	Rachel		F							304
RASLAS	Yenta		F			Rachel				304
RASLAS	Ya'akov		M			Rachel				304
RASLAS	Mendel		M			Rachel				304
RASLAS	Meir		M			Rachel				304
RAIDER	Gitel		F	Widow			Ben-Zion			304
RAIDER	Shmuel		M	Married	Ben-Zion	Gitel	Shprintza		The widow of the judge R' Ben-Zion	304
RAIDER	Shprintza		F	Married			Shmuel			304
RAIDER	David		M	Married	Ben-Zion	Gitel	Ita			304
RAIDER	Ita		F	Married			David			304
ROSENFELD	Rachel		F							304
ROSENFELD			M			Rachel				304
ROSENFELD	Shmuel		M	Married						304
ROSENFELD			F	Married			Shmuel			304
ROSENFELD	Moshe		M		Shmuel					304
ROSENFELD	Nisan		M	Married			Temma			304
ROSENFELD	Temma		F	Married			Nisan			304
ROSENFELD	Moshe		M		Nisan	Temma				304
RAAB	Yisrael		M					His family		304
	Esther	ROSENFELD	F					Her family		304
	Milka	ROSENFELD	F					Her family		304
	Lifsha	ROSENFELD	F					Her family		304
RUTENBERG	Zelig		M					His family		304
RUTENBERG	Yisrael		M							304
	Feiga	RUTENBERG	F					Her family	The sister of Yisrael RUTENBERG	304
ROSENBLUM	Yosef		M	Married			Sheindel			304
ROSENBLUM	Sheindel	GOLDHOVER	F	Married			Yosef			304

REITER	Sheindel		F							304
REITER	Batya		F							304
	Liba	REITER	F			Batya		Her family		304
	Meika	REITER	F			Batya		Her family		304
RABIN	Avraham Eliezer		M					His family		304
RABIN	Eliyahu		M					His family		304
REICHMAN	Sarel		F							304
REICHMAN	Bluma		F			Sarel				304
ROTENTELER	Fani		F							304
ROTENTELER	Mordecai		M			Fani				304
ROTENTELER	Yisrael		M			Fani				304
ROSENBERG	Meita		F							304
ROSENBERG	Yehoshua		M	Married		Meita	Gitel			304
ROSENBERG	Gitel		F	Married			Yehoshua			304
REITER	Shalom		M	Married			Esther	Their family		305
REITER	Esther		F	Married			Shalom	Their family		305
REIF	Risel									305
ROSMARIN	Esther Leah		F							305
RAAB	Leibel		M	Married			Reila			305
RAAB	Reila		F	Married			Leibel			305
RAAB	Avraham		M		Leibel	Reila				305
RAAB	Reizel		F		Leibel	Reila				305
RAAB	Ya'akov Moshe		M		Leibel	Reila				305
RAAB	Sarah		F		Leibel	Reila				305
RUBINSTEIN	Chaim		M	Married			Hinda			305
RUBINSTEIN	Hinda	FARBER	F	Married			Chaim			305
RUBINSTEIN	Yocheved		F		Chaim	Hinda				305
REIVER	Mordecai		M					His family		305
REITER	Rachel	CHAZANWALD	F							305
REITER			M			Rachel				305
REITER	Esther		F					2 sisters		305
SHIN										
STEINBERG	Shalom		M	Married			Mintzi			305
STEINBERG	Mintzi		F	Married			Shalom			305
STEINBERG	Moshe		M		Shalom	Mintzi		His family		305
SPIRER	Moshe		M	Married			Perl	Children, number not recorded		305
SPIRER	Perl		F	Married			Moshe	Children, number not recorded		305

SPIRER	Gala		F							305
SPIRER	Henya		F			Gala				305
SHNOL	Baruch Zvi		M	Married			Baila			305
SHNOL	Baila		F	Married			Baruch Zvi			305
SHNOL	David		M		Baruch Zvi	Baila				305
SHNOL			F		Baruch Zvi	Baila				305
SHEINERMAN	Yehezkel		M	Married			Feiga			305
SHEINERMAN	Feiga		F	Married			Yehezkel			305
SHEINERMAN	Samel		M		Yehezkel	Feiga				305
SHEINERMAN	Ya'akov		M		Yehezkel	Feiga				305
SHEINERMAN	Mendel		M		Yehezkel	Feiga				305
SHEINERMAN	Yitzhak		M		Yehezkel	Feiga				305
SHEINERMAN	Batsheva		F		Yehezkel	Feiga				305
SHEINERMAN	Chana		F		Yehezkel	Feiga				305
SHEINERMAN	Gitel		F		Yehezkel	Feiga				305
SHEINERMAN	Zvi		M	Married			Henya	Children, number not recorded		305
SHEINERMAN	Henya		F	Married			Zvi	Children, number not recorded		305
SHEINERMAN	Eliyahu		M	Married			Bracha			305
SHEINERMAN	Bracha		F	Married			Eliyahu			305
SHEINERMAN	Moshe		M		Eliyahu	Bracha				305
SHEINERMAN	Hinda		F		Eliyahu	Bracha				305
SHEINERMAN	Chana		F		Eliyahu	Bracha				305
SHEINERMAN	Zvi		M		Eliyahu	Bracha				305
SAFRAN	Michael		M	Married			Batya			305
SAFRAN	Batya	ROSMARIN	F	Married	Yosef		Michael			305
SAFRAN	Ya'akov		M		Michael	Batya				305
SHEINBRON	Arieh		M							305
SHEINBRON	Eliezer		M		Arieh					305
SHTIMER	Avraham		M	Married			Tzirel			305
SHTIMER	Tzirel	ROSMARIN	F	Married		Sheindel	Avraham			305
SHTIMER	Chaim		M		Avraham	Tzirel				305
SHTIMER	Moshe		M		Avraham	Tzirel				305
SHTIMER	Sheindel		F		Avraham	Tzirel				305
SHEINTOP	Rabbi Yehoshua		M	Married			Reshi	Children, number not recorded	His profession is listed as Rabbi & rabbinic judge	305
SHEINTOP	Reshi		F	Married			Yehoshua	Children, number not recorded		305

SHEINMAN	Sheindel		F		Yisrael					305
SCHLECHTER	Rabbi Avraham		M						He was a Rabbi & a shochet (slaughterer of kosher meat)	305
SHLECHTER	Berel		M	Married	Avraham		Rachel	Children, number not recorded		305
SHLECHTER	Rachel		F	Married			Berel	Children, number not recorded		305
SHLECHTER	Fridel		F		Berel	Rachel				305
SHLECHTER	Shlomo		M		Berel	Rachel				305
SHLECHTER	Shimon		M		Berel	Rachel				305
SHLECHTER	Chava		F		Berel	Rachel				305
	Chana	SHLECHTER	F		Avraham					305
	David		M			Chana			The son of Chana who was the daughter of Avraham SHLECHTER the Shochet	305
SHULAV	Rachel Dovrish		F		Yisrael					305
SPEISER	Mordecai		M	Married			Batya			305
SPEISER	Batya	FANIK	F	Married			Mordecai			305
SPEISER	Baila		F		Mordecai	Batya				305
SPEISER	Tzipora		F		Mordecai	Batya				305
SHLECHTER	Moshe		M	Married			Miriam			305
SHLECHTER	Miriam		F	Married			Moshe			305
SHLECHTER	Fishel		M		Moshe	Miriam				305
SHLECHTER	Shimon		M		Moshe	Miriam				305
SHLECHTER	Zisha				Moshe	Miriam				305
SHATKAN	Yisrael		M	Married	Eliezer		Rachel			306
SHATKAN	Rachel		F	Married			Yisrael			306
SHATKAN	Avraham		M		Yisrael	Rachel				306
SHNOL	Moshe		M	Married			Bilha	2 children		306
SHNOL	Bilha		F	Married			Moshe	2 children		306
SHNITER	Chaim		M		Avraham					306
SHMELTZ	Asher		M					His family		306
SHLEIFER	Aharon		M							306
SHLEIFER	Mindel		F							306
SHLEIFER	Gedalia		M							306
SHLEIFER	Dudik		M							306

SHLEIFER	Moshe		M							306
SHLEIFER	Batya		F							306
SHLEIFER	Yehoshua		M							306
SHIFER	Yosef		M	Married			Hodel			306
SHIFER	Hodel		F	Married			Yosef			306
SHIFER	Yisrael		M	Married			Etil			306
SHIFER	Etil		F	Married			Yisrael			306
SHIFER	Shlomo		M	Married						306
SHIFER			F	Married						306
SHIFER	Pinchas		M	Married	Shlomo		Dina	Children, number not recorded		306
SHIFER	Dina	ROFF	F	Married			Pinchas	Children, number not recorded		306
	Temma	SHIFER	F		Shlomo			Her family		306
SHAMASH	Mordecai		M	Married						306
SHAMASH			F	Married			Mordecai			306
SHARER	Yosef		M	Married			Rivkah	Children, number not recorded		306
SHARER	Rivkah		F	Married			Yosef	Children, number not recorded		306
	Sarah	KRIMER	F		Arieh			Her family		306
	Sarah	MILSTEIN	F			Breindel		Her family		306
	Shmuel		M						His occupation is listed as water drawer	306
SHTORM	Avraham		M	Married						306
SHTORM			F	Married			Avraham			306
SHTORM	Sarah		F		Avraham					306
SHTORM	Moshele		M		Avraham			His family		306
STERN	Michael		M	Married			Rosha	Children, number not recorded		306
STERN	Rosha		F	Married			Michael	Children, number not recorded		306
SHPAK	Zelig		M	Married			Chaya	Children, number not recorded		306
SHPAK	Chaya		F	Married			Zelig	Children, number not recorded		306
SHLEIFER	David		M		Aharon			His family		306
SHLEIFER			F						The mother of David SHLEIFER & wife of the Rabbi	306
SHPIER	Elazar		M					His family		306

SHROIT	Ya'akov		M	Married			Fradel			306
SHROIT	Fradel		F	Married			Ya'akov			306
SHROIT	Shmuel		M		Ya'akov	Fradel				306
SHROIT	Gitel		F		Ya'akov	Fradel				306
SHAMASH	Arieh		M	Married	Mordecai		Shifra			306
SHAMASH	Shifra	FARBER	F	Married			Arieh			306
SHAMASH	David		M		Arieh	Shifra				306
SHEINERMAN	Zvi		M					His family		306
SHEINERMAN	Sarah		F							306
SHEINERMAN	Tovah Esther		F			Sarah				306
SHEINERMAN	Mindel		F			Sarah				306
SPEISER	David		M	Married			Bluma			306
SPEISER	Bluma	HALPERIN	F	Married			David			306
SPEISER	Nachman		M		David	Bluma				306
SHTREIMAL	Yosef		M					His family		306
SHTREIMAL	David		M					His family		306
SHTREIMAL	Sheindel		F					Her family		306
SHTREIMAL	Sarah		F					Her family		306
SHTREIMAL	Sender		M	Married			Bluma	Children, number not recorded		306
SHTREIMAL	Bluma		F	Married			Sender	Children, number not recorded		306
SHTREIMAL	Yona		M		Ichel			His family		306
SHEINERMAN	Hersh		M	Married						306
SHEINERMAN			F	Married			Hersh			306
	Sheindel	SHEINERMAN	F		Hersh			Her family		306
SHLEIFER	Chaim Zev		M					His family		306
	Fruma	SHLEIFER	F		Chaim Zev			Her family		307
SHLEIFER	Moshe		M		Chaim Zev			His family		307
SHLEIFER	Yitzhak		M		Chaim Zev			His family		307
	Rachel	SHLEIFER	F		Chaim Zev			Her family		307
SHAPIRO	Avraham		M	Married			Hinda			307
SHAPIRO	Hinda	POPLIS	F	Married			Avraham			307
SHTORM	Dov		M	Married			Freida			307
SHTORM	Freida	POPLIS	F	Married			Dov			307
SHTORM	Leibel		M		Dov	Freida				307
SHTORM	Kalman		M		Dov	Freida		His family		307
	Roza	SHTORM	F		Dov	Freida		Her family		307
	Sarah		F		Hersh Yosha					307
SCHWARTZ	Michael		M					3 sisters		307

SCHWARTZ			F						The mother of Michael SCHWARTZ	307
SHIFER	Yosef		M					His brother & 3 sisters		307
SHIFER			F						The mother of Yosef SHIFER	307
SHPRINGER	Moshe		M					His family		307
SPIEGEL	Shalom		M					His family		307
SPIEGEL	Ben Zion		M					His family		307
SPIEGEL	Shlomo		M					His family		307
SACK	Moshe		M					His family		307
SACK	Natan		M		Moshe Chaim			His family		307
SACK	Hersh		M		Moshe Chaim			His family		307
	Perl	SACK	F		Moshe Chaim			Her family		307
SHTAL	Yitzhak		M							307
SHTAL	Riva		F							307
SHTAL	Chaim		M							307
SHTAL	Sarah		F							307
SHTAL	Chava		F							307
SPEISER	Batya		F							307
SPEISER	Rachel		F			Batya				307
SHPAK	Kalman		M					His family		307
SHPAK	Yosef		M					His family		307
SPIEGEL	Yisrael		M					His family		307
	Chana	SPIEGEL	F		Yisrael			Her family		307
	Zelda	SPIEGEL	F		Yisrael			Her family		307
SHTAL	Mordecai		M					His family		307
SHLEIFER	Gedalia		M		Aharon			His family		307
SHEINERMAN	Shmuel		M	Married			Sarah			307
SHEINERMAN	Sarah	KORNFELD	F	Married			Shmuel			307
SHEINERMAN	Moshe		M		Shmuel	Sarah				307
SHUSTER	Ezra		M							307
SHUSTER	Yenta		F							307
SHUSTER	Toiba		F							307
SHUSTER	Moshe		M							307
SHNERK	Shmuel		M					His family		307
	Shlomo		M						His occupation is listed as shoemaker	307

	Shalom		M		Shlomo			His family	The son of Shlomo the shoemaker	307
	Yosef		M		Shlomo			His family	The son of Shlomo the shoemaker	307
	Shlomo		M		Zisha			His family		307
	Yosef		M					His family		307
	Shlomo		M						He occupation is listed as a wheelwright	307
SHLECHTER	Yosef		M	Married			Devorah	Their sons, number not recorded		307
SHLECHTER	Devorah		F	Married			Yosef	Their sons, number not recorded		307

[Page 308]

Fallen for the Homeland

Translated by Ala Gamulka

"Thou shalt make an altar unto me…" (Exodus, 20:21)

Yaakov Cohen

A.

I met him in Jerusalem. In his face were reflected the feelings and thoughts of an immigrant searching a place for himself in a new life. A life swirling around him.

In his soul there was the romantic dream shared by many of those aspiring to make Aliyah. They dream of Eretz Israel. He was trying to dismiss the tiny sense of doubt gnawing at his beliefs.

[Page 309]

Yaakov Cohen knew the demands of life in Eretz Israel in those difficult times. Rumors of doom came from Eretz Israel, but that did not influence him. He accepted, with love, the long difficult years of preparation. He waited patiently to fulfil his life's dreams. He had a distressing time for the first three months after his arrival. As his ship docked, he was immediately thrust into the fiery front of Ramat Hakovesh. There was much fighting and destruction.

It was difficult for Yaakov to get used to new conditions, but he fulfilled his duties with knowledge and loyalty.

He loved life. His face always reflected smiles. His eyes showed happiness. He was blessed to be able to understand the meaning of life. His seriousness and willingness were accompanied by a happy disposition. It was as if he had forgotten to show sadness and suffering.

I. Gotlieb

B.

We knew Yaakov by his deeds and not by his speeches. I met him when he came from Vishkov to the preparatory kibbutz in Grochov. He stood out with his simplicity and great smile, even in bad times in our lives. He did not stop smiling even when he spoke about personal problems. He spent five years in the preparatory kibbutz. He overcame difficulties there. He also had problems integrating in Eretz Israel, especially when it came to his job. All his colleagues praised his devotion. He had much to criticize in our lives, but he was happy with every success and always happily spoke about it.

Michael

C.

He was born in Ustiluh, Poland in 1906. He studied in yeshiva. In April 1933 he started the preparatory kibbutz. He was one of the conquerors of Vengrov for the benefit of the preparatory kibbutz. He made Aliyah in March 1938.

Yaakov was modest and quiet. He did not stand out with special traits. He devoted himself to his work in a simple way. He was a good friend and was loved by all. Here, in Ramat Hakovesh, he worked hard with dedication and diligence.

We were together in the preparatory kibbutz and on Aliyah.

We used to meet after work and speak about Eretz Israel and the kibbutz. He dearly wished to see the country, but he did not dare ask the members committee for time off.

One evening, before he died, we sat together. We were a group of friends from Grochov and we talked. Yaakov spoke of the fear he had on a daily basis at work. He was afraid he would not return. The next day Yaakov went to work and did not return. This is how the life of a young, healthy man was cut down.

I cannot forget him– my dear, devoted friend.

Fruma

(from the booklet "In Memory of the Eight")

[Page 310]

Yehuda Fleisher

(On the twentieth anniversary of his death– 18 Tamuz, 1940)

Yehuda was 14 when the Balfour Declaration was made in 1917. He was already active in Zionist functions and was totally devoted to these activities. He was one of the founders of Hashomer Hatzair and he then moved on to Hechalutz. He established the local chapter. He dedicated all his efforts to this group until he made Aliyah. He helped with preparatory kibbutzim in the area and he educated a generation of pioneers. Many of them are with us here, in Israel. He was active in the drama group, the Hebrew library, Jewish National Fund, Keren Hayesod and the Orphans committee. Everywhere he was either a committee member or an ordinary worker. He always fulfilled his tasks with loyalty. I was sometimes a member of these committees and he always accepted any task.

In 1925, my husband and I were ready to make Aliyah. However, there was a great depression. We received distressing news from Eretz Israel. Many of those who made Aliyah returned to the Diaspora. Although I was married, my parents' influence was strong. They did not allow us to make Aliyah. Yehuda had been drafted by the Polish army, but was liberated. He made us a proposition: he would go to Eretz Israel for two years –the time he would have spent in the army. During that time, he would investigate the situation and tell us what to do. We agreed and he made Aliyah and stayed there. Here, too, he was very active in defence for Hapoel in Haifa.

In 1929 he came for a visit to our town. He met a young woman and brought her to Eretz Israel in 1933. He established a family. He still continued his public service.

In spring 1940, he was in our house and he read in the newspaper that Italy was joining Hitler in WWII. It was as if he felt that this was his last spring on earth and he said: "I am done for. I will be the first to be killed by the enemy". That is what happened. Six weeks later he was among the first victims of the bombing by the enemy in Haifa. The young tree was cut down at the age of 36.

It is still difficult to accept the fact that Yehuda is no longer with us. May his memory be a blessing!

Tzila

[Page 311]

"If one were to fall holding a rifle against a fiery background, the earth will mourn and suffer. The scenery will be enveloped n the bones of man"

I.Rabinov

Aaron Blander

He was the son of David and Hannah and was born on May 6, 1912 in Ustiluh. His parents were traditional. In spite of his parents' objection, he left home at a young age and applied himself to pioneering work. He went to preparatory kibbutz in 1936 in Sokel. From there he moved to Kielce. He was very active and fulfilled all tasks with dedication and responsibility.

In 1939 he came to Eretz Israel on the ship Colorado. He joined kibbutz Gevat and worked in its water works. His integration into the work world was not easy, but he overcame all difficulties by sheer will. He did various jobs and was proud of the successes of his kibbutz. In 1945 he became a guard in Atlit. There he came into contact with all newcomers. He wrote about his experiences in the kibbutz journal.

He suggested to the United Kibbutz executive to commemorate the names of the last fighters in Poland.

On 29 June 1946, on the day of many arrests in the Jewish community, he was taken by the British and sent to Rafiach. He was one of the last to return from there. On June 11, 1948 he went with other members of kibbutz Gevat to guard the road between the kibbutz and several Arab villages. There was a concentration of enemy forces in the area. He did not return from this outing. He was buried in Gevat.

He left behind a wife and two children.

Aaron was beloved and admired by all his friends. This fact came to light in a compilation published by the kibbutz on the first anniversary of his death. The words expressed are emotional and his character is highly admired. His many activities during preparatory kibbutz and in Eretz Israel are highly praised. Some of his writings are included.

We will never forget him.

Gevat

Some of his writings:

Remembering the dead at camp

The deepest experience that shook me to my core was – remembering the dead at camp on holidays. The shack dedicated to the synagogue was filled with men, women and children. It was lit with candles

[Page 312]

Prepared in advance– inside hollowed out potatoes. A large table was used for these candles. It looked like a small cemetery…

The candles stood quietly, in rows and rows. Each candle represented a soul. Each candle was a gravestone. If you looked deeply at the candles, you saw eyes. These were tearless eyes, eyes with a frozen flame, eyes telling the stories of simple, honest young lives. They told of lives torn through no blame of their own. The eyes looked straight into your eyes and showed their sorrow.

When the candles began to die out, I saw a man (young? Old?) clasping his hands and sobbing. He was crying and saying: the candle is no longer lit; the eyes are darkened. Who by fire and who by water…?

Have you ever seen a man cry?

And so, I, too, stood silently. I thought to myself: how many candles should I light?

I later found out some details about this man: he came from Yugoslavia and was all alone. His entire family was burned in a small town called Dobitza, by a low–flying German airplane. The building was completely burned down.

Diary of the kibbutz, May 17, 1945

Aaron

Avraham Korenfracht

He was the only child of his parents Moshe and Tamar. He was born on 21 Iyar 1930 in Ustiluh. When he was four years old the family made Aliyah. He had a complete religious education. He first attended the Mizrachi school in Kfar Saba and then yeshivot in Petach Tikvah and Jerusalem.

Avraham was a dear person and was modest in his behavior. He belonged to B'nei Akiva and also was a counselor there. At the same time, he learned machinery and worked in the Egged garage in Tel Aviv. He joined Haganah at a young age and spent four years in the movement. He fulfilled all tasks with dedication and exceptional loyalty. He joined the army in the War of Independence and served in the Alexandroni division as a mortar operator. He took part in the battle of Latrun to liberate Jerusalem and fell there on 16 Iyar, 1948.

Everyone who knew him cried, together with his bereaved parents, over the loss of this innocent victim who sacrificed himself for his homeland.

He was buried on Mount Herzl, Jerusalem, on 25 Heshvan 1940.

His soul is in heaven.

A.A.

[Page 313]

Passed Away

Translated by Ala Gamulka

In memory of my parents *(may their souls be in paradise)*

My father, Moshe, son of Yaakov, Rosmarin, z"l, was born in 1850 in Ustiluh. His parents were well–off and they educated him In Torah and good behavior. I was told that he was engaged at the age of 12. When he came for the first holiday to his bride's house in Trisk, he carved himself a wood whistle.

[Page 314]

The parents of the bride saw this as a natural phenomenon. They were proud that in addition to his knowledge of Torah, he had "golden hands".

After the wedding, he did not wish to be dependent on his father–in–law. He rented the Vishtzteyn farm near Ustiluh. There he had a large family.

Two years after the birth of her sixth child, his young wife died. It can be understood how great was his sorrow and mourning, but he had to overcome it and to bring another woman into the household. His little orphans needed a mother and the house had to be managed. After a year he married my mother– she was a widow with a child.

Father learned farming and loved it and was devoted to it.

[Page 315]

He spent his spare time learning Torah. He finished studying the Mishna twice and he also read other scholarly books. He was an enthusiastic follower of the Maggid from Trisk– the author of Shield of Abraham. Later he followed the Maggid's eldest son Leibeinu. When the latter visited Ustiluh, he stayed in our home.

My mother had three children with him– my late sister Pessia, my brother Rabbi Dr. Aaron Rosmarin now in the United States and me.

My father really wished to make Aliyah and to work the land there. In 1920 he asked Norman Bentvitz, at the recommendation of Prof. Israel Friedlander, z"l, my mother's nephew, to help him make Aliyah. However, he was not fortunate to fulfill his dream. In the month of Iyar 1921 he became very ill. My mother and I spent a month in Warsaw with him. In spite of all the efforts of the doctors, we returned home without any hope for his recuperation. He died on 29 Tamuz of that year. He was 71 years old.

My mother Breindel (Brontzia), the daughter of Yossel and Hannah Erlich, was born in Kovel in 1862. Her family was an enlightened religious one. Once, the city of Kovel sent a delegation to the old Tsarina Maria and my mother's brother was part of it. He was Hershel Erlich who spoke Russian well. My mother had also studied Russian and could speak and write it.

My mother was first married to a young intellectual from the Izrael family, well–known in Brisk. She was pregnant with her second child when her husband died. Three years later she married my father who already had three children.

My mother was a beautiful woman, educated and very clever. My paternal grandmother used to say: "Anyone who speaks for an hour with my daughter–in–law will stay smart for a year". My mother was gentle, energetic and intelligent and she captured the hearts of the family. It was many–faceted. Her step children adored and respected her. In town she was nicknamed "the one with the brain of a male". She built her home with knowledge and intelligence. The house was open to the needy, be they family or strangers. I remember what father said before he died, that it was thanks to mother that he was able to bring guests for Shabbat, from the synagogue. He had a partner in all matters of charity and assistance. We, the children, were educated in an advanced, traditional manner. We were able to participate in our Zionist, cultural or philanthropic activities. We could bring home friends and to conduct meetings there. This is how life continued until the depression after WWI.

In 1920, when hundreds of young people immigrated, my brother and sisters went to the United States. A few years later, I made Aliyah. Soon, my mother joined us and lived with us until 1942. She had a clear mind until the end– age 80. A day before she died, when three doctors came for a consultation, she said to them:" Nu, doctors, what do you say? My daughter thinks that if there will be a few doctors

[Page 316]

my "passport" will be renewed. However, if the one above decides, no else can help". The doctors were amazed at her manner of speaking. She died the next day– 25 Adar 1942.

May her soul be bound among the living.

Tzila Fleisher

Feiga from across the river (Eichenboim)

She was called Feiga from across the river because she and her family lived in a settlement on the other side of the Bug river–west of town. I knew her a little at home, but I really got to know her in Eretz Israel.

It is quite acceptable to refer to educated people as intelligent. She, Feiga, was not educated, but she had native intelligence. It must have been a gift from above that she was even more intelligent than learned people. She was modest and was always ready to help the needy. Her home was open to any passing guest and she was devoted to all those near her. These attributes she also implanted in her children– a son and a daughter who are with us in Eretz Israel. She made Aliyah in 1929 and died, at an old age, in 1948.

May her soul be bound among the living.

Tzila

Yosef Eidelshteyn

Yosef (Yozhi) Eidelshteyn, z"l, was a true son of the Jewish people. He fought for the freedom and independence of his homeland. From early childhood he could not accept the lot of the Jewery living in towns and villages in foreign lands. He was absorbed by the teachings of Jabotinsky and undertook the difficult task of imbuing the youth of Ustiluh with the recognition that the future of the people and the individual are in their homeland of Eretz Israel.

As the commander of the Beitar branch in Ustiluh he loyally took care of the national education of the youth and the possibility of illegal immigration to the homeland.

In the midst of this blessed activity, WWII broke out and Yosef, z"l, arrived with other refugees in Vilna.

[Page 317]

He immediately dedicated himself to continue all Beitar activities. This was quite dangerous in Soviet times.

He was unafraid and his room became the center for meetings and for hiding people and arms.

In order not to become a burden on his friends, Yosef carried on a small business. He did not forget his friends who were suffering in jail in Vilna. His heart, his ears and his pocket were always open to any demand.

Yosef, z"l, was a good and loyal friend. He showed these traits during the most difficult times in the Diaspora and in Eretz Israel.

In 1941, after much suffering and tribulations, Yosef, z"l, arrived in Eretz Israel. He immediately offered his services to the Irgun which had waved its rebellion flag against the foreign rulers. He wanted independence for Eretz Israel.

Here, too, as in the Diaspora, Yosef, z"l, always stood with his friends, in hard times and good ones.

Yosef had a physical disability and it is quite common that such people become bitter, angry and indifferent.

Yosef, z"l, was the exact opposite. He was always full of energy, belief and dedication.

His friends loved and admired him because of these traits. They always found him to be a true friend who was ready with deed and advice.

During the rebellion against the British in 1947, he was arrested and held in Latrun detention camp. Later he was moved to Atlit together with mayors and national leaders.

In spite of the fact that detention was difficult for him he did not lose his sense of humor and was beloved by everyone who met him.

Yosef, z"l, was a talented organizer and he was successful in his position as the manager of a Workers Health clinic in Ramat Gan.

He also held positions as a member of the national Herut executive, a leader of the local branch and of the workers Union in Ramat Gan. For some time, he was also a member of work agency of H.E.L.

Yosef's friends were deeply shocked when they heard the tragic news that Yosef Eidelshteyn was no longer among us.

[Page 318]

It is with deep pain that we said good bye to him in the Kiryat Shaul cemetery. We will not forget him.

Yosef Eidelshteyn, z"l, will always serve as an example of friendship and loyalty. His family can be proud of their Yosef. His friends from his hometown will always remember him as a true member of the Jewish people who began his dreams in Ustiluh. He managed to fulfill some of them.

David Yotan

Aaron Dror (Shovalev)

He was the son of Simcha and Tzartel and was born in Ustiluh in 1899. His parents were religious, but enlightened. His mother died when he was 16. He had technical talents and studied carpentry. His father, Simcha, the teacher, had no way of earning a living during WWI and Aaron was very helpful to him. The two older sons had moved far away.

Unfortunately, he came down with a chronic illness in his leg and he had to be bedridden, at times. Aaron did not let it stop him and continued working.

When the branch of Hechalutz Hamizrachi was founded in Ustiluh, Aaron joined. In 1924 he received a certificate for Aliyah. Soon he was able to also bring his fiancÃ©e Leah, daughter of the cantor Akhiezer. A few years later he also brought his father. At first, he settled in Afula where he lived for 4 years. He then moved to Haifa and after 4 more years he built a home in Kiryat Haim.

In Eretz Israel he continued with his profession in a construction cooperative, in the oil distillery and in the Vulcan factory. His childhood illness finally overtook him and he died on 13 Nisan 1957 after much suffering. He was only 58 years old. He left a wife and two sons.

Aaron was a gentle person, like his parents. In spite of the physical suffering, he always had a smile on his lips. He took good care of his family and was totally devoted to all his friends and relatives.

May his soul be bound among the living.

A.A.

[Page 319]

Reuven Rotenberg

Reuven was born in 1902 to a religious family. His education was according to their beliefs. He was an excellent student and learned with Rabbi Wertheim, z"l. He studied Torah together with Pinchas, son of the Rabbi. When he grew up, he studied secular subjects privately, without his parents' knowledge. After we became family because my brother married his sister, he was able to read books and newspapers in our home. This is how he spent his spare time. After he finished dealing in business in the villages, he spent time reading. When the branch of Zeirei Mizrachi was founded in Ustiluh, Reuven joined and was an active member. In 1925 he received a certificate and made Aliyah, in spite of his parents' objections.

He had difficulty being absorbed in Eretz Israel. For the first two years, he was ill and unemployed and stayed in Haifa. He then moved to Binyamina and went to work at PKA in Habara. He worked hard for 4 years in order to receive land for settlement. During that time, he also dreamed of having a family. There was less work and his dreams were not fulfilled. He was let go and returned, disappointed, to Haifa. After a few difficult months he began a steady job. In 1932 I made Aliyah and joined him. Slowly, our family life began. In 1934, our daughter Hadassah was born and a year later we moved to Kiryat Haim. Time passed with hard work and various difficulties. The war between Ethiopia and Italy and the events of 1936 brought their own desperate times. In the meantime, our son Dror was born in 1945. The next few years brought economic success and we overcame our problems. Reuven was taken suddenly from us. He was only 52 and had not yet seen true happiness.

Reuven was an honest and modest man in everything he did. He was warm and kind towards others. He was always ready to help with good advice, money and his own efforts. He was devoted to his family and beloved by all who knew him.

May his memory remain with us forever.

Sima

[Page 320]

Yenta Gurevitz

Yenta knew suffering and hard work from an early age. Her father was a trusted employee of a Jew who leased the whiskey distillery of the wealthy owner. He died young and left a wife and three daughters. There was also a son who had polio and remained incapacitated for the rest of his life. The father's boss, a generous man, helped the family to open a tavern and Yenta was the manager. The business flourished thanks to her intelligence, honesty and energy. Everyone, Jews and gentiles alike, loved and respected her. Unfortunately, her mother did not live much longer and Yenta had to take the place of both parents for her young sisters and invalid brother. Yenta was so devoted to her family that she did not want to get married before her sisters. When it was her turn to be wed, her condition to her groom was that her brother would live with them. Her husband was an honest person and had a good trade and he agreed. They lived together happily and raised their children in a proper way. They prospered until WWII broke out.

It is said that Yenta's family was killed in the first action, but that she, herself, miraculously remained alive. After much wandering and frightful experiences– she was on the "Exodus"– Yenta arrived in Eretz Israel at the end of the War of Independence. She was completely worn out physically and emotionally. Her situation here was difficult because she depended on assistance from the Welfare department and from former residents of our town. (Help came mainly from those of us living in Haifa), Eventually she received funds from the Claims Conference in Germany.

Her bitter lot did not allow her to enjoy an easier life. This lonely woman was suddenly afflicted with a disease and she died quickly.

May her soul be bound among the living.

Daughter of Moshe

Zehava (Golda) Eidelshteyn

She was born in Ustiluh in 1911 to an important and wealthy family. However, her parents died when she was quite young and she and her little brother were raised by an uncle. He was their father's brother and they had, together, owned a large commerce. A few years later, her brother died and she was left alone. Zehava grew into a beautiful and clever young woman. Se was a member of the Zionist organization and made Aliyah in 1935. Here, she married a very fine young man, but the marriage did not last. Zehava married a second time and was very happy.

[Page 321]

Sadly, the good days did not last. She became ill and died at the age of 37.

May her memory be a blessing.

M.K.A.

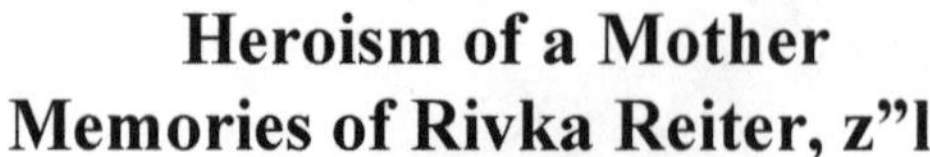

Heroism of a Mother
Memories of Rivka Reiter, z"l

Rivka was born in 1911 in Ustiluh. Her family was modest and poor. Her father was a teacher of young boys and her mother ran a notions store. The father died young and left his wife a widow with young children. They grew up and were educated and learned trades. One of the sons even became a Hebrew teacher.

Rivka was a member of Hechalutz and made Aliyah in 1936. She married a fine young man and they had a son. They were quite happy. Her cruel fate was to become deathly ill. Prior to being taken to the hospital she asked the doctor to test her husband and three–year–old son. She was afraid that she had infected them.

When I came to visit her in the hospital, just before her death, she said to me: "I wish to die in peace and this is why I asked for the tests". She added: "Believe me, I have not kissed my son and he is almost four –years–old…"

I was astonished by her generous spirit. She fought her illness and was fearful for her child. She managed to overcome her feelings and denied herself a last enjoyment– the kiss of a young dying mother to her child!

Her soul returned to God on 15 Adar 1944.

She was 33 years old.

May her memory be a blessing.

Her townmate

[Page 322]

Ben Zion Goldhaber

He was born in 1900 in the village of Ludin, near Ustiluh. His family was a well–off rural one. His grandfather, Baruch Ludiner, was well known as a donor of potatoes to the needy before Passover. (Another donor was Shmuel Leib Bortnover). Just before WWI, Ben Zion's mother died and his father was left alone with five children. The oldest, 14 years old, showed a talent in art. He studied at the Art Schools in Warsaw and Krakow and became a famous artist. Ben Zion and the other children were also talented, but the war stopped them from continuing their education appropriately. They attended a regular school. In 1928, Ben Zion married a teacher of Polish from Zmushets. They had a son and lived happily together until WWII broke out. Many difficulties pursued them. They hid in bunkers and in displaced persons camps. They made Aliyah in 1949.

They were well absorbed here. Ben Zion worked in a canning factory in Haifa bay. They lived in Kiryat Haim. Everyone, bosses and co–workers alike, liked and respected him. He was a pleasant man with a good disposition.

One morning, on 7 Tishrei, 1961, he did not feel well. He did not want to scare his wife and he left for work. He felt worse there and a doctor was summoned. He had died, by then, He was 60 years old.

May his memory be a blessing.

TZ.P.

Pinhas Sapir–Chen

My father, a dear man, Pinhas, son of Eliyahu Sapir–Chen, z"l, was born in the village of Osvoba, near Stepan, Volyn, in 1912. He was sent to learn in a Heder at a young age, as were all other children. At the age of 12 he went to study in the Yeshiva in Koretz. He stayed there for two years and returned home. He began to look for new horizons, but he could not find them in his village. He decided to go to Warsaw. He was only 14 years old, but he was accepted in the Seminary for teachers and rabbis– Tachkemoni.

Conditions at home were bad and young Pinhas did not receive any funds from them, unlike his colleagues. He studied in the seminary, but he had to earn his keep.

[Page 323]

He gave private lessons until late at night. Only then was he able to do his own homework. There were nights when he did not sleep, but he kept up his school work.

A year after he came to Warsaw, his father also sent his younger brother to study. Understandably, the older brother received the younger one in a grand manner. He even gave up his own food to him. This is how he managed during his studies.

He studied in the seminary for 6 years. After successfully completing his studies he began to teach. At first, he taught at the high school in Kovel and later in the Tabut school in Lublin. It was run by Israel Shalita.

He especially loved Hebrew literature and he spent many nights researching the language. He taught his students in the spirit of renewal of the Hebrew language.

In 1936, 24–year–old Pinhas decided to fulfill his dream and make Aliyah. And so, he did.

Here, in Eretz Israel, he devoted himself completely to work in the field of Hebrew literature. At first, he worked in the Masada publishing house and then in other houses. He continuously worked in editing, punctuating, proofreading and translating. He did this work with great love and devotion.

Many different books went through his hands. Each book had its own difficulties until it came out of the printing press. Each book was prepared by father in his easy, pleasant and simple style. He was appreciated in every publishing house in which he worked for his love of Hebrew books. For certain, every book lover with taste would have liked him, but to them he was anonymous. His name was not listed in the book. He was very modest.

His friends all knew him as a noble soul. He radiated love to his surroundings. He was honest and bright. Many people turned to him when they were in trouble. He, in turn, would comfort and encourage them.

Even when he was on his death bed, he managed to seem calm. He knew what was coming, but he never complained. He did not bother anyone and behaved with kindness towards all.

Many people cried when this special man left us at the age of 47. Just as he never wished to bother anyone, even on the day he died, he continued in that vein.

[Page 324]

He died on the first day of the month of Elul 1960. On that day, there are no eulogies, so no one had to be disturbed.

May his soul be bound among the living.

His son Gideon

Pinhas Sapirstein, z"l, as described above, was not born in Ustiluh. However, after he married Yehudit Helfman from Ustiluh, he became close to the former residents of our town. He participated in happy and sad events. He attended our activities as if he were one of us, even though he had never been there. He knew much about it and spoke of the town with great love and interest. This is why we considered him an adopted son of Ustiluh. It was our blessing. We feel his absence and we are mourning his death together with his family.

M.K.A

Rivka Ingber

My mother, Rivka, daughter of Liptche Eisenberg, made Aliyah with her family in December 1935.

During the bloody times after the Russian revolution, she lost a husband and three children. Still, her spirits were high. She remarried and began a new family. Here, in Eretz Israel, life was not easy and she suffered during the attacks. In spite of everything, she remained hopeful. She was in dire economic conditions, but she managed to give her children a good education.

My mother resembled her father – she was gentle, bright and kind. She inherited, from her mother, a sense of humor. This is why she was beloved by all who knew her.

During the War she suddenly became ill. After three days, on 14 December, 1941, she died at the age of 52.

May her soul be bound among the living.

Miriam Blechman

Rivka Wasserman

I met her under special circumstances, when she was three–years old. When we began our charitable work, as I mentioned in my article "Kindness of Youth", we decided to give assistance to

[Page 325]

orphaned and neglected children. This was in the years 1919–1920. The first activity was a visit, in twos, the poor sections in order to research the economic and familial conditions. In one house, on Danche street, we found (my partner was Mordechai Privner, z"l), little Rivka enveloped in rags. Her body was full of sores caused by hunger and dirt. After a short conversation with her, we discovered that she had no mother or father. Her older brother was learning tailoring and her sister was a maid in one of the houses down town. She, this little girl, was all alone all day at home. On a nice day she went to the neighbors to ask for food.

That evening, when the investigators met, the idea of founding a special home for the neediest was born. We did not have the budget for a large home. The institution was opened and Rivka was among the first to arrive. Soon, her sores healed and she became a beautiful girl. When I made Aliyah, she was still in the orphanage– healthy, happy, a good student learning a trade.

I did not know what happened to her afterwards for some years. She made Aliyah with her husband and children, about three years ago. She came to visit us. We were very happy to see her. She told us how she and her family survived and how happy they are. The main purpose was to invite us to her daughter's wedding. We were delighted to be invited. Rivka was even more beautiful and shone with contentment when she introduced her family. We all rejoiced together.

There is a saying: when a person is in a bad situation and eventually conditions improve, Satan interferes and takes his life. This is what happened to Rivka.

She was suddenly taken from us about six months after her daughter's wedding.

May her soul be bound among the living

Tzila Fleisher

Yossel and Nachman Burlyant

As the book was being prepared for publication, we received the sad news from New York. These two brothers died young. They were among the elite of Ustiluh during the period between the two wars. Their articles are included in this collection.

Readers will find a description of the Burlyant family in the article by A. Schlachter – "Figures". Another article about Nachman, in Yiddish, is by Tz. Fleisher.

May their memories be blessed.

The Editors

[Page 326]

Vision of the Dry Bones
Ezekiel 37

Translated by Ala Gamulka

The hand of the Lord came upon me, and carried me out in the spirit of the Lord, and set me down in the midst of the valley, and that was full of bones.

And He made me pass by them round about, and lo! they were exceedingly many on the surface of the valley, and lo! they were exceedingly dry.

Then He said to me; "Son of man, can these bones become alive?" And I answered, "O Lord God, You [alone] know."

And He said to me, "Prophesy over these bones, and say to them, 'O dry bones, hear the word of the Lord.'

So says the Lord God to these bones; Behold, I will cause spirit to enter into you, and you shall live!

And I will lay sinews upon you, and I will make flesh grow over you and cover you with skin and put breath into you, and you will live, and you will then know that I am the Lord."

So I prophesied as I was commanded, and there arose a noise when I prophesied, and behold a commotion, and the bones came together, bone to its bone!

And I looked, and lo! sinews were upon them, and flesh came upon them, and skin covered them from above, but there was still no spirit in them.

Then He said to me, "Prophesy to the spirit, prophesy, O son of man, and say to the spirit, 'So says the Lord God: From four sides come, O spirit, and breathe into these slain ones that they may live.'"

And I prophesied as He had commanded me, and the spirit came into them, and they lived and stood on their feet, a very great army, exceedingly so.

Then He said to me, "Son of man, these bones are all the house of Israel. Behold they say, 'Our bones have become dried up, our hope is lost, we are clean cut off to ourselves.'

Therefore, prophesy and say to them, So says the Lord God: Lo! I open your graves and cause you to come up out of your graves as My people, and bring you home to the land of Israel.

Then you shall know that I am the Lord, when I open your graves and lead you up out of your graves as My people.

And I will put My spirit into you, and you shall live, and I will set you on your land, and you shall know that I, the Lord, have spoken it and have performed it," says the Lord.

And the word of the Lord came to me, saying:

"And you, son of man, take for yourself one stick and write upon it, 'For Judah and for the children of Israel his companions'; and take one stick and write upon it, 'For Joseph, the stick of Ephraim and all the house of Israel, his companions.'

And bring them close, one to the other into one stick, and they shall be one in your hand.

And when the children of your people say to you, saying, 'Will you not tell us what these are to you?'

Say to them, So says the Lord God: Behold I will take the stick of Joseph, which is in the hand of Ephraim and the tribes of Israel his companions, and I will place them with him with the stick of Judah, and I will make them into one stick, and they shall become one in My hand.

And the sticks upon which you shall write shall be in your hand before their eyes.

And say to them, So says the Lord God: Behold I will take the children of Israel from among the nations where they have gone, and I will gather them from every side, and I will bring them to their land.

And I will make them into one nation in the land upon the mountains of Israel, and one king shall be to them all as a king; and they shall no longer be two nations, neither shall they be divided into two kingdoms anymore.

And they shall no longer defile themselves with their idols, with their detestable things, or with all their transgressions, and I will save them from all their habitations in which they have sinned, and I will purify them, and they shall be to Me as a people, and I will be to them as a God.

And My servant David shall be king over them, and one shepherd shall be for them all, and they shall walk in My ordinances and observe My statutes and perform them.

And they shall dwell on the land that I have given to My servant, to Jacob, wherein your forefathers lived; and they shall dwell upon it, they and their children and their children's children, forever; and My servant David shall be their prince forever.

And I will form a covenant of peace for them, an everlasting covenant shall be with them; and I will establish them and I will multiply them, and I will place My Sanctuary in their midst forever.

And My dwelling place shall be over them, and I will be to them for a God, and they shall be to Me as a people.

And the nations shall know that I am the Lord, Who sanctifies Israel, when My Sanctuary is in their midst forever."

[Page 328]

Memorial Assembly for Victims of the Holocaust from our town 1961 Tel Aviv

[Page 329]

Participants in the Memorial Assembly

[Page 330]

Board of the Organization of Former Residents of Usiluh in New York

[Page 331]

The Surviving Remnant

The Yizkor Book committee

Translated by Ala Gamulka

"Ye shall be gathered one by one. O ye children of Israel" (Isiah 27:12)

"But in Mount Zion there shall be those that escape and it shall be holy" (Obadiah 1:17)

While we were searching for ways of strengthening the ties among our former residents in Israel and abroad, we came up with the idea of publishing the names and addresses of our townspeople in all countries. We intended to publicize, at the very least, the partial lists in our possession or those we could obtain. Our townspeople in the Diaspora stopped us from doing it, with good reasons. We were obliged, therefore, to limit our effort to Israel. Still, we are not prepared to give up on the idea. However, it is not for this book. We contacted our active members in the United States, Canada, Argentina, Brazil, Mexico, Cuba and European countries. We asked them to find a way to prepare these lists and to send them to us. We will look after their publication either in another booklet or as an addendum to this book.

In Israel, there are–according to the enclosed list– about 90 households of townspeople (in many of them, both members of the couple came from Ustiluh). Many of them made Aliyah in the period between the two wars. Some arrived after the Holocaust and a very few were here before WWI. Our people are scattered throughout the country, in towns, settlements and kibbutzim. A great majority are in Haifa and surrounding areas. Most of them are workers: artisans, laborers, farmers, clerks, teachers, etc. There are a few in business and industry.

Once a year, on 19 Elul, we gather in one of the larger towns to hold a Memorial Assembly for our Holocaust victims. We also discuss issues pertaining to the organization. In addition, there are occasional meetings and celebrations when visitors come from abroad. Members from the entire country come to these events. Also, we have many occasions to celebrate together weddings, Bar Mitzvahs, etc.

This mutual feeling of closeness is also evidenced in collective help to the needy. We do not have a specific fund for this purpose. However, when the need arises we can collect the funds. For some time, to our great delight, there was no need for such a fund. Two years ago, a family of survivors arrived. They were in poor health and we must support them. It is probably a good idea to create a permanent fund for this case and other future ones. Let us hope we will not need it!

[Page 332]

List of Former Ustiluh Residents in Israel

Translated by Ala Gamulka

AHARONI, Leah, 15 Habanim, Ramat Gan
AVINADAV (Tabakhandler), Aryeh, Kfar Ganim B., Petach Tikvah
BEN-YOCHANAN (YOKHENZON), Menashe, 29 Hagefen, Haifa
BEKER, Avraham, Uziel street, Kiryat Motzkin
BERGENZON, Hava, 83 Sheinkin, Givatayim
BERGER, Mendel, Shikun Motzkin, Bloc 6, Apt. 3, Kfar Saba
BINSHTOCK, Yafa, 25 Grandos, Ramat Gan
BITERMAN, Yaakov, Shikun Noah Zait 69, Lod
BLECHMAN, Miriam, Haifa
BOIM, Shmuel, Bustan Hagalil, Doar Haifa
DIMANT, Shmuel, Gan Warburg, Azor
DROR (SHOVALEV), Leah, 71 Daled, Kiryat Haim
EICHENBOIM, Yehoshua, 5 Sde Boker, Givatayim
EIDELSHTEYN, Manis, Hamatmid 19, entrance 3, Ramat Gan
EIDELSHTEYN, Eliezer, 28 Hacherut, Ramat Gan
EIDELSHTEYN, Bella, 36 Fireberg, Tel Aviv
EIGER, Gershon, 6 Yekhezkel, B'nei Brak
EINIS, Baruch Zvi, 15 Gideon, Haifa
EINIS, Yosef, 46 Hatavor (Michael), Haifa
FARBER, Yitzhak, 15 Yael, Kiryat Motzkin
FEFER, Esther, (KREMER), 66 Kibbutz Galuyot, Haifa
FLEISHER, Mordechai and Tzila, 162 Ibn Gevirol, Tel Aviv
GOLDHOVER, Yosef, 29 Reines, Tel Aviv
GOLDHOVER, Avner, 18 Bar Giora, Haifa
GOLDMAN, Menucha, 6 Hevron, B'nei Brak
GROBER, Rivka, Neve Shaanan, near Haifa

GUR-ARYEH, Sara, 28 Anzio Sereny, Givat Rambam
GURFINKEL, Malka, 10/1 Akiva, Shikun Rasko, Holon
HADARI (POMERANTZ), Zvi, Kibbutz Amir, Upper Galilee post
HALPERIN Betzalel and Penina, 104 Bialik, Ramat Gan
[Page 333]

HARKABY (REITER), David, 53 Nachmani, Tel Aviv
HERBST, Ben Zion, 20 Gruzberg, Tel Aviv
HOVAL, Issachar, 44 Vav, Kiryat Haim
ILAN (Boim), Shmuel, Kibbutz Rosh Hanikra, Western Galilee post
KARSH, Eliyahu, 5Aleph, Azor
KATZ, Shmuel, 10 Hahashmonaim, Tel Aviv
KATZ, Miriam, 19/4 Shikun Rasko, Kiryat Motzkin
KESSEL, Menachem, Bustan Hagalil, Doar Haifa
KHAZENWALD, Yaakov, 21 Alexander Yanai, Tel Aviv
KOHAN (FLEISHER) Devorah, 91 Abas, Haifa
KORNFELD, Hillel, Atlit
KORNFELD, Shlomo, 2 Pevsner, Haifa
KORNFRACHT, Moshe Aryeh, Shikun Hapoel Hamizrachi A, Shal Street, Kfar Saba
KREITZER, Bracha, 40 Atzmaut, Bat Yam
KRIGSHER, Moshe, 26 Sderot Chen, Tel Aviv
KOKVA, Sheindel, 15 Kaplan, Kiryat Ono
KOPIT, Esther, (née VURTZEL), 27 Yehuda Hanasi, Kiryat Tivon
LANGA, Bluma (nee GOLDHOVER), 91 Derech Hashalom, Yad Eliyahu, Tel Aviv
LICHTMAN, Yaakov, 36 Hatzipornim, Kiryat Tivon
LIPINSKI, Libel, 25 Hatichon, Neve Shaanan, Haifa
LIPINSKI, Shmerl, 2 Betzalel, Haifa
LISHTCHENKER, Mordechai, 58 Hatavor (Michael), Haifa
MASTBOIM, Etel, 47 Moshe Shapira, Ramat Yitzhak
MATEH (SHTEKN), Yeshayahu, Kibbutz Afek, Doar Haifa
MELTZMAN, Yeshayahu, Kfar Hamesubim (Hiria), near Tel Aviv
MILLER, Avish, 42 Hashiluach, Haifa
MIROTZNIK, Moshe, 71 Shikun Ein Hatchelet, Netanya
OVENTAL, Zeev, Carmela Hotel, 8 Deganiot, Tivon
PERLMUTER, Elchanan, Rabbi, 48 Shikun Ezrachi, P.B. 23, Hadera

[Page 334]

POMP, Zvi, Shikun Zafon 26/3, Acco
RAFNER, Yona, 30 Haportzim, Ramat Gan
REITER, Peretz, 7 Hanotrim, Holon
ROSENFELD, Natan, Shikun Oved Ben Ami, Netanya
ROSMARIN, Binyamin, 45 Gideon, Ramat Gan
ROTENBERG (GOLDBERG), Sima, 44 Vav, Kiryat Haim
ROTENSHTEYN, David, Talmei Yechiel, Doar Na, Hof Ashdod
SAPIR-CHEN, Yehudit (nee HELFMAN), 4 Betzalel, Tel Aviv
SCHARBROT, Menashe, 19 Aliya, Bat Galim, Haifa
SHTIMER, Aryeh, 69 Shlomo Hamelech, Tel Aviv
SHTIMER, Mordechai Zvi, Marmorek St., Tel Aviv
SHMUKLER, Esther, 2 Aminadav, Ramat Yitzhak, Kiryat Borochov
SHLECHTER, Eliyahu, 20 Zhabotinsky, Acco
SHLECHTER, Nissan, 15 Zayin, Kiryat Haim
SHEINMAN, Zvi and Mina, Kibbutz Afek, Doar Haifa
SHPRINGER, Rashi, 62 Keren Kayemet, Kiryat Bialik
SHLESINGER, Malka, 3 Betzalel, Hadar Hacarmel, Haifa

SHNEIDER, Feiga, 20 Balfour, Bat Yam
SOBOL, Bluma, 4 Pinat Herzl, Haifa
SOBOL, Miriam
STOLIAR, Azriel, 11 Ben Ziv, Ramat Gan B
STOLIAR, Haim, Kibbutz Tel Amal, Doar Beit Alfa
TAGERMAN, Pinchas and Leah, 27 Yehuda Hanasi, Tivon
TERNER, Eliezer, 59 Yahalom, Ramat Gan
TESSLER, Bella, 60 Sheinkin, Tel Aviv
TVOL, Yosef, 7 Hanotrim, Holon
VEIGER, Moshe, Beit Hakerem, Shikun Amami, Bloc B, entrance 7, Jerusalem
VINSHEL, Yosef, 75 Kaf Het, Kiryat Haim
VOPNIARSKY, Moshe, 30 Arlozorov, Holon
ZEHAVY, Shamai, 25 Kish, Netanya
ZEMEL, Moshe, Atlit
ZMIRIN, Golda, 24 Samech Bet, Kiryat Haim

NAME INDEX

A

A.A., 270, 276
Abramowitz, 214
Achi–Frida, 113
Adlerman, 213
Agras, 214
Agrontchik, 122
Aharoni, 290
Alboim, 211, 244
Alinik, 213
Anis, 213
Ansky, 130
Applebaum, 213, 215
Atlas, 214
Avinadav, 12, 109, 195
Avinadav, 290
Avunadav, 2

B

Ba'al Shem Tov, 8, 16
Bandura, 112
Banis, 216, 218
Barak, 51
Becker, 195
Becker, 216
Beker, 290
Beliankin, 41, 51, 148, 168
Beltzer, 216
Benderovtsky, 189
Benderovtzis, 112, 192
Ben–Dov, 63, 84
Beno, 217
Bentvitz, 272
Ben-Yochanan, 290
Bergelson, 144
Bergenzon, 290
Berger, 215, 216, 290
Berkes, 48, 51
Berliant, 81, 82
Bernfeld, 63
Bernstein, 217
Bialik, 68, 139, 291
Bialy, 192, 195
Bicher, 216, 218
Bieliankin, 23, 48, 51, 62, 165
Bier, 215
Biliankin, 79, 81
Binshtock, 290
Biterman, 82
Biterman, 215, 290
Bitterman, 187, 188
Blander, 158, 268
Blatt, 51
Blatt, 216, 217, 253
Blechman, 284
Blechman, 290
Bley, 218
Bliander, 101
Bliander, 217, 238
Blinder, 9
Bodenstein, 218, 240
Boigel, 217
Boim, 47, 167, 291
Boim, 290
Boimel, 225
Bojm, 215, 219, 248
Bok, 134
Bokser, 137
Bokser, 217
Borg, 217
Borliant, 3
Bortnover, 281
Bortnoyer, 86
Boxer, 103
Branek, 187, 188, 189, 191
Bree, 218
Brenner, 217, 231
Brif, 156
Brik, 58, 137
Brik, 217
Broit, 217
Budenstein, 102
Burlyant, 43, 54, 58, 136, 149, 150, 151, 156, 158, 176, 178, 182, 285
Burlyant, 216, 217
Byksenholcz, 216

C

Chasid, 232
Chazanwald, 232, 258
Chazzan, 26, 151
Chometzki, 151
Chrein, 232
Cohen, 9, 55, 130, 265
Cohen, 218, 235, 236
Cooperstein, 254
Czar Nicholas Ii, 20
Czar Nikolay I, 78

D

Dan, 8
Danziger, 171
Danziger, 224
Dartva, 224
Darwin, 85
David, 12
Dayan, 12, 24, 25, 26, 52, 64, 99, 131, 134, 139, 144
Diamant, 184, 188
Diamant, 223, 224

Dimant, 171
Dimant, 290
Dimentstein, 224
Dina's, 43, 194
Dovrishes, 34
Dror, 290
Druker, 224

E

Eichenboim, 68, 88, 167, 171, 173, 174, 274
Eichenboim, 212, 213, 214, 250, 290
Eidel, 214
Eidelshteyn, 174, 206, 274, 275, 279
Eidelshteyn, 290
Eiger, 202
Eiger, 212, 290
Einis, 211, 212, 290
Eisenberg, 12, 54, 79, 158, 169, 174, 284
Eisenstein, 214, 234, 240
Eksmit, 54, 93
Elbaum, 79, 81
Engle, 245
Erlich, 99, 272

F

Fadim, 247, 248
Fanik, 94, 131
Fanik, 245, 246, 260
Farber, 66, 69, 116, 169
Farber, 2, 232, 245, 258, 262, 290
Fefer, 290
Fein, 247
Feldman, 247, 248
Feler, 248
Feltz, 58
Fenik, 100, 197
Feniks, 173, 176, 177
Fenix, 179
Finger, 246
Finkelstein, 248
Fishel, 54, 79, 92, 113, 114, 158, 169, 173, 174
Fishman, 247
Fleischer, 58
Fleisher, 51, 52, 55, 68, 71, 75, 89, 97, 150, 158, 169, 267, 273, 285
Fleisher, 2, 290, 291
Flim, 246
Fliszer, 78
Frankfurt, 248
Franzak, 247
Freiman, 246
Freizinger, 171
Friedlander, 272
Friedman, 248
Frij, 8, 136, 147, 178
Frishberg, 148
Frishberg, 246, 247
Frumer, 248

G

Garbatch, 171, 186
Garber, 223
Garstenblit, 222
Geillis, 147, 148
Giderberg, 158
Ginsburg, 164, 169
Ginsburg, 220, 221, 223
Ginzburg, 194
Glaz, 176
Glazer, 220, 221, 223
Glizer, 222
Gloz, 212, 222
Gobel, 171
Gold, 165
Gold, 220
Goldberg, 44, 51, 74, 94, 136, 147, 197
Goldberg, 219, 221, 223, 291
Goldfeder, 222
Goldhaber, 55, 98, 178, 281
Goldhaber, 219
Goldhover, 65, 199, 200
Goldhover, 217, 220, 221, 223, 246, 252, 257, 290, 291
Goldman, 118
Goldman, 290
Goldschmidt, 95, 198
Goldschmidt, 219, 220
Goldzemer, 222, 223
Gordin, 154, 156, 158
Gorgal, 223
Gorvatch, 222, 223
Gostetsky, 187
Gotlieb, 266
Goval, 220, 221, 223
Graber, 223
Grabowski, 79, 80
Greenberg, 219, 221, 222, 223
Greenboim, 222
Greiz, 221
Grinberg, 131, 137, 158
Gritchuk, 185, 187
Grober, 291
Gruber, 221, 222, 223
Gur-Aryeh, 291
Gurevitch, 48
Gurevitz, 278
Gurfinkel, 291
Gurion, 172
Gurvatz, 219
Gut, 51

H

Hadari, 291
Haddasses, 136
Hallel's, 185
Halperin, 105, 114, 115, 116, 171
Halperin, 2, 224, 225, 262, 291
Hammer, 225, 226
Harkaby, 291
Hecht, 226

Heinischs, 173
Helfman, 83, 283
Helfman, 225, 291
Heller, 134
Herbst, 225, 226, 291
Hering, 225, 226
Herlich, 226
Herschels, 19
Herzl, 53, 54, 60, 79, 162, 270, 292
Himber, 226
Hirschbein, 154, 163
Hitler, 92, 114, 164, 169, 170, 171, 183, 267
Hoar, 226
Hoichman, 226
Hoivan, 226, 227
Holtz, 225, 226, 227
Holtzer, 198
Holtzer, 227
Hon, 225, 226
Hornstein, 225
Horowitz, 227
Hoval, 291
Hubel, 224, 225, 226, 227
Hugenberg, 170

I

Idelstein, 211, 214, 243
Ilan, 291
Ilboim, 213
Ingber, 284
Isenberg, 91, 92, 94
Isenberg, 214

J

Jacobs, 8, 9, 18, 19
Jennings, 170
Jochenson, 235, 245, 255

K

Kafka, 253
Kaminka, 85
Kaminsky, 172
Kanat, 137, 148, 159, 160
Kandiner, 58, 65
Kandiner, 242, 251
Karp, 252, 255
Karsh, 185, 186, 187, 189
Karsh, 222, 250, 251, 253, 254, 291
Kasel, 253
Katchke, 47
Katsav, 99
Katz, 236, 239, 254, 291
Katzer, 255
Katzner, 253, 254
Kaufman, 254
Kavsovitzer, 251
Kelner, 252
Kent, 54
Kent, 251
Kessel, 77
Kessel, 291
Khazenwald, 291
Khaznonlad, 47
Kilim, 253
Kimmel, 51, 161
Kirzchner, 245
Kiser, 148
Kitai, 254
Kitika, 253
Kleiner, 167, 171
Kleiner, 253
Kleinman, 251, 252
Kliger, 180
Kloper, 163
Kohan, 291
Kokva, 291
Kol, 252
Kolton, 251, 252, 253
Koltun, 156, 163
Kondas, 255
Konstantin, 48
Kopf, 252
Kopit, 109
Kopit, 291
Kopp, 8, 136, 147, 178
Korenfracht, 270
Koris, 252, 253
Kornfeld, 51, 137, 138, 159, 176
Kornfeld, 252, 254, 255, 263, 291
Kornfracht, 68
Kornfracht, 291
Kornfrecht, 250
Kotika, 253
Kotzki, 255
Kozlovska, 125
Krainer, 252
Krakover, 200, 201
Krakover, 218, 235, 250
Krakower, 53, 54, 93, 110, 178
Kramer, 252, 253, 254, 255
Kreiner, 66
Kreitzer, 291
Kremer, 290
Krigsher, 171
Krigsher, 251, 291
Krimer, 235, 261
Krishtal, 251, 252, 253
Kritz, 89
Krongold, 248, 250
Krotch, 252
Kultin, 8, 136, 147, 178
Kutchkov, 40
Kvassevitzer, 156
Kvitel, 252, 254

L

Lachman, 239, 251
Lakritz, 238
Landau, 239
Landsberg, 238

Langa, 291
Larach, 239
Laroch, 238
Lateiner, 163
Lebensboim, 238
Leder, 238
Lefel, 239
Leibeniu, 135
Leiezerel, 8
Leitsis, 101
Leitzes, 192
Leitzis, 238
Lemberger, 34, 35
Lerer, 239
Lerner, 236, 238
Lev, 239
Levertov, 224, 238
Lialtzuk, 239
Liashuk, 111
Lichtboim, 239
Lichtman, 23, 109
Lichtman, 237, 238, 291
Lilka, 238
Linder, 186
Lipinski, 48, 101
Lipinski, 291
Lipsky, 84
Lishchinker, 236, 237, 238
Lishtchenker, 291
Lishtchinker, 171
Lodiner, 253
Lorber, 239
Ludiner, 281
Lutvak, 238, 239

M

M.K.A., 93, 279
Machlok, 243
Maltzman, 171
Mamet, 99, 168
Mamet, 240, 243
Mandelbaum, 240, 241, 242
Mandelker, 58
Mandelkern, 240, 241
Mandelyok, 240, 241
Manerdron, 239, 240, 242, 243
Manises, 48, 89
Markevitch, 187, 191
Markizer, 242
Mastboim, 291
Mastenbaum, 242, 243
Mateh, 291
Mayerson, 239
Mehl, 240
Melamed, 110
Melamed, 240, 241, 242, 243, 244
Melech, 169
Meltzman, 99
Meltzman, 240, 248, 291
Milgroim, 240
Miller, 171
Miller, 241, 242, 291
Milstein, 242, 243, 261
Miltz, 243
Mirotznik, 291
Montag, 241
Moshkas, 245
Moshkis, 99
Muzikanski, 240
Muzikansky, 101, 111, 186

N

Nadel, 244
Natz, 59, 74
Nigal, 243

O

Ochsmut, 213, 214
Odes, 158
Odissist, 41
Optowsky, 212
Orfin, 212
Orils, 105
Ovental, 291
Oventhal, 212, 256

P

Palis, 248
Pansevitz, 118, 121, 122, 126
Papir, 248
Patika, 33
Patoritz, 245
Pavlovich, 13
Peltz, 246, 248
Peretz, 48, 66, 76, 87, 139, 154, 163, 168, 291
Perlman, 248
Perlmuter, 247, 248, 291
Philipon, 77
Platnik, 247
Pletzel, 247
Pofelis, 51, 99
Pomerantz, 34, 69, 173
Pomerantz, 246, 291
Pomp, 248, 291
Poplis, 226, 228, 245, 262
Posh, 248
Potika, 247, 255
Preisinger, 247
Printsches, 48
Privner, 285
Privner, 248
Pulka, 247

R

Raab, 257, 258
Rabin, 255, 256, 258
Rabinov, 268
Rafner, 291

Raider, 257
Raslas, 257
Rechtshaft, 256
Reichman, 222, 256, 258
Reider, 9, 55, 64
Reif, 216, 258
Reiter, 280
Reiter, 258, 291
Reiver, 256, 258
Reiz, 151, 153, 159
Roff, 222, 240, 246, 255, 261
Rosenberg, 255, 256, 258
Rosenblum, 257
Rosenfeld, 257, 291
Rosmarin, 5, 58, 60, 98, 132, 152, 203, 204, 205, 271, 272
Rosmarin, 228, 253, 255, 256, 258, 259, 291
Rotenberg, 79, 205, 277
Rotenberg, 2, 291
Rotenshteyn, 291
Rotenstein, 189, 190, 191
Rotenteler, 258
Rothstein, 187
Rubinshteyn, 66
Rubinstein, 255, 256, 258
Rutenberg, 74
Rutenberg, 256, 257

S

Sack, 263
Safran, 259
Sapir–Chen, 83, 282
Sapir-Chen, 291
Saposov, 111, 112
Sapp, 245
Sass, 245
Satalnik, 244, 245
Scharbrot, 291
Schlachter, 9, 47, 89, 93, 156, 163, 285
Schlechter, 77
Schlechter, 260
Schwalb, 33, 137
Schwartz, 8, 41
Schwartz, 262, 263
Secharbrot, 91
Sekular, 159
Shafran, 54, 89, 100, 110, 175, 178, 179, 206
Shalom Aleichem, 48, 151, 154
Shamash, 246, 261, 262
Shamayas, 8
Shapiro, 262
Sharer, 261
Shatkan, 260
Sheinborn, 107, 156, 163
Sheinbron, 259
Sheinerman, 80, 178
Sheinerman, 259, 262, 263
Sheinman, 90
Sheinman, 260, 291
Sheintop, 259
Shifer, 248, 254, 261, 263
Shinerman, 68, 99, 110, 158, 171
Shinman, 80
Shintop, 9, 56, 99
Shlachter, 2, 3
Shlechter, 249, 260, 264, 291
Shleifer, 260, 261, 262, 263
Shlesinger, 292
Shmayes, 135, 176
Shmeltz, 260
Shmukler, 291
Shneider, 292
Shnerk, 263
Shniter, 260
Shnol, 259, 260
Shnop, 264
Sholev, 68
Shovalev, 86, 87, 276
Shovalev, 290
Shpak, 261, 263
Shpeizer, 171
Shpier, 261
Shpigel, 66
Shpirer, 54, 66, 68, 82, 94, 137, 147, 148, 149
Shpringer, 263, 291
Shroit, 66
Shroit, 236, 262
Shtal, 263
Shtekn, 291
Shternberg, 138, 140, 141, 142, 143, 144, 145, 146, 147
Shtimer, 47, 205
Shtimer, 259, 291
Shtorm, 261, 262
Shtravitsky, 60
Shtreimal, 241, 262
Shturm, 58
Shulav, 260
Shuster, 168
Shuster, 263
Singer, 231
Smiyatitzki, 245
Sobol, 244, 292
Sodovnik, 47
Sofer, 49, 96
Sokoler, 51, 137, 138
Sokolovsky, 14
Spasov, 185, 187
Speiser, 225, 260, 262, 263
Spiegel, 80
Spiegel, 263
Spirer, 258, 259
Sposov, 245
Stalin, 114
Starer, 84
Stav, 13, 14, 36, 64, 66, 79, 91, 150, 156, 158
Steinberg, 258
Stelnik, 171
Stern, 261
Stolar, 66, 80, 127, 169, 171
Stoler, 244
Stoliar, 9
Stoliar, 292
Sutnik, 241

T

Tabakhandler, 45, 94, 290
Tabakhendler, 219, 227, 234
Tagerman, 292
Takatch, 8
Tanenbaum, 235
Tanerman, 234
Taub, 138, 139, 142, 146
Tchil, 66
Tebel, 25
Tefer, 234
Teig, 171, 186, 187, 188, 189
Teig, 233, 235
Teitel, 106, 171
Teitel, 233
Teitelbaum, 235
Tenerman, 109
Terner, 54, 58, 173, 197
Terner, 222, 233, 246, 292
Teshel, 234
Tesler, 234
Tessler, 292
Tiles, 55, 93
Tisch, 233, 241
Tish, 68
Tkatch, 3
Topoler, 101, 171
Topoler, 232, 233
Tovel, 187
Toyer, 234
Trachtenberg, 156
Trakeltoib, 248
Trumpeldor, 54
Tsingalovsky, 187, 188, 189
Tsuker, 107, 169, 194
Tubal, 233
Turem, 235
Tversky, 55
Tvol, 292
Tzelnik, 219
Tzigal, 249
Tzigel, 83, 84, 86, 87, 137
Tzila, 2, 58, 150, 153, 268, 273, 274, 285, 290
Tzimering, 233, 249, 250
Tzirl, 183, 205
Tzitrin, 249
Tzuperfine, 249

U

Unger, 212, 213

V

Varsha, 25
Vasler, 229
Vegenfeld, 88
Veiger, 227, 292
Veinshel, 165, 169
Vensky, 189, 190
Verbenmacher, 135
Vertzal, 228
Veverik, 105, 169
Vevrik, 228, 229
Vidler, 229
Vidra, 228, 247
Vinehauser, 8, 9, 55, 131, 132, 164, 171, 183
Vinshel, 292
Vogenfeld, 14, 23, 54, 178
Volf, 58, 97, 133
Vopaniarsky, 102, 171
Vopniarsky, 292
Vorik, 110, 111
Vortzel, 109, 110
Vortziner, 110
Vurtzel, 291

W

Wagonfeld, 228, 229, 238
Wapner, 229, 230
Wapniarski, 218, 229
Wasserman, 285
Wasserman, 229, 230
Weiner, 198
Weiner, 227
Weinfeld, 43
Weinreb, 229
Weinrib, 228
Weinshel, 161
Weinshel, 227, 228, 229, 230
Weiss, 229
Weitzman, 228, 229
Werber, 230
Wertheim, 18, 55, 58, 130, 160, 277
Wertheim, 3
Winemaker, 39
Wolf, 8, 9, 18, 19, 50, 79, 93, 148, 160
Wolf, 248

Y

Yaabetz, 85
Yaikes, 176
Yekes, 160
Yellen, 235, 236
Yevilevitch, 136
Yochanson, 78, 79
Yocht, 235
Yokenzon, 148
Yokhenzon, 9, 16, 18, 19, 54, 58, 68, 97, 101, 136, 150, 156, 160, 171, 203
Yokhenzon, 290
Yudel, 25, 27, 28, 49, 136

Z

Zachartchuk, 185, 186, 191, 193
Zack, 55
Zack, 227, 230
Zak, 131, 163
Zaltz, 232
Zehavy, 292

Zeidel, 231
Zelgs, 99
Zemel, 230, 231, 292
Zhak, 64
Zigelboim, 230
Zilberstein, 232
Zipper, 54, 138
Ziske, 182
Ziskind, 231
Zlotorewski, 163
Zmirin, 292
Zonshine, 231
Zuberman, 231
Zucker, 249, 250
Zweig, 51
Zweig, 249
Zylber, 231, 232

www.ingramcontent.com/pod-product-compliance
Lightning Source LLC
Chambersburg PA
CBHW082004150426
42814CB00005BA/218

* 9 7 8 1 9 5 4 1 7 6 2 1 8 *